The Chicken Cookbook

The Chicken Cookbook

by BEVERLEE SIAS

South Brunswick and New York: A. S. Barnes and Company
London: Thomas Yoseloff Ltd

A. S. Barnes and Co., Inc.
Cranbury, New Jersey 08512

Thomas Yoseloff Ltd
108 New Bond Street
London W1Y OQX, England

SBN: 498 06886 2
Printed in the United States of America

To Marian Anderson

Contents

Preface

This is a book about chicken: chicken cooking, chicken eating, chicken history, preparation of chicken, regional chicken, cosmopolitan chicken, its culinary history around the world and the way each country prepares the bird in its own particular style, the masterly chicken dishes created by celebrated chefs—in fact, just about everything I could find out about chicken.

Why chicken? I might answer because of its fascinating adaptability to so many wonderful combinations. I know of no other meat which lends itself so beautifully to blending with herbs, spices, and condiments. The addition of wines and liquors adds glamour to the flavor and transforms the chicken into a gustatory specialty. It is universally enjoyed whether boiled, broiled, sautéed, roasted, or fried. Fried! The mere mention of the words "Fried Chicken" is enough to bring the average American male to his knees with nostalgic memories of childhood days and the sumptuous Sunday dinners at Grandmother's house and the remembered taste and smell of her crisp golden fried chicken.

Chicken is delicious whole, halved, quartered, or by the piece. It can go to a picnic or to a backyard barbecue or preside with dignity at the most elegant dinner. Today there isn't a better buy on the market than chicken. It is generally thrifty and is available every day of the year in practically every market in the country. Chicken is inexpensive and may be purchased whole or in convenient cut-up pieces so that each person can choose exactly the right amount of chicken to suit his or her needs. One may also buy packaged breasts, wings, thighs, drumsticks, backs, and necks so that it is easy to select the type and quantity needed for any recipe.

The recipes which are contained in the first part of this book are completely American. You have heard about Southern cooking, Creole cooking, New England cooking, Pennsylvania Dutch cooking, Southwestern cooking; these are the regional recipes of America, the recipes of our Pilgrim forefathers, the exotic distinctive cuisine of the Creoles, the best of the old Southland, the recipes brought to us by the Spaniards and the Mexicans—some of them have been favorites since the days of Cortez. Then there are those recipes whose origin can be traced to other lands, these are the favorite dishes brought to us by the many peoples who immigrated to our country and which we have adopted as our own. I have put these recipes under a section called Cosmopolitan Cooking. I have included in this section many dishes we have created ourselves out of the vast bounty of our land and which show the great versatility in the American cuisine.

The second section of this book takes a gastronomic chicken tour around the world. Included are the great chicken recipes of France, Italy, Spain, Hungary, Germany, Austria, and other countries of Europe as well as those of the Near and Far East, the South Pacific and South America. Every country in the world has contributed some method of serving up a chicken, from the clay and mud-baked chickens of antiquity to the cultivated, truffled extravagant chickens of classic French cuisine. Many and varied are the ways of cooking chicken and it always looks, smells, and tastes delicious.

I can vouch for the quality of all the chicken recipes included in this book. I have had help from many sources and this book could not have been finished without the help of friends of foreign and domestic background or without the help of their friends who have all given me much needed help and information and recipes. Everyone has been most generous with ideas for new dishes and wonderful about taste-testing. We have tested and sampled them all—a major project, I assure you; it is astonishing how many chicken dishes one can eat without growing tired of the flavor of chicken. A change in the herbs or spices used in a recipe will transform the dish completely. A distinctly different flavor is easily obtained by adding a few ounces of wine, sherry, or Brandy.

This is by no means an all-inclusive collection of chicken recipes. I have tried to be selective in choosing only those recipes that seemed to me characteristic of each country and region, and those which I considered the best. Possibly I should have included more recipes than I have to make a complete book on chicken but since the ways of preparing chicken are virtually endless I am afraid it would have been a rather overwhelming volume in both size and content. There are hundreds, or even thousands, of recipes for ordinary chicken dishes in standard cookbooks, in women's magazines, in the columns of home economists, but these were not the recipes I wanted for my book. I wanted recipes that were not only authentic but excitingly different and delicious. I hope I have weeded out all the run-of-the-mill kind, and that this book is a representative collection of the most delectable chicken dishes enjoyed by everyone around the world.

Acknowledgments

I would like to acknowledge first my great debt to my dear friend, Marian Anderson, who not only helped me with research but laid at my disposal her treasured store of recipes, her kitchen, and her time. Without her generous assistance I am sure this book could never have been written.

I am grateful as well to the many people of domestic and foreign background who have given me much needed help and information and ideas for recipes on chicken. My thanks go also to people who have helped me in many different ways: to Professor Ernest K. Mundt, head of the Art Department at San Francisco State and an author of several cookbooks himself, who in the beginning gave me excellent advice; to Betty Smith Stevenson, Director of Home Economics for Foster Farms Poultry Producers, and to Mrs. L. Bailey, advertising manager of Mississippi Federated Cooperatives, for their kind assistance. I wish to especially thank Adena Robinson, home economist at Marin High School, as well as all the other kind people who have donated recipes. Also I wish to thank the Chinese restaurant proprietors and chefs for their fine help on Chinese methods of cooking. Especially I wish to thank Kee Joon of Empress of China, Helen Jung of Sai Yen, and Leonard Wong of Sun Hung Heung, who all so generously gave me their recipes. Mention should be made here too of my mother-in-law, Florence Sias, whose knowledge of New England cooking has been invaluable and the debt I owe my husband, Dick, and my son, Steve, who have tried with me so bravely almost all the chicken recipes in this book.

Beverlee Sias

The Chicken Cookbook

Measures

	American	English
1 cup of breadcrumbs (fresh)	1½ oz.	3 oz.
1 cup of flour or other powdered grains	4 oz.	5 oz.
1 cup of sugar	7 oz.	8 oz.
1 cup of icing sugar	4½ oz.	5 oz.
1 cup of butter or other fats	8 oz.	8 oz.
1 cup of raisins, etc.	5 oz.	6 oz.
1 cup of grated cheese	4 oz.	4 oz.
1 cup of syrup, etc.	12 oz.	14 oz.

1 English pint	20	fluid ounces
1 American pint	16	fluid ounces
1 American cup	8	fluid ounces
8 American tablespoons	4	fluid ounces
1 American tablespoon	½	fluid ounce
3 American teaspoons	½	fluid ounce
1 English tablespoon	⅔	to 1 fluid ounce (approx.)
1 English tablespoon	4	teaspoons

The American measuring tablespoon holds ¼ oz. flour.

The Story of Chicken

The domesticated chicken of today has a long and impressive lineage that goes back thousands and thousands of years into the primitive jungles of Southeast Asia. Evolving somewhere in the dim distant past from a reptile into a wild jungle fowl, the ancestor of our domesticated chicken was a beautiful bird with orange-red and shiny green plumage. He and his mate, a plain brown spotted hen, roamed through the dark jungles of antiquity and managed to survive and multiply.

Primitive man discovered the chicken and brought it out of the jungle almost before the discovery of fire and cookery. Ancient records show that the Chinese began using it as food as early as 1400 B.C. And so with the help of man, the chicken always an adventurous bird at heart, crossed the road from its native Southeast Asia and began its travels east and west, north and south around the world.

It journeyed with the Polynesians from island to island in their great migrations across the Pacific. It roamed through India and brought itself esteem in curry dishes. It lent itself to many exotic dishes for the Persians and Greeks and in Rome became so popular that the Roman senators found it necessary to pass a law restricting the use of it. In France two of the most celebrated French rulers paid homage to the chicken, Henri IV with his Poule au Pot and Napoleon with Chicken Marengo. The great chefs of France embraced the chicken and rose to glory with it. It moved across Europe lending itself to innumerable gustatory whims and taking on a different character in each new country it visited.

When the Spanish Conquistadors explored the New World the chicken went with them. The English colonists brought more, and after the first dreadful starving years at Jamestown the colonists began raising them for breeding purposes only. In fact in 1611 the colony passed a law condemning to death anyone found killing a chicken. Later when the Pilgrims landed at Plymouth so did the chicken and again as the pioneers migrated westward the chicken moved westward with them.

The domestic chicken has come a long way from its original primitive jungle existence. It is now the most civilized of all birds. It can produce tender, edible flesh with far less trouble than any other living creature. The tremendous size and efficiency of the American chicken farms are beyond belief. Thousands and thousands of chickens are raised to uniform size and excellence in streamlined palaces and given more care than we give our children. In clean sanitary surroundings their health is protected from the moment they hatch out as baby chicks until they blossom forth as plump young broilers or fryers or fat roasting hens ready for the market. They are kept in comfortable air-conditioned surroundings, given plenty of vitamins and good food, and in easygoing contentment dream out their short lives until the moment they are killed, cleaned, graded, packed with incredible efficiency, and shipped to market.

There is no other meat or bird that has become more cosmopolitan than chicken. It has been served on the table of almost every nation and certainly no other food is so universally admired. Chickens thrive in almost any climate under a great variety of conditions. Our barnyard friend, the chicken, pecking and scratching in search of food, is a common sight throughout the world. Chickens are raised everywhere except possibly at the highest altitudes. The early-morning crowing of the rooster has served the farmer as an alarm clock for thousands of years. Very few people tire of chicken because the meat is delicious and tasty no matter how it is cooked, and since that long-ago day when our early ancestors brought the chicken forth from its jungle home it has become the darling of the dinner table, feted in the banquet halls of the nobility, glorified and raised to undreamed of gustatory heights, praised and enjoyed in every corner of the earth.

Selecting the Chicken

While the versatile fryer is the star of many of my recipes because it can be used for almost any method of cooking, the chicken still has many sizes from the tiny squab chicken to the portly stewing hen. Chicken is easily obtainable the year round and it is economical; watch the specials in your local newspaper and see.

For Broiling: A plump young chicken under 3 pounds is best. A typical broiler usually ranges in age from 13 to 18 weeks and weighs between 1 and 2½ pounds. A broiler may be split in half lengthwise, quartered, or cut in pieces.

For Frying, Sauteeing, Baking, Quick Braising: The fryer, that all-purpose bird, lends itself easily to a wide range of recipes. A fryer of any size may be used. They weigh from 2½ to 3½ pounds usually and range in age from 14 to 20 weeks old. They are sufficiently young and soft-meated to be cooked tender by frying.

For Roasting: Choose a chicken weighing from 3 to 5 pounds and ranging in age from 5 to 9 months old. They are usually heavier-breasted and should be well fatted. They may be stuffed or not. They are very tasty and practical for serving over 4.

The Capon: Usually roasted but they can also be cooked in a number of delectable ways. They usually weigh from 6 to

10 pounds. They have rounded well-fleshed bodies and pale combs. They are easily identified by the "capon pick" from which only some of the feathers have been removed. They are roosters that have been gelded to improve the flesh and increase the growth.

For Soups, Stews, and Fricassees: Choose a fowl which is a mature chicken of any weight. Fowls need long, slow cooking but they are very flavorful.

Preparing the Chicken

Once upon a time chicken was a Sunday treat but today with modern production and marketing methods chickens can be purchased in any form all year round. They come in three major forms: fresh, frozen, canned.

Fresh Chickens: Fresh chickens usually come to the market clean and drawn, tagged with brand name and weight, and shipped fresh on chipped ice to market. They have a much better flavor than frozen ones so look for them and buy them when you can. Fresh chickens are better when stored a day before using, as it improves their flavor. They can be bought whole or by the piece for sautéing, baking, or frying. They can be washed, dried, seasoned, and coated with flour or bread crumbs, and kept cold in the refrigerator until ready to use. The convenient packages of cut-up parts makes it very convenient for the busy housewife to select exactly what she needs, both for her pocketbook and family.

While chickens are usually bought clean and drawn, it is still helpful to know the proper method of doing it.

To Singe: Hold chicken with one hand on neck and the other hand on feet and turn bird constantly over a flame to expose all of the surface to the heat, thus burning off tiny feathers and down.

To Dress and Clean: Although a chicken is usually dressed at market it is still a good idea to examine it carefully to make sure it has been properly done. Cut off the head and pull off the pinfeathers, using a small pointed knife. Remove tendons by cutting through the skin around the leg an inch below the leg joint and taking care not to cut the tendons. Place cut on leg over the edge of a board, press downward to snap the bone; then take the foot in your right hand, holding the chicken firmly in your left hand, and pull off the foot and with it the tendons.

To Draw: Make an incision through the skin below the breast-bone large enough to admit the hand. Remove:

Entrails and giblets (gizzard, heart, liver). Set aside the giblets to use in soup, gravy, dressing, etc.

Gall bladder (on under surface of right lobe of liver). Be careful not to break, as even a small amount of the bile will give a bitter flavor. Cut away any part of the liver that may be stained.

Lungs (spongy red flesh on either side of backbone between ribs). Remove every particle carefully.

Kidneys (in hollow near the end of the backbone).

Windpipe and crop. Feel under skin close to neck with first two fingers and pull out windpipe and crop which is attached to skin close to breast.

Cut neck down the center of the back to the shoulders, cutting off neck close to body and leaving skin long enough to fasten under the back. Remove oil sac at the base of tail by cutting under the sac to the backbone and up towards the tail. Wash chicken by running cold water into the cavity to remove any remaining entrails. Rinse well with more cold water, drain, and dry thoroughly.

Store the prepared chicken in a shallow pan in the coldest part of the refrigerator and keep cold until ready to cook. Whole chickens keep better than when they are cut up.

Frozen Chickens: Frozen chickens come ready to cook too.

They come whole or cut-up or you can buy separate parts. Completely thaw frozen chickens before you use them. To thaw, leave the wrapped chicken in the food compartment of the refrigerator overnight. Or for a quicker method, unwrap the chicken and thaw it by running cold water over it until unfrozen. Always cook within a day after it has been unfrozen because the flavor of chickens deteriorates quickly. Never re-freeze poultry.

Canned Chickens: Canned chickens may be purchased whole or in parts. They come in such forms as Chicken Fricassee with gravy, Chicken à la King, and in many other cooked chicken dishes.

Serve chicken immediately after cooking. Always refrigerate any leftover chicken at once. As a caution never stuff poultry ahead of time as there may be danger of food poisoning. Wait to stuff the chicken just before roasting and always remove all the leftover stuffing from the chicken and refrigerate it separately.

Cooking Time for Chicken: Giving the exact time a chicken is done depends always on a chicken's age and size. I can state the finished cooking time as nearly correct as I can make it, but each cook's own good judgment and common sense must prevail. Every cook should test for the bird's tenderness herself. Chickens should never be overdone, but they should always be cooked through thoroughly and completely.

Cutting Up the Chicken

Grasp the wing, bend it back and away from the carcass, and cut through the skin, flesh, and joint. Repeat for the second wing.

Next the legs. Hold leg away from body and cut skin from leg joint near the backbone. Cut through the remaining skin.

Divide the leg into thigh and drumstick. Repeat for the second leg.

Separate back and breast. Cut through all rib joints towards the shoulder joints. Break the joints to complete the cut.

Locate end of breastbone and cut through flesh and small joint in front part of breast making two breast pieces.

Locate last rib in back piece and cut right in back of it. Locate joint in middle of back and break joint. Cut through to make two pieces of the back.

To Divide Chicken Broilers into Serving Portions

Lay chicken on its back and split lengthwise, cutting down flesh at one side of breastbone and cutting through to the other end of the breast. Cut through the rib joints just to one side of the backbone on the same side as the first cut. Cut through ribs and tail to separate into halves. For four portions, divide each half as above and then cut crosswise into two portions again so there are two leg and two breast pieces.

Trussing the Chicken

METHOD I—Insert trussing needle through body of chicken below knee joint and pull through. Continue cord through wings. Tie tightly to hold wings close to body. Stuff neck opening of chicken with stuffing and tuck end of neck skin under cord. Using another piece of cord insert needle through legs near joint. Stuff body cavity and truss opening with trussing pins or cord. Draw cord from legs around tail piece and tie legs down close to body.

METHOD II—Draw thighs close to body and hold by inserting a steel skewer under middle joint, running it through body, coming out under the middle joint on other side. Cross legs, tie securely with a long string, and fasten to tail. Place wings close to body and hold them by inserting a second skewer through wing, body, and wing on opposite side. Draw neck skin under back and fasten with a small skewer. Turn chicken on its breast. Cross string attached to tail piece and draw it around each end of lower skewer. Again cross strings and draw around each end of upper skewer. Tie string in a tight knot.

METHOD III—Have incision for drawing cut near one leg instead of down the middle. Fill neck cavity with stuffing and fasten neck skin to back with skewer or cord. Tie a cord firmly around lower end of leg. Fill body cavity with stuffing. Overlap edges of skin at the incision, pressing leg down firmly to hold edges together and tie both legs with cord to tail piece, holding them firmly against body. Cross cord over back, catch around the wings, pull wings close to body, and tie.

For an easier method that I use most of the time myself, simply tie the wing tips onto the back firmly, which holds the neck skin. Next tie the legs together and then tie them to the tail. This works just as effectively, I believe, although one should be familiar with the recommended methods of trussing. The main reason for keeping the legs and wings close to the body is so that the heat of cooking will not force them apart and the meat cook too dry.

Boning the Chicken

Boning a chicken is quite an art but it is not very difficult to master, and when you are slicing and serving your first de-boned chicken you will feel quite a glow of accomplishment. A fryer or roaster chicken may be used for boning. Remove pin feathers, singe, and wash, but do not draw.

Cut along center back from neck downward, completing cut down either side of tail and around vent.

Cut in a circle through flesh of wing and leg bones; scrape flesh loose from bones and pull bones out.

1—Cut off head, wings up to second joint, and legs at knee joint. This loosens skin and flesh for easier removal of bones.

2—Using a small sharp knife, cut along center back from the neck downward, completing the cut down either side of tail and around vent.

3—Cut the flesh away from the back and ribs down to the keel bone trying not to tear the skin and working with your fingers. Insert knife into each hip joint and turn so as to break joint. This separates the legs from the body. Break wing joints in the same way. For the bones that extend towards the joints and the tiny bones scrape alongside with the knife lightly. Very often they will slip out easily.

4—Push the breast flesh away from the breast bone until they are connected only by the vent and below the tip of the breast bone. Separate by cutting through the thin layers of flesh and skin.

5—Remove bones from legs and wings by working down from inside of body, leaving outside skin intact.

6—Cut through thigh-bone flesh to bone from inside; avoid scraping the flesh. Cut through flesh between thigh and drumstick and pull out the bone.

7—Cut in a circle to the smaller end of the drumstick and cut and scrape flesh loose from bones. Pull bone out. Cut out the wishbone which has remained in the breast.

Place the deboned chicken on a board and sew the chicken together so that it retains its natural shape. When it is stuffed and cooked your guests will gasp with surprise and pleasure.

Carving the Chicken

1—Place chicken on back on platter. Hold drumstick firmly with fingers and with serving knife in right hand cut through skin between leg and body. With knife pull back leg and disjoint from body. Then cut off wing. Remove leg and wing from other side.

2—Hold leg on serving plate and separate drumstick and thigh by cutting down through the joint to the plate. Then divide wings at joint.

3—Beginning at the front of the breast carve breastmeat in thin crosswise slices. The slices should fall away from the chicken as they are cut. Carve just enough meat for first servings. Carve more chicken if needed.

4—To serve stuffing remove skewers or thread from cavity openings and spoon out the stuffing onto a platter.

Regional Chicken

The chicken tour of America starts with a number of regional recipes which are renowned from California to the rocky shores of Maine. These are typical American dishes that bring back memories of the early years at Plymouth, the lordly plantations of the Southland, the old farm kitchens with their spicy, savory smells. These are the recipes of our forefathers, the recipes brought to us by the Spaniards and by the Mexicans, the simple hearty dishes of early colonial life, the magic cookery of the Creoles, the famous dishes prepared in the great tradition of Southern cooking. They are as much a part of our national heritage as our history, literature, and art. Chicken Maryland, Brunswick Stew, Kentucky Burgoo, Vermont Potpie, Southwest Tamale—to name just a few—they all carry with them the beliefs and customs and folklore of our rich and colorful past.

New England Chicken

New England cooking: chowder and fishcakes, lobster and cod, baked beans and brown bread, red flannel hash, a boiled salted dinner—these have been the mainstays of New Englanders since the days of our Pilgrim fathers. That they were able to subdue the inhospitable rock-strewn wilderness and to thrive in the severe climate has been a minor miracle. They flourished in the new environment and created out of unpalatable materials savory foods which have influenced to a great extent what we in America eat today.

That first winter the Pilgrims were unprepared for life in the American wilderness. They would have starved to death if they had not learned from the Indians the value of corn as a food. With this "immortal maize," which was a staple of life to the Indians in New England, and with the clams they were able to dig up along the ocean shore they managed to survive. The woods were bursting with game: elk, moose, deer, wild turkeys, bear; ducks, geese, pheasants, partridges were plentiful; fish abounded in the lakes and swift-flowing rivers. There were over two hundred varieties of fish as well as lobsters, oysters, and clams along the seacoast, but the Pilgrims were neither fishermen nor hunters. They were townspeople, craftsmen, artisans, tradesmen, or farmers, so they pounded the Indian corn to a powder and learned to make corn cakes and pone and pudding.

In the spring under Indian guidance the Pilgrims planted corn, squash, pumpkin, beans, as well as the seeds of wheat and rye they had brought with them from England. Wheat did not take well to the new climate but rye thrived to provide along with corn the main staple food for those early years. Pigs waxed fat on the corn to give them salted and pickled pork for the next winter. Preserves and pickles made from cabbage, green walnuts, barberries, and nasturtium buds began to add variety to their diet. They soon learned to fish well, and it was not long before New England fishing boats were bringing in huge catches of cod, haddock, and mackerel. Some of the catch was eaten fresh but most of it was preserved by salting or drying. The dried salted fish was used in trade with the West Indies and such items as spices, molasses, and raisins began to enrich New England cooking.

At home the New Englanders found many uses for the dried salted fish. Cod was soaked overnight, then shredded and combined with mashed potatoes and eggs, rolled into balls, and fried in hot fat until crusty and browned. In Massachusetts the crusty codfish cakes soon became a Sunday-morning breakfast tradition. It was not all fish in New England, however. The Pilgrims invented many dishes of their own which have made Yankee cooking famous: brick-oven-baked beans fragrant with the flavors of salt pork, mustard, molasses, served with dark moist bread dotted with raisins; Indian pudding, the Thanksgiving turkey, cranberry sauce, blueberries in pie and muffins, pumpkin pie, maple syrup, all the fish and chicken chowders; and no dish is more typically Yankee than chowder. They invented all of these simple old-fashioned dishes and many more. Even today they are considered among the best in American cooking.

The center of New England life was the old colonial kitchen with its great open fireplace which furnished all of the heat and most of the light. The cooking was done over on open log fire in the fireplace. Long-legged skillets were thrust into the burning coals to cook corn cakes and fry meat. Spits for roasting or broiling meats were common. A "Dutch" oven, built into the wall at one side of the fireplace, was used for baking. However, most of the food the New Englanders ate came out of heavy black iron pots hung from a large crane. From these iron pots came the stews, the chowders, and the famous New England boiled dinner. Corned beef was responsible for the popularity of the boiled dinner, and during the winter months when no fresh meat was to be had it was eaten at least twice a week. There were boiled chicken dinners too and they still hold a place among the traditional dishes of New England cookery.

The built-in fireplace brick "Dutch" oven was used twice a week for baking. Midweek and on Saturday morning a fire was built in the oven and when it had burned down the coals were removed and the ashes swept out with a husk broom. Loaves of bread made from rye or cornmeal were placed in the back of the oven. Chicken and meat pies went in next, then the pot of beans and an Indian pudding made from Indian meal, molasses, and whole milk; and last, the pies and the cakes and the cookies were arranged in the front. The iron door was shut tight and remained shut until the pies and cakes and cookies and bread were baked. The beans and the Indian pudding were left in the slow heat of the fireplace oven to cook all day.

Thanksgiving has always been a special holiday for New Englanders. That first hard year the crops were good and at harvest time Governor Bradford called on his people to give thanks to God for their deliverance in the new land. As well as the Pilgrims, many Indians came bringing gifts of venison and other game. There were all kinds of wild game and shellfish served, but even at that first Thanksgiving it was the turkey that was the star of the feast. It is doubtful that the first Thanksgiving turkey resembled the plump tender domesticated bird we are so familiar with or that any of the traditional mouth-watering "fixings" were served but it was not too many years before the New Englanders had made a wonderful feastday of Thanksgiving with a plump golden-brown turkey filled with savory butternut stuffing, accompanied by ruby red cranberry sauce, mashed potatoes, golden giblet gravy; there were vegetables of many kinds; cucumber pickles and pungent green-tomato relish; for dessert there was mince and apple pie and steamed pudding; and pumpkin pie that was always a must. In fact, pumpkin pie was almost as important to the success of a New England Thanksgiving dinner as was the turkey.

Clam chowder was a first-of-the-week dish and it was often followed the next day by a chicken stew topped with feather-light dumplings, or possibly a tasty veal stew, or a Yankee potroast surrounded by golden carrots and plum little onions. At the end of the week leftovers went into a dish of red flannel hash colored by beets and beet juice. Saturday the traditional New England supper was baked beans and homemade steaming brown bread accompanied by green-tomato pickle and a dish of cole slaw tangy with vinegar and cream, with a little sugar added for sweetness. Indian pudding was a favorite Saturday-night dessert served with thick yellow cream and still warm from the oven it had shared with the beans in the last hours of baking. Codfish cakes on Sunday morning and always pie—apple, blueberry, gooseberry, pumpkin. . . .

There are also many wonderful chicken dishes that are typically Yankee: Chicken Potpie, Chicken Stew, Chicken Chowder, Chicken Friscassee with dumplings as only the New Englanders know how to make them. Plymouth Succotash, that most famous of all New England dishes which was served in a number of Plymouth households on December 21 each year to celebrate the landing of the Pilgrims (1620). Fried chicken has never held the place in New England that it has in the rest of the country. I don't know why, except possibly the chicken fricassee or stew or chowder that could be put in an iron pot and cooked for hours without further attendance was a great advantage to the very busy New England housewife. The New Englanders had several interesting ways of tenderizing an old tough fowl. One was to soak it in buttermilk for fourteen or sixteen hours and, incidentally, the buttermilk imparted a very delicious flavor. Another method which was called "potting the chicken" was to pack the pieces tightly into a bean pot, cover them with boiling water, and cook the chicken for hours and hours in the slow heat of the fireplace oven.

In cold weather the great fireplace radiated a comforting warmth and mingled with the spicy smells of cookies and cakes and pies baking in the old built-in brick oven. There is a certain nostalgia about those days and about the simple hardy dishes of our forefathers; they are still wonderfully good eating and New England holds a very special place in the American cuisine.

Plymouth Succotash

Plymouth Succotash, traditionally served in Plymouth households on December 21, Founder's Day. The dish was originally made by the Pilgrims and handed down from generation to generation.

2 cups pea beans
5-pound fowl cut into pieces
2 pounds corned beef
½ pound salt pork
4 quarts water
2 bay leaves
1 onion sliced
1 rutabaga peeled and cut into cubes
3 medium potatoes peeled and cut into cubes
2 medium cans of hominy

Soak the beans overnight. The next morning drain, cover with cold water, and cook slowly for 2½ hours. Drain and mash or blend in an electric blender. Set aside. Put the chicken pieces, corned beef, and salt pork in a large kettle. Add the 4 quarts water, bay leaves, and sliced onion. Cook over a low heat about 2½ hours or until the meats are tender. If the chicken and salt pork become tender before the corned beef remove them and set aside. In the meantime cook the rutabaga and potatoes until tender. When the corned beef has become tender remove it from the kettle and cut into serving portions. Return it to the kettle along with the chicken and salt pork. Stir in the bean puree, cooked potatoes, cooked rutabaga, and hominy. Heat through and serve in deep heated bowls.

Serves 8

Cape Cod Chicken Fricassee with Dumplings

This is a genuine New England chicken fricassee with light fluffy dumplings as only a New Englander knows how to make them.

½ pound fat salt pork diced
5-pound chicken cut into pieces
Boiling water
1 teaspoon salt
2 turnips peeled and diced
4 onions sliced
4 medium potatoes peeled and diced
Dumplings

Try out the salt pork in a large heavy kettle and then add the chicken pieces. Add boiling water to cover and salt. Cover the kettle and simmer for 30 minutes. Add the turnips and onions. Cook 15 minutes longer. Add the potatoes and continue cooking until the chicken and the vegetables are tender. Put in the dumplings 12 minutes before serving and steam covered tightly. Place the chicken pieces on a large hot platter surrounded by the vegetables and dumplings. Pour over the gravy and serve at once.

Dumplings
2 cups flour

½ teaspoon salt
3 tablespoons baking powder
1 cup thin cream

Sift dry ingredients together. Add cream and stir in quickly to make a medium-soft batter. Drop by teaspoonfuls on top of the chicken fricassee, making sure the dumplings do not settle down into the liquid. Cover tightly and steam 15 minutes without removing the cover.

Serves 6

New England Hen and Beans
My mother-in-law, Florence Sias, lived most of her life in Massachusetts and one of her favorite cold weather suppers was a succulent chicken baked in a pot with homemade Boston Beans. This is her recipe.

1 large chicken cut into pieces
1 quart pea beans
½ pound fat salt pork
1½ teaspoons brown sugar
½ cup molasses
1 teaspoon dry mustard
boiling water
½ cup cream

Wash the beans and soak overnight in cold water. In the morning drain, cover with fresh water, and let simmer until the skins burst. Drain the beans. Place the chicken pieces in the bottom of a bean pot. Cover with the beans, score the salt pork and press it into the beans so only the rind is above the surface. Add sugar, molasses, and mustard. Add boiling water to cover. Cover the pot and bake in a slow 250° oven for 6 hours, adding water as needed to keep the beans covered.

The last half hour of baking time add ½ cup cream and uncover to brown.

Serves 8

Vermont Potpie

Famous Vermont Potpie has been one of the mainstays of New Englanders since the days of our forefathers.

5-pound chicken cut into pieces
1 turnip cut in half
1 stalk celery
3 sprigs parsley
1 medium onion
6 peppercorns
1 teaspoon salt
2 cups sifted flour
½ teaspoon salt
2 eggs
2 tablespoons water
3 large potatoes sliced
2 tablespoons chopped parsley

Place the chicken pieces in a large kettle with the turnip, celery, parsley, onion, peppercorns, and 1 teaspoon salt. Cover with water and simmer over a low heat for 1 hour or until the chicken is tender. Remove the vegetables and discard them. Keep the chicken and broth hot. Make a pie dough by sifting the flour and ½ teaspoon salt together in a bowl. Make a well in the center and drop in the eggs. Mix quickly to make a stiff dough, adding the water as needed. Roll out as thin as possible on a lightly floured board and cut into small squares with a knife. Drop the pastries along with the sliced potatoes into the hot broth. Cover tightly and cook over a

medium heat for 20 minutes. Serve in deep bowls with chopped
parsley sprinkled on top.

Serves 6

Old-Fashioned Chicken Pie
A genuine old-fashioned Yankee chicken pie is as good as
anything you can eat.

5-pound chicken cut into pieces
Water to cover
1 teaspoon salt
¼ teaspoon pepper
Flour
Pastry dough

Place the chicken in a large kettle with water to cover. Add
salt and pepper, cover, and simmer over a low heat 1½ hours
or until the chicken is tender. Line a baking dish with the
pastry dough and place the chicken pieces in the dish. Add
enough flour to the broth the chicken was cooked in to make
3 cups medium thick gravy. Pour the gravy over the chicken.
Place a pastry top over the dish and make slits with a knife
so the steam can escape. Bake in a preheated 450° oven for
15 minutes. Reduce heat to 350 and continue baking about
30 minutes longer when the crust should be nicely browned.

Pastry
2½ cups flour
½ teaspoon salt
¾ cup shortening
⅓ cup cold water

Sift the flour and salt together. Cut in the shortening. Add
the water a little at a time, stirring in quickly, and handling

as little as possible. Roll out on a floured board to make the bottom and top crusts.

Serves 4

New England Chicken Stew
Florence Sias is again responsible for this good plain Yankee chicken stew.

5-pound chicken cut into pieces
3 potatoes diced
2 large onions sliced
Boiling salted water
3 tablespoons butter
1 cup thin cream
Salt and pepper to taste
8 common crackers
Cold milk

Place the chicken pieces in a large heavy kettle with the diced potatoes and sliced onions. Cover with boiling salted water and simmer over a low heat for 1½ hours or until the chicken is tender. Add the butter and the thin cream and cook until just heated through. Season to taste with salt and pepper. Split the common crackers in half and moisten them in cold milk. Add to the chicken stew and serve at once.

Serves 6

Chicken and Clam Pie
Another Yankee dish that has long been a favorite in New England.

2 tablespoons butter
½ cup chopped celery
12 small white peeled onions

2 cups cooked chicken cut into chunks
2-7½ ounce cans clams chopped
1 cup diced cooked potatoes
1 teaspoon salt
¼ teaspoon pepper
Dash of cayenne
1 tablespoon flour
½ cup thin cream
¼ cup clam juice
Pie crust topping

Sauté the celery and small white onions in the butter until soft. Add the cooked chicken, clams, diced potatoes, salt, pepper, and a dash of cayenne. Simmer for 5 minutes. Blend the flour with the thin cream until smooth and add to the chicken mixture along with the clam juice. Cook, stirring constantly until thickened, about 5 minutes. Pour into a greased casserole and place the pie crust over the top. Make slits in the crust so the steam will escape and bake 30 minutes in a preheated 425° oven or until the crust is golden brown.

Serves 6

Chicken and Rice, New England Style
A tasty New England dish from Duxbury, Massachusetts.

5-pound chicken cut into pieces
1 carrot sliced
2 stalks celery chopped
1 onion sliced
1 teaspoon salt
Water to cover
2 tablespoons butter
3 tablespoons flour
Salt to taste
1 cup cream

Boiled rice

Place chicken pieces in a large kettle with the carrot, celery, onion, and salt. Cover with water and simmer covered over a low heat for 1½ hours or until the chicken is tender. Strain the vegetables from the broth and reserve. Melt 2 tablespoons butter in a saucepan and blend in the flour. Slowly add 2 cups hot chicken broth from the kettle. Add the cream and stir over a low heat until thickened and smooth. Taste for seasoning and add the cooked vegetables. Place the boiled rice in a large hot serving platter. Pile the chicken pieces on top of the rice and cover with the vegetables and sauce.

Serves 6

Potted Chicken

This was the way thrifty New Englanders made use of an aging fowl. There is no real point in using an old hen today when fryers, which are a better buy anyway, can be cooked in one fourth the time.

4-pound chicken fryer cut into pieces
16 small white onions peeled
½ cup butter melted
1 cup cream
Salt and pepper

Place the chicken pieces in a bean pot with the onions and butter. Cover the pot tightly and bake in a 350° preheated oven for 45 minutes or until the chicken is tender. Remove the chicken and onions to a hot serving platter. Add the cream to the pot and cook until just heated through stirring and scraping up all the browned particles from the bottom of the pot. Season to taste with salt and pepper and pour over the chicken.

Serves 4

New Hampshire Chicken Chowder

Chicken Chowder is one of the wonderful New England dishes that have made Yankee cooking famous for its simple but excellent quality.

5-pound hen cut into pieces
2 quarts cold water
¼ pound salt pork cubed
2 medium onions sliced
4 cups hot water
6 medium potatoes diced
2 teaspoons salt
3 cups milk scalded
1 cup thin cream scalded
4 tablespoons butter

Place the chicken pieces in a kettle with 2 quarts cold water and simmer covered over low heat for 2 hours or until the chicken is tender. Remove the chicken from the kettle, free the meat from the bones, and cut into small pieces. Try out the salt pork in a frying pan, add the sliced onions, and cook over a low heat until the onions are a light golden in color. Then put the onions and salt pork in a large kettle, add the diced potatoes and the salt. Simmer over a low heat until the potatoes are tender. Add the chicken meat and the broth and simmer 20 minutes longer. Add the scalded milk and cream. Add the butter and cook over a low heat until the butter is melted.

Serves 8

Vermont Cream of Chicken Soup

A simple but delicious New England soup good for cold weather eating.

½ cup finely chopped celery

½ cup scraped diced carrots
3 cups chicken broth
2 tablespoons flour
2 tablespoons butter
1 cup cream
½ teaspoon salt
Common crackers split and toasted

Add the celery and carrots to the chicken broth and cook over a low heat about 30 minutes or until tender. Melt the butter in another pan and blend in the flour. Slowly add the chicken broth and vegetables. Cook over a low heat, stirring constantly, until thickened. Add the cream and salt and cook slowly 10 minutes longer. Serve hot with the split toasted crackers.

Serves 4

Southern Chicken

Southern cooking has a mouth-watering appeal which brings back memories of stately white-columned mansions with broad sweeping lawns, of plantation life before the Civil War, and the incomparable Negro cooks who created so many wonderful and tantalizing dishes. The dining halls of the old South and the magnificence of the tables laden with good things to eat and drink. There were huge Virginia hams home-cooked to perfection, great succulent roasts of mutton and pork and beef; enormous platters of fried chicken, well seasoned, dredged with flour, and browned crisp in sizzling fat. There were rich soups and bisques, shellfish of many varieties, little pigs in blankets, turkey with oyster stuffing, hush puppies, innumerable vegetables. White-jacketed Negroes passed large silver trays filled with delicious hot breads: Sally Lunn, hoe cakes, ash cakes, cornbread, the famous Maryland beaten biscuits fresh out of the oven and feathery light. The lordly plantations served an overabundance of good things to eat and the cooking of the Negro cooks has never been equaled. The dining tables glowed with goblets of imported wines, fancy jellies, brandied preserved fruits. Many rich desserts were served: trifle, poundcake, fruit and berry pie, strawberry shortcake, English steamed pudding, floating island, crisp pastries filled with fresh sugared peaches cooked down to a thick jam and sprinkled with powdered sugar. There were cheeses and fruits of every variety. The cloths were thick white damask, there was the unhurried clink of silver on fine china, the pace was leisurely.

A rich regional cookery grew up in the Southland. It combined English influences, Negro cooking skills, and the natural food resources of the country. Southern plantation life with its abundance and variety became something to remember. The plantations were vast estates with great houses adorned by tall graceful Grecian columns and surrounded by sloping green lawns, shade trees, and flower gardens. No food was cooked in the great plantation houses. A separate building contained the kitchen and the food was carried by Negro slaves in enormous covered silver dishes from the kitchen building to the dining hall. In addition to the kitchen annex the plantation had an assortment of other buildings: a schoolhouse, stables, carriagehouse, blacksmith shop, carpentry shop, laundry, smokehouse, icehouse, henhouses, dairy. The dairy was often referred to as the springhouse, as it was actually built directly over a flowing spring. Here crocks of butter, milk, and cream were kept fresh and sweet in the cold flowing water. Behind the plantation outbuildings were the slave quarters. Some of the slaves were house servants, some worked in the shops spinning and weaving or making things for the plantation, but most of the slaves worked out in the fields.

Southern plantation life was a lavish social and sporting life patterned after the landed gentry of England. The plantation owner did none of the actual labor. He was a gentleman from an aristocratic family brought up in the old tradition to live like an English country gentleman. He worked only at planning, hiring overseers, buying and trading slaves, selling his crops, and much of his time was spent in hunting, horse racing, drinking, graciously entertaining guests. Most of the responsibility for running the huge household fell not on the planter but on his wife. The lady of the manor, efficient, softspoken, moved with quiet grace around her menage superintending the household. It was she who managed the kitchen and staff and saw to the planning of the abundant meals. In her capable hands she kept both the keys and the recipes and she managed both with grace and dignity.

Southern fried chicken was the most popular of all Southern dishes. There were naturally differences of opinion throughout the South as to its method of preparation. Some cooks dredged the chicken pieces with flour before frying them. Others dipped the chicken pieces first in beaten egg, then into flour, cornmeal, or breadcrumbs; while others dipped the chicken into a batter of flour, milk, and eggs before frying. Whatever method they used in preparing the chicken, a cream gravy was invariably made from the drippings in the pan and at the last minute poured hot over the crisp fried chicken.

Fried chicken was only one of many famous chicken dishes in the Southland. Burgoo, the best known of all Kentucky regional dishes, was a thick stew prepared with chickens, squirrels, beef, hogs, lambs, and a wide assortment of vegetables and seasonings. It was served in Kentucky on Derby Day as well as at political rallies and elections. It was usually cooked outdoors in great iron kettles, and if the crowd was very large the quantities required of each ingredient reached a staggering proportion.

A popular regional chicken dish in Georgia was Country Captain, named after an English army captain homeward bound from India, so the story goes, who stopped off in Savannah long enough to introduce the recipe to his Southern friends. The dish is well-flavored with Indian spices and it is still served frequently in Georgia households. Then there is Chicken à la Maryland, one of the most delectable of all chicken dishes. The dish is said to have originated in St. Clement Island and was later introduced into Maryland by Lord Baltimore. Chicken shortcake, another Southern favorite, was a rich creamed chicken served between squares of cornbread like a shortcake.

Brunswick Stew is one of the most famous of all Southern dishes. Supposedly it originated in Brunswick County, Virginia, but there are authentic recipes for it from every section of Dixie. At first it was made with squirrels and no vegetables but onions. Later chicken became the main ingredient and fresh lima beans, corn, okra, and even tomatoes were added. It was cooked in enormous steaming kettles and served at barbecue parties. Barbecues were big events in the Southland and guests came from far-distant plantations to attend them. Every plantation had its own long barbecue pits for roasting meats and poultry, and the night before a party the barbecue fires were lighted up to burn down slowly during the night so that whole quarters of beef, whole calves, pigs, turkeys, and chickens could roast in pits of burning embers. The meats and poultry were turned on spits over the hot coals and their juices tricking down into the glowing embers made the air pungent with rich meat smells. Brunswick Stew was served as a prelude to the barbecue and its savory smells whetted the appetites of the guests. Long-trestled picnic tables were set up for the barbecue, covered with the finest linen, and laden with platters of Georgia country ham, Virginia ham, sugar-coated ham, and various other assorted meats. Between the courses slaves ran back and forth with silver trays of dainties and with a dozen or more kinds of fresh hot breads.

Yes indeed, the Southern plantation life was a pleasant, slow, leisurely way of life, but time ran out for the plantation Southland. The Civil War with its invasion and chaos and bloodshed ended it abruptly. The Southern geneleman wore the gray uniform of the Confederacy and fought and died for a cause he believed was right. The glory of the plantation disappeared with the South's defeat but the memory of its princely hospitality, its charm, its golden slow-paced life, the finest of its recipes has never faded.

Brunswick Stew

Brunswick Stew was one of the most famous of all Southern dishes and there are authentic recipes for it from every section of Dixie. Many of the original recipes called for squirrels instead of chicken although the historic recipes of Georgia and the Carolinas mention chicken as the essential ingredient. Whether or not it was squirrel in its original form, squirrels have gradually disappeared from the recipes and chicken is now more or less accepted as the major ingredient for Brunswick Stew.

1 large plump chicken cut into pieces
1 teaspoon salt
¼ teaspoon pepper
½ cup flour
¼ cup bacon drippings
5 cups boiling water
1 bay leaf
2 onions sliced
2 cups fresh or canned tomatoes
1½ cups fresh or frozen lima beans
1½ cups fresh or frozen corn kernels
1 cup fresh or frozen okra cut in ¼ inch slices
1 tablespoon Worcestershire sauce
2 tablespoons chopped parsley

Mix the salt, pepper, and flour together and roll the chicken pieces in the seasoned flour. In a deep pot melt the bacon drippings and when hot fry the chicken pieces until well browned on both sides. Then pour off the fat and add the boiling water to the pot. Add bay leaf, onions, tomatoes, lima beans, corn kernels, okra, Worcestershire sauce, and chopped parsley. Cover and simmer over low heat for 1 hour or until the chicken and vegetables are tender. Serve in deep bowls.

Southern cooks would sometimes thicken the broth with fine bread crumbs.

Serves 6–8

Brunswick Stew Virginia
Brunswick County, Virginia, has for many years laid claim to the origin of Brunswick Stew and most of the early recipes

called for both squirrels and chickens. Here is a variation of a typical one.

1 large plump chicken or 2 squirrels
1 ham bone from baked Virginia ham
2½ quarts water
1 onion sliced
1 bay leaf
2 cups tomatoes
½ cup chopped celery and leaves
1 cup fresh or frozen lima beans
1 cup fresh or frozen corn kernels
½ cup fresh or frozen okra
½ cup butter
Salt and pepper

Place the chicken or squirrels in a large kettle with the ham bone, water, sliced onion, and bay leaf. Cook covered over a low heat until the meat is tender enough to fall from the bones. Remove meat and ham bone. When the meat has cooled free from the bones and cut into pieces. Set aside. To the broth in the kettle add the tomatoes, chopped celery and leaves, lima beans, corn kernels, and okra. Cook over a low heat until the beans are tender. Return the meat to the kettle and continue cooking until the mixture is of the consistency of a rich thick soup. Add the butter and salt and pepper to taste. Cook until the butter has melted and ladle into bowls.

Serves 8 or more

Kentucky Burgoo

Kentucky Burgoo came to be associated with Kentucky because of its great popularity at Kentucky political rallies and outdoor gatherings. It was made in huge iron pots and served in enormous quantities. In fact, one old recipe called for 1400 pounds of meat and poultry. Needless to say, I have cut the quantity down considerably but it is still a dish worth trying.

4 tablespoons bacon fat
1 pound beef shin bones
1 pound shoulder of veal
1 large plump chicken cut in pieces
2 quarts water
1 teaspoon salt
2 onions chopped
1 clove garlic minced
1 cup potatoes diced
4 stalks celery chopped
4 tomatoes chopped
1 green pepper diced
4 cloves
1 bay leaf
1 tablespoon Worcestershire sauce
¼ teaspoon cayenne pepper
1 cup fresh or frozen okra
1 cup fresh or frozen corn kernels
Flour
¼ cup butter
¼ cup chopped parsley

Melt 2 tablespoons bacon fat in a large heavy pan. Add beef bones, shoulder of veal, and brown well all over. Add the chicken, 1 teaspoon salt, and the water. Cover and cook over low heat until the meat is tender. Remove the meat and cool. Cut the meat from the bones into small pieces and return to the pan. In a frying pan melt 2 tablespoons bacon fat and cook the chopped onions until soft. Add them to the pan along with the garlic, potatoes, celery, tomatoes, green peppers, cloves, bay leaf, Worcestershire sauce, and cayenne pepper. Cover and cook slowly for 1½ hours. Then add the okra and corn kernels and cook 15 minutes longer. Thicken the Burgoo with the flour mixed with a little cold water. Stir in the butter and when melted ladle the Burgoo into soup bowls. Sprinkle with chopped parsley.

Serves 10

Country Captain
An English army captain homeward bound from India, so the story goes, stopped off in Savannah and introduced this recipe to his southern friends.

1 large chicken fryer cut into pieces
1 teaspoon salt
¼ teaspoon pepper
½ cup flour
¼ cup butter melted
1 cup chopped onions
1 green pepper chopped fine
1 clove garlic minced
1 tablespoon curry powder
1½ cups canned tomatoes
½ cup dried currants
Hot boiled rice

Mix the salt and pepper with the flour and roll the chicken pieces in the seasoned flour. Melt 2 tablespoons of the butter in a large heavy frying pan and add the chopped onions, chopped green peppers, minced garlic, and curry powder. Cook until soft but not browned. Remove the vegetables and set aside. Add the rest of the butter to the pan and brown the chicken well on both sides. Return the vegetables to the pan along with the canned tomatoes. Mix in well, cover the pan, and simmer over a low heat for 30 minutes or until the chicken is tender. Add the dried currants and cook a few moments longer. Serve over hot boiled rice.

Serves 4

Chicken à la Maryland
Chicken à la Maryland was one of the most delectable dishes
to delight the southern palate. This recipe is from Louis P.
DeGouy's Gold Cookbook, used with permission from Chilton
Book Company, Philadelphia. I have tried many recipes for
Chicken à la Maryland and I consider this particular recipe
the best.

2 milk-fed chickens, 2 pounds each
Salt and pepper
Milk
Flour
Melted lard
Scalded rich milk
2 well beaten egg yolks

Quarter the chicken and remove necks and backbones. Clean
thoroughly, wash and dry, then season with salt and pepper.
Dip each piece in milk, roll in flour, and cook in an inch of
melted lard in a hot pan until golden brown, turning frequently. Transfer them to another pan, cover, and place in a
moderate 375° oven until they are thoroughly steamed
through. Meanwhile, sprinkle the necks and the backbones
lightly with seasoned flour, and brown them in the pan in
which the chicken was cooked. Add enough scalded rich milk
to make a medium-thick cream sauce which is then enriched
with 2 well beaten egg yolks. Pour this sauce onto a hot platter
and arrange the chicken on it. Garnish with corn fritters,
strips of broiled bacon, and small potato croquettes.

Serves 6

Maryland Chicken in Sherry Sauce
My aunt found the original of this one in an old southern
recipe book.

4 pound chicken
5 cups water
2 teaspoons salt
½ pound medium egg noodles
2 tablespoons butter
Sherry sauce
4 tablespoons toasted shredded almonds

Put the chicken in a kettle with 5 cups water and 2 teaspoons salt. Cover and cook over low heat until tender about 1 hour. Remove the chicken and when cool free the meat from the bones and cut into large pieces. Set aside. Cook the egg noodles in boiling water to cover until tender. Drain. Pour hot water over them and drain again. Return the noodles to the pan and add 2 tablespoons butter. Mix thoroughly. Place the buttered noodles in a greased casserole and lay the chicken pieces on top of them. Pour over the sherry sauce and sprinkle the toasted shredded almonds over the top. Bake in a pre-heated 425° oven for 15 minutes or until lightly browned.

Sherry Sauce
¼ cup butter melted
6 tablespoons flour
2 cups chicken stock
2 cups heavy cream
½ teaspoon salt
¼ teaspoon paprika
½ pound mushrooms sliced
2 tablespoons butter
⅔ cup sherry

Melt the butter in a saucepan. Add the flour and blend in well. Slowly add the chicken stock and the heavy cream. Cook over a low heat until thickened. Sauté the mushrooms in 2 tablespoons butter and add to the sauce along with ½ teaspoon salt and ¼ teaspoon paprika. Add the sherry and blend until smooth.

Serves 4

Chicken Pudding
Chicken Pudding is a favorite old Virginia dish.

4-pound chicken fryer cut into pieces
½ cup flour
1 teaspoon salt
¼ teaspoon black pepper
¼ cup butter melted
1½ cups flour
1 teaspoon salt
1½ teaspoons baking powder
4 eggs well-beaten
1½ cups milk
3 tablespoons butter melted

Add the salt and pepper to the flour and roll the chicken pieces in the seasoned flour. Melt ¼ cup butter in a heavy frying pan and brown the chicken well on both sides. In the meantime make a batter by sifting the flour, salt, and baking powder together. Beat the eggs well and add the milk and 3 tablespoons melted butter. Add the dry ingredients and beat until smooth. Turn the batter into a well-greased baking dish and place the chicken in the batter so it is partly covered. Bake in a preheated 375° oven for 45 minutes or until the batter is puffed and browned and the chicken tender.

Serves 4

Baked Ham Bethany
The name of this dish intrigued me and especially so when a chicken cooked this way with crusty cornbread fixings comes straight from Dixie.

1 fat stewing hen
1 teaspoon salt
1 onion
1 stalk celery with leaves
Water to cover
3 cups cornbread crumbs
1 teaspoon poultry seasoning
1 teaspoon celery salt
½ teaspoon salt
Melted butter
2 tablespoons flour
1 cup chicken stock
1 cup cream

Put the chicken in a kettle with the salt, onion, celery and leaves, and enough water to cover. Bring to a boil, lower heat, and simmer covered 1½ hours or until chicken is tender. Meanwhile combine the cornbread crumbs, celery salt, poultry seasoning, and ½ teaspoon salt. When the chicken is tender place it in a shallow baking pan and let it cool. Strain the stock and moisten the cornbread mixture with it. Set 1 cup of the strained chicken stock aside. Stuff the chicken lightly with the cornbread mixture and arrange any leftover stuffing around the chicken in the baking pan. Brush the chicken well with melted butter and bake in a preheated 425° oven until the skin is well browned and the stuffing crusty. Brush frequently with melted butter. Remove the chicken and stuffing to a hot platter. Add enough melted butter to the drippings in the pan to make two tablespoonfuls. Blend in the flour and gradually add the reserved cup of chicken stock and the cream, stirring constantly over the heat until thickened. Taste for seasoning and serve with the chicken and stuffing.

Serves 6

Chicken Tallyrand

This dish is a good example of the creations of the Negro cooks. The dish was probably named after Talleyrand, a great French epicurean in the 18th century.

4-pound chicken fryer cut into pieces
3 cups chicken stock
1 stalk celery cut into pieces
2 sprigs parsley
½ teaspoon thyme
1 bay leaf
2 tablespoons butter
2 tablespoons flour
¾ cup chicken stock
½ cup Madeira wine
Baked Virginia ham sliced thin

Put the chicken pieces in a kettle and cover with 3 cups chicken stock, adding water if necessary to barely cover the chicken. Add celery, parsley, thyme, and bay leaf. Simmer covered over a low heat for 45 minutes or until chicken is tender. Remove the chicken and keep hot. Strain the stock and reserve. In a saucepan melt 2 tablespoons butter and blend in the 2 table-spoons flour. Gradually add ¾ cup of the chicken stock and cook over the heat, stirring constantly until the sauce is smooth and thick. Add ½ cup Madeira and stir over a low heat until smooth. Arrange the chicken pieces on a serving platter and lay a thin slice of Virginia baked ham over each piece. Pour the sauce over the top and serve at once.

Serves 4

Southern Fried Chicken

What dish can be more Southern or truly American, for that matter, than old-fashioned Southern-fried chicken? Well-sea-soned, rolled in flour, sizzled in hot lard, it has long been a national favorite.

2—2½-pound chicken fryers cut into pieces
Milk
1 egg slightly beaten
½ cup milk
1 teaspoon salt
¼ teaspoon pepper
½ cup flour
½ cup lard or Crisco
3 cups scalded milk (approximately)
4 tablespoons flour

Cover the chicken pieces with milk and let them stand for
1 hour. Beat 1 egg slightly with ½ cup milk. Add the salt and
pepper to the flour. Drain the chicken and dip it first in the
egg-milk mixture and then in the seasoned flour. Melt the
lard or Crisco in a heavy skillet and when the fat bubbles add
the chicken. Cook the chicken until golden brown on both
sides, turning frequently so that it browns evenly. Cover the
skillet, lower the heat, and cook slowly for 15 minutes. Remove the lid, turn the chicken over, and continue cooking
15 minutes longer or until the chicken is tender. Remove the
chicken to a serving platter and keep hot. My grandmother
used to remove it to a hot oven for 5 or 10 minutes to crisp
it before serving.

Drain off all but 4 tablespoons of the drippings. Add 4 tablespoons flour and stir smooth. Slowly add enough scalded milk
—about 3 cups—to make a medium-thick cream gravy. Season
to taste. Pour into a gravy boat and serve separately with the
chicken along with piping hot biscuits and honey.

Serves 4

Fried Chicken in Cornmeal Batter
Golden-brown chicken fried in cornmeal batter is another
typically Southern dish.

2 egg yolks
1 cup cornmeal
1 cup grated Cheddar cheese
1½ teaspoons salt
½ teaspoon white pepper
2 egg whites beaten stiff
4-pound chicken fryer cut into pieces
½ cup butter melted

Beat the egg yolks until thick and yellow colored. Stir in the cornmeal, Cheddar cheese, salt, and white pepper. Fold in the stiffly beaten egg whites. Dip the chicken pieces in this mixture coating them well all over. Let them set for half an hour to dry out. Melt the butter in a heavy frying pan and fry the chicken in it, turning frequently, until the chicken is browned and tender, about 45 miuntes.

Serves 4

Fried Chicken and Virginia Ham
Fried crisp chicken and spicy Virginia ham make a delightful combination.

3½-pound chicken fryer cut into pieces
4 thin slices Virginia ham
1 teaspoon salt
¼ teaspoon pepper
½ cup flour
¼ cup lard
2 heaping tablespoons flour
2 cups thin cream

Fry the slices of Virginia ham in a large heavy skillet until browned and crisp on both sides. Set aside and keep hot. Add the salt and pepper to the flour and roll the chicken pieces in the seasoned flour. Melt the lard in the skillet the ham was cooked in and add the chicken pieces. Fry until browned and tender, turning frequently to brown both sides evenly. When chicken is fork tender transfer to a platter and keep hot. Pour off all but 4 tablespoons of the drippings. Stir in the 2 heaping tablespoons flour and cook a few minutes. Then pour in the thin cream. Cook, stirring constantly, until the sauce is smooth and thick. Pour the sauce over the hot chicken and garnish with the fried Virginia ham.

Serves 4

Chicken Shortcake

Creamed chicken, served between squares of cornbread sliced in half like a hot biscuit, has always been a favorite dish in the Southland.

5-pound chicken
Cold water to cover
2 teaspoons salt
1 onion
2 stalks celery
1 bay leaf
3 cups chicken broth
1 cup heavy cream
4 tablespoons chicken fat or butter
4 tablespoons flour
½ teaspoon salt
1 pound mushrooms sliced and sautéed in 2 tablespoons
     butter

Cornbread
2 cups white cornmeal
¾ cup flour
½ teaspoon salt
2 eggs well-beaten
½ cup milk
2 tablespoons butter melted

Put the chicken in a kettle with cold water to cover. Add 2 teaspoons salt, the onion, celery, bay leaf; cover, and simmer over low heat for 1½ hours or until the chicken is tender. Remove the chicken, strain the broth, and let it cool. Skim off the fat and reserve. Remove the skin and bones from the chicken and cut the meat into cubes. Sauté the mushrooms in butter. In a saucepan melt 4 tablespoons of the chicken fat or butter and blend in the 4 tablespoons flour. Gradually add 3 cups of the chicken broth, stirring constantly over a low heat until the sauce has thickened. Add 1 cup heavy cream and continue cooking until the sauce is smooth and of a medium thickness. Add the chicken and the mushrooms, ½ teaspoon salt, and cook a few moments longer. Keep hot while you make the shortcake.

Sift together the cornmeal, flour, salt, and baking powder. Beat the eggs and mix with the milk. Stir the egg mixture into the dry ingredients and gradually add 2 tablespoons melted butter. Pour into a greased rectangular pan and bake in a 400° oven for 25 minutes. Cut the shortcake into 4-inch squares and split them in half. Butter them lightly. Spread the bottom piece with a heaping spoonful of the creamed chicken mixture, cover with the shortcake top, and cover the square with more of the hot creamed chicken.

Serves 4

Creole Chicken

The traditional Creole cookery of New Orleans is famous the world over for its excellence. It is a luscious blend of the best classical cookery of France and Spain, the ingenuity of the refugee Cajuns, the native Indian use of wild herbs and seasonings, and, last but not least, the magic cooking talent of the Negro cooks, all of which contributed to give Creole cooking its exotic and distinctive flavor. Such delectable dishes as daube glacé, thick gumbo, jambalaya, pompano en papillotes, sugared pecans, and pralines are like nothing else on earth.

The gay, colorful, glamorous city of New Orleans was the heart of Creole cooking. The charm of the old historic French Quarter, the colored women with trays of delicious breakfast cakes called callas on their heads, whose familiar chant, *"Bel callas tout chaud,"* was heard on Canal Street Sunday mornings after church. It was the custom for churchgoers to buy the hot cakes and take them home for breakfast to be served with café au lait—coffee and hot milk in equal proportions. The fame of the Mardi Gras with the parades and masquerading and merrymaking . . . all the rich eating and gay living . . . no wonder New Orleans intrigues visitors as few other cities can. The picturesque food market with row upon row of stalls filled with all manner of foodstuffs stretching out beyond a quarter of a mile became a great sightseeing attraction. The strategic position of New Orleans at the mouth of the Mississippi drew into its lap all the exotic foods and fruits from the West Indies and South America, not to mention the farm produce and meats from the whole Midwest brought by steamship and barge down the Mississippi River. Add to this the abundance of local game in the surrounding wooded areas, the many varieties of fish in lakes and streams, and all the seafood of the gulf, and it is easy to see how it was possible for New Orleans to create such a succulent cuisine.

The fame of Creole cooking was spread quickly by the French Quarter restaurants where their superb cuisine soon captivated visiting gourmets. Restaurants like Antoine's, Broussard's, Galatoire's, became a delight for tourists. The narrow romantic cobblestoned streets, the lacy wrought-iron gratings and trellised balconies, the shaded patios glimpsed briefly behind stuccoed walls among palm, banana, and magnolia trees, all charmed the out-of-town visitors. Visiting tourists were captivated by the restaurants with their high culinary traditions, the cool, spacious dining rooms opening onto garden courtyards; snowy cloths on tables gleaming with polished silver; immaculate dusky waiters dignified and formal. In the unpretentious subdued setting food and drink were the primary concern—the menus in French and the food magnificent.

The dishes created by master chefs became famous among gourmets of all nationalities. There were delicate soups of the bisque family; bouillabaisse, the most celebrated of all Louisiana fish soups because of the unsurpassed flavor of the fish caught in the Gulf of Mexico; jambalaya with chicken, oyster, shrimp; shellfish and other saltwater delicacies served in a dozen different ways, each more delicious than the other. The superb pompano en papillotes topped with an elegant sauce of crayfish, crab, or shrimp. Gumbo was the most distinctive of all the exotic Creole dishes. Gumbo was not a soup exactly, not a stew, not a ragout, but a pungent mixture inherited from Africa and the West Indies and perfected by the Cajuns. The most famous Gumbos were made from chicken, squirrel, rabbit, crab, shrimp, or herbs, each one of which was a completely different dish. The secret ingredient of Gumbo was filé powder which was dried sassafras leaves ground to make a rich green powder. The filé powder was manufactured from the tender young leaves of the sassafras plant by the native Indians. The leaves were gathered by the squaws and spread out in the sun to dry thoroughly. Then they were pounded to a fine powder and passed through a hair sieve. Twice a week the Indians brought the sassafras powder to the French food market in New Orleans. It is easily obtainable now in any gourmet food shop in one of the larger cities.

In preparing a Gumbo, the filé powder is added after the pot has been removed from the fire. The powder is poured in slowly and as it is stirred it binds and thickens. After the filé powder is added, the Gumbo must never be reheated or it is liable to become stringy and unpalatable.

Chicken Gumbo

Gumbo, that pungent mixture inherited from Africa and the West Indies and perfected by the Cajuns, represents the most distinctive dish in Creole cuisine.

5-pound roasting chicken cut into pieces
1½ tablespoons salt
½ cup shortening
½ cup flour
2 cups chopped onions
1 cup chopped green peppers
2 cloves garlic minced
2 cups hot water
2 tablespoons Worcestershire sauce
1 tablespoon lemon juice
1 teaspoon black pepper
pinch of thyme
2 pounds uncooked cleaned shrimp
½ cup celery chopped
½ cup green onions chopped

1 teaspoon filé powder (ground dried sassafras leaves)
½ cup chopped parsley

Season chicken with 1½ tablespoons salt. Heat the shortening in a large pot or Dutch oven and brown the chicken well on both sides. Remove the chicken and add ½ cup flour to the shortening in the pan. Stir over low heat until the flour is a light brown. Add the chopped onions, chopped green peppers, and the minced garlic. Cook for 1 minute and then add 2 cups hot water. Return the chicken to the pot and add 2 teaspoons salt, 2 tablespoons Worcestershire sauce, 1 tablespoon lemon juice, 1 teaspoon black pepper; and a pinch of thyme. Cover and simmer over low heat about 45 minutes or until the chicken is tender. Add 2 pounds uncooked shrimp, the chopped celery and green onions. Simmer 30 minutes longer. Remove the chicken pieces to a large platter and keep hot. Bring the sauce to a boil, stirring constantly. Remove from the heat and stir in the filé powder. Pour the sauce over the chicken and sprinkle with chopped parsley. Serve with Creole Rice.

Serves 6

* Never reheat the gumbo after the filé powder is added or it is liable to be stringy.

Creole Rice
1 large onion sliced thin
1 cup green pepper chopped
4 tablespoons butter melted
1 cup rice
¼ pound fresh mushrooms sliced
1 cup canned tomatoes
½ cup pitted black olives sliced
1 teaspoon salt
¼ teaspoon black pepper

½ teaspoon dried thyme
1 tablespoon chopped parsley
¼ teaspoon crushed red peppers
1 clove garlic minced
2 cups boiling water
2 tablespoons Worcestershire sauce

Cook the sliced onion and chopped green pepper in 4 tablespoons melted butter for 5 minutes over a low heat, stirring constantly. Gradually stir in the rice and cook until the rice turns yellow. Add the sliced mushrooms, canned tomatoes, pitted black olives, 1 teaspoon salt, black pepper, thyme, chopped parsley, and crushed red peppers. Add the minced clove of garlic and 2 cups boiling water to which has been add the Worcestershire sauce. Cover and simmer over low heat for 45 minutes. Serve with the Chicken Gumbo.

Creole Chicken
A composite of Creole cookery at its best.

5-pound roasting chicken cut into pieces
⅓ cup butter melted
1 teaspoon salt
⅛ teaspoon black pepper
1 cup thinly sliced onions
2 green peppers sliced thin
2 cups stewed tomatoes
1 cup dry white wine
12 pitted green olives sliced
1 cup mushrooms sliced
2 whole cloves
Bouquet garni
8 slices bacon
1 teaspoon filé powder

Season the chicken pieces with salt and pepper and brown

in the ⅓ cup butter in a heavy pan or Dutch oven. When the chicken is well browned on both sides remove it and set aside. Add the sliced onions to the pan along with the 2 sliced green peppers. Cook over low heat until soft and lightly browned. Add the stewed tomatoes, dry white wine, pitted green olives, sliced mushrooms, cloves, bouquet garni composed of parsley, thyme, bay leaf, peppercorns, all tied together in a cheese-cloth bag so that they can be removed before serving. Return the chicken to the pan, cover, and cook over a low heat for 45 minutes or until the chicken is tender. Fry the bacon until crisp and drain on absorbent paper. When the chicken is tender, crumble the bacon and add it to the sauce. Simmer covered 5 minutes longer. Remove the chicken pieces to a large hot platter. Remove the sauce from the heat and stir in the filé powder. Pour the sauce over the chicken and serve with plain boiled rice or with Creole rice.

Serves 6

Chicken Jambalaya

Creole Jambalaya which in some respects is a sort of Creole Arroz con Pollo is a mixture of imagination and toothsome ingredients blended subtly to make a delightful dish.

5-pound roasting chicken cut into pieces
¼ cup butter melted
2 cups chopped onions
1 cup chopped celery
1 cup chopped green peppers
2 cloves garlic minced
3 cups hot chicken stock plus 3 cups hot water
3 cups uncooked rice
4 tablespoons chopped green onions
3 tablespoons chopped parsley
Salt and pepper to taste
1 teaspoon filé powder

Melt ¼ cup butter in a large pot. Add the chicken pieces and brown well on both sides. Add the chopped onions, chopped celery, chopped green peppers, and the minced garlic. Cook with the chicken until the vegetables are lightly colored and tender. Add the 3 cups hot chicken stock plus the 3 cups hot water, the uncooked rice, chopped green onions, chopped parsley, and continue cooking, covered, over low heat for about 1 hour or until the chicken is tender. Remove the chicken to a hot serving platter. Remove the pot from the fire and add 1 teaspoon filé powder. Mix in well and pour the sauce over the chicken.

Serves 6

Louisiana Chicken
Creole herbs and spices give this Louisiana dish a piquant flavor.

4-pound chicken fryer cut into pieces
1 teaspoon salt
¼ teaspoon pepper
¼ cup butter melted
¼ cup chopped onions
½ cup chopped green peppers
1 tablespoon chopped parsley
1 cup rice
½ teaspoon salt
⅛ teaspoon pepper
1 teaspoon Worcestershire sauce
Dash of cayenne
Dash of Tabasco sauce
Pinch of thyme
2½ cups hot chicken broth
Chopped parsley

Season chicken pieces with salt and pepper and brown in the

melted butter until golden on both sides. Remove the chicken and keep hot. Add to the pan the chopped onions, chopped green peppers, chopped parsley, and cook until lightly browned. Add the rice, ½ teaspoon salt, ⅛ teaspoon pepper, Worcestershire sauce, cayenne, Tabasco, and thyme. Cook 5 minutes stirring occasionally. Return the chicken to the pan, add the hot chicken broth, and simmer covered over low heat about 30 minutes or until chicken is tender and rice has absorbed all the liquid. Arrange the rice on a hot platter with the chicken on top. Sprinkle with the chopped parsley.

Serves 4

Chicken Creole Curry

Creole Curry with onions and tomatoes and herbs and spices is another mouth-watering Creole delight.

4-pound chicken fryer cut into pieces
¼ cup butter melted
1 cup onions chopped fine
2 medium tomatoes peeled and chopped
1½ teaspoons curry powder
1 teaspoon chopped parsley
1 clove garlic minced
½ teaspoon ginger
1 cup warm chicken broth
Creole rice

Melt the butter in a heavy frying pan and brown the chicken pieces well on both sides. Add the chopped onions and let them simmer with the chicken for 5 minutes. Add the chopped tomatoes and cook for 15 minutes. Mix the curry powder, chopped parsley, minced garlic, and ginger together and add the warm chicken broth. Stir well with a spoon and pour over the chicken. Simmer over a low heat for 1 hour or until the chicken is tender. This will not be a very liquid sauce. Serve with Creole rice.

Serves 4

Chicken Creole Ragout with Almonds

A rich sauce of cream and mushrooms and shredded toasted almonds distinctively flavors this Creole classic.

4-pound chicken fryer cut into pieces
½ cup flour
1 teaspoon salt
¼ cup butter melted
1 cup hot chicken broth
1 medium onion chopped fine
½ cup heavy cream
3 tablespoons flour
½ teaspoon white pepper
½ teaspoon nutmeg
1 cup canned mushroom slices
1 cup shredded toasted almonds

Add the salt to the flour and roll the chicken pieces in the seasoned flour. Melt the butter in a heavy frying pan and brown the chicken well on both sides. Add the hot chicken broth and the chopped onion. Cover and simmer over low heat for 40 minutes or until the chicken is tender. Blend the heavy cream with the 3 tablespoons flour. Add the white pepper and nutmeg. Stir into the pan with the chicken and cook over low heat, stirring constantly, until thickened. Add the mushroom slices and the shredded toasted almonds. Cook 1 minute longer and serve over rice.

Serves 4

Chicken Sauté New Orleans

Another exciting dish from New Orleans.

4-pound chicken fryer cut into pieces
½ cup flour

1 teaspoon salt
⅛ teaspoon pepper
¼ cup butter melted
2 tablespoons chopped green onions
1 clove garlic minced
½ cup mushrooms sliced
½ cup dry white wine
1 bay leaf crumbled
½ teaspoon chervil
12 oysters and liquor

Add the salt and pepper to the flour and roll the chicken pieces in the seasoned flour. Melt the butter in a heavy skillet and brown the chicken pieces well on both sides. Remove the chicken. Add to the pan the chopped green onions, minced garlic, sliced mushrooms, bay leaf, and chervil. Cook until the green onions and mushrooms are lightly browned. Return the chicken to the pan and add ½ cup dry white wine. Cover and simmer over low heat for 40 minutes or until the chicken is tender. Add the oysters and their liquor and let cook a few minutes longer over medium heat until the edges of the oysters begin to curl. Serve with rice.

Serves 4

Chicken à la Chevalière
A masterpiece of New Orleans cuisine, Chicken à la Chevalière, is a dish fit for a king.

3½-pound chicken boned
½ cup sausage meat
1 egg white
¼ cup sour cream
½ teaspoon salt
⅛ teaspoon pepper
⅛ teaspoon Tabasco sauce

½ teaspoon chervil
½ teaspoon tarragon
1 teaspoon chopped parsley
Several slices cooked lean ham
Several slices cooked smoked tongue
½ pound chicken livers
3 truffles
4 slices lean bacon

Sauce
2 cups chicken broth
2 teaspoons meat glaze
¼ cup Madeira wine
1 tablespoon cornstarch diluted in 2 tablespoons water

Bone the chicken carefully or ask your butcher to do it. Spread the chicken on a board. In a bowl mix the sausage meat, sour cream, egg white, salt, pepper, Tabasco sauce, chervil, tarragon, and parsley. Cover the top of the chicken with this mixture. Cover with the slices of cooked lean ham and the slices of cooked lean tongue. On top of this place the chicken livers and the truffles. Roll up carefully and sew with thread. Place the chicken in an open roasting pan and cover the top with the slices of lean bacon. Roast in a preheated 350° oven for 2 hours, basting frequently with the following sauce: Combine in a saucepan the chicken broth, meat glaze, Madeira, and the 1 tablespoon cornstarch diluted in 2 tablespoons cold water. Stir over the heat until it comes to a boil and baste the chicken frequently with this sauce. When chicken is done remove to a platter and add the rest of the sauce to the pan in which the chicken was cooked. Stir over the heat until the sauce comes to a boil scraping up all the browned particles from the bottom. Slice the chicken into thin slices and pour over the hot sauce.

Serves 4

New Orleans Chicken Pilaf
Another example of Creole ingenuity.

3 tablespoons butter
¼ cup chopped green pepper
½ cup chopped onion
¼ cup chopped celery
1 cup rice
2 cups canned tomatoes
2 cups chicken broth
1 teaspoon salt
Few drops Tabasco
2 cups chopped cooked chicken

Melt the butter in a large heavy frying pan and sauté the chopped green pepper, chopped onion, and chopped celery until soft but not browned. Add the rice, the canned tomatoes, chicken broth, salt, and the Tabasco. Bring to a boil and stir well. Add the chicken, cover, and cook over a low heat for 20 minutes or until the rice is tender and has absorbed most of the liquid.

Serves 4

Chicken Pie Creole
A flaky golden top covering a creamy chicken dish of delicate flavor.

1 plump chicken cut into pieces
2 tablespoons butter melted
¼ cup flour
2 cups chicken stock
2 cups heavy cream
½ teaspoon salt
¼ teaspoon white pepper
Pie crust

Place the chicken in a pot with water to cover and simmer over a low heat about 2 hours or until tender. Cut the meat from the bones in large chunks and arrange in a buttered baking dish. Blend the 2 tablespoons butter with the flour in a saucepan and gradually add 2 cups of the chicken stock. Stir over a low heat until thick and smooth. Add the 2 cups heavy cream, the salt, and the white pepper. Cook, stirring constantly, until the sauce is smooth and creamy. Pour 3 cups of the sauce over the chicken in the baking dish and reserve the rest to serve on the side in a gravy boat.

Pie Crust
2 cups sifted flour
4 teaspoons baking powder
1 teaspoon salt
2 tablespoons butter melted
1 egg well-beaten
¾ to 1 cup milk

Sift together flour, baking powder, and salt. Combine melted butter, egg, and milk. Add the liquid to the dry ingredients, stirring in quickly to make a soft dough. Drop by spoonfuls over the chicken and gravy in the baking dish. Bake in a pre-heated 425° oven for about 20 minutes and the crust is nicely browned. Serve hot with the extra gravy passed in a gravy boat.

Serves 6

Creole Omelet
While I was working my way through Creole chicken a friend in Sausalito, Barbara Carter, sent me this recipe and suggested I might like to use it. I found it an unusual dish and am delighted to include it here.

2 cups cooked chicken cut into chunks
8 French pancakes

¼ cup butter
1 onion chopped
¼ cup chopped celery
2 tablespoons chopped parsley
2 tomatoes peeled and chopped
¼ cup green pepper chopped
1 teaspoon crushed red peppers
1 tablespoon tomato puree
1 tablespoon flour
2 cups chicken stock

Prepare the French pancakes and keep warm. Then make the sauce: melt the butter in a saucepan and cook the chopped onion until a light golden in color. Add the celery, parsley, tomatoes, green peppers, crushed red peppers, and the tomato puree. Cook over a medium heat about 5 minutes or until the vegetables are soft. Turn heat to high and let all the liquid evaporate in the pan. Sprinkle 1 tablespoon flour over the vegetables and mix in well. Slowly add the chicken stock and cook over a medium heat, stirring constantly, until the mixture has thickened slightly. Blend the sauce with the cooked chicken and place several spoonfuls in the middle of each pancake. Carefully roll up the pancakes and place two on each serving plate. Pour the rest of the sauce over the tops. Serve at once.

Serves 4

French Pancakes
3 eggs
¾ cup flour
1 tablespoon sugar
Pinch of salt
½ cup milk

Blend the eggs, flour, sugar, and salt together until smooth, or better yet blend them in an electric blender. Add the milk and blend until of a smooth eggnog consistency. Heat a skillet and when a few drops of water will dance on it the skillet is hot enough for even browning. Pour in 1½ tablespoons batter, tilting the pan so the batter covers the bottom of the pan evenly. Cook for about 1 minute or until lightly browned, then turn over and cook until lightly browned on the other side. Grease pan before cooking each pancake. They should be very thin.

New Orleans Fried Chicken

Chicken fried the New Orleans way and covered with a rich sherry flavored sauce is a dish that should melt in your mouth.

1 teaspoon salt
1 teaspoon cayenne pepper
½ cup flour
4-pound chicken fryer cut into pieces
¼ cup butter melted
1½ cups heavy cream
½ cup sherry
1 teaspoon Worcestershire sauce

Mix salt, cayenne, and flour together and roll the chicken pieces in the seasoned flour. Make sure each piece of chicken is well coated. Melt the butter in a heavy frying pan and fry the chicken, turning each piece of chicken frequently, until the chicken is tender and evenly browned on both sides. Remove to a serving platter and keep hot. Add the heavy cream and the sherry to the drippings in the pan, stirring hard to collect all the browned particles at the bottom. Add the Worcestershire sauce and stir over low heat until smooth. Pour over the chicken and serve immediately.

Serves 4

Cajun Fried Chicken

I have included this unusual recipe for Cajun Fried Chicken from Peggy Harvey's distinguished anthology of recipes, *The Horn Of Plenty*, Copyright © 1964 by Peggy Harvey, with permission granted by Atlantic, Little, Brown and Company. The author was given this recipe on an interesting trip to Avery Island, Louisiana, where Tabasco sauce is made.

2 disjointed frying chickens
1 quart milk
2 well-beaten eggs
1 teaspoon Tabasco
Salt to taste
½ cup flour
½ cup breadcrumbs
Crisco

Soak 2 disjointed chickens overnight in refrigerator in a mixture of 1 quart milk, 2 well-beaten eggs, 1 teaspoon Tabasco and salt to taste. Next day roll each piece of chicken in a mixture of half flour and half breadcrumbs—about ½ cup of each.

Heat 1½ inches of Crisco in a skillet that is just large enough to hold the pieces of chicken. When the fat bubbles, add the chicken and brown quickly on all sides. Cover the skillet, lower the heat and cook for 15 minutes. Remove the lid, turn the pieces of chicken and cook 15 minutes longer or until chicken is tender. Serve hot or cold.

Serves 6

Pennsylvania Dutch Chicken

Southeastern Pennsylvania is the home of the colorful Pennsylvania Dutch people and their delicious cuisine. Here for over three hundred years they have built up an American regional cuisine that can hold its own with the best. Pennsylvania Dutch food is as good as the people who live by it and their well-cultivated farms grow just about everything they eat. Their homes are solid and built soundly of stone, their barns bursting with fodder, their cattle sleek in the pastures, their fields so skillfully managed that they yield crops as good now as the day they were first plowed. It is a land of peace and plenty and the Pennsylvania Dutch people cherish their land and respect their bounty:

In the lush green hills of Southeastern Pennsylvania the Pennsylvania Dutch created a distinct culture of which their food is only one part. Persecuted for centuries because of their religious beliefs, they were finally driven from their homeland in the Palatinate, a province of the Rhineland in Germany, to America where they became united in Pennsylvania to build up the culture that became known as Pennsylvania Dutch. The Mennonites came first, then the Amish, Baptists, Dunkards, and Moravians. The Lutherans and the Reformers came later, and by the time of the Revolutionary War they almost outnumbered the British in Pennsylvania. Their peculiar dialect was responsible for giving them the name of Dutch, for in those days anyone speaking a variant of the German tongue was automatically thought to be Dutch.

These migrants from the Palatinate spread all over the southeastern part of Pennsylvania. They cleared the land and established their farms of unsurpassed bounty. They were good farmers and they toiled ceaselessly in the wilderness to produce such bountiful crops. The women cooked and baked and filled their larders with food. They bought very little besides salt and spices. They were good craftsmen and could make for themselves just about everything they needed. They built their houses of native stone, made all their own furniture, adorning the chairs and chests and tables with religious motifs and painting them in bright colors. The "Folks," as they called themselves, were deeply religious. They believed in a separateness from the world, in pacifism, piety, and hard work. They came together to feast, to worship, sometimes to mourn, but their religious ties rejected many aspects of modern civilization and thus they remained more or less separate from other Americans. There in Pennsylvania they created their own distinctive culture and a rich regional cookery as well.

Theirs was a cuisine of abundance, thrift, and hard work. The busy Pennsylvania Dutch housewives had a natural gift for being able to make something delicious out of the simplest foods. No one else could make pancakes quite the way they did, or tender golden waffles, or crullers, or doughnuts. No one else could fry delicately seasoned homemade sausage or bake crisp crunchy bread or sticky sweet buns and breakfast cakes, strickle sheets, coffee wreaths, citronenkuchen (lemon tarts) just the way they did. Their own special creations like rich dark apple butter, scrapple, Philadelphia Pepperpot, chicken corn soup, shoo-fly pie drenched in molasses and an inch deep in crumbs, marvelous cheesecake, have long been accepted as part of our national diet.

Dumplings and noodles form a substantial part of many Pennsylvania Dutch dishes. One of the best-known specialties is Schnitz un Knepp made with sliced dried sweet apples soaked back to original size and served in a steaming dish with thick slices of tender ham and feather-light dumplings.

Apples yielded an abundant crop in Pennsylvania Dutch country and every year the thrifty Pennsylvania Dutch housewives dried sliced apples and other fruits for use throughout the winter months.

The Pennsylvania Dutch celebrated many religious holidays, but Christmas was always the climax of all their feasting for the year. Cookies were baked by the bushel in every home along with tarts, doughnuts, Lebkuchen (a rich honey cake containing citron, orange peel, and almonds), and mince pies by the score. The holiday board contained the most appetizing array of food to be found anywhere. It included the colorful superstition of seven sweets and seven sours, a cherished tradition. Among the sweets there were likely to be such homemade concoctions as apple butter, ginger pears, pickled watermelon rind, spiced pears, fox-grape jelly, corn relish; for the sours, pickled oysters, pepper relish, green-tomato pickle, dill pickle, sweet pickle, marinated vegetables, pickled beets. There were smoked hams and homemade sausages, and for the main dish roast goose preceded by chicken corn soup and goose livers in jelly. Potato pancakes or hot potato salad, corn pudding, and green beans in vinegar sauce all customarily went with the goose. For desserts there were two or three kinds of pie as well as stacks of gay Christmas cakes and cookies.

The Pennsylvania Dutch had a way with chicken too. Chicken with waffles, chicken with biscuits, plump roast chicken with potato stuffing, chicken-noodle pie—a dish containing chunks of tender chicken and broad noodles swimming in creamy golden sauce topped with flaky pie crust. Chicken potpie, one of the basic dishes they brought with them from the farms and villages of Germany, has remained a favorite dish to this day. There was the famous chicken corn soup with tender sweet kernels of corn floating in rich chicken broth. Chicken and rivel soup was another specialty. The rivels were tiny specks of dough made by rubbing flour, salt, and egg together until crumbly, then tossing the crumbs into boiling chicken broth. When cooked they looked like tiny dumplings. Yes, they made all these good chicken dishes in southeastern Pennsylvania, and even today the old-fashioned Pennsylvania Dutch cooking is among the most distinctive of all American cuisine.

Pennsylvania Dutch Potpie

Chicken Potpie has been a favorite with the Pennsylvania Dutch since the days they cleared the first woodlands in Southeastern Pennsylvania and this recipe which came to me from an old friend of my aunt's is a typical one.

2 medium potatoes sliced thin
Biscuit dough cut into 1-inch squares
2 medium onions sliced thin
½ teaspoon salt
⅛ teaspoon pepper
1 teaspoon minced parsley
3 cups cooked chicken cut into chunks
2 tablespoons flour
2 tablespoons chicken fat or butter
1 cup chicken stock
1 cup cream

Line the bottom of a Dutch oven with the sliced potatoes. Place a layer of the biscuit dough squares on top of them. Then a layer of sliced onions. Sprinkle with salt, pepper, and minced parsley. Add a layer of chicken. Repeat until all of the chicken has been used up, finishing with a layer of the biscuit dough squares with spaces between. Blend the flour with the chicken fat or butter and add 1 cup chicken stock. Cook over a medium heat until thick and smooth. Add the cream and cook until heated through, stirring constantly. Pour over the chicken potpie and cover tightly. Cook covered over low heat for 20 minutes. Serve at once.

Biscuit Dough

1 heaping tablespoon butter

2 cups flour
1 teaspoon salt
2 eggs well beaten
2 tablespoons milk

Mix the butter, flour, and salt together. Add the well-beaten eggs and the milk. Mix lightly. Roll out on a floured board as thin as possible. Let stand for ½ hour then cut into 1 inch squares.

Serves 4

Pennsylvania Dutch Chicken Pie
A fragrant chicken pie in the best tradition of Pennsylvania Dutch cooking.

5-pound chicken cut into pieces
1 carrot
1 onion
1 stalk celery
3 sprigs parsley
1 teaspoon salt
¼ teaspoon pepper
4 tablespoons butter
4 tablespoons flour
2 cups chicken stock
1 cup cream
Pastry dough

Put the chicken pieces in a kettle with water to cover. Add the carrot, onion, celery, parsley, salt, and pepper. Cover the kettle and cook over a low heat about 1½ hours or until the chicken is tender. Remove chicken and let it cool. When cooled discard skin and bones and cut the meat into large pieces. Strain the chicken stock and measure out 2 cups. Melt the butter in a saucepan. Blend in the flour and stir until smooth. Slowly add the 2 cups strained chicken stock and cook, stirring constantly, until the sauce is thickened. Add the cream and continue cooking until of the consistency of a medium white sauce. Make the pastry.

Pastry
2 cups sifted flour
½ teaspoon salt
4 teaspoons baking powder
½ cup butter
¼ cup milk (approximately)

Sift the flour, salt, and baking powder together. Add the butter and mix with your fingers until of a mealy consistency. Add milk gradually and turn out on a floured board. Knead for 1 minute. Divide pastry in half and roll out half of it for the bottom crust. Line the bottom and sides of a round baking dish. Arrange the chicken meat on top of the pastry and pour over the cream sauce. Cover with the remaining pastry and make slits in the top for the steam to escape. Bake in a 450° preheated oven for 30 minutes or until the crust is golden brown.

Serves 6

Chicken and Corn Pie

For many years chicken and corn pie has been a cherished recipe of Pennsylvania Dutch cooks. This is my version of that wonderful dish.

4-pound chicken fryer cut into pieces
Boiling water
1 onion sliced
½ teaspoon salt
Rich pie pastry
3 cups canned corn kernels

4 eggs well beaten
2 cups heavy cream
Strained chicken stock
Salt and pepper to taste
Butter

Place the chicken in a kettle and cover with the boiling water. Add the sliced onion and ½ teaspoon salt. Simmer covered for about 1 hour or until the chicken is tender. In the meantime make a rich pie pastry, roll it out very thin, and line a deep pie dish with the bottom crust. When the chicken is done remove it from the kettle and cut the meat from the bones into chunks. Strain the stock and reserve. Combine the chicken with the corn kernels, well-beaten eggs, heavy cream, and 1 cup of the strained chicken stock. Season to taste with salt and pepper and pour into the pie shell. Dot with the butter and place the top crust over the pie. Make several cuts in the crust so the steam can escape and bake in a preheated 400° oven for about 30 minutes or until the top crust is delicately browned. Thicken any leftover chicken stock with a flour and water paste and serve on the side for extra gravy.

Serves 6

Chicken and Noodle Pie
A chicken-noodle pie with chicken and noodles swimming in golden gravy makes delicious eating.

5-pound chicken cut into pieces
1 large onion
1 teaspoon salt
½ pound flat egg noodles
Chicken giblets
4 tablespoons chicken fat
4 tablespoons flour

1 cup chicken stock
1 cup cream
2 tablespoons minced celery
2 tablespoons minced onion
Rich pastry topping

Put the chicken in a kettle with the onion and cover with cold water. Add salt, bring to a boil, then lower heat and simmer covered for 1½ hours or until chicken is tender. Remove chicken and when cooled cut all the meat from the bones into chunks. Strain 1 cup chicken stock and set aside. Add the flat egg noodles to the rest of the chicken stock and cook for 8 minutes or until tender. Cook the giblets in salted water until tender. Drain and mince. Drain the egg noodles and set aside. Melt the chicken fat in a saucepan and blend in the flour. Slowly add the reserved cup of chicken stock and the cream. Cook, stirring constantly, over a low heat until the sauce is creamy and smooth. Add the minced celery, minced onion, and minced giblets. Cook a few moments longer. Butter a baking dish and place the chicken and noodles in the dish. Cover with the sauce. Place a rich pastry top over the dish and bake in a 450° preheated oven for 30 minutes or until the crust is golden brown.

Serves 6

Pennsylvania Dutch Braised Chicken with Onions
A plump chicken braised with onions is a most delicious dish.

4-pound chicken fryer cut into pieces
¼ cup flour
4 tablespoons butter
1 teaspoon salt
⅛ teaspoon pepper
5 medium onions sliced

Dredge the chicken pieces with the flour and brown well on both sides in a heavy Dutch oven in the 4 tablespoons butter. Sprinkle with salt and pepper. Lay the sliced onions over the chicken, cover, and braise over low heat for 1 hour or until the chicken is tender. Shake the pan occasionally but do not stir. The onions and the chicken braise down to a lovely golden color.

Serves 4

Chicken Fricassee with Waffles

Chicken Fricassee with waffles is a Pennsylvania Dutch creation and a very tasty one.

1 plump chicken cut into pieces
Water to cover
1 large onion sliced
Salt and pepper
3 tablespoons butter
3 tablespoons flour
1½ cups chicken stock
1½ cups heavy cream

Place the chicken in a kettle with water to cover. Add the sliced onion and salt and pepper. Cover and cook over low heat about 1½ hours or until chicken is tender. When chicken is done melt 3 tablespoons butter in a saucepan and blend in the flour. Slowly add the chicken stock and heavy cream. Cook over a low heat, stirring constantly, until the sauce is smooth and thickened. Serve the chicken pieces on top of the waffles smothered with the creamed sauce.

Waffles
1 teaspoon soda
2 cups sour cream
¼ cup butter melted

3 eggs well beaten
½ cup milk
1 teaspoon salt
2½ cups flour

Mix the soda with the sour cream. Beat the eggs with the milk
and add with the melted butter. Add the salt and flour and
mix in well. Cook in preheated waffle iron until brown and
serve with the chicken.

Serves 4

Pennsylvania Dutch Fried Chicken
Even with fried chicken the Pennsylvania Dutch know how
to add a special flair.

3½-pound chicken fryer cut into pieces
1 egg well beaten
½ cup flour
¼ teaspoon baking powder
½ teaspoon salt
¼ cup butter melted
Cream

Add the flour, baking powder, and salt to the well-beaten egg
and mix well. Dip the chicken pieces in this batter and fry
in the melted butter in a heavy frying pan. When well
browned on both sides, cover tightly, and cook over a low
heat about 40 minutes or until tender. Remove the chicken
to a hot serving platter. Thin the balance of the batter with
a little cream and some of the drippings from the pan and
blend together for a cream gravy.

Serves 4

Baked Chicken
Another yummy Pennsylvania Dutch treat.

2 chicken broilers about 1½ pounds each
2 tablespoons butter melted
1 cup hot water
Salt and pepper
Giblets
1 small onion
1 tablespoon flour

Split the chickens in half. Place then in a baking pan with the butter and hot water. Sprinkle with salt and pepper and bake in a 400° preheated oven for 30 minutes. Turn and baste frequently with the drippings in the pan. Lower heat to 350° and bake 15 minutes longer when the chicken should be browned and tender. In the meantime cook the giblets with the onion in water to cover until tender. When the chicken is done remove to a hot serving platter and keep warm. Blend the flour into the drippings in the baking pan and add enough water to make a smooth gravy. Chop the giblets and add to the gravy. Serve hot with the chicken.

Serves 4

Roast Chicken with Potato Stuffing
A chicken roasted the Pennsylvania Dutch way with a wonderful potato stuffing.

5-pound roasting chicken
Softened butter
1 teaspoon salt
Flour
Potato Stuffing
½ small onion
Chicken giblets

Potato Stuffing
2 cups mashed potatoes

½ cup minced onion
¼ cup chopped celery
2 tablespoons butter melted
1 egg well beaten
¼ cup flour
1 teaspoon salt
¼ teaspoon poultry seasoning
¼ teaspoon thyme
1 teaspoon chopped parsley

Sauté the onions and celery in 2 tablespoons melted butter. Mix the beaten egg with the mashed potatoes and flour. Add the salt, poultry seasoning, thyme, and chopped parsley. Add the onion, celery, butter mixture and mix thoroughly.

Rub the cavity of the chicken with softened butter, then stuff it with the potato stuffing. Sew the opening closed and truss. Rub the outside of the chicken well with softened butter, sprinkle with salt and dredge lightly with flour. Place in an open roasting pan and roast in a 375° preheated oven allowing approximately 20 minutes to the pound. Baste frequently with the drippings in the pan. The last 20 minutes of roasting time turn the chicken over to brown the underside. Cook the giblets and onion in water until tender. Mince and save along with the water in which they were cooked. When the chicken is done remove it to a hot serving platter. Blend a little flour and water together to form a paste and brown it in the roasting pan. Thin to the desired consistency with the giblet broth, add the minced giblets, and serve with the chicken and stuffing.

Serves 6

Pennsylvania Dutch Curried Turnovers

Marian Anderson found this tasty tidbit on a scrap of paper in her bulging recipe file. We tried it and found it so good I decided to use it in this section under Pennsylvania Dutch chicken.

Pastry
1 cup sifted flour
¼ pound butter
1 3-ounce package cream cheese
Salt
Curry powder

Sift the flour. Work into it the ¼ pound of butter and the cream cheese. Form into a roll and wrap in waxed paper. Chill in the refrigerator for 2 hours. Roll out very thin on a floured board and cut into 2 inch circles. Place a spoonful of filling on each round circle and fold over. Press the edges tightly together to seal. Bake in a preheated 400° oven for about 8 minutes or until the turnovers are well browned. Sprinkle lightly with salt and curry powder. Serve hot.

Filling
¾ cup boiled chicken livers
2 hard-cooked eggs
1½ teaspoon grated onion
½ teaspoon salt
⅛ teaspoon black pepper
1 teaspoon curry powder
4 tablespoons heavy cream

Chop the chicken livers and eggs very fine, then press through a fine sieve. Add the onion, salt, pepper, curry powder, and the heavy cream. Mix well and use as filling for the turnovers.

Serves 4

Chicken Corn Soup with Rivels
Chicken Corn Soup with Rivels is one of the most famous

Pennsylvania Dutch dishes. When cooked, the Rivels look like minute dumplings or grains of rice floating in the soup.

1 plump chicken cut into pieces
1 large onion chopped fine
3 quarts water
1 teaspoon salt
8 ears fresh or frozen corn grated
½ cup diced celery
1 tablespoon minced parsley

Place the chicken pieces in a large pot with water to cover. Add the onion and salt. Cover the pot and cook over low heat about 1½ hours or until the chicken is tender. Remove chicken from the stock and cut the meat from the bones. Return the chicken meat to the stock. Add the grated corn kernels, the diced celery, and the minced parsley. Cover and simmer for 30 minutes longer. Add the Rivels, cover, and cook 15 minutes longer.

Rivels
1 cup flour
⅛ teaspoon salt
1 egg
Milk to blend

Mix the flour, salt, egg, and enough milk together in a bowl with your fingers until the crumbs are like grains of rice. Drop them into the soup and cook covered for 15 minutes.

Serves 6

Chicken Corn Soup with Butter Balls
A chicken corn soup with butter balls was another favorite.

1 plump chicken cut into pieces

1 teaspoon salt
1 cup diced celery
½ cup onion chopped fine
2 10-ounce packages frozen corn kernels
2 tablespoons parsley chopped fine
Butter balls

Place the chicken in a pot with water to cover and the salt. Cook covered over a low heat for 1½ hours or until tender. Remove the chicken from the stock and when cool enough to handle discard the skin and cut the meat from the bones. Return the chicken meat to the pot. Add the celery, chopped onion, and corn kernels. Cover and simmer for 30 minutes. Add the butter balls, cover, and cook 5 minutes longer.

Butter Balls
2 tablespoons butter
1 cup sifted flour
½ teaspoon salt
3 or 4 tablespoons milk

Mix the butter, flour, and salt with your fingers until crumbly. Add just enough milk so that the dough will stick together. Form into small balls about the size of a marble and chill in the refrigerator until ready to add to the soup.

Serves 6

Southwest Chicken

The great open spaces of the Southwest stretch westward from central Texas across New Mexico and through Arizona. It is a land of sun-baked plateaus, arid wastelands with mesquite, cactus, and yucca, steep mesas and buttes, gorges and precipices, but it is also a land that contains some of the most beautiful scenery in the world—the Grand Canyon, the Painted Desert, and the Petrified Forest. Spanish and Mexican influences on food are very strong in the Southwest but the Pueblo Indian and the American cowboy have also contributed to the unique flavor of Southwest cookery.

The roots of Spanish and Mexican cooking grow deep. Until fairly recent years Arizona, New Mexico, Texas were all a part of Mexico, so it is not surprising that there are Spanish and Mexican dishes in the Southwest that have been popular for hundreds of years. The tortilla, for instance, that unleavened corncake made from dried corn flattened by pounding between the hands, and finally baked on a big flat pan. The thin brown tortilla cakes have always been one of the basic foods of the Mexican in the Southwest and they are used in a variety of food combinations.

There was the enchilada, a tortilla fried in fat, then dipped in hot chili pepper sauce and sprinkled with sharp grated cheese, chopped onions, chopped green peppers, chopped green olives, then rolled up, splashed with more hot chili pepper sauce and topped with shredded lettuce. For a tacos, the tortilla was folded in half and fried crisp, then filled with beans, cheese, vegetables, chopped meat or chicken. The tacos could also be filled first and then fried. There was the

94

tostado, a tortilla fried flat and heaped high with beans, grated cheese, chopped meat, chopped chicken, minced onion, and shredded lettuce.

Then there was the chicken and beef tamales which were served to Cortez by the Aztecs when he first arrived in Mexico City. They were a combination of dried cornhusks, cornmeal paste, and well-seasoned meat or chicken. The husks were softened in water until pliable, then spread with a layer of cornmeal paste and the meat or chicken, and rolled up lengthwise. The tamales were tied with strips of cornhusk or strung into bundles and cooked by steaming over boiling water in a tightly covered kettle. Delicious and hot in their cornhusk wrappers, they have preserved their identity throughout the centuries to become a part of the regional cookery of the Southwest.

Frijoles, the pinto beans the cowboys ate at their chuckwagon meals on the open range, are still one of the standard daily foods of many Southwesterners. They are used in soups, meat stews, chili con carne, chicken dishes, as fillings for tacos and enchiladas, or in the popular dish frijoles refritos—refried beans. In this popular dish the beans are cooked in water until tender, then mashed and fried in hot fat until crisp. Frijoles fritos are cooked beans which are mashed with bean liquid and lightly fried to a thick mush.

The most colorful contribution of the Americans to the Southwest was the chuck wagon, the rolling kitchen of the American cowboy on the long cattle drives that sometimes stretched into months. The chuck wagon was a traveling kitchen that contained the necessary provisions needed for the trail cook to prepare three meals a day for the outfit. Pinto beans—frijoles—and bread formed the basic part of the diet. The only fresh food served on the roundup was beef, and steaks and stews were everyday chuck-wagon fare. When the crew tired of beef there was always fresh game to be had for the shooting: deer, buffalo, wild turkey, squirrel, prairie chicken.

Outdoor cooking has always been an important part of Southwestern life from the simple open-pit range cooking of the cowboys to the lavish beef barbecues of the cattle barons. The old-time range cooks quite often used a clay pack for cooking fish and fowl when utensils were not available. Chicken was considered delicious cooked that way. The bird was killed and bled, but it was neither plucked nor gutted. The feathered bird was plastered all over with a thick pack of moist clay about an inch thick and buried carefully in the smoldering embers of an open fire to cook. The clay baked hard as pottery, and when tapped neatly with a hammer the feathers stripped off with the baked clay to reveal a fine-flavored, moist, tender chicken.

Of course I believe most of us would prefer to have the chicken cleaned and gutted with the head and feet removed first. The insides can be stuffed solidly with a good bread stuffing and the cavities sewed tightly so that no clay will seep in. Or better still, cover the openings with foil. The old-timers recommend leaving the feathers on as they not only strip off easily when the clay pack is broken but they also give the chicken an unusual flavor. A chicken baked in clay is one of the most ancient methods of cooking chicken, but this dish is also served as a specialty in one of San Francisco's finest Chinese restaurants.

Chicken Tamale
What could be more typical of Southwestern cooking than the ancient Aztec tamale in its cornhusk wrapper.

1 large fat hen cut into pieces
Water to cover
1 small onion
1 teaspoon salt
1 cup cornmeal
12 red peppers
4 tablespoons butter

2 tablespoons flour
Bundle of corn husks

Stew the chicken for 2 hours in water to cover with the onion and salt. Remove the chicken and let it cool. Thicken the chicken stock with 1 cup cornmeal and cook over low heat for ½ hour. Pour boiling water over the 12 red peppers and let them stand for 10 minutes. Scrape the meat off the red peppers. They should be thick like a sauce. Blend 4 tablespoons butter with 2 tablespoons flour and mix with the hot water that was poured over the red peppers. Add to the pepper scrapings and cook over a low heat for 5 minutes, stirring constantly. Pour boiling water over the corn husks and lay them flat. On one husk lay 2 tablespoons of the meal, then over this a good-sized chunk of the chicken which has been skinned and boned. Add 1 tablespoon of the red-pepper sauce. Over this lay another husk spread with the cornmeal paste, then with chicken and topped with red-pepper sauce. Over this lay another husk, adding as many husks as you wish, although 7 or 8 are enough for one bundle. Roll the layered husks up carefully and tie the ends with string. Place the rolled corn husks gently in a steamer and steam for 2 hours over boiling water.

Chicken Tamale Pie

A Southwestern variation of the tamale is the tamale pie, a cooked mixture of meat or chicken, onion, tomatoes, green pepper, green olives, well seasoned with chili powder and baked between layers of cornmeal mush.

3½ teaspoons salt
3 cups water
1 cup cornmeal
3 tablespoons shortening
1 large onion chopped
1 green pepper chopped

2 cups cooked chicken meat cut into large pieces
2 tablespoons chili powder
4 medium tomatoes sliced
1 cup green stuffed olives sliced

Bring 3 cups water with 1½ teaspoons salt to the boiling
point. Add 1 cup cornmeal, stirring constantly, and cook
over low heat for 10 minutes. Remove from the heat. Melt
3 tablespoons shortening in a skillet, add chopped onions,
chopped green pepper, and cook over low heat until soft but
not browned. Add the chicken meat along with the chili
powder and 1½ teaspoons salt. Stir until well blended and
cook over a low heat for 1 minute. Spread half the cooked
cornmeal mixture in the bottom of a casserole. Cover with a
layer of sliced tomatoes and ½ the sliced green stuffed olives.
Next put in all of the chicken mixture. On top of that place
the rest of the cooked cornmeal and then the remaining tomato
slices and sliced green olives. Bake in a preheated 375°
oven for 30 minutes.

Serves 4

Ranchero Chicken with Frijoles
A typical Southwestern chicken dish is this one served with
the ever popular frijoles.

4-pound chicken fryer cut into pieces
⅓ cup butter
1 onion chopped fine
1 chili pepper crushed
1 teaspoon paprika
Salt and pepper to taste
6 tablespoons chili sauce
½ cup cream

Melt the butter in a heavy pan and let it turn brown. When

it is a brown color add the chicken pieces and let them brown well on both sides. Remove the chicken from the pan. Add the chopped onions to the pan along with the crushed chili pepper and the paprika. Cook over a medium heat until the sauce is a dark brown. Return the chicken to the pan and season with salt and pepper to taste. Add the chili sauce, cover, and simmer over low heat about 30 minutes or until the chicken is tender. Remove the chicken to a serving platter and keep hot. Sprinkle the flour over the sauce and when well blended add the cream. Stir over low heat until thickened and pour the sauce over the chicken. It should be a dark rich brown in color. Serve with an accompanying dish of frijoles.

Serves 4

Frijoles
The ever popular Southwest cowboy bean dish.

1 pound pink or pinto beans
1 large onion sliced
1 bay leaf
1 teaspoon salt
2 cloves garlic
2 medium onions chopped fine
1 tablespoon brown sugar
¼ teaspoon cayenne
4 tablespoons finely chopped chives
Garlic

Cover the beans with cold water and soak overnight. Drain and place in a kettle with cold water to cover with the sliced onion, bay leaf, 1 teaspoon salt, and the cloves of garlic. Cook until the beans are tender. In a casserole put the 2 medium chopped onions and sprinkle over them the brown sugar. Drain the water from the beans and add them to the casserole. Season with cayenne and the finely chopped chives. Rub the lid of the casserole with garlic, cover the casserole, and place in a preheated 350° oven. Bake about 30 minutes or until the beans are almost but not quite dry. Serve with the Ranchero Chicken.

Barbecued Chicken
There is no festivity in the Southwest more popular than the outdoor barbecue. The barbecue sauce is strongly Mexican in flavor and usually contains chili peppers.

4-pound chicken fryer
1 teaspoon salt
⅛ teaspoon pepper
½ cup butter
½ cup hot water
2 teaspoons Worcestershire sauce
1 teaspoon chili powder
1½ teaspoons sugar
1 teaspoon salt
1½ teaspoons flour
Dash of cayenne

Rub the chicken well with salt and pepper. Tie the legs and wings together and place the chicken on a revolving spit over glowing charcoal embers. Baste every 5 minutes with the barbecue sauce.

To make the sauce melt ½ cup butter in a saucepan and add to it ½ cup hot water. Add the Worcestershire sauce, chili powder, sugar, salt, flour, and a dash of cayenne. Blend well together and cook for 3 minutes over a medium heat or until mixture thickens slightly. Baste the chicken every few moments with the sauce as it broils.

Serves 4

Mexican American Chicken
For chicken *aficionados.*

4-pound chicken fryer cut into pieces
1 teaspoon salt
¼ teaspoon pepper
½ cup flour
¼ cup butter melted
1½ cups chopped onions
¾ cup chopped green peppers
2½ cups canned tomatoes
2 cups fresh or canned corn kernels
2 cloves garlic minced
3½ tablespoons tarragon flavored vinegar
2 tablespoons chili powder

Add the salt and pepper to the flour and roll the chicken pieces in the seasoned flour. Brown the pieces in ¼ cup melted butter in a heavy pan. As each piece is browned remove from pan and put in the bottom of a casserole. Sauté the chopped onions and green peppers in the same pan the chicken was cooked in until soft. Add the tomatoes, corn kernels, minced garlic, tarragon vinegar, and chili powder. Stir over low heat for 1 minute then pour the mixture over the chicken in the casserole. Bake covered in a 350° preheated oven for 1 hour or until the chicken is tender.

Serves 4

Breast of Chicken Mexican
From the wide open spaces of the Southwest comes this dish with a Mexican flavor.

4 chicken breasts
Water to cover

1 teaspoon salt
1 tablespoon butter melted
1 medium onion chopped fine
1 green pepper chopped fine
1 clove garlic minced
1 cup stewed tomatoes
Pinch of sugar
1 teaspoon chili powder
Dash of cayenne
1 teaspoon cornstarch

Put the chicken breasts in a kettle with water to cover. Add the salt and simmer covered 30 minutes or until the chicken breasts are tender. Remove the chicken and discard the skin and bones trying to keep the breasts in one piece. Set aside. Melt the butter in a heavy frying pan and add the chopped onions, chopped green peppers, garlic, and cook until the vegetables are soft. Add the tomatoes, pinch of sugar, chili powder, and dash of cayenne. Return the chicken to the pan, cover, and cook over low heat for 5 minutes. Mix the cornstarch with a little of the hot sauce and add to the pan. Cook stirring constantly a few minutes or until the sauce has thickened slightly.

Serves 4

Chicken New Mexico Style
This Southwestern dish with onions, garlic, red chili pepper, herbs, olives, and sherry shows both a Mexican and Spanish heritage.

4-pound chicken fryer cut into pieces
2 medium onions chopped
3 cloves garlic chopped fine
2 bay leaves crushed
1 teaspoon salt

⅛ teaspoon rosemary
1 pod red chili pepper crushed
1 cup black pitted olives
¾ cup sherry

Place the chicken in a kettle with water to just barely cover
and add the chopped onions, garlic, bay leaf, salt, rosemary,
and crushed chili pepper. Simmer for 30 minutes or until
the chicken is barely tender. Turn heat to high and let sauce
reduce to ⅓ of original amount. Add the pitted black olives
and the sherry. Simmer covered for 10 minutes and serve over
rice.

Serves 4

Chicken Enchiladas

Chicken enchiladas smothered in hot chili pepper sauce and
filled with a tasty chicken mixture splashed with nippy cheese
is one of the most popular Mexican dishes in the Southwest.

12 tortillas either frozen, canned, or homemade
2 cups ground cooked chicken
2 onions chopped fine
2 cloves garlic minced fine
2 tablespoons olive oil
1 cup tomato hot sauce
1 teaspoon salt
1 tablespoon chili powder
1 cup pitted ripe olives chopped fine
1 cup grated sharp Cheddar cheese
2 ounces of chili powder
½ cup flour
Water
¼ cup grated sharp Cheddar cheese
Shredded lettuce
Chopped green onions

Heat the olive oil in a skillet and fry the onions and garlic until soft but not browned. Add the ground cooked chicken and the tomato hot sauce and cook over a medium heat for 5 minutes, stirring constantly. Add the chopped olives and the 1 cup grated cheese. Cook until the cheese has melted. Mix the 2 ounces of chili powder with the flour and enough water to make a thin smooth paste. Cook over a medium heat until of the right consistency, adding more water if it becomes too thick. Dip the tortillas in this sauce, then lay them flat in a baking pan. Place 2 tablespoons of the chicken mixture in the center of each tortilla. Roll up and spoon the rest of the hot chili sauce over each one. Sprinkle with 1/4 cup grated cheese and place in a hot oven until the cheese has melted. Sprinkle with shredded lettuce and chopped green onion.

Serves 6

Chicken Tacos
Tacos are another favorite Mexican dish in the Southwest. Tacos are tortillas folded in half like a sandwich, fried crisp, and filled with chopped meat or poultry.

12 tortillas frozen, canned, or homemade
Deep fat for frying
2 cups shredded cooked chicken
Shredded lettuce
Chopped green onions
Grated sharp Cheddar cheese
Ripe olives

Fold the tortillas in half and fry them until crisp in deep hot fat. Make sure the fold stays open enough to put the filling inside as they fry. Drain them on absorbent paper then fill them with the shredded cooked chicken, shredded lettuce, chopped green onions, and grated Cheddar cheese. Garnish with ripe olives. A hot chili sauce may be poured over the tacos if desired.

Serves 6

Southwest Arroz con Pollo

Although still basically the old favorite from Spain there are local touches in this dish of the Southwest.

4-pound chicken fryer cut into pieces
½ cup olive oil
1 onion chopped
3 cloves garlic minced
1 green pepper chopped
1 cup stewed tomatoes
2½ cups water
1 bay leaf crumbled
1 tablespoon salt
1 tablespoon chili powder
1 cup raw rice

Heat the olive oil in a heavy frying pan. Add the chicken and brown well on both sides. Add the chopped onion, minced garlic, and chopped green pepper. Cook 5 minutes. Stir in the stewed tomatoes, crumbled bay leaf, salt, chili powder, and 2½ cups water. Stir well and add the raw rice. Cover and cook over low heat for 20 minutes or until the chicken is tender and the rice done.

Serves 4

Clay-Baked Chicken

A chicken bundled in clay and baked in the embers of an open fire was a method quite often used by oldtime range cooks in the Southwest. It can also be cooked easily in the oven of your own kitchen. My friend Marian Anderson made up her own clay out of flour, salt, and water, and gave me this particular recipe. The clay can be bought commercially too in most art supply stores. Ask for Grumbacher's Moist Modeling Clay No. 753. It sells for about $1.20 for a 5-pound pack. Incidentally little cutouts of dough can be made from any leftover clay to fancy it up for a special occasion.

3-pound chicken
1 teaspoon salt
½ cup butter melted
Bread stuffing
Heavy-duty aluminum foil

Clay
 1 cup flour
2 cups salt
1 cup water

Rub the chicken well inside and out with the salt. Then rub the melted butter liberally over the outside of the chicken as well as in the body cavity. Stuff with any good bread stuffing and sew the openings tightly. Place the chicken on a heavy piece of aluminum foil and wrap the chicken tightly in the foil.

Make the clay by mixing the flour, salt, and water together in a bowl. Mix well and, as Marian Anderson directed me, knead h--- out of it. Roll it out with a rolling pin into a large circle about ½ to ¾ inch thick. Place the foil wrapped chicken in the center of the clay circle and wrap the clay solidly around the chicken, molding it with your fingers so that the chicken is completely covered. Preheat your oven to 500° and bake the chicken at this hot temperature for 1½ hours. Serve the chicken wrapped in its clay mold on a napkin. Crack the clay smartly with a hammer and it will come off easily. Peel off the foil and it will reveal the white breast and legs of a tender moist finely-flavored chicken. Carve and serve.

Serves 3

Cosmopolitan Chicken

American, cosmopolitan, cosmo-American—call it what you will, as richly varied as America herself are her foods and cooking customs. All the natural raw materials of the country, a wonderfully wide and varied selection of foreign foodstuffs, originality, imagination, and the best recipes of innumerable nations have combined to give us one of the best eating cultures in the world. Many culture groups have contributed to our cuisine: the Dutch in old New York, the Germans in Pennsylvania and the Midwest, the Puritans, the French aristocrats of Louisiana, the Spanish, the Mexicans, the Negroes, the Chinese, the Italians, the hardy pioneers, not to mention the basic contributions of the Indians, have all added to the diversity of American cooking. As American colonists moved westward to new frontiers they were joined by settlers from many lands in Europe. Germans, Dutch, Swiss, Scandinavians, Italians, Cornish, Irish—they have all helped to give us an exciting American cuisine.

The happy melding of a vast foreign population has inspired us to concoct chicken dishes that are new and rewardingly different. Foreign herbs and spices, fragrant condiments, the provocative use of wines and liqueurs, have added great zest to the dishes. We have our own New World versions of many Old World favorites, and since we are dealing here strictly with chicken, we have been able to do many wonderful things to a chicken to make it sublime. There are so many foods that can be harmoniously combined with chicken—chicken with pineapple, oranges, grapes, and other fruits are combinations that occur in many exotic recipes. Chicken also goes well with almonds or walnuts or peanuts; all the herbs and spices and spirits that give distinction to so many foreign dishes; in fact, the combinations that one can use with chicken are virtually endless.

The nations of Europe poured millions of people with varied tastes and customs into this country. New York City became the melting pot of the world with immigrants from many lands. There were the Irish, the Jews, Chinese, Austrians, Russians, English, Scottish, Hungarians, Bohemians, Swedes, Norwegians, Danes; Greeks and their Greek resturants; there were Portuguese, Swiss, Dutch, Germans and Spanish. Pennsylvania attracted many foreigners—the Swedes, the Finns, the English Quakers, and soon after the Germans, Welsh, and Scotch-Irish. Later coal mining brought Italians, Poles, Lithuanians, Hungarians, and Yugoslavs to work in Pennsylvania. All these nationalities have contributed something to our food culture.

To the Southern cities came Africans and West Indians. To Maryland came French planters with their cooks, driven from Hispaniola by the slave revolt at the beginning of the nineteenth century. Charleston received the French Huguenots; the Florida Keys the Cubans. The discovery of gold in California attracted many immigrants including Irish, Yugoslavs, Scandinavians, Cornishmen. Thousands of Chinese were brought in to work on the transcontinental railroad. All these nationalities have influenced American cooking.

In the beginning, language difficulties and discrimination kept the foreign population segregated. In fact, most Americans of Anglo-Saxon Protestant stock had a real prejudice against anything foreign. The strong tastes and smells of foreign cooking, the garlic and onions of the Mediterranean, the smelly cheeses and cabbages of Germany, all the unfamiliar foods of different nationalities they found unpleasant, but little by little foreign foods began to be acceptable. Hired domestics and cooks working in American households cooked their gravy-rich pot roasts and paprikas and their delicate pastries. The Germans, who had long been excellent sausage makers, opened delicatessens in the larger towns and cities with such enticing items as sausage, sauerkraut, potato salad, pickles, cheeses. Small foreign restaurants originally opened for fellow countrymen who yearned for old-country cooking began to draw the more adventurous Americans. They soon became accustomed to foreign cooking and began to like the different dishes from other lands.

Chinese cooking came into popularity first with Chop Suey and later with more authentic Chinese dishes. Now we have many chicken dishes with a Chinese accent. Mexico has given us interesting variations. Many of our foods have a definite Mexican heritage—the chili powder we use, the beans we serve with barbecues, the tomato sauce we toss into so many dishes. Italian restaurants became very popular with their bountiful meals with pasta and red wine, and as a result Italian cooking has had a tremendous influence on our eating habits. Scandinavian cooking too has left its mark in the well-known smorgasbord which we accepted enthusiastically.

The cooking featured in these restaurants helped tremendously to enrich the American palate. Then, with an increase in wealth and worldliness, a dazzling array of elegant dining establishments came into being. Delmonico's, Sherry's, the Knickerbocker Grill; through their doors passed the highest ranks of finance, fame, and society. Guests were served with magnificent grandeur all kinds of rich and exotic dishes. In San Francisco the Palace Hotel made culinary history with its lavish fare. Chefs outdid themselves in preparing extravagant dishes, and by the time those fabulous days were gone many Americans had acquired a taste for fine food.

No wonder spices, herbs, and condiments began to enrich American cooking. We were given a gastronomic legacy that is unequaled. Our continent is vast and no other country has had such a variety of foodstuffs as we have or such contrasts in food, and the result has given us a wonderfully imaginative array of chicken dishes which are now as completely American as Southern Fried Chicken and Yankee Potpie, although many of them retain the flavors of other lands.

Bourbon Chicken
Bourbon whiskey and herbs give this chicken dish a decidedly distinctive flavor.

4-pound chicken fryer cut into pieces
¼ cup butter melted
¼ cup bourbon whiskey
1 medium onion diced
2 tablespoons minced parsley
1 teaspoon thyme
½ teaspoon salt
⅛ teaspoon pepper
½ cup bourbon whiskey
¼ cup heavy cream

Melt the butter in a heavy frying pan and brown the chicken pieces well on both sides. When browned add ¼ cup bourbon whiskey and ignite. When the flame has burned down add the diced onions, parsley, thyme, salt, pepper, and ½ cup bourbon whiskey. Mix in well, cover the pan, and cook over low heat 40 minutes or until the chicken is tender. Just before serving add the heavy cream to the sauce and stir well into the juices in the pan.

Serves 4

Scotch Chicken
Don't let the title of this recipe throw you. The addition of Scotch actually gives the chicken a piquant and delicious flavor.

4-pound chicken fryer cut into pieces
3½ cups chicken stock

1 teaspoon salt
¼ teaspoon pepper
2 cups small white onions
½ cup butter
2 cups cream
1 cup uncooked rice
½ cup Scotch whiskey

Put the chicken pieces in a kettle with the chicken stock and the salt and pepper. Cover and simmer over low heat about 45 minutes or until the chicken is tender. Peel the small white onions and cook them in a pan with ½ cup butter over a low heat for about 40 minutes or until they are tender. When the chicken is done place it in a casserole. Reserve the stock. Cover the chicken with the cooked buttered onions. Add the cream. Bring the chicken stock to a boil and add the uncooked rice. Turn heat to low and simmer covered for 30 minutes or until tender. Drain the rice and add it to the casserole with the chicken. Heat through and stir in the Scotch whiskey. Serve from the casserole.

Serves 4

Irish Chicken
A chicken dish with an Irish flair and the zesty flavor of Irish whiskey.

4-pound chicken fryer cut into pieces
½ cup flour
1 teaspoon salt
⅛ teaspoon pepper
¼ cup butter melted
½ pound bacon diced
4 small yellow onions chopped
1 clove garlic minced
¾ cup Irish whiskey

1 cup rich brown gravy
¼ cup tomato sauce
¼ cup white wine
1 teaspoon thyme
1 cup sliced canned mushrooms
Salt and pepper to taste

Add the salt and pepper to the flour and roll the chicken pieces in the seasoned flour. Melt the butter in a heavy frying pan and brown the chicken pieces well on both sides. When browned, remove the chicken and drain off all but 1 tablespoon of the butter. Add the diced bacon, chopped onions, and garlic. Cook until bacon is crisp and onions browned. Return the chicken to the pan and add ¼ cup of the Irish whiskey. Ignite, and when the flame has burned down add ½ cup Irish whiskey, the rich brown gravy, tomato sauce, and white wine. Mix in well and add the thyme and sliced mushrooms. Cover the pan and cook over low heat about 40 minutes or until the chicken is tender. Remove the chicken and vegetables to a hot serving platter. If the sauce seems too thin turn heat to high and let the sauce reduce. Pour the sauce over the chicken and serve.

Serves 4

Gin-Sautéed Chicken
The addition of gin adds a piquant flavor to this dish.

4-pound chicken fryer cut into pieces
1 teaspoon salt
½ cup chicken stock
½ cup gin
½ cup grape jelly
Juice and rind of 1 lemon
¼ cup butter melted

Rub the chicken pieces well with the salt and place them in a flat dish. In a saucepan combine the chicken stock, gin, grape jelly, and juice and rind of 1 lemon. Bring to a boil, then turn heat to low and let simmer for 10 minutes. Pour this hot sauce over the chicken and let it marinate for several hours. Melt the butter in a heavy frying pan and brown the chicken pieces well on both sides. Pour over the marinade, cover the pan tightly, and cook over low heat for 40 minutes or until the chicken is tender. Serve in the sauce.

Serves 4

Chicken in Chablis Wine
A chicken dish delicately flavored with Chablis.

4-pound chicken fryer cut into pieces
1 teaspoon salt
1/4 teaspoon pepper
1/2 cup flour
1/4 cup butter melted
3 tablespoons green onions chopped fine
1/2 cup mushrooms sliced
3 tomatoes peeled and chopped
1/2 cup Chablis wine
1 avocado peeled and sliced
2 tablespoons butter
1 tablespoon chopped parsley

Mix the salt and pepper with the flour and roll the chicken pieces in the seasoned flour. Melt 1/4 cup butter in a heavy frying pan and brown the chicken well on both sides. Turn heat to low and continue cooking the chicken until tender about 40 miuntes, turning frequently during the cooking. Remove the chicken to a serving platter and keep hot. To the butter left in the pan add the chopped green onions, the

sliced mushrooms, and the chopped tomatoes. Cook over low
heat for 5 minutes. Add the Chablis wine and the sliced
avocado. Continue cooking for 10 minutes longer, stirring in
the 2 tablespoons butter bit by bit. Add the chopped parsley
and pour over the chicken. Serve at once.

Serves 4

Chicken in White Burgundy
A chicken cooked in white Burgundy makes a wonderful dish.

4-pound chicken fryer cut into pieces
¼ cup butter melted
1 heaping tablespoon flour
1½ cups white Burgundy
¼ cup green onions finely chopped
½ teaspoon salt
⅛ teaspoon pepper
1 tablespoon grated lemon rind

Melt the butter in a heavy frying pan and when hot add the
chicken. Brown well on both sides. When browned, sprinkle
over the heaping tablespoon flour and stir into the pan. Add
the chopped green onions and the white Burgundy. Season
with salt and pepper, cover the pan, and cook over low heat
for 40 minutes or until the chicken is tender. Remove the
chicken to a serving platter and keep hot. Turn heat to high
and let the sauce reduce to half. Add the grated lemon rind
and pour over the chicken.

Serves 4

Chicken in Champagne
The champagne gives chicken a lovely flavor.

4-pound chicken fryer cut into pieces
½ teaspoon salt

⅛ teaspoon pepper
¼ cup butter melted
1 heaping tablespoon flour
Dash of nutmeg
1 cup dry champagne
1 cup heavy cream
2 egg yolks beaten with 2 tablespoons cream

Rub the chicken with the salt and pepper. Melt the butter in a heavy frying pan and brown the chicken well on both sides. Sprinkle over the flour and stir until the flour disappears. Add ½ cup of the champagne and mix in well. Cover the pan and cook over low heat for 40 minutes or until the chicken is tender. Remove the chicken to a serving platter and keep hot. Add the rest of the champagne to the sauce in the pan and cook over high heat, stirring constantly, until the sauce is reduced to half. Add the cup of heavy cream and cook over a low heat for 2 minutes, stirring constantly. Add the 2 egg yolks which have been beaten with 2 tablespoons cream and continue cooking over low heat until the sauce has thickened slightly. Pour the sauce over the chicken and serve.

Serves 4

Savory Chicken with Vermouth

Dry French vermouth gives this savory chicken dish quite an unusual flavor.

4-pound chicken fryer cut into pieces
3 tablespoons butter melted
½ teaspoon salt
¼ teaspoon black pepper
¾ cup dry French vermouth

Brown the chicken pieces quickly in 3 tablespoons melted butter in a heavy frying pan. Season with salt and pepper.

Cover the pan. Turn heat to low and cook about 35 minutes or until chicken is tender, turning the chicken pieces occasionally. Remove the cover and turn the heat to high. Pour the dry French vermouth over the chicken and cook at high heat until the vermouth has cooked down to a tablespoon or two. Stir constantly so the chicken will not stick to the bottom of the pan or burn. Serve at once.

Serves 4

Chicken in Vermouth Sauce
The combination of sweet and dry vermouth makes a wonderful sauce for this chicken dish.

4-pound chicken fryer cut into pieces
1 teaspoon salt
⅛ teaspoon pepper
½ cup flour
¼ cup butter melted
2 green onions chopped fine
1 clove garlic minced
¾ cup sweet vermouth
¾ cup dry vermouth
1 tablespoon lemon juice

Add the salt and pepper to the flour and roll the chicken pieces in the seasoned flour. Melt the butter in a frying pan and brown the chicken pieces well on both sides. Add the chopped green onions and the minced garlic and cook 1 minute longer. Add the sweet and dry vermouth, cover the pan tightly, and cook over low heat for 40 miuntes or until the chicken is tender. Remove the chicken to a hot serving platter. Turn heat to high and reduce the sauce down to ½. Add the lemon juice and pour over the chicken.

Serves 4

Chicken with Port
The Port wine may give this dish a subtle flavor but it was Marian Anderson who suggested adding the *pâté de foie gras.*

3½-pound chicken fryer cut into pieces
1 teaspoon salt
¼ teaspoon pepper
2 tablespoons butter
2 medium onions chopped
1 clove garlic minced
1 tablespoon flour
1 cup port wine
3 tablespoons *pâté de foie gras*
Pinch of ginger
½ cup chicken stock
¼ cup minced parsley
Juice of 1 lemon

Rub the chicken well with salt and pepper. Melt 2 tablespoons butter in a skillet and brown the chicken well on both sides. Remove the chicken from the pan and add the chopped onions and garlic. Brown in the pan juices. When browned add 1 tablespoon flour and stir in well. Add the port, *pâté de foie gras,* pinch of ginger, and ½ cup chicken stock. Mix well and return the chicken to the pan. Cover and cook over low heat for 40 minutes or until the chicken is tender. Add the minced parsley and the juice of 1 lemon. Serve at once.

Serves 4

Chicken in Port and Cherry Sauce
Charles Samson, who prided himself on his gourmet cooking, gave me this recipe and I think you will agree that it is unusual.

4-pound chicken fryer

1 teaspoon salt
¼ teaspoon pepper
4 tablespoons *pâté de foie gras*
4 tablespoons chopped mushrooms
4 tablespoons soft butter
½ cup port wine
1 cup pitted black cherries
1 teaspoon cornstarch

Rub the chicken well inside and out with the salt and pepper. Combine the *pâté de foie gras* with the chopped mushrooms and stuff the cavity of the chicken with the mixture. Rub the outside of the chicken well with the soft butter, truss, and roast in a 375° oven allowing 20 minutes to the pound, basting frequently with the drippings in the pan. The last 20 minutes of roasting time turn the chicken over to brown the underside. When the chicken is done remove it to a serving platter and keep hot. To the juices in the pan add the ½ cup Port and stir in well scraping up all the brown particles from the bottom. Reduce over a high heat to ½ of its original quantity. Add the pitted black cherries and cook over low heat a few moments. Mix the cornstarch with a little of the hot sauce and pour into the pan. Stir over low heat until thickened. Carve the chicken and serve with the sauce poured over it.

Serves 4

Chicken Rosé
Rosé wine and sour cream give this chicken dish a very light, delicate flavor.

4-pound chicken fryer cut into pieces
1 teaspoon salt
¼ teaspoon pepper
½ teaspoon paprika

2 tablespoons flour
3 tablespoons butter melted
½ cup rosé wine
½ cup sour cream

Rub the salt, pepper, paprika, and flour well into the chicken. Melt 3 tablespoons butter in a skillet and brown the chicken pieces well on both sides. When browned add the rosé wine, cover and cook over a low heat for 30 minutes or until the chicken is tender. Remove the chicken to a serving platter and keep hot. Add the sour cream to the drippings in the pan and stir until well blended and heated through. Pour the sauce over the chicken and serve at once.

Serves 4

Chicken in Wine and Brandy Sauce

This chicken in wine and brandy sauce is a simple dish to make but redolent with the special ingredients that go to make up a gourmet specialty.

4-pound chicken fryer cut into pieces
1 teaspoon salt
⅛ teaspoon pepper
½ cup flour
¼ cup butter melted
1 cup sliced mushrooms
2 medium tomatoes diced
1 cup dry white wine
1 jigger brandy
1 tablespoon Worcestershire sauce
2 teaspoons minced parsley
2 teaspoons minced green onion
½ clove garlic minced

Add the salt and pepper to the flour and roll the chicken

pieces in the seasoned flour. Melt the butter in a heavy frying pan and brown the chicken well on both sides. When browned add the sliced mushrooms and diced tomatoes. Cook over medium heat for 10 minutes. Add the white wine, brandy, and Worcestershire sauce. Cover the pan and simmer over low heat for 40 minutes or until the chicken is tender. Remove the chicken to a serving platter and keep hot. Add the minced parsley, green onion, and garlic to the pan. Turn heat to high and let the sauce reduce to half. Pour over the chicken and serve.

Serves 4

Chicken Raphael Weill

A famous dish renowned in San Francisco and created by that great epicure Raphael Weill for whom the dish is named. He was a cook of considerable talent and his picture, complete with chef's cap, hangs in the Bohemian Club in San Francisco. There seems to be some question as to whether Mr. Weill actually invented the dish or whether it was named in his honor.

3-pound chicken fryer cut into pieces
¼ cup butter melted
Salt and white pepper
Finely chopped shallots, about ½ cup
1 jigger brandy
½ cup chicken stock
½ cup white wine
Bouquet garni

Sauce
1½ cups heavy cream
2 tablespoons sherry
Salt and white pepper
3 egg yolks
Juices in casserole in which chicken was cooked

Melt the butter in a casserole and add the chopped shallots and
the chicken pieces. Season with salt and white pepper. Cook
until lightly colored but do not brown. Flame with a jigger
of brandy. When flame burns down add the chicken stock
and a bouquet garnis. Add the white wine and cook covered
until tender about 40 minutes. Remove the chicken to a hot
serving platter and to the juices in the pan add the heavy
cream. Stir well and add the sherry and salt and white pepper.
Thicken with the 3 egg yolks by beating a little of the warm
cream into the egg yolks and adding the egg yolks gradually
to the rest of the sauce beating constantly until heated through
over low heat.

Serves 4

Chicken à la Ritz
The fine hand of a French chef shows itself in this famous
gourmet recipe.

4-pound chicken fryer cut into pieces
½ cup flour
1 teaspoon salt
¼ teaspoon pepper
¼ cup butter melted
6 small green onions chopped fine
½ pound mushrooms sliced
Dash of allspice
1 cup cream
¼ pound cooked ham cut in strips
2 tablespoons butter
2 tablespoons sherry
2 egg yolks beaten with 2 tablespoons water
1 tablespoon cream

Mix the salt and pepper with the flour and roll the chicken
pieces in the seasoned flour. Brown well on both sides in ¼

cup melted butter. Add the chopped green onions, sliced mushrooms, and a dash of allspice. Cover tightly and cook over a low heat for 30 minutes. Add 1 cup cream and cook 10 minutes longer. Heat the ham strips in 2 tablespoons butter. Add the sherry and mix in well. Add the ham and sherry to the chicken and cook 5 minutes. Remove from the heat and add the 2 egg yolks beaten with 2 tablespoons water. Mix in well and add the 1 tablespoon cream. Serve the chicken hot with the sauce.

Serves 4

Sherried Chicken with Vegetables

Sherry, vegetables, and rich brown gravy make a gourmet sauce for chicken.

4-pound chicken fryer cut into pieces
½ cup flour
1 teaspoon salt
¼ teaspoon pepper
¼ cup butter melted
12 small white onions
12 small whole mushrooms
12 small baby carrots
4 artichoke hearts cut into wedges
½ cup sherry
1 cup rich brown gravy (You can use a package mix for this)
Minced parsley

Mix the salt and pepper with the flour and roll the chicken pieces in the seasoned flour. Melt the butter in a heavy frying pan and brown the chicken pieces well on both sides. When browned, remove the chicken pieces. Add to the pan the small white onions, small whole mushrooms, and artichoke wedges. Cook until lightly browned and return the chicken to the pan.

Add the sherry and the rich brown gravy. Cover and cook over low heat for 40 minutes or until the chicken is tender. Serve with the sauce and vegetables with parsley sprinkled over the top.

Serves 4

Chicken with Mushrooms and Olives

A chicken cooked with mushrooms and olives makes a very tasty dish.

4-pound chicken fryer cut into pieces
1/2 cup flour
1 teaspoon salt
1/4 teaspoon pepper
1/4 cup butter melted
2 tablespoons brandy
2 bay leaves crumbled
1/4 teaspoon thyme
Pinch of nutmeg
1 cup sliced mushrooms
1 1/4 cups scalded cream
1 cup sliced pitted black olives

Add the salt and pepper to the flour and roll the chicken pieces in the seasoned flour. Melt 1/4 cup butter in a heavy frying pan and brown the chicken well on both sides. When browned pour the brandy over the chicken and ignite. Let the flame burn down and add the crumbled bay leaves, thyme, nutmeg, and sliced mushrooms. Cook for 5 minutes over medium heat. Add the scalded cream and the sliced pitted black olives. Cover tightly and cook over low heat for 40 minutes or until the chicken is tender.

Serves 4

Olive Chicken

A hearty main dish that is both robust and delicious. For a change of pace I highly recommend it.

5-pound stewing chicken cut into pieces
¼ cup butter melted
4 cups chicken stock
1 tablespoon salt
1 large onion chopped
1 cup chopped celery
1 cup chopped green pepper
1 cup stuffed green olives cut in half
1 cup pitted black olives cut in half
1 pound spaghetti broken into pieces
2 cups grated Cheddar cheese
Salt and pepper to taste

Melt ¼ cup butter in a skillet and brown the chicken pieces well on both sides. Transfer the chicken to a kettle and add 4 cups chicken stock and 1 tablespoon salt. Cover and cook over low heat until tender about 1½ hours. Cool. Cut the meat from the bones in large pieces discarding the skin and bones. Return the chicken pieces to the broth. To the skillet the chicken was browned in add the chopped onion, celery, and green pepper. Cook until tender. Add to the chicken and stock. Heat the kettle to boiling and then add the spaghetti that has been broken into pieces. Boil until the spaghetti is tender, adding water if necessary. Add the stuffed green olives and the black pitted olives. Add the grated Cheddar cheese and continue cooking until the cheese has melted. Season to taste with salt and pepper.

Serves 6

Chicken Sauté with Artichokes

Here's a chicken dish for your special guests.

4-pound chicken fryer cut into   pieces
1 teaspoon salt
⅛ teaspoon pepper
¼ cup butter melted
8-ounce package frozen artichoke hearts
1 clove garlic minced
1 cup white wine
2 egg yolks
1 cup heavy cream
1 teaspoon lemon juice

Sprinkle the chicken pieces with salt and pepper and brown them in the melted butter. When well browned on both sides add the artichoke hearts and the minced clove of garlic. Cook for 2 minutes and add the white wine. Cover the pan and simmer over low heat about 40 minutes or until the chicken is tender. Remove the chicken and artichoke hearts to a serving platter and keep hot. Beat the egg yolks with the heavy cream and add to the sauce in the pan. Cook over low heat until thickened, stirring constantly. Add the lemon juice and pour over the chicken.

Serves 4

Chicken with Carrots
This chicken with carrots offers an interesting adventure in flavor.

4-pound chicken fryer cut into pieces
1 teaspoon salt
⅛ teaspoon pepper
¼ cup butter melted
1 onion sliced thin
¼ cup sliced mushrooms
8 carrots scraped and sliced thin
1 tablespoon flour

½ cup white wine
1 cup chicken stock
1 bay leaf
½ teaspoon tarragon
1 teaspoon sugar
½ cup heavy cream
¼ cup chopped parsley

Sprinkle the chicken pieces with salt and pepper. Melt the butter in a heavy frying pan and brown the chicken well on both sides. Remove the chicken from the pan and add the sliced onion, sliced mushrooms, and carrot slices. Cook until the onions are soft but not browned. Blend in the flour and return the chicken to the pan. Add the white wine, chicken stock, bay leaf, tarragon, and sugar. Cover the pan and cook over a low heat for 40 minutes or until the chicken is tender. Remove the chicken and carrots to a serving platter and keep hot. Turn heat to high and cook the liquid left in the pan down until it has reduced to half. Add the cream and cook until just heated through. Do not let the sauce boil again. Pour the sauce over the chicken and carrots, sprinkle the parsley over the top, and serve at once.

Serves 4

Chicken Romaine
The accent of this dish is Italian.

4-pound chicken cut into pieces
¼ cup flour
1 teaspoon salt
¼ teaspoon pepper
¼ cup grated Parmesan cheese
1 teaspoon paprika
¼ cup butter melted
½ cup sliced mushrooms

1 large tomato peeled and sliced
4 medium zucchini sliced

Mix the flour, salt, pepper, Parmesan cheese, and paprika together. Roll the chicken pieces in this mixture and brown in ¼ cup melted butter in a heavy skillet. When well browned on both sides add the sliced mushrooms, tomato slices, and the zucchini slices. Cover and cook over low heat for 30 minutes or until the chicken is tender.

Serves 4

Chicken Italienne

Here's another Italian treatment of chicken with Mozzarella, Monterey jack, and Parmesan cheese.

4 chicken breasts boned
1 tablespoon butter melted
1 tablespoon olive oil
1 large onion chopped
1 clove garlic minced
1 carrot grated
2 tablespoons minced parsley
4 cans tomato hot sauce
½ teaspoon oregano
½ teaspoon salt
⅛ teaspoon pepper
1 teaspoon Worcestershire sauce
¼ cup flour seasoned with 1 teaspoon salt
4 tablespoons butter melted
4 thin slices Monterey jack cheese
4 thin slices Mozzarella cheese
Grated Parmesan cheese

Heat 1 tablespoon butter with 1 tablespoon olive oil in a saucepan. Add the chopped onion, minced garlic, grated carrot, and minced parsley. Cook over low heat for 5 minutes. Add the 4 cans tomato hot sauce, oregano, salt, pepper, and Worcestershire sauce. Stir well and let simmer for 10 minutes. Keep hot. Dredge the chicken breasts in the seasoned flour and brown in 4 tablespoons butter. Turn heat to low and continue cooking about 20 minutes longer, or until tender, turning frequently so the chicken will brown evenly. Remove the chicken breasts to a shallow baking dish. Pour ½ of the tomato sauce over the chicken. Place the slices of Monterey Jack cheese on top. Cover with the sliced Mozzarella cheese and sprinkle heavily with grated Parmesan. Place under the broiler until it bubbles. Spoon more sauce over the chicken and serve with the rest of the sauce in a dish on the side.

Serves 4

Chicken with Chestnuts
A chicken cooked in a gourmet sauce with chestnuts makes a rich dish for special guests.

1 plump stewing hen
1 pound chestnuts
1 cup sliced mushrooms
16 small white onions
⅓ cup butter
1 cup dry white wine
1 cup chicken stock
2 cups heavy cream
2 tablespoons tomato paste
3 egg yolks
Salt and white pepper to taste
Chopped parsley

Put the chicken in a kettle with salted water to cover and cook over a low heat for 1½ hours or until tender. Remove the chicken from the kettle and when cooled cut the meat from the bones in good-sized pieces. Discard the skin and bones. Put the chestnuts in a kettle of boiling water and boil for 10 minutes. Drain and peel while still warm. The inner shell should come off easily as well as the shell. Melt the butter in a large heavy frying pan and sauté the sliced mushrooms and small white onions until soft. Add the chicken, chestnuts, and the dry white wine. Cook over a medium heat until the white wine is almost absorbed. Turn heat to low and add the chicken stock, heavy cream, and the tomato paste. Simmer for 5 minutes. Add the egg yolks and stir over low heat until thickened slightly. Season to taste with salt and white pepper. Turn into a serving dish and sprinkle with chopped parsley.

Serves 6

Chicken with Celery
This chicken and celery dish is a taste sensation.

4-pound chicken fryer cut into pieces
¼ cup butter melted
5 medium onions sliced thin
2 cups diced celery
4 tomatoes peeled and cut into pieces
1 teaspoon salt
¼ teaspoon pepper

Melt the butter in a heavy frying pan and brown the chicken pieces well on both sides. Add the sliced onions and the diced celery and cook them over low heat with the chicken until soft and lightly colored. Add the tomatoes, salt, and pepper, and cook covered over a low heat for 40 minutes or until the chicken is tender. Serve the chicken with the celery and vegetables.

Serves 4

Chicken with Capers

A chicken cooked with capers is particularly good.

4-pound chicken fryer cut into pieces
1 teaspoon salt
¼ teaspoon pepper
½ cup flour
¼ cup melted butter
1 tablespoon flour
1 tablespoon vinegar
1 cup chicken stock
2 egg yolks beaten with 2 tablespoons cream
Juice of ½ lemon
Grated rind of ½ lemon
¼ cup capers

Add the salt and pepper to the ½ cup flour and roll the chicken pieces in the seasoned flour. Melt the butter in a heavy frying pan and brown the chicken pieces well on both sides. Sprinkle the tablespoon of flour over the chicken and stir in well. Add the vinegar and cook a few minutes over medium heat, stirring constantly. Add the chicken stock, mix in well, cover pan tightly and cook over low heat 40 minutes or until the chicken is tender. Remove the chicken to a serving platter and keep hot. Beat the egg yolks with the cream until they are thick and yellow. Add the lemon juice, lemon rind, and the capers. Mix into the sauce in the pan and cook over low heat until it has thickened slightly. Pour over the chicken and serve.

Serves 4

Russian Chicken

This chicken dish flavored with dill and sour cream and Madeira has a decidedly Russian character.

4-pound chicken fryer cut into pieces

½ cup flour
1 teaspoon salt
¼ teaspoon pepper
4 tablespoons butter melted
¼ cup Madeira
1 teaspoon tomato paste
1 tablespoon flour
½ cup chicken stock
1 cup sour cream
2 tablespoons finely chopped dill

Mix the salt and pepper with the flour and roll the chicken pieces in the seasoned flour. Brown the chicken well on both sides in the melted butter. Pour over the Madeira and cook for 1 minute. Remove the chicken and add to the pan the tomato paste and 1 tablespoon flour. Stir in well and add ½ cup chicken stock. Cook until the mixture thickens, stirring constantly. Add 1 cup sour cream and 2 tablespoons dill. Stir until smooth and return the chicken to the pan. Cover and cook over a low heat for 30 minutes or until the chicken is tender. Arrange the chicken pieces on a large serving platter and cover with the sauce.

Serves 4

Chicken Vichyssoise
Vichyssoise has even taken our chicken under its influence.

4-pound chicken fryer cut into pieces
1 teaspoon salt
¼ teaspoon pepper
½ cup flour
¼ cup butter melted
½ cup chicken consommé
½ cup dry white wine
2 cups diced potatoes

1 cup chopped leeks or green onions
1 cup sour cream

Add the salt and pepper to the flour and roll the chicken pieces in the seasoned flour. Brown the pieces in melted butter and when well browned on both sides add the ½ cup chicken consommé and the ½ cup dry white wine. Cover and simmer over a low heat for 15 minutes. Add the diced potatoes and the chopped leeks or green onions. Simmer covered 30 minutes longer. Remove the chicken to a hot serving platter. Add the sour cream to the sauce. Stir smooth and cook over low heat for five minutes. Pour the sauce over the chicken and serve at once.

Serves 4

Chicken Sauté with Onions
A very satisfying dish.

4-pound chicken fryer cut into pieces
1 teaspoon salt
¼ teaspoon pepper
½ teaspoon sweet basil
4 tablespoons butter melted
3 large Bermuda onions sliced
½ cup brandy

Rub the chicken well with the salt, pepper, and sweet basil. Melt the butter in a heavy frying pan and add the chicken pieces and the onion slices. When the chicken and onions are well browned add the brandy, cover, and simmer over low heat for 45 minutes or until the chicken is tender. The onions and chicken will cook down to a deep golden brown.

Serves 4

Chicken Sauté with Garlic
Very flavorful is this chicken sauté with garlic.

4-pound chicken fryer cut into pieces
1/4 cup butter melted
1 teaspoon salt
1/4 teaspoon pepper
1/2 cup white wine
2 cloves garlic minced fine
Chopped parsley

Melt the butter in a frying pan and brown the chicken pieces well on both sides. Add the minced garlic and cook 5 minutes longer. Add the salt and pepper. Add the white wine and cook uncovered over a low heat, turning frequently, until chicken is tender. Remove chicken to a hot platter and pour the pan juices over it. Garnish with chopped parsley.

Serves 4

Chicken with Bleu Cheese
To impress gourmets try this unusual chicken with bleu cheese.

4-pound chicken fryer cut into pieces
1 teaspoon salt
1/4 teaspoon pepper
1/2 cup flour
1/4 cup butter melted
3 ounces bleu cheese
3 ounces liver pâté
2 tablespoons brandy
1/2 cup white wine
1/2 cup heavy cream
Salt and pepper

Add the salt and pepper to the flour and dredge the chicken pieces with the seasoned flour. Melt the butter in a heavy frying pan and brown the chicken well on both sides. When browned remove the chicken from the pan. Blend the bleu cheese with the liver pâté and add to the butter in the frying pan. Stir until melted, scraping up all the browned particles in the bottom of the pan. Add the brandy and cook over a low heat, stirring constantly, for 1 minute. Return the chicken to the pan and add the white wine. Cover and cook over low heat for 40 minutes or until the chicken is tender. Remove the chicken to a hot serving platter. Add the heavy cream and cook until just heated through. Season to taste with salt and pepper and pour the sauce over the chicken.

Serves 4

Chicken Coriander
The overtones of this chicken dish are Indian.

4-pound chicken fryer cut into pieces
3 tablespoons grated onion
2 cloves minced garlic
¼ cup butter melted
1 teaspoon tumeric
1 teaspoon chili powder
½ teaspoon ground ginger
1 tablespoon ground coriander
½ cup flour
1 teaspoon salt
¼ teaspoon pepper
2 tablespoons flour
2 cups hot chicken stock
15 small white onions
½ cup sliced carrots
½ cup sliced mushrooms

Melt ¼ cup butter in a heavy pan and cook the onion and garlic until a light golden in color. Add the tumeric, chili powder, ground ginger, and coriander. Blend well and cook 1 minute over low heat. Mix the salt and pepper with the ½ cup flour and roll the chicken pieces in the seasoned flour. Add the chicken pieces to the pan and cook until they are evenly browned all over. Sprinkle 2 tablespoons flour over the chicken and stir in well. Add 2 cups hot chicken stock and stir over medium heat until sauce has thickened slightly. Add the small white onions, the sliced carrots, and sliced mushrooms. Cover and simmer over low heat about 35 minutes or until the chicken is tender. Serve with the sauce over fluffy white rice.

Serves 4

Pineapple Chicken with Rum
A delightful and exotic chicken dish.

4-pound chicken fryer cut into pieces
Juice of 1 lemon
¼ cup flour
1 teaspoon salt
⅛ teaspoon pepper
¼ cup butter melted
1 medium onion chopped fine
1 cup crushed pineapple
¼ teaspoon tomato puree
4 tablespoons currants soaked in ½ cup water for 15 minutes
2 tablespoons brown sugar
¼ cup dark Puerto Rican rum

Rub the chicken pieces well with the juice of 1 lemon. Add the salt and pepper to the flour and roll the chicken in the seasoned flour. Melt the butter in a frying pan and brown the chicken well on both sides. When browned add the chopped onion and cook for 5 minutes. Add the crushed pine-apple, tomato puree, currants, brown sugar, and the ¼ cup rum. Cover and simmer over low heat for 40 minutes or until the chicken is tender.

Serves 4

Chicken with Lime Juice

Anyone with a true appreciation of delicately blended flavors will love this dish. Indeed, it has always been one of my favorites.

4 tablespoons grated onion
2 cloves garlic minced
¼ cup butter melted
4-pound chicken fryer cut into pieces
½ cup flour
1 teaspoon salt
¼ teaspoon pepper
½ teaspoon tumeric
½ teaspoon chili powder
⅛ teaspoon ground ginger
1 tablespoon ground coriander
¼ cup hot chicken broth
¼ cup Rose's Sweetened Lime Juice
2 tablespoons flour

Mix 1 teaspoon salt and ¼ teaspoon pepper with ½ cup flour and roll the chicken pieces in the seasoned flour. Melt ¼ cup butter in a heavy pan and add the grated onion, minced garlic, tumeric, chili powder, ground ginger, and coriander. Cook over low heat for 2 minutes, stirring constantly. Add the chicken pieces and brown well on both sides over a medium high heat. Sprinkle with 2 tablespoons flour and mix in well. Add ¼ cup hot chicken broth and stir over medium high heat until the sauce has thickened slightly. Reduce heat to low, cover, and cook about 35 minutes or until the chicken is tender. Stir in ¼ cup Rose's Sweetened Lime Juice and cook 1 minute longer, stirring constantly. Serve with fluffy white rice.

Serves 4

Chicken in Grape Juice

Marian Anderson spent long hours experimenting with me on fruit and chicken combinations. She is responsible for this delightfully different chicken and grape dish.

4-pound chicken fryer cut into pieces
2 cups seedless white grapes
1 teaspoon salt
4 tablespoons butter melted
2 tablespoons minced parsley
1 cup dry white wine

Blend 1 cup of white grapes in an electric blender until liquid. Season the chicken with salt. Melt the butter in a heavy frying pan and brown the chicken pieces well on both sides. Stir in the parsley, then add the grape juice and white wine. Turn heat to low, cover the pan, and cook over low heat for 40 minutes or until chicken is tender. Uncover the pan, turn heat to high, and let the sauce reduce down to about ⅓ cup. Stir constantly. Add the rest of the seedless white grapes and cook until just heated through. Serve at once.

Serves 4

Chicken with Bananas

A chicken dish with rum, bananas, and maple syrup that is quite different. The rum and bananas have been tried before but the pure maple syrup was suggested by Robert Mosher, a gourmet friend with an open and inquiring mind. Incidentally, it adds a delightful touch.

4-pound chicken fryer cut into pieces
1 teaspoon salt
⅛ teaspoon pepper
¼ cup butter melted
½ cup dark Puerto Rican rum
Pinch of ginger
¼ cup pure maple syrup
5 bananas

Add the salt and pepper to the flour and roll the chicken pieces
in the seasoned flour. Melt the butter in a heavy frying pan
and when bubbling hot add the chicken pieces. Brown well
on both sides and when well browned add the ½ cup rum.
Ignite and let the flame burn down. Add a pinch of ginger
and the maple syrup. Cover and cook over a low heat for 40
minutes or until the chicken is tender. Turn over once while
cooking. Peel the bananas and slice into rounds. Add them to
the chicken and cook 5 minutes longer. Place the chicken on
a hot serving platter and pour over the sauce and bananas.

Serves 4

Chicken with Grapefruit
The addition of grapefruit to this sauce may sound rather
odd but actually it gives the chicken a delicious, indefinable
flavor.

4-pound chicken fryer cut into pieces
½ cup flour
1 teaspoon salt
¼ teaspoon pepper
¼ cup butter melted
4 tablespoons brandy
½ cup chicken broth
½ cup sherry
1½ grapefruit
Grated rind of ½ grapefruit

Add 1 teaspoon salt and ¼ teaspoon pepper to the flour and roll the chicken pieces in the seasoned flour. Melt the butter in a heavy frying pan and brown the chicken pieces well on both sides. When browned add 4 tablespoons brandy and ignite. When the flame has burned down add the chicken broth and the sherry. Cook covered over a low heat for 30 minutes or until the chicken is tender. Remove the chicken to a serving platter and keep hot. Add the grated grapefruit rind to the sauce and stir in well. Add the sections of the ½ grapefruit from which the white rind has been removed. Add the juice of 1 grapefruit and stir well, loosening all the browned particles from the bottom of the pan. Cook until just heated through, pour the sauce over the chicken, and serve.

Serves 4

Chicken with Apples
Chicken and apples combine to make a surprisingly good chicken dish.

4-pound chicken fryer cut into pieces
1 teaspoon salt
¼ teaspoon pepper
4 tablespoons butter melted
1 Bermuda onion sliced thin
3 tart apples peeled and cut into rings
1 heaping tablespoon flour
1 cup chicken stock
¼ cup brandy
Pinch of nutmeg
¼ cup heavy cream

Season the chicken pieces with salt and pepper and brown well on both sides in the melted butter. When browned remove the chicken from the pan and add the sliced Bermuda onion and apples. Cook until the onions are soft. Blend in the flour and stir until smooth. Add the chicken stock and stir over a low heat until the sauce is smooth and thickened. Add the brandy and pinch of nutmeg. Mix in and return the chicken to the pan. Cover and cook over low heat about 40 minutes or until the chicken is tender. Remove the chicken to a hot serving platter along with the apples and onions. Add the heavy cream and cook until just heated through. Pour over the chicken and serve.

Serves 4

Apricot Chicken
Chicken and apricots blend harmoniously to make a delight-ful dish.

4-pound chicken fryer cut into pieces
1 teaspoon salt
1/8 teaspoon white pepper
1/2 cup flour
1/4 cup butter melted
1/4 cup dark Puerto Rican rum
1 large onion chopped fine
Pinch of ginger
1/2 cup chicken broth
1 cup dried apricots
1/2 cup water
1/4 cup rum
1 tablespoon brown sugar
Pinch of ginger

Add the salt and pepper to the flour and roll the chicken pieces in the seasoned flour. Melt the butter in a heavy frying pan and brown the chicken well on both sides. Pour over 1/4 cup rum and ignite. When the flame has burned down add the chopped onions and a pinch of ginger. Cook for 5 minutes then add the chicken broth. Cover the pan and cook over a low heat for 40 minutes or until the chicken is tender. Meanwhile cook the dried apricots in ½ cup water for 15 minutes or until barely tender. Add to the chicken when it is done along with ¼ cup rum, the brown sugar, and a pinch of ginger. Mix in well, stirring up all the brown particles from the bottom of the pan, and cook 1 minute longer. Serve the chicken and apricots in the sauce.

Serves 4

Chicken and Oranges

Marian Anderson shares equal honors with me in the development of this orange chicken dish and we are both proud of the result.

4-pound chicken fryer cut into pieces
½ cup butter
½ cup chopped onions
12-ounce can frozen orange juice, undiluted
½ cup orange marmalade—English style that is not too sweet
1 teaspoon Worcestershire sauce
4 oranges cut in thin wedges
Grated rind of 1 orange

Melt the butter in a large heavy frying pan and brown the chicken pieces well on both sides. Remove the chicken from the pan. Add the chopped onions to the drippings and cook until soft but not browned. Combine the undiluted orange juice, orange marmalade, and Worcestershire sauce. Add to the onions and cook over a medium low heat for 1 minute, stirring and scraping to loosen all the browned particles from the bottom of the pan. Return the chicken to the pan, cover, and simmer for 40 minutes or until the chicken is tender. Add the thin orange wedges and continue cooking until just heated through. Arrange the chicken and orange slices on a serving platter and pour over the sauce. Sprinkle the top with grated orange rind.

Serves 4

Chicken Oriental
The use of herbs and spices and coconut blends delicately with the chicken to give this dish a new personality.

4-pound chicken fryer cut into pieces
1 teaspoon salt
¼ teaspoon pepper
¼ cup butter melted
1 medium onion chopped fine
1 clove garlic minced
½ teaspoon chili powder
½ teaspoon ginger
1 cup packaged shredded sweetened coconut
½ cup water

Season the chicken pieces with salt and pepper and rub in well. Melt the butter in a heavy pan and brown the chicken well on both sides. Add the onions, garlic, chili powder, ginger, coconut, and water. Cover tightly and cook over low heat for 40 minutes or until tender.

Serves 4

Curried Chicken in Cream
There is the hint of the East in this dish of Curried Chicken in Cream.

¼ cup butter melted
1 onion chopped fine
2 teaspoons curry powder
4-pound chicken fryer cut into pieces

½ cup cream
2 tablespoons tomato puree
2 tablespoons chicken broth
6 tablespoons packaged shredded sweetened coconut

Melt ¼ cup butter in a heavy skillet and brown the onion until it is golden in color. Add 2 teaspoons curry powder and mix well. Add the chicken pieces and brown on both sides. When browned add ½ cup cream, 2 tablespoons tomato puree, and 2 tablespoons chicken broth. Cook over low heat for 40 minutes until tender. Add 6 tablespoons shredded coconut to the sauce and serve at once over rice.

Serves 4

Chicken Smothered in Oysters

This is a variation of a dish from an early American cookbook.

4-pound chicken fryer cut into pieces
1 teaspoon salt
¼ teaspoon pepper
¼ cup butter melted
½ cup milk
1 pint small oysters
1 cup cream

Rub the salt and pepper well into the chicken pieces and brown them in the melted butter. When well browned on both sides place the chicken pieces in a flat baking dish. Pour over them ½ cup milk, cover the baking dish, and bake in a 375° preheated oven for 45 minutes. Add 1 pint of small oysters and 1 cup of cream. Bake 15 minutes longer. Remove the chicken to a hot serving platter and pour the oysters and cream sauce around the chicken.

Serves 4

Smothered Chicken
Simple but tasty.

4-pound chicken fryer cut into pieces
1 teaspoon salt
¼ teaspoon pepper
½ cup flour
¼ cup butter melted
¼ cup Crisco or lard melted
4 cups chicken stock
¼ cup flour

Add the salt and pepper to the flour and roll the chicken pieces in the seasoned flour. Melt the butter and lard together in a heavy Dutch oven and when bubbling hot brown the chicken quickly on both sides. Remove the chicken pieces and add ¼ cup flour to the fat in the pan. Stir until smooth and browned. Add the chicken stock a little at a time, stirring constantly, and cook until thickened. Return the chicken to the thickened sauce and cook covered over low heat for 40 minutes or until the chicken is tender. Serve the chicken in the sauce.

Serves 4

Batter-Fried Chicken
Simple and flavorsome.

4-pound chicken fryer cut into pieces
1 cup flour
1½ teaspoons salt
¼ teaspoon pepper
1 teaspoon sugar
½ teaspoon paprika
1 egg slightly beaten
1 cup milk

¼ cup butter melted

Combine the flour, salt, pepper, sugar, and paprika in a mixing bowl. Beat the egg into the milk and stir into the dry ingredients. Dip the chicken pieces in the batter until they are well coated. Brown them in ¼ cup melted butter in a large skillet. Turn frequently to brown evenly all over, cooking over medium heat until the chicken is tender, about 30 minutes.

Serves 4

Fried Chicken in Tarragon Batter
This chicken fried in tarragon batter is very tasty.

4-pound chicken fryer cut into pieces
1 teaspoon salt
¼ teaspoon pepper
½ cup flour
2 eggs
½ cup milk
2 teaspoons tarragon
2 cups fresh breadcrumbs
½ cup butter

Add the salt and pepper to the flour and roll the chicken pieces in the seasoned flour. Beat the eggs with the milk. Add 2 teaspoons tarragon to the 2 cups fresh breadcrumbs. Dip the chicken pieces in the egg-milk mixture, then in the seasoned breadcrumbs. Let dry out for ½ hour. Melt the butter in a heavy frying pan and brown the chicken in the hot melted butter. When well browned on both sides, cover the pan, turn heat to low, and cook gently about 40 minutes or until tender. Uncover, turn heat to high, and cook 5 minutes longer to crisp the chicken.

Serves 4

Glazed Chicken Breasts

A mixture of tart jelly, port wine, and Swiss cheese forms the glaze that distinguishes this chicken dish.

3 tablespoons butter
4 whole chicken breasts halved
1 teaspoon salt
¼ teaspoon pepper
¼ cup tart currant jelly
2 tablespoons honey
4 tablespoons port wine
1 teaspoon lemon juice
½ cup shredded Swiss cheese

Melt the butter in a heavy frying pan and brown the chicken well on both sides. Sprinkle with salt and pepper and cook over a medium low heat until tender, turning frequently. Combine the tart currant jelly, honey, port wine, and lemon juice in a saucepan. Heat slowly until currant jelly and honey are melted and mixture is blended. When chicken is tender pour over this sauce and sprinkle the Swiss cheese over the top. Place under the broiler until the cheese is bubbly.

Serves 4

Breast of Chicken Piemontaise

There are many dishes called Chicken Piemontaise but I think this is a very good one.

4 chicken breasts
4 tablespoons flour
1 teaspoon salt
½ teaspoon white pepper
2 tablespoons butter
4 large mushrooms sliced and sautéed in butter

4 very thin slices Swiss cheese

Season the flour with the salt and white pepper and roll the chicken pieces in the seasoned flour. Cook in 2 tablespoons hot melted butter until the chicken is tender and browned on both sides, about 20 minutes in all. Turn frequently to brown evenly. Remove the chicken to a shallow baking dish. Arrange large mushroom slices on each breast. Cover with a slice of Swiss cheese. Put under the broiler just long enough for the cheese to melt. Serve at once.

Serves 4

Parmesan Breast of Chicken Mosier

Robert Mosier, who is chef at the Der Wedeln in Mount Shasta, California, as well as cook at the ski lodge at Mt. Ashland, Oregon, gave me this recipe which he invented himself.

6 chicken breasts
1 teaspoon salt
¼ teaspoon white pepper
¼ cup butter melted
2 eggs well beaten
Parmesan cheese

Sprinkle the chicken breasts with salt and pepper. Heat ¼ cup butter in a heavy skillet until hot and bubbling. Beat the 2 eggs well and then add enough Parmesan cheese to make a stiff batter. Dip the chicken breasts in the batter and make sure they are well coated all over. Let them dry out for about half an hour. Brown them in the hot melted butter until they are a deep golden color on both sides and cooked through. They should cook about 20 minutes. Turn frequently so they brown evenly on both sides.

Serves 3

Breast of Chicken with Cream
A divine dish with a French flair.

4 chicken breasts boned and halved
1 teaspoon lemon juice
½ teaspoon salt
⅛ teaspoon white pepper
4 tablespoons butter
¼ cup chicken stock
¼ cup brandy
1 cup heavy cream
Salt and pepper
½ teaspoon lemon juice
2 tablespoons chopped parsley

Sprinkle the chicken breasts with salt and pepper and rub well into the chicken with 1 teaspoon lemon juice. Melt 4 tablespoons butter in a pan and cook the chicken breasts until tender and browned on both sides about 30 minutes in all. Remove to a platter and keep hot while making the sauce. Add ¼ cup chicken stock to the butter in the pan and when hot add ¼ cup brandy. Cook over a high heat until the liquid has reduced to half. Stir in the cup of heavy cream and boil down again until the cream has thickened slightly. Remove from heat and season to taste with salt and pepper. Add the lemon juice and pour the sauce over the chicken. Sprinkle with chopped parsley and serve at once.

Serves 4

Breast of Chicken on Sliced Ham
Chicken breasts on slices of thick ham makes a very tasty dish.

4 chicken breasts
4 tablespoons butter melted

4 green onions chopped
1 clove garlic minced
4 tablespoons chopped parsley
1 cup mushrooms sliced
¼ cup brandy
2 cups thick white sauce
4 thick slices cooked ham

Cook the chicken breasts in 4 tablespoons butter until browned and tender, about 30 minutes. Remove to a platter and keep hot. Sauté the green onions, minced garlic, parsley, and sliced mushrooms in the pan the chicken was cooked in until soft. Add the brandy and cook 1 minute longer. Add to the 2 cups thick white sauce and cook and stir over a low heat for 5 minutes. Arrange the 4 thick slices of cooked ham in a greased baking dish. Place the chicken breasts on top of the ham. Pour over the white sauce and bake in a 350° preheated oven for 10 minutes.

Serves 4

Chicken Breasts with Horseradish

You will find that the addition of horseradish, sour cream, and sherry gives this dish an original flavor.

4 chicken breasts
1 teaspoon salt
¼ cup butter melted
1 tablespoon butter
2 tablespoons flour
1 cup milk
1 cup sour cream
½ teaspoon salt
⅛ teaspoon white pepper
½ cup prepared horseradish
¼ cup sherry

Sprinkle the chicken breasts with 1 teaspoon salt and brown in ¼ cup melted butter in a heavy skillet. Turn frequently and cook about 30 minutes in all until breasts are well browned and tender. Melt 1 tablespoon butter in a saucepan and blend in the flour. Gradually add the milk and the sour cream, stirring constantly over a medium low heat until smooth and thickened. Add ½ teaspoon salt, ⅛ teaspoon white pepper, and the prepared horseradish. Add the sherry and cook over a low heat a few moments longer. Pour over the chicken breasts and serve.

Serves 4

Breast of Chicken with Eggplant
There is the flavor of the Mediterranean world in this chicken dish with eggplant and tomato.

4 chicken breasts
4 tablespoons flour
½ teaspoon salt
⅛ teaspoon pepper
½ cup butter
½ cup sherry wine
1 cup rich brown gravy or packaged gravy mix
1 large eggplant
2 tomatoes sliced
¼ cup dry white wine

Mix the salt and pepper with the flour and roll the chicken breasts in the seasoned flour. Brown them well on both sides in ¼ cup melted butter. Pour over the sherry and cook for 1 minute. Add the brown gravy, cover the pan, and cook over a low heat for 30 minutes. Meanwhile peel the eggplant and cut into slices. Melt the rest of the butter in a skillet and fry the eggplant until browned on both sides. Arrange in the bottom of a serving platter and keep hot. Brown the tomato slices in the same skillet and place on top of the eggplant. When the chicken breasts are tender arrange them on top. Add the dry white wine to the pan the chicken was cooked in, stir to scrape up all the browned particles from the bottom, and let the sauce boil up once. Pour over the chicken and serve.

Serves 4

Chicken with Lemon Cream Sauce

Undisputedly Dione Lucas is one of the most outstanding figures in the gourmet field and this chicken with lemon cream sauce is one of Madame Lucas' most delightful chicken recipes. Copyright 1947 by Dione Lucas, published by Little, Brown and Co. Reprinted by permission.

1 4-pound chicken
½ cup butter
1 tablespoon sherry
1 tablespoon white wine
1 large lemon
1 small orange
2 teaspoons lemon juice
Salt and pepper
1 cup thin cream
Little grated cheese

Cut the chicken up carefully, as for casserole. Cook until brown all over in foaming butter. Cover with the lid and continue sautéing over a slow fire until nearly cooked. Remove the chicken and stir into the pan the sherry and white wine. Add the grated rind of the large lemon, the grated rind of the orange, the lemon juice, and season with salt and pepper. Turn up the fire and stir in the cream slowly. Put back the chicken and toss over the fire for a few minutes. Arrange on a serving dish. Pour over the sauce and sprinkle with the grated cheese. Put a few thin slices of lemon and a few small pieces of butter on top. Brown under the broiler.

Serves 4

Chicken in Mustard Sauce
This dish should be served at once because it can stand neither reheating nor being kept warm. Like many Chinese dishes it should go immediately from stove to stomach.

4-pound chicken fryer cut into pieces
½ cup flour
1 teaspoon salt
¼ teaspoon pepper
¼ cup butter melted
1 cup dry white wine
1 tablespoon butter
1 heaping tablespoon flour
1 cup thin cream
1 egg yolk
1 tablespoon prepared mustard

Add the salt and pepper to the flour and roll the chicken pieces in the seasoned flour. Melt ¼ cup butter in a heavy frying pan and brown the chicken well on both sides. When browned add the dry white wine. Cover the pan and cook over low heat for 40 minutes or until the chicken is tender. Meanwhile melt the 1 tablespoon butter in a saucepan and blend in the flour. Slowly add the thin cream and cook over low heat, stirring constantly, until thickened. Remove from heat and stir in the egg yolk and the prepared mustard. Keep warm over hot water. When the chicken is done slowly add the sauce from the chicken pan to the mustard mixture and blend in well. Pour this mustard sauce over the chicken and cook over low heat, basting the chicken continually with the sauce until all of the chicken is well coated with the sauce. Serve very hot and be sure to serve at once.

Serves 4

Buttermilk Chicken
A spicy dish to set your taste buds tingling.

4-pound chicken fryer cut into pieces
1½ cups buttermilk
2 cloves garlic minced fine
¼ cup butter melted
1½ cups onion chopped fine
1 teaspoon salt
½ teaspoon powdered ginger
½ teaspoon powdered cloves
1 teaspoon curry powder
½ cup slivered almonds
1 tablespoon flour

Combine 1 cup buttermilk with 2 cloves minced garlic and marinate the chicken pieces in the mixture for 4 hours, turning them several times. In a heavy frying pan melt ¼ cup butter, add the chopped onions along with the salt, ginger, and powdered cloves. Cook over a low heat for 5 minutes. Add the curry powder and the slivered almonds and blend in well. Add 1 tablespoon flour and cook until slightly thickened stirring constantly. Blend in the buttermilk marinade and add the chicken pieces. Cover and cook over low heat for 40 minutes or until the chicken is tender. Transfer the chicken to a hot serving platter and pour over the sauce.

Serves 4

Chicken with Walnuts
In the days when I lived on Telegraph Hill, Austin Mallet established himself as a chef of imagination in our small

community. His special knack was in preparing exotic dishes out of unusual ingredients. Chicken with walnuts is one of his creations.

4-pound chicken fryer cut into pieces
1 teaspoon salt
¼ teaspoon pepper
½ cup flour
¼ cup butter melted
1 cup onions chopped fine
1 clove garlic minced
1 teaspoon grated ginger root
1 bay leaf crumbled
1 cup red wine
½ cup brandy
2 cups walnut meats
Juice of 1 lemon
1 teaspoon grated orange peel
1 teaspoon grated lemon peel

Add the salt and pepper to the flour and roll the chicken pieces in the seasoned flour. Melt the butter in a heavy pan and brown the chicken well on both sides. Remove the chicken and add to the pan the chopped onions, minced garlic, grated ginger root, and crumbled bay leaf. Cook over medium low heat until the onions are soft but not browned. Return the chicken to the pan. Add the red wine and the brandy. Cover the pan and simmer over a low heat for 30 minutes. Meanwhile chop the walnuts fine or blend them in an electric blender. Add them to the chicken along with the lemon juice, grated orange peel, and grated lemon peel. Cook uncovered 10 minutes longer. The sauce should be slightly thick. If it seems too thin boil it down over a high heat. Pour the chicken and sauce into a deep dish to serve.

Serves 4

Chicken with Peanuts
An adventurous chicken dish that is unusual.

4-pound chicken fryer cut into pieces
4 tablespoons butter
1 large onion chopped
2 large tomatoes chopped
½ teaspoon chili powder
1 cup roasted peanuts
¼ cup chicken stock
¼ cup sherry
Salt and pepper to taste

Melt the butter in a heavy frying pan and brown the chicken pieces well on both sides. In an electric blender blend together the chopped onion, chopped tomatoes, chili powder, and roasted peanuts. Add the blended mixture to the chicken in the pan. Stir in well and add the chicken stock and the sherry. Cover the pan and simmer over a low heat for 40 minutes or until the chicken is tender. Taste for seasoning and serve.

Serves 4

Chicken Farmer Style
A robust old-fashioned meal-in-one chicken dinner.

4-pound chicken fryer cut into pieces
½ teaspoon salt
⅛ teaspoon pepper
¼ cup butter melted
1 large onion chopped
1 medium green pepper chopped
½ cup celery diced
1 teaspoon thyme
1 teaspoon Worcestershire sauce

1-pound can tomatoes
8-ounce can string beans
Salt and pepper to taste
Chopped parsley
Hot cooked rice

Sprinkle the chicken pieces with salt and pepper. Melt the butter in a large heavy skillet and brown the chicken pieces well on both sides. Remove the chicken from the skillet. Add the chopped onion, chopped green pepper, and diced celery. Cook for 5 minutes. Add the thyme, Worcestershire sauce, can of tomatoes, and the chicken pieces. Heat to boiling, cover, reduce heat and simmer for 40 minutes or until the chicken is tender. Turn into a serving dish and add salt and pepper to taste. Sprinkle with chopped parsley and serve over hot cooked rice.

Serves 4–6

Spicy Chicken

A lively chicken dish with a zesty sauce in which the star ingredient is saffron. It is considered the world's most expensive spice but fortunately only minute quantities of saffron are required in most recipes. Tumeric is often used as a substitute but most supermarkets carry it now in small quantities on their spice racks.

1 stewing chicken cut into pieces
1 tablespoon salt
1 onion sliced
½ lemon sliced
3 sprigs parsley
1 bay leaf
1 cup raisins
½ cup dry white wine
4 tablespoons butter melted

3 tablespoons flour
2 cups cream
Salt to taste
Pinch of saffron
Pinch of allspice
1 cup blanched almonds chopped
½ cup chopped red pimiento
Cooked rice

Put the chicken pieces in a kettle and cover with cold water. Add 1 tablespoon salt, the onion, lemon, parsley, and bay leaf. Cover and cook over low heat 1½ hours or until chicken is tender. Remove chicken from the kettle, strain the stock, and reserve 1½ cups. Soak the raisins in ½ cup wine until they plump up. Melt the butter in a saucepan and blend in the flour. Slowly add the chicken broth and cream, cooking over a low heat until the mixture is smooth and thickened. Add salt to taste, the saffron, allspice, raisins and wine. Blend well and add the blanched chopped almonds and chopped red pimiento. Return the chicken to the pan, heat through, and serve hot over rice.

Serves 6

Chicken with Mayonnaise
Do not use a commercial brand mayonnaise for this one. A good homemade mayonnaise consisting of nothing but egg, oil, a pinch of salt, and lemon juice is what makes this dish.

4-pound chicken fryer cut into pieces
¼ cup butter melted
2 green onions chopped fine
½ clove garlic minced fine
2 tablespoons tarragon
1 teaspoon salt
½ cup dry white wine
1½ cups mayonnaise

Melt the butter in a heavy frying pan and add the chicken pieces. Brown well on both sides. Add chopped onions, minced garlic, and tarragon. Add salt and dry white wine. Cover the pan tightly and cook over low heat for 40 minutes or until the chicken is tender. Meanwhile make the mayonnaise with lemon juice and spread it on a serving platter. Place the hot chicken pieces on top of the mayonnaise and serve immediately.

Mayonnaise
1 whole egg
1 teaspoon lemon juice
Pinch of salt
1 cup oil
Extra lemon juice

Put egg, 1 teaspoon lemon juice, and salt in the container of an electric blender. Add 3 tablespoons of the oil. Cover and blend thoroughly, about 5 seconds. Without stopping the blender remove the cover and gradually pour in the rest of the oil in a fine thin stream. Stop blending when all of the oil has been added. Taste for seasoning and add more salt and lemon juice if needed.

Serves 4

Viennese Chicken
The blending of sherry, onions, garlic, tomatoes, sour cream, and Swiss cheese gives a subtle and delicious flavor to this dish.

4-pound chicken fryer cut into pieces
¼ cup butter melted
2 tablespoons sherry
1 clove garlic minced
2 tablespoons onion minced
3 medium tomatoes sliced

1 tablespoon tomato paste
3 tablespoons flour
1½ cups chicken stock
¼ cup shredded almonds
1 teaspoon salt
1 bay leaf
¾ cup sour cream
½ cup grated Swiss cheese

Melt the butter in a heavy frying pan and brown the chicken pieces well on both sides. When browned add the sherry and cook 1 minute longer. Remove the chicken from the pan and add the garlic, onion, tomatoes. Cook 3 minutes. Remove from the heat and stir in the tomato paste and flour, blending until smooth. Add the chicken stock and stir over the heat until it comes to a boil. Add the shredded almonds, salt, and bay leaf. Return the chicken to the pan, cover, and cook over low heat for 40 minutes or until the chicken is tender. Remove the chicken and place it in a shallow baking pan. Add ¾ cup sour cream to the sauce and ½ cup grated Swiss cheese. Simmer a few moments until the sour cream and cheese are blended. Pour over the chicken. Sprinkle with more grated Swiss cheese and brown under the broiler.

Serves 4

Chicken Fricassee
An old favorite with a dash of mace to give it a piquant flavor.

1 large plump chicken cut into pieces
3 tablespoons butter
1 cup chicken broth
1½ teaspoons salt
¼ teaspoon pepper
¼ cup butter
½ pound fresh mushrooms sliced

1 cup cream
¼ teaspoon mace
Chopped parsley

Melt 3 tablespoons butter in a heavy saucepan and brown the chicken pieces evenly on both sides. When well browned add 1 cup chicken broth, 1½ teaspoons salt, and ¼ teaspoon pepper. Cover and simmer over low heat for 1½ hours or until chicken is tender. Melt ¼ cup butter in a pan. Add the sliced fresh mushrooms and cook for 5 minutes. Add the mushrooms to the chicken. Add 1 cup cream and ¼ teaspoon mace. Cook over low heat for 10 minutes. Arrange chicken pieces on a hot serving platter and spoon over the sauce. Sprinkle with chopped parsley and serve.

Serves 4

Deep Dish Chicken Pie
There are many ways to make a good American chicken pie. I have tried a number of recipes, adapting ideas here and there, and this deep-dish chicken pie is my favorite.

5-pound roasting chicken
1 onion sliced
1 carrot sliced
1 stalk celery
1 teaspoon salt
1 bay leaf

Sauce
2 tablespoons butter
3 tablespoons flour
1½ cups chicken broth
½ cup cream
1 cup cooked baby carrots sliced thin
¼ teaspoon thyme

Dash of cayenne
Salt and pepper to taste

Crust
1½ cups flour
4 tablespoons lard
3 egg yolks
2 tablespoons water
1 teaspoon salt

Put the chicken in a kettle with water to cover. Add onion, carrot, celery, salt, and bay leaf. Cover tightly and simmer over low heat for 1 hour or until the chicken is tender. Remove chicken and cut the meat from the bones into large pieces. Discard the skin and bones. Strain the broth. Add to the following sauce:

Melt the butter in a saucepan and blend in the flour. Slowly add 1½ cups chicken broth and stir over the heat until the sauce thickens. Add the ½ cup cream and cook 1 minute longer. Add the chicken meat, sliced baby carrots, sliced mushrooms, thyme, cayenne, and salt and pepper to taste. Fill a deep baking dish with this mixture and cover with the following crust:

Put 1½ cups flour in a bowl and make a well in the center. In the well put 4 tablespoons lard, 3 egg yolks, 2 tablespoons water, and 1 teaspoon salt. Work into a smooth paste with your fingers and slowly work the paste into the flour. Roll out not too thin on a floured board and cover the top of the baking dish. Seal the edges tightly and make slits in the top so the steam can escape. Bake in a preheated 400° oven until the crust is browned.

Serves 6

Chicken Pie with Biscuit Topping

A chicken pie made with biscuit dough will awaken the whole family.

5-pound roasting chicken
2 stalks celery and tops
1 medium onion sliced
1 teaspoon salt
1 bay leaf
5 tablespoons butter
5 tablespoons flour
1 cup cream
Biscuit dough

Put the chicken in a kettle with cold water to cover. Add celery, onion, salt, and bay leaf. Cover and cook over low heat for 1 hour or until chicken is tender. Remove the chicken from the broth, take off the skin, and separate all the meat from the bones, keeping the meat in large pieces. Return the bones and skin to the broth and simmer for another hour. Strain and cool the broth and skim off the fat. Melt 5 tablespoons butter and blend in the 5 tablespoons flour. Add 2 cups chicken broth and cook over a medium low heat, stirring constantly until thickened and smooth. Add 1 cup cream and the chicken meat and cook 1 minute longer. Season to taste with salt and pepper and pour the chicken and gravy into a shallow casserole. Cover with biscuit dough rolled ¼ inch thick, fitting it carefully over the top and making slits so the steam will escape. Or top with individual biscuits if you prefer. Use a mix or make the biscuits yourself.

Serves 6

Chicken and Mushroom Patties

For that special ladies' luncheon party creamed chicken and mushrooms served in patty shells are always sure-fire to please.

Baked patty shells
Boiling salted water
5-pound roasting chicken
2 tablespoons butter
2 tablespoons flour
1 cup chicken stock
1 cup heavy cream
1 cup sliced canned mushrooms
2 tablespoons sherry
Salt and pepper to taste

Put the chicken in a kettle with boiling salted water to cover and cook over a low heat for about 1 hour or until the chicken is tender. Remove the chicken from the broth. Skin and cut the meat from the bones into small pieces. Blend the butter with the flour in a saucepan. Slowly add 1 cup of the chicken broth and 1 cup of heavy cream. Cook over a medium low heat until the sauce is thickened stirring constantly. Add the chicken meat and the sliced canned mushrooms. Add the sherry and season to taste with salt and pepper. Heat the patty shells and pour the hot filling into the shells.

Patty Shells
2 cups sifted flour
½ teaspoon salt
1 teaspoon lemon juice
¾ cup water approximately
1 cup butter
2 egg yolks mixed with 2 tablespoons cream

Put flour in a bowl and make a well in the center. Add salt, lemon juice, and ½ cup water. Using one hand, work flour and liquid together to make a firm slightly sticky dough. If necessary add more water gradually. Knead the sticky dough on a floured board until it is elastic and smooth. Cover the dough and let it rest for 10 minutes in the refrigerator.

While the dough rests, roll butter into an oval shape and sprinkle with flour. When dough is ready roll it out on a large floured cloth and place the butter in the center. Fold over the edges of the dough to seal in the butter and chill for 10 minutes. Roll out the dough to a long rectangle. Fold the end nearest you to the center. Fold the other end to the center. Then fold together again as though closing a book. There will be 4 layers of dough. Chill dough 20 minutes. Then lay dough so narrow ends are nearest you and roll out into a rectangle again. Fold in the same way as before and chill 20 minutes again. Repeat the process until the dough has been rolled and folded 5 times in all. Chill 3 hours before using. Roll out ½ inch thick and cut out 3 inch rounds with a scalloped cookie cutter. Using a slightly smaller plain cutter press into the center of each round about ⅔ of the way through the dough. Chill 20 minutes. Brush tops with beaten egg and place on an ungreased cookie sheet. Bake in a preheated 350° oven for 45 minutes or until the patty shells are well puffed and browned. With a knife loosen and remove the center round. Scrape out any soft dough remaining in the shells. Fill the shells with the creamed chicken and use the little center round as a cap.

Makes 12 patty shells

Chicken and Tarragon Aspic
A superior aspic worth all the loving care you can give it.

2 1½-pound broilers split in half
3 tablespoons soft butter
1 teaspoon salt
¼ teaspoon pepper
4 teaspoons lemon juice

Aspic
1¾ cups hot chicken broth

1 envelope plain gelatin
1 tablespoon dried tarragon
1 tablespoon tarragon vinegar
1 tablespoon lemon juice
¼ teaspoon salt
Dash of pepper

Carefully remove all the bones except the leg and wing bones from the broilers. Rub well with the soft butter and sprinkle with salt and pepper. Arrange the boned broiler halves on a broiler rack skin side down and put 1 teaspoon lemon juice over each half chicken. Broil 7 inches from the heat for 15 minutes. Turn over and broil 15 minutes on the other side. Remove from pan and chill.

Mix the gelatin into the hot chicken broth. Place over the heat and stir until the gelatin is dissolved. Remove from the heat and add tarragon, tarragon vinegar, lemon juice, salt, and pepper. Cool until almost jelled. Arrange the chicken halves on a platter and spoon half the gelatin mixture on top. Place in the refrigerator and chill until set. Spoon the rest of the gelatin over the top. Refrigerate overnight.

Serves 4

Cold Lemon Chicken
For a real summer treat this is superb.

3½-pound chicken fryer
Boiling salted water to barely cover
Peel from ½ lemon
2 egg yolks
1 heaping tablespoon cornstarch
½ cup sugar
1 cup water
2 tablespoons butter

Pinch of salt
Juice and grated rind from 2 lemons
1 cup heavy cream

Put the chicken in a kettle with boiling salted water to barely cover. Add peel from ½ lemon, cover the kettle, and cook over low heat about 1 hour or until the chicken is tender. Remove the chicken and when cooled discard the skin and bones and cut the meat into large pieces. Mix the egg yolks, cornstarch, sugar, water, butter, and salt together in a saucepan. Cook together over a low heat, stirring constantly, until thick and smooth. Add the lemon juice, grated lemon rind, and heavy cream. Cook 1 minute longer. Add the cooked chicken and pour into a shallow dish. Chill thoroughly in the refrigerator. Serve very cold.

Serves 4

Braised Chicken
A simple, flavorful way to prepare an American chicken.

4-pound chicken fryer cut into pieces
1 teaspoon salt
¼ teaspoon pepper
½ cup flour
3 tablespoons butter
½ cup water

Add the salt and pepper to the flour and roll the chicken pieces in the seasoned flour. Brown the chicken well on both sides in 3 tablespoons butter in a heavy Dutch oven. When browned add the water, cover tightly, and simmer 40 minutes or until the chicken is tender.

Serves 4

Braised Stuffed Chicken
A braised chicken with a dash.

4-pound roasting chicken
2½ cups bread crumbs
1 small onion minced
½ cup celery chopped fine
½ teaspoon salt
⅛ teaspoon pepper
¼ teaspoon poultry seasoning
5 tablespoons butter melted
Water
½ cup dry white wine
1 teaspoon butter
1 teaspoon flour
¼ cup toasted chopped almonds
2 egg yolks beaten with 2 tablespoons cold water

Make a stuffing for the chicken by mixing the bread crumbs, minced onion, celery, salt, pepper, poultry seasoning, and melted butter together. Stuff the chicken with this and sew up the opening tightly. Truss and place the chicken in a heavy Dutch oven. Barely cover with cold water and add ½ cup dry white wine. Set over a high heat and boil rapidly for 10 minutes. Reduce heat to low and simmer 10 minutes longer. Then transfer the Dutch oven to a 350° preheated oven and cook covered 40 minutes longer. Remove the chicken to a hot serving platter and keep warm. Place the Dutch oven over a high heat on top of the stove and let the pan gravy boil a few moments. Add 1 teaspoon butter blended with 1 teaspoon flour and stir over the heat until smooth. Remove from the heat and blend in the 2 egg yolks which have been beaten with 2 tablespoons water. Add the chopped toasted almonds and serve with the chicken and stuffing.

Serves 4

Chicken à la King

There are many stories about the origin of Chicken à la King. One version is that it was first created by Foxhall Keene and served at Delmonico's in New York as Chicken à la Keene. Anyway, it has long been an American favorite.

4 tablespoons chicken fat
1 cup fresh mushrooms sliced
1 green pepper sliced thin
1 pimiento chopped fine
1½ tablespoons flour
1½ cups heavy cream
½ cup chicken stock
½ cup sherry
1 teaspoon salt
Dash of cayenne
¼ teaspoon paprika
4 egg yolks beaten well
½ cup heavy cream
3 cups cooked chicken in large chunks

Melt the chicken fat in a saucepan. Add the sliced mushrooms, green pepper, and pimientoes. Simmer 5 minutes. Add the flour and blend in well. Add the 1½ cups heavy cream and the chicken stock. Cook over a low heat until thickened, stirring constantly. Add the sherry and stir in well. Season with salt, cayenne, and paprika. Combine the egg yolks with ½ cup heavy cream and stir slowly into the sauce. Add the chicken and heat through but do not let the sauce boil. Serve on toast triangles or in patty shells.

Serves 6

Minced Chicken with Almonds

This is an excellent dish for a luncheon or a light summer meal.

1 plump chicken cut into pieces
4 cups chicken broth
1 teaspoon salt
1 onion
3 sprigs parsley
1 stalk celery and top
2 tablespoons butter
2 tablespoons flour
1 cup strained stock
1 cup heavy cream
¼ teaspoon nutmeg
1 teaspoon salt
¼ teaspoon white pepper
3 tablespoons Madeira wine
12 sliced mushrooms
1 tablespoon butter
Chervil
1 cup thinly sliced toasted almonds

Put the chicken pieces in a kettle and cover with the 4 cups chicken stock. Add salt, onion, parsley, celery and top. Cook covered over low heat about 1½ hours or until chicken is tender. Remove chicken from the kettle and cut the meat into chunks discarding the skin and bones. Melt 2 tablespoons butter in a pan and blend in the flour. Slowly add 1 cup strained chicken stock mixed with 1 cup heavy cream. Cook over low heat until thickened, stirring constantly. Add nutmeg, salt, white pepper, and Madeira. Mix in well. In a separate pan sauté the sliced mushrooms in 1 tablespoon butter for 5 minutes. Add to the sauce along with the chicken and ½ of the sliced toasted almonds. Pour into a serving dish and sprinkle with chervil and the rest of the sliced toasted almonds.

Serves 6

Oven Barbecued Chicken
A practicable and thoroughly American way to serve a chicken.

2 1½-pound broilers split in half
1 tablespoon olive oil
2 tablespoons instant minced onion
1 cup water
½ cup catsup
½ teaspoon Tabasco
1 teaspoon Worcestershire sauce
½ teaspoon garlic salt
1 teaspoon grated lemon rind
2 tablespoons lemon juice
2 tablespoons brown sugar

Preheat oven to 425°. Brush a baking pan with 1 tablespoon olive oil. Combine onion, water, catsup, Tabasco, Worcestershire sauce, garlic salt, lemon rind, lemon juice, and brown sugar. Cook over low heat for 5 minutes. Coat the split broiler halves well on both sides with the sauce and arrange skin side down in the baking pan. Bake for 20 minutes in a hot 425° oven. Reduce the heat to 375°, turn the chicken pieces over, and brush with the remaining sauce. Bake 10 minutes longer or until tender.

Serves 4

Chicken Kabobs
Outdoors or indoors chicken kabobs are always good.

Kabobs
3 chicken breasts boned and quartered
¼ pound chicken livers
12 squares cut from 2 green peppers
1 tomato cut into 6 wedges
6 mushroom caps

Marinade

½ cup soy sauce
⅔ cup olive oil
¼ cup sugar
3 tablespoons sherry
1 clove garlic minced

Combine all the ingredients for the marinade and let the chicken and livers marinate in it for 2 hours. Then take 2 long skewers and arrange alternating pieces of chicken, green pepper squares, mushroom caps, chicken livers, and tomato wedges on the skewers. Brush with the marinade and place under the broiler about 4 inches from the heat. Broil 25 minutes, brushing with the marinade and turning often.

Serves 2

Roast Chicken

Roasting chickens are usually from five to ten months old and weigh 3½ to 6 pounds. A fryer or roaster of any weight may be roasted, however, but the chicken should be plump and weigh at least 3 pounds for best results.

While there has been much controversy as to whether a chicken should be roasted at high heat with constant basting or a lower heat and longer cooking, I would not dare to disagree with the experts on the subject but personally I prefer to roast a chicken at 375°, allowing 20 minutes to the pound, approximately, with excellent results.

I am also a great believer in frequent basting, and unless a recipe specifically states otherwise I use melted butter kept warm on the stove for that special flavor. And I always turn the chicken over during the last 20 minutes of cooking time so that the underside will be perfectly browned as well as the breast side. To turn without breaking the skin, pick the chicken up by the neck and legs, using several layers of clean cloth as a holder.

Always be sure to truss the chicken, because unless the chicken is trussed the heat of the oven forces the legs and wings away from the body and the meat is apt to cook dry.

When cooking several chickens at one time in one oven keep the temperature somewhat higher or too much steam forms and the chickens are apt to taste more steamed than roasted.

Test chicken for doneness by pressing the meaty portion of the drumstick with your fingers. When it feels soft and the drumstick moves up and down easily the chicken is done. Never pierce the meat with a fork.

A chicken may be roasted either stuffed or not.

Roast Stuffed Chicken: Chickens should always be stuffed just before roasting. Allow 1 cup large breadcrumbs for each pound ready to cook weight. Crumble the bread or cut into cubes. When measuring, pile it lightly into the cup. Heat oven to 375°. Rinse the chicken with cold water, drain, and pat dry. Fill neck cavity with stuffing and sew or skewer neck skin to back. Spoon stuffing into body cavity lightly. Never pack it. Close the opening by placing skewers across it or sew with needle and thread. Truss by tying wing tips onto back firmly. Tie drumsticks together and then tie them to the tail.

Place the chicken in a shallow open roasting pan breast side up. Rub well with soft butter. If you are using a meat thermometer insert it so the bulb is in the center of the inside thigh muscle or the thickest part of the breast meat. Be sure the bulb is not touching the bone. Put the chicken in the preheated oven and roast, allowing 20 minutes to the pound until the chicken is tender and browned. Baste the chicken frequently, especially any dry areas around the legs. Test for doneness by pressing with fingers. The last 20 minutes of cooking time turn the bird over so the underside will brown nicely too.

Chicken Roasted in Foil: Chickens roasted in foil do not have to be basted and there is no spattering in the oven. There are two ways of doing it—wrapping, and tenting.

For the wrapping method heat the oven to 450°. Stuff and truss the chicken exactly as for roast chicken. Brush the skin with soft butter. Use heavy wide aluminum foil. Place the chicken breast side up in the center of a piece of foil 12 inches longer than the chicken. To prevent puncture wrap small pieces of foil around the legs and wings. Bring edges of foil together over breast of chicken and secure tightly. Bring sides up high enough to prevent drippings from escaping into pan. The foil should not be airtight. Place the chicken in a shallow open roasting pan and roast to within 30 minutes of total roasting time. Open foil carefully and fold back to edge of pan. This will allow the chicken to brown during the last half hour of roasting time.

For the tenting method heat oven to 350°. Stuff and truss the chicken as for roast chicken. Tear off a piece of foil five inches longer than the chicken and crease it lengthwise. Rub the chicken with soft butter and place in a shallow roasting pan. Place the creased foil over the chicken like a tent and pinch it at the legs and the breast to anchor it. If the breast or legs begin to brown too quickly press the foil tent down over these parts so that they will not become too browned. The last 20 minutes of cooking time remove the foil and turn the chicken over to brown the underside.

Rotisserie Roasted Chicken: Any chicken that can be roasted can be spit roasted, either in an electric rotisserie in the oven or over the barbecue. Two or three chickens can usually be roasted on the spit at one time. Follow the manufacturer's directions on the equipment for best results. Cooking time is about the same as for ordinary roasting but it is a good idea to use a thermometer or test the meaty portion of the drumstick with your fingers to be sure the bird is done.

Gravy for Roast Chicken: Remove the chicken from the roasting pan when it is done and keep hot. Drain off all but 4 tablespoons of the drippings and make the gravy. A delicious pan gravy can be made by swishing a little stock or wine around in the pan juices, stirring in all the brown bits that cling to the bottom of the pan, and letting it boil up once. A giblet gravy is made by adding 4 tablespoons flour to the pan and cooking and stirring until browned. Add 2 cups of stock in which the giblets were cooked and let the gravy cook over medium heat until thickened and smooth. Then add the chopped giblets. Or a nice rich cream gravy can be made by using milk or cream in place of the stock. If you wish add a dash of wine to give an extra zip.

Roast Chicken
The delicate flavor of chicken takes very well to roasting.

1 large roasting chicken
4 tablespoons butter
Salt and pepper

Sprinkle the chicken with salt and pepper and place the heart and liver inside. Rub the chicken well with the butter and place in an open roasting pan. Place the chicken in a preheated 375° oven and roast uncovered allowing 20 minutes to the pound. Baste frequently with the juices in the pan adding more butter if necessary. The last 20 minutes of roasting time turn the chicken over so the underside will brown nicely too. When the chicken is tender transfer to a heated platter. Add a little boiling water to the juices in the pan and scrape all the particles sticking to the bottom of the pan. Season to taste with salt and pepper and pour the sauce into a heated bowl. Serve with the chicken.

Serves 6

Old-Fashioned Roast Chicken
A wonderful roast chicken with a simple old-fashioned stuffing the way my grandmother made it.

5-pound roasting chicken
Softened butter
1 teaspoon salt
1/8 teaspoon pepper
2 1/2 cups dried breadcrumbs
1 medium onion chopped fine

½ cup celery chopped fine
½ cup butter melted
½ teaspoon salt
⅛ teaspoon pepper
¼ teaspoon poultry seasoning

Make the stuffing first. Melt ½ cup butter in a heavy pan and sauté the onion and celery gently until they are soft but not colored. Mix the onion, celery, and butter into the dried breadcrumbs. Add ½ teaspoon salt, ⅛ teaspoon pepper, and ¼ teaspoon poultry seasoning. Mix together well and stuff the chicken cavities lightly with the stuffing. Sew or skewer the opening closed. Truss.

Rub the outside of the chicken well with softened butter and sprinkle with 1 teaspoon salt and ⅛ teaspoon pepper. Place breast side up in an open roasting pan and roast uncovered in a 375° oven allowing 20 minutes to the pound until the chicken is tender. Baste frequently with the juices in the pan and add more butter if necessary. The last 20 minutes of cooking time turn the chicken carefully breast side down so the underside can brown.

Serves 6

Herb Roasted Chicken
Herb roasted chicken is a good reason for serving roast chicken, delicately flavored with garlic, rosemary, basil, and white wine.

4-pound chicken fryer
1 teaspoon garlic salt
1 teaspoon rosemary crushed
½ cup butter melted
½ cup dry white wine
1 teaspoon rosemary crushed

1 teaspoon sweet basil crushed
1 teaspoon chopped parsley
½ teaspoon salt
¼ teaspoon pepper

Heat oven to 375°. Sprinkle the neck and body cavities of
the chicken with the garlic salt and 1 teaspoon of the crushed
rosemary. Melt the butter in a pan, add the dry white wine,
1 teaspoon crushed rosemary, 1 teaspoon crushed sweet basil,
1 teaspoon chopped parsley, ½ teaspoon salt, and ¼ teaspoon
pepper. Cook over low heat a few moments until thoroughly
blended. Truss the chicken, place in an open roasting pan,
and brush well with the butter-wine sauce. Place in a 375°
preheated oven and roast 20 minutes to the pound until the
chicken is tender. Baste frequently with the sauce. The last
20 minutes of roasting time turn the chicken over to brown
the underside. When tender remove the chicken to a serving
platter and carve into serving pieces.

Serves 4

Roast Chicken with Onions
The onions give a delicious flavor to the chicken and they
are good to eat too.

5-pound roasting chicken
Softened butter
1 pound small white onions
1 teaspoon salt
¼ teaspoon pepper
Salt and pepper

Rub the cavities of the chicken well with softened butter.
Mix 1 pound small white onions with 1 teaspoon salt and ¼
teaspoon pepper. Place them in the body cavity and sew or
skewer the opening closed. Sprinkle salt and pepper over the

chicken and rub well with softened butter. Place the chicken in an open roasting pan and roast uncovered in a 375° oven allowing 20 minutes to the pound until browned and tender. Baste frequently with the drippings in the pan. The last 20 minutes of cooking time turn the chicken over so the underside can brown too. Carve and serve the chicken with the onions.

Serves 6

Lemon Roasted Chicken
A dish that is both piquant and delicious.

5-pound roasting chicken
Juice of ½ lemon
1 onion minced
2 tablespoons butter
2 cups soft bread crumbs
1 teaspoon salt
½ teaspoon pepper
¼ teaspoon thyme
¼ teaspoon savory
⅛ teaspoon nutmeg
⅛ teaspoon tarragon
1 tablespoon chopped parsley
2 tablespoons melted butter
¼ cup lemon juice
Salt and pepper
4 tablespoons melted butter
4 tablespoons lemon juice
Juice of ½ lemon

Rub the chicken cavities well with lemon juice. Then make the stuffing. Melt 2 tablespoons butter in a pan and cook the onion until soft but not browned. Mix with the breadcrumbs. Add salt, pepper, thyme, savory, nutmeg, tarragon, chopped parsley, and 2 tablespoons melted butter. Mix well and add ¼ cup lemon juice. Stuff the chicken lightly with this mixture and sew or skewer the openings closed. Truss. Salt and pepper the chicken and rub well with softened butter. Squeeze the juice of ½ lemon over the chicken and roast in a preheated 375° oven, allowing 20 minutes to the pound or until the chicken is browned and tender. During roasting, baste frequently with a mixture of 4 tablespoons melted butter and 4 tablespoons lemon juice. Be sure to turn chicken over during the last 20 minutes of roasting so the underside will brown too.

Serves 6

Roast Chicken Tarragon

The elusive flavor of tarragon is delightful; no additional sauce or gravy is needed.

5-pound roasting chicken
1 bunch tarragon leaves or 1 tablespoon dried tarragon
Salt and pepper
Softened butter
¼ cup butter melted

Put 1 bunch fresh tarragon leaves inside the cavity of the chicken. If they are not available use 1 tablespoon dried tarragon instead. Rub well inside the cavity. Sprinkle the chicken with salt and pepper and rub it well with soft butter. Place the chicken in an open roasting pan and roast in a preheated 375° oven allowing 20 minutes to the pound or until browned and tender. Turn over the last 20 minutes of cooking time to brown the underside. Baste the chicken frequently with melted butter and when it is used up continue basting with the juices in the pan.

Serves 6

Roast Chicken with Anchovy Butter
This roast chicken is toothsome and tantalizing.

5-pound roasting chicken
Salt and pepper
Softened butter
6 finely chopped anchovy fillets
3 tablespoons unsalted butter

Sprinkle the chicken with salt and pepper and rub well with softened butter. Truss and roast in an open roasting pan in a 375° preheated oven allowing 20 minutes to the pound. Baste frequently with drippings in the pan. Turn the chicken over 20 minutes before it is done and let the underside brown. When the chicken is tender take out of the oven and fill the inside with softened anchovy butter made by mashing the anchovy fillets with 3 tablespoons unsalted butter. Carve the chicken and serve with a few spoonfuls of pan gravy around each serving. The anchovy butter will melt and run into the gravy. Spoon a little of the combined anchovy butter and pan gravy on the plate with the chicken.

Serves 6

Roast Chicken with Spinach Stuffing
Italian housewives quite often stuff a chicken with a garlicy spinach cheese dressing. This recipe was given to me by Tina Rossi who lives in San Francisco's North Beach.

5-pound roasting chicken
1 10-ounce package frozen chopped spinach
2 tablespoons butter
½ pound chopped mushrooms
½ cup chopped parsley
1 clove garlic crushed
1 teaspoon basil

1 cup fine French breadcrumbs
1 teaspoon salt
½ teaspoon pepper
1 egg well beaten
½ cup grated Parmesan cheese
Salt and pepper
Softened butter
½ cup butter melted
¼ cup brandy
¼ cup white wine
1 teaspoon basil

Cook the chopped spinach according to directions on the package. Drain and set aside. Melt 2 tablespoons butter in a pan and add the chopped mushrooms, chopped parsley, crushed garlic, and 1 teaspoon basil. Sauté for 5 minutes. Mix into the spinach and add the dry French breadcrumbs. Season with salt and pepper. Add the well beaten egg and the grated Parmesan cheese.

Fill the chicken cavity with this stuffing and skewer or sew the openings closed. Truss the chicken. Rub with salt and pepper and softened butter. Roast in an open roasting pan in a preheated 375° oven allowing 20 minutes to the pound roasting time until the chicken is tender and browned. The last 20 minutes turn the chicken over to brown the underside. Baste frequently with a sauce made from ½ cup melted butter, ½ cup brandy, ¼ cup white wine, and 1 teaspoon basil. Carve and pour some of the juices from the pan over each serving.

Serves 6

Roast Chicken Kamemehameha
This is the creation of a dear friend of mine from Hawaii who has served this dish at many festive dinners both in the islands and on the mainland.

1 large roasting chicken
Softened butter
Salt and pepper
1 loaf French bread
Giblets plus 5 extra chicken livers
¼ cup butter melted
1 bay leaf crumbled
Salt and pepper
½ cup red wine
Sage
½ cup beef bouillon
½ cup walnuts

Sprinkle the chicken with salt and pepper and rub it well with softened butter. Then make the dressing. Scoop out 1 loaf of French bread and put it through the meat grinder or blend in an electric blender. It should be of a fine consistency. Cut the giblets and the chicken livers into small pieces and brown them with 1 clove minced garlic in ¼ cup melted butter. When browned add the crumbled bay leaf, salt, pepper, and ½ cup red wine. Sauté for 30 minutes. Dissolve the sage in ½ cup beef bouillon and add to the breadcrumbs. Add the liver mixture and ½ cup walnuts to the breadcrumbs. Mix well together until of sausage like consistency. Stuff the chicken lightly with this stuffing and sew or skewer the openings closed. Place the chicken in an open roasting pan and roast in a preheated 375° oven allowing 20 minutes to the pound or until the chicken is browned and tender. Baste frequently with the juices in the pan. The last 20 minutes of roasting time turn the chicken over to brown the underside.

Serves 6

South American Roast Chicken
Steeped in the spicy flavors of Latin America this dish is for those who like their chicken well seasoned.

5-pound roasting chicken
1 teaspoon salt
¼ teaspoon black pepper
Softened butter
2 tablespoons olive oil
½ cup minced onions
1 cup uncooked rice
2 cups hot chicken broth
¼ teaspoon dried green chili peppers crushed
2 tablespoons minced parsley
2 tablespoons butter

Season the chicken with salt and pepper. Rub with softened butter. Heat the olive oil in a pan and sauté the minced onions until soft. Stir the rice in until it is well-coated. Add the broth and the chili peppers. Cover and cook over low heat for 20 minutes. Mix in the parsley. Taste for seasoning and stuff lightly into the chicken. Sew or skewer the openings closed. Truss. Melt 2 tablespoons butter in an open roasting pan and place the chicken in it. Roast in a preheated 375° oven allowing 20 minutes to the pound or until the chicken is browned and tender. Baste frequently with the melted butter. The last 20 minutes of roasting time turn the chicken over to brown the underside.

Serves 6

Pork Stuffed Chicken
A chicken stuffed with pork, almonds, and raisins, makes a dish good for a party.

1 large roasting chicken
1 teaspoon salt
¼ teaspoon black pepper
3 tablespoons softened butter
1 clove garlic minced

1 pound ground pork
½ cup minced onions
1 tomato chopped fine
1 cup seedless raisins
½ cup slivered almonds
1 clove minced garlic

Mix the salt, pepper, softened butter, and 1 clove minced garlic together. Rub the chicken well with this mixture. Mix together the ground pork, minced onions, tomato, raisins, almonds, and 1 clove of minced garlic. Stuff the chicken lightly with this mixture and sew or skewer the openings closed. Truss. Place the chicken in an open roasting pan and roast in a preheated 375° oven allowing 20 minutes to the pound or until the chicken is tender and browned. Baste frequently with the drippings in the pan. Turn chicken over the last 20 minutes of roasting time to brown the underside.

Serves 6

Alsatian Roast Chicken

Where the name Alsation came from I don't know because the recipe was given to me, but it is an original and tasty way to serve up a roast chicken.

5-pound roasting chicken
1 teaspoon salt
¼ teaspoon pepper
1 clove garlic split
4 tablespoons softened butter
1 package frozen peas
¼ pound noodles
1 cup grated Parmesan cheese
½ cup butter melted
1 teaspoon oregano
2 tablespoons white wine

Rub the chicken well with the salt, pepper, and split clove of garlic. Then rub with the softened butter. Truss. Place in an open roasting pan and roast in a preheated 375° oven allowing 20 minutes to the pound or until the chicken is tender and browned. The last 20 minutes of cooking time turn the chicken over to brown the underside. Baste frequently with the drippings in the pan. Cook the peas in boiling salted water until tender. Cook the noodles in boiling salted water until tender. When the noodles and peas are done, drain, and mix together with the grated Parmesan cheese, melted butter, and oregano. Carve the chicken into pieces. Place the noodle mixture on a heated serving platter and put the chicken on top. Add the white wine to the roasting pan and let it come to a boil on top of the stove, scraping the juices and browned particles to blend them into the wine. Pour over the chicken and noodles.

Serves 6

Bohemian Roast Chicken
For a roast chicken with real eye appeal this glossy glazed bird is an impressive sight.

¼ cup melted butter
¼ cup soy sauce
¼ cup crushed canned pineapple
5-pound roasting chicken

In a saucepan combine the melted butter, soy sauce, and crushed pineapple. Cook over a medium heat until just heated through. Brush the inside of the chicken with this mixture. Truss the chicken and place it in an open roasting pan. Coat the chicken liberally with the soy sauce pineapple mixture and place it in a preheated 375° oven allowing 20 minutes to the pound or until the chicken is tender. The last 20 minutes of cooking time turn the chicken over. Baste frequently with the sauce and when it is used up continue basting the chicken liberally with the browned butter-soy sauce-pineapple mixture gathered in the bottom of the pan. The sauce should form a glossy brown glaze.

Serves 6

Roast Chicken Au Gratin
Utterly delicious and the cheese sauce gives the chicken a new zest.

4-pound fryer chicken
1 teaspoon salt
¼ teaspoon pepper
2 tablespoons softened butter
3 tablespoons butter melted
4 tablespoons flour
2 cups scalded milk
½ teaspoon salt
2 egg yolks
⅓ cup grated Swiss cheese
⅓ cup grated Parmesan cheese
2 tablespoons grated Swiss cheese
2 tablespoons grated Parmesan cheese

Sprinkle the chicken with salt and pepper and rub well with the softened butter. Truss. Place in an open roasting pan and roast in a preheated 375° oven allowing 20 minutes to the pound or until the chicken is tender and browned. Baste frequently with the pan juices. The last 20 minutes of roasting time turn the chicken over to brown underside. Melt 3 tablespoons butter in a saucepan and stir in the flour. When well blended add the scalded milk a little at a time and stir until smooth and thickened. Add ½ teaspoon salt and the 2 egg yolks mixing them in well. Add ⅓ cup grated Swiss cheese and ⅓ cup grated Parmesan cheese. Cook over low heat, stirring constantly, until the cheese has melted. When the chicken is done carve it into serving pieces. Pour the cheese sauce over the chicken and sprinkle with 2 tablespoons grated Swiss cheese and 2 tablespoons grated Parmesan cheese. Place under the broiler a few moments for the cheese to melt.

Serves 4

Roast Stuffed Chicken with Grapes
Grapes and white wine makes a pleasing change.

5-pound roasting chicken
7 slices dry crumbled bread
1 onion chopped fine
1 cup white seedless grapes
6 tablespoons melted butter
1 teaspoon chopped parsley
¼ teaspoon sweet basil
½ teaspoon salt
½ cup dry white wine
Salt and pepper
Softened butter

Make a stuffing of the dry crumbled bread, chopped onion, white seedless grapes, melted butter, chopped parsley, sweet basil, and ½ teaspoon salt. Stuff this mixture lightly into the cavities of the chicken and sew or skewer the openings closed. Truss. Sprinkle the chicken with salt and pepper and rub well with the softened butter. Place in an open roasting pan and roast in a preheated 375° oven allowing 20 minutes to the pound or until the chicken is browned and tender. The last 20 minutes of roasting time turn over to brown the underside. Baste frequently with the dry white wine.

Serves 6.

Roast Spring Chicken in Casserole
So easy to prepare and yet so good.

2½-pound broiler chicken
½ teaspoon salt
⅛ teaspoon pepper
3 tablespoons butter
½ cup boiling water

Truss the chicken and rub it with salt and pepper. Melt the
3 tablespoons butter in a heavy Dutch oven. Add ½ cup boiling water and place the chicken in the Dutch oven. Put it in
a 375° preheated oven and roast uncovered about 1 hour or
until the chicken is tender and browned. Baste and turn the
chicken often so that it is the same even brown all over. Should
the liquid in the Dutch oven reduce too fast add a little more
boiling water. Serve plain with the juices from the casserole.

Serves 2

Chicken Stuffing

The stuffing that fills a roasted chicken is actually what makes the chicken. A plump golden chicken filled with a taste-tingling spicily seasoned dressing is the test of your ability as a gourmet chef. A properly made stuffing adds flavor and zest to the chicken. There are a wide and interesting variety of ingredients that can go inside a fowl. They are the secret success of a deliciously roasted chicken.

Stuff, truss, and roast, are the directions repeated over and over in recipes for roast chicken. The stuffing or dressing is needed to keep the fowl filled out in its natural shape. Also the stuffing releases its own spicy flavors into the flesh of the chicken while at the same time absorbing the juices as they exude and trickle down during the roasting.

The variety of stuffings is endless. You can use white bread, cornbread, rice, or potatoes. You can add celery, onions, mushrooms, oysters, sausage, chestnuts, and nutmeats. You can season with almost anything aromatic.

Any extra stuffing can be baked in a covered greased casserole right along with the chicken. Uncover the last 15 minutes of cooking time for a crisp top.

And remember—never stuff the chicken until just before roasting time. Always remove any leftover stuffing from the cavity and store in a separate dish in the refrigerator!

Old-Fashioned Bread Stuffing

¼ cup butter melted
½ cup onion chopped fine

½ cup chopped celery
4 cups cubed white bread
1 teaspoon salt
1 teaspoon poultry seasoning
1 tablespoon chopped parsley
½ cup cream

Melt ¼ cup butter in a pan. Cook the onions and celery until soft and yellow but not browned. Combine with the bread crumbs. Add the salt poultry seasoning, chopped parsley, and the ½ cup cream. Mix well and stuff lightly into chicken cavities.

For a 5-pound chicken

Cornbread Sausage Stuffing

¼ pound sausage meat
½ cup chopped onion
3 cups crumbled cold cornbread
⅛ teaspoon finely chopped parsley
⅛ teaspoon finely chopped green pepper
⅛ teaspoon chopped green onion
1 teaspoon salt
⅛ teaspoon black pepper
½ teaspoon powdered sage
¼ teaspoon thyme
¼ teaspoon mace
1 small clove garlic mashed
1 egg beaten
Cold milk

Brown the sausage meat over a medium high heat breaking the sausage into small pieces with a fork as it cooks. Remove the sausage meat and set aside. Cook the chopped onions in the sausage drippings until soft. Combine with the sausage meat. Add the crumbled cornbread, parsley, green pepper, and green onions. Season with salt, black pepper, sage, thyme, mace, and garlic. Add the beaten egg and mix in well. If stuffing is not moist enough add a little cold milk to moisten. Stuff lightly into chicken cavities.

For a 5-pound chicken

Savory Rice Stuffing

2½ cups raw rice
Water
3 chicken bouillon cubes
½ cup butter
1 cup chopped onions
½ teaspoon salt
⅛ teaspoon pepper
½ teaspoon thyme
½ teaspoon sage
1 teaspoon chopped parsley

Cook the rice in water according to directions on the package, adding the chicken bouillon cubes to the water. Melt the butter in a frying pan and cook the chopped onions until soft but not browned. Combine the cooked rice, onion, butter, salt, pepper, thyme, sage, and chopped parsley. Mix well and stuff lightly into chicken cavities.

For a 5-pound chicken

Oyster Stuffing

½ cup butter melted
1 large onion chopped fine
½ cup chopped celery
1 tablespoon finely chopped parsley
1 tablespoon finely chopped green pepper

½ teaspoon salt
⅛ teaspoon pepper
½ teaspoon sage
¼ teaspoon mace
¼ teaspoon thyme
3 cups toasted breadcrumbs
1 pint oysters with liquid

Melt ½ cup butter in a heavy frying pan and cook the onions, celery, parsley, and green pepper until soft. Mix with the toasted breadcrumbs. Season with salt, pepper, sage, mace, thyme, and mix in thoroughly. Chop the oysters and add them along with their liquid to the mixture. Mix well and stuff lightly into the chicken cavities.

For a 5-pound chicken

Brazil-Nut Stuffing

½ cup butter
1 cup sliced Brazil nuts
1 cups onions chopped fine
2½ cups soft breadcrumbs
½ teaspoon poultry seasoning
½ teaspoon salt
⅛ teaspoon pepper
¼ teaspoon nutmeg
¼ cup chicken broth

Melt ½ cup butter in a frying pan and sauté the Brazil nuts and onions until the onions are soft but not browned. Add the breadcrumbs, poultry seasoning, salt, pepper, nutmeg, and mix thoroughly. Add the chicken broth and stir in well. Stuff lightly into the chicken cavities.

For a 5-pound chicken

Wild Rice Mushroom Stuffing

1 package wild rice mix
2 tablespoons butter
2 tablespoons chopped onion
½ cup chopped mushrooms
1 tablespoon chopped parsley

Cook the wild rice according to directions on the package. Melt the butter in a frying pan and cook the onions and mushrooms until soft. Add the parsley and cooked wild rice to the onion-mushroom mixture. Mix well and stuff lightly into the chicken cavities.

For a 5-pound chicken

Chestnut Stuffing

½ pound chestnuts
Chicken stock
¼ cup butter melted
¼ cup finely chopped onions
2 tablespoons finely chopped parsley
2 tablespoons finely chopped chives
1 teaspoon salt
½ teaspoon sage
Pinch of thyme and nutmeg
3 cups soft breadcrimbs

Cover the chestnuts with hot chicken stock and cook about 20 minutes. Drain. Remove shells and inner brown skin. Chop them coarscly. Melt the butter in a skillet and cook the onions until they are soft but not browned. Add the parsley, chives, salt, sage, thyme, and nutmeg. Add the soft breadcrumbs and the chopped chestnuts. Mix thoroughly and stuff lightly into the chicken cavities.

For a 5-pound chicken

Pecan Stuffing

½ cup butter
½ cup chopped onion
2 tablespoons minced parsley
½ teaspoon thyme
¼ teaspoon sage
¼ teaspoon powdered cloves
½ teaspoon salt
⅛ teaspoon pepper
¼ teaspoon nutmeg
3 cups soft stale breadcrumbs
½ cup parsley chopped pecans

Melt the butter in a skillet and cook the onion, parsley, thyme, sage, powdered cloves, salt, pepper, and nutmeg until the onions are soft but not browned. Stir constantly over a low heat. Add the breadcrumbs and the chopped pecans and mix well. Stuff lightly into the chicken cavities.

For a 5-pound chicken

Broiled Chicken

Broilers are in a class by themselves. They are young, tender, usually no more than 7 to 12 weeks old and ranging in weight from 1½ to 2½ pounds. When buying a broiler look for a flexible breastbone for this is a sign of a very young and tender chicken. Be sure too that you choose a plump bird.

Broilers are usually cooked by direct heat from hot coals, a gas flame, or an electric element. Always place them skin side down in the pan first as this prevents the skin from shrinking away. Keep your eye on your chicken as it broils, and baste and turn it frequently so the meat will not dry out. When done a broiled chicken should be tender and succulent on the inside and just the right golden brown on the outside. For a perfect broiled chicken baste frequently with oil or a sauce or a marinade. Not only does this prevent dryness but it also gives a crisp golden brown appearance.

A young broiling chicken takes about 45 minutes to cook through. When more than 3 broilers are cooked allow a little longer cooking time. The cooking temperature should be about 350° and the broiler rack placed from 5 to 7 inches from the heat. Turn the chicken frequently during the last 15 minutes of cooking time so that all portions of the chicken may be thoroughly cooked.

When splitting broilers in half usually allow ½ a split broiler per person. To split a broiler in half, cut from neck end to tail along one side of backbone, which should be discarded, splitting the breast along one side of the keel bone.

Another suggestion for broiling is to cut through the joints so that the chicken fits flatter on the broiler pan. You can carefully press the chicken back into plump compact shape before serving.

Broiled Chicken
Crisp broiled chicken will never fail you.

2 broilers split in half
½ teaspoon salt
⅛ teaspoon pepper
8 teaspoons butter

Split 2 broilers in half. Rub well with ½ teaspoon salt and ⅛ teaspoon pepper. Put 1 teaspoon butter in the hollow of each broiler half. Place the broilers skin side down on a broiler rack and broil under the heat for 20 minutes. Turn over, dot with 1 teaspoon butter for each broiler half, and broil for 20 minutes longer. Serve immediately.

Serves 4

Marinated Broiled Chicken
This makes a delicious supper with crunchy green salad and hot rolls.

2 broilers split in half
¾ cup olive oil
2 cloves garlic mashed
⅓ cup chopped parsley
½ teaspoon salt
½ teaspoon Tabasco
Dash of cayenne
1 teaspoon Worcestershire sauce

Split the broilers down the back. Combine the olive oil, mashed garlic, parsley, salt, Tabasco, cayenne, and Worcestershire sauce. Marinate the chicken in this mixture overnight in the refrigerator. Drain off the marinade. Arrange the split broiler halves skin side down on a broiler rack placed about 5 inches from the heat. Broil for 45 minutes, turning often to broil both sides evenly and basting often with the marinade. Serve at once on a hot platter.

Serves 4

Broiled Lemon Chicken
This is one of my specialties. It's good.

2 broilers split in half
½ teaspoon salt
⅛ teaspoon pepper
½ cup butter
Juice of 2 lemons
Parsley and lemon wedges for garnish

Split the broilers in half and rub well with salt and pepper. Melt ½ cup butter in a pan and add the juice of 2 lemons. Roll the broiler halves well in the lemon butter. Then put the broilers on the rack of a broiler pan and broil about 6 inches from the heat until browned. Turn and broil the other side until browned. Remove from the rack and place in the broiler pan. Pour the remainder of the lemon butter over the chicken and bake in a 300° oven for 30 minutes, basting frequently with the juices in the pan. Arrange the chicken on a hot platter, pour some of the drippings from the pan over the chicken, and garnish with the parsley and lemon wedges.

Serves 4

Broiled Chicken in Barbecue Sauce
This tastes equally good indoors or out.

2 broilers split in half
½ teaspoon salt

⅛ teaspoon pepper
2 tablespoons butter melted
½ cup butter
½ cup hot water
2 teaspoons Worcestershire sauce
½ teaspoon Tabasco
1½ teaspoons sugar
1 teaspoon salt
1½ teaspoons flour
Dash of cayenne

Split broilers in half. Sprinkle with salt and pepper and brush with melted butter. Place on broiling rack skin side down about 6 inches from the heat. Broil 15 minutes. Turn and broil the other side. Turn again in 15 minutes allowing about 45 minutes for broiling chicken in all. Baste every few moments while broiling with the barbecue sauce.

To make the barbecue sauce, melt ½ cup butter in a pan and add to it ½ cup hot water. Add the Worcestershire sauce, Tabasco, sugar, salt, flour, and a dash of cayenne. Blend well and cook about 3 minutes over medium heat until mixture thickens slightly. Baste the chicken often with the sauce as it broils.

Serves 4

Broiled Chicken with Cucumber Sauce
Crisp broiled chicken served with a chilled cucumber sauce is something your guests won't forget.

2 broilers split in half
½ teaspoon salt
⅛ teaspoon pepper
8 teaspoons butter
1 cup diced unpeeled cucumber
2 tablespoons lemon juice

1 teaspoon onion salt
¼ teaspoon celery salt
1 cup whipped cream

Rub the split broilers with salt and pepper and put 1 teaspoon
butter in the hollow of each broiler half. Place the broilers
skin side down on a broiler rack and broil under the heat for
20 minutes. Turn over, dot with 1 teaspoon butter for each
broiler half, and broil 20 minutes longer.
For the sauce blend the cucumber, lemon juice, onion salt,
and celery salt in an electric blender until smooth. Combine
with 1 cup whipped cream and stir until smooth and creamy.
Serve chilled with the hot broiled chicken.

Serves 4

Stuffed Baked Broilers
This broiled stuffed chicken is a fine holiday dish.

2 broilers split in half
½ teaspoon salt
⅛ teaspoon pepper
4 tablespoons melted butter
½ cup bread crumbs
½ cup milk
2 4½-ounce cans deviled ham
2 tablespoons prepared mustard
1 tablespoon chopped parsley
6 small green onions chopped fine
Pinch of thyme
½ bay leaf crushed
1 egg
Breadcrumbs
Butter

Brush the broiler halves with 4 tablespoons melted butter

and sprinkle with salt and pepper. Place in a shallow pan on the broiler rack skin side down and broil for 5 minutes. Turn and broil for 5 minutes on the other side. While the broilers are cooking soak the breadcrumbs in the milk and squeeze them dry. Combine with the deviled ham, prepared mustard, chopped parsley, chopped onions, thyme, crushed bay leaf, and egg. Blend well. Remove chicken from the oven and turn skin side down. Fill centers with the stuffing, piling it towards the center. Sprinkle the tops with bread crumbs and dot with butter. Bake for 30 minutes in a 375° oven basting frequently with butter.

Serves 4

Broiled Tomato Chicken
This always makes a hit.

2 broilers split in half
½ teaspoon salt
⅛ teaspoon pepper
4 tablespoons soft butter
2 onions chopped fine
2 tablespoons flour
2 tablespoons tomato paste
2 teaspoons Worcestershire sauce
1 teaspoon sugar
1 teaspoon dry mustard
2 cups hot beef broth
2 tomatoes

Sprinkle the broiler halves with salt and pepper and rub well with the soft butter. Cook the chopped onions in 2 tablespoons of the butter. Add 2 tablespoons flour, the tomato paste, Worcestershire sauce, sugar, and the dry mustard. Mix until smooth and add the hot beef broth. Cook stirring frequently until thickened and smooth. Place the chicken skin side down on a broiler rack 6 inches from the heat and brush generously with the tomato sauce. Broil for 15 minutes, basting frequently with the sauce. Turn and broil the other side 15 minutes basting frequently with the sauce. Remove from the rack and place the chicken in the broiler pan. Pour the rest of the sauce over the chicken and bake in a 300° oven for 15 minutes or until the chicken is tender. Remove the pan from the oven and keep hot. Cut the 2 tomatoes crosswise in half. Broil them quickly. Arrange the chicken and tomatoes on a hot platter and pour the sauce over them.

Serves 4

Broiled Pineapple Chicken
Guests will demand this recipe.

2 broilers split in half
2 cups pineapple juice
4 tablespoons butter melted
1 teaspoon salt
1 cup pineapple chunks
1 cup vinegar
1 tablespoon catsup
1 teaspoon soy sauce
3 tablespoons sugar
Cornstarch for thickening

Split the broilers down the back. Cover with 2 cups pineapple juice and marinate for 2 hours turning frequently to soak chicken all over. Drain chicken and dry. Brush well with the melted butter and season with salt. Place skin side down on a greased preheated broiler rack. Broil 20 minutes. Turn and broil the other side 20 minutes. In the meantime melt 1 tablespoon butter in a pan. Add the vinegar, catsup, soy sauce, 1/4 cup pineapple juice from the marinade, sugar, and a pinch of salt. Cook over high heat to boiling point, then reduce heat to low. Thicken with a cornstarch paste so that the sauce is of the consistency of a medium cream sauce. Add 1 cup pineapple chunks and simmer over low heat until they are heated through. When chicken is done place on a hot serving platter and pour the sauce over the chicken.

Serves 4

Broiled Chicken à La Tartare
Simple, yet a classic French dish.

2 broilers split in half
½ teaspoon salt
⅛ teaspoon pepper
¼ cup olive oil
2 cups soft bread crumbs
1 teaspoon dry mustard
1 tablespoon chopped parsley
1 teaspoon chervil
1 teaspoon tarragon
½ teaspoon onion salt
½ teaspoon garlic salt
Remolade sauce

Split the broilers in half and rub well with salt and pepper. Season 2 cups soft bread crumbs with 1 teaspoon dry mustard, the chopped parsley, chervil, tarragon, onion salt, and garlic salt. Dip the broiler halves in olive oil soaking them well all over. Roll them in seasoned bread crumbs and place skin side down on a broiler rack 6 inches from the heat. Broil 15 minutes then turn and broil the other side for 15 minutes. Cook 15 minutes longer turning frequently. Serve hot accompanied by a side dish of remolade sauce.

Remolade sauce—to 1 pint mayonnaise add 1 tablespoon prepared mustard, 1 tablespoon chopped gherkins, 1 tablespoon capers, 1 tablespoon chopped parsley, 1 tablespoon chervil,

1 tablespoon tarragon, and 1 teaspoon anchovy paste. Mix well and let set in refrigerator 1 hour before serving.

Serves 4

Broiled Chicken Breslin
Utterly delicious yet easy to fix.

3 tablespoons butter
1 tablespoon tarragon
½ teaspoon salt
Juice of ½ lime
2 broilers split in half
Salt, pepper, tarragon for seasoning

In a small saucepan combine the butter, tarragon, salt, and the juice of ½ lime. Stir over low heat until the butter has melted. Then sprinkle the split broiler halves with salt, pepper, and tarragon. Brush well with the sauce and place the broiler halves skin side down on the broiler rack. Broil for 15 minutes, basting frequently with the sauce. Turn the broilers over and broil for 15 minutes basting frequently with the sauce. Turn again and broil another 15 minutes basting and turning frequently. Place the broiler halves on a warm serving platter. Add the juices from the broiler pan to the remaining sauce, heat through, and pour the sauce over the chicken.

Serves 4

Broiled Ginger Chicken
Ginger marmalade gives this broiled chicken a tangy touch.

2 broilers split in half
Juice of ½ lemon
1 teaspoon salt
¼ teaspoon pepper

¼ cup butter
1 cup ginger marmalade

Brush the split broiler halves with the juice of ½ lemon.
Sprinkle with salt and pepper. Melt ¼ cup butter in a pan
and brush well over the chicken. Place the broiler halves skin
side down on the broiler rack and broil 10 minutes, basting
frequently with the melted butter. Brush heavily with the
ginger marmalade and broil 5 minutes longer. Turn the
chicken over and brush with the melted butter and then with
the ginger marmalade. Broil 15 minutes brushing first with
butter and then with the ginger marmalade. Turn again and
broil 15 minutes longer, brushing with butter and then with
ginger marmalade.

Serves 4

Broiled Deviled Chicken
You will encounter this dish in fine restaurants but it's easy
to prepare.

2 broilers split in half
½ cup olive oil
1 tablespoon crushed red pepper flakes
½ teaspoon salt
¼ cup dry white wine

Crush the split chicken halves with a meat mallet. Brush both
sides with olive oil and sprinkle with crushed red pepper
flakes and salt. Place on a broiler rack 6 inches from the heat
skin side down and broil 15 minutes. Turn and broil the
other side for 15 minutes. Turn again allowing 45 minutes for
broiling in all. Baste frequently all the while with olive oil.
Transfer the chicken to a hot dish and keep warm. Put the
broiler pan with the drippings over a low heat and stir in ¼
cup dry white wine. Bring to a boil and pour over the chicken.

Serves 4

Broiled Chicken alla Milano

An Italian favorite. Use your chafing dish for this.

2 broilers split in half
¼ cup olive oil
½ teaspoon salt
¼ teaspoon pepper
4 bay leaves crushed
1 cup brandy warmed

Brush broiler halves with olive oil well on both sides. Season with salt and pepper and crushed bay leaves. Broil chicken on a broiler rack about 6 inches from the heat. Turn frequently until browned and tender about 45 minutes in all. Place the broiler halves in a chafing dish at the table. Pour over the warmed brandy and set aflame. Serve as soon as the flame burns down.

Serves 4

Charles' Broiled Chicken

Whenever Charles Samson gave a dinner party you could be sure of some unusual dish. Here is a recipe for a wonderfully extravagant broiled chicken according to his directions.

2 broilers split in half
Juice of ½ lemon
½ cup butter melted
1 clove garlic minced
8 large mushrooms sliced thin
1 teaspoon tarragon chopped fine
1 teaspoon chives chopped fine
2 jiggers rum
2 jiggers gin
2 jiggers green chartreuse

Rub the split broiler halves well with lemon juice. Melt ¼ cup butter and add to it the minced clove of garlic. Place the broiler halves skin side down on a broiler rack and brush generously with the garlic butter. Broil for 15 minutes basting frequently with the garlic butter. Turn over and broil 15 minutes basting frequently with the garlic butter. Melt the other ¼ cup butter in a pan. Add the mushrooms, tarragon, and chives. Cook over low heat for 5 minutes. Place the broiler halves in a baking pan. Mix the juices from the broiler pan with the mushroom butter mixture and pour over the chicken in the baking pan. Bake in a 300° oven for 20 minutes or until the chicken is very tender. Arrange the chicken on a hot serving platter and pour the sauce over it. Pour a mixture of 2 jiggers each of rum, gin, green chartreuse over all and set aflame. Let the flame burn down and serve at once.

Serves 4

Baked Chicken

Baked chicken is probably the easiest way to cook it and it invariably comes out juicy, tender, and beautifully browned. All you have to do is season or coat the chicken parts with a crust, pop it in the oven, and forget about it for the next 50 or 60 minutes.

There is a variety of crust that may be used in baking a chicken. The choice is personal. For a heavier crust dip the chicken in crumbs, then in 2 eggs beaten with $\frac{1}{4}$ cup water and again in crumbs.

A quick simple method is to dip each piece of chicken in oil and melted butter in equal parts and then in the crumb mixture.

Soak chicken in sweet cream, then dip in crumb mixture and sauté before baking.

If there is time allow the chicken to stand for $\frac{1}{2}$ hour before baking to allow the crumb mixture to dry out. It stays on so much better that way and your chicken comes out of the oven with its crumb coating crisply browned.

Favorite Baked Chicken
A baked chicken that rates superb.

2 eggs
$\frac{1}{2}$ cup milk
1 cup flour
1 cup fine breadcrumbs
$\frac{1}{2}$ teaspoon pepper

1 teaspoon salt
2 teaspoons chervil
2 tablespoons chopped parsley
4-pound chicken fryer cut into pieces
3 tablespoons butter
½ cup Madeira wine
½ cup sliced mushrooms

Beat together 2 eggs and ½ cup milk. Combine 1 cup flour, 1 cup fine bread crumbs, salt, pepper, chopped parsley. Dip the pieces of chicken in the egg-milk mixture and then coat with the seasoned flour-breadcrumb mixture. Brown the chicken pieces in 3 tablespoons butter and when well-browned on both sides place in a shallow baking dish. Pick up all the brown from the frying pan with ½ cup Madeira wine. Pour it over the chicken. Add the sliced mushrooms and bake in a 350° oven about 50 minutes or until the chicken is tender.

Serves 4

Baked Crumbled Chicken
A crisp, crumbly, delicious baked chicken.

2 eggs
½ cup milk
3 cups cornflake crumbs
½ teaspoon pepper
1 teaspoon salt
2 teaspoons paprika
2 tablespoons fresh chopped parsley
2 teaspoons sweet basil
4-pound chicken fryer cut into pieces
¼ cup butter melted

Beat together 2 eggs and ½ cup milk. Combine 3 cups cornflake crumbs with pepper, salt, paprika, parsley, and sweet basil. Dip the pieces of chicken in the egg-milk mixture and then coat thoroughly with the seasoned cornflakes. Arrange the crumbled chicken in a shallow baking pan, pour ¼ cup melted butter over the chicken, and bake in a 400° oven for 50 minutes or until the chicken is browned and tender. Use more butter if needed.

Serves 4

Baked Parmesan Chicken
Parmesan cheese gives this baked chicken plenty of good flavor.

2 eggs
½ cup milk
2 cups stale breadcrumbs
2 cups grated Parmesan cheese
¼ cup chopped parsley
1 clove garlic minced
2 teaspoons salt
¼ teaspoon pepper
4-pound chicken fryer cut into pieces
¼ cup butter melted

Beat the eggs and milk together. In a separate bowl combine the breadcrumbs, Parmesan cheese, parsley, garlic, salt, and pepper. Dip the pieces of chicken in the egg-milk mixture, then in the seasoned eggs and bread crumbs. Arrange the coated chicken pieces in a shallow baking pan. Pour over the melted butter and bake in a 400° oven for 50 minutes or until the chicken is tender. Use more butter if needed.

Serves 4

Baked Chicken Tarragon
Tarragon and white wine make a gourmet-baked chicken.

4-pound chicken fryer cut into pieces
1 tablespoon tarragon

1 tablespoon chopped parsley
¾ cup dry white wine
½ cup flour
1 teaspoon salt
¼ teaspoon pepper
¼ cup butter melted

Make a marinade of the tarragon, chopped parsley, and dry white wine. Marinate the chicken pieces in this mixture for 4 hours, turning the chicken several times. Mix the salt and pepper with the flour and roll the chicken pieces in the seasoned flour. Arrange in a shallow baking pan. Pour over the marinade and the melted butter. Bake in a 400° oven about 50 minutes or until the chicken is tender. Serve at once.

Serves 4

Baked Chicken with Rosemary
Chicken baked with sherry and rosemary makes a delicious entree.

2 broiler chickens about 1½ pounds each
½ cup chicken broth
¼ cup sherry
½ teaspoon salt
⅛ teaspoon pepper
1 clove garlic minced fine
1 bay leaf
¼ cup butter melted
1 teaspoon rosemary

Split the broilers in half and arrange them in a flat baking pan. Combine the chicken broth, sherry, salt, pepper, garlic, bay leaf, and butter. Let cook over a low heat for 2 minutes then pour the butter sauce over the chicken and marinate for 2 hours turning frequently. Bake in a 400° oven for 40 minutes or until the chicken is tender. Crush the rosemary, and after the first 20 minutes of cooking time sprinkle it over the chicken. When the chicken is tender arrange on a serving platter and spoon the sauce from the pan over the top.

Serves **4**

Baked Chicken with Honey
Chicken baked with honey—an exotic dish.

4-pound chicken fryer cut into pieces
3 tablespoons butter melted
1 cup finely chopped onions
1/4 teaspoon cinnamon
1/2 cup softened butter
1/2 cup honey

Arrange the chicken pieces in a buttered baking dish. Cook the chopped onions in 3 tablespoons melted butter until soft. Add them to the chicken in the baking dish and sprinkle the cinnamon over the top. Cream the honey and softened butter together and coat the chicken pieces thickly with this mixture. Bake in a preheated 400° oven for 50 minutes or until the chicken is tender. Baste frequently with the honey butter juices. Serve with the juices poured over the chicken.

Serves 4

Baked Chicken Supreme
An Italian sauce with sour cream is a pleasing combination in this baked chicken.

4-pound chicken fryer cut into pieces
1/4 cup butter melted
1 clove garlic minced
1 onion chopped fine
2 cups sour cream

1 tablespoon tomato paste
1 teaspoon salt
1 teaspoon oregano
¼ cup grated Parmesan cheese

Cook the chicken pieces in the melted butter until they are
well browned on both sides. Remove them to a shallow greased
baking pan. Add the minced garlic and chopped onion to the
pan and cook until soft but not browned. Add the sour cream,
tomato paste, salt, and oregano. Cook for 1 minute over low
heat and add the Parmesan cheese. Mix well and pour the
sauce over the chicken in the baking pan. Bake in a preheated
400° oven for 45 minutes or until chicken is tender.

Serves 4

Baked Cashew Nut Chicken
Always a hit; cashew nuts make this dish unusual.

4-pound chicken fryer cut into pieces
¼ cup melted butter
1 cup ground toasted salted cashew nuts

Brush the chicken pieces liberally with the melted butter.
Roll each piece in the ground toasted salted cashew nuts.
Place the chicken pieces in a buttered baking pan and bake
in a 400° preheated oven for 50 minutes or until browned
and tender. Serve immediately.

Serves 4

Baked Chicken in Orange Sauce
Here's a baked chicken with an unforgettable flavor.

4-pound chicken fryer cut into pieces
¼ cup butter melted

1 12-ounce can frozen orange juice concentrate, thawed
½ cup raisins
½ cup almonds ground fine
½ teaspoon ginger

Brown the chicken pieces well on both sides in the melted butter. Place them in a shallow baking pan. Combine the orange juice, raisins, ground almonds, and ginger. Cook over a low heat for 3 minutes stirring constantly. Pour over the chicken and bake in a 400° oven for 50 minutes or until the chicken is tender. Baste frequently with the sauce in the baking pan.

Serves 4

Baked Chicken in Cherry Sauce
For a baked chicken with a new flavor, try this one.

4-pound chicken fryer cut into pieces
¼ cup butter melted
1½ cups pitted dark sweet cherries
1 cup cherry sauce
1 tablespoon cornstarch
2 tablespoons water
1 teaspoon grated onion
2 teaspoons grated lemon peel
2 teaspoons grated orange peel
2 tablespoons brandy

Brown the chicken well on both sides in the melted butter. When browned place in a shallow baking pan and pour the drippings from the pan over the chicken. Bake in a 400° oven for 50 minutes or until the chicken is tender. Meanwhile make a paste of the cornstarch and 2 tablespoons water. Thicken the cherry juice with this mixture and add the grated onion, lemon peel, and orange peel. Cook over a medium heat until thickened. Add the dark sweet cherries and the brandy. Pour over the chicken.

Serves 4

Baked Fruit-and-Nut-Stuffed Chicken Breasts

While I was digging through countless recipes for ways to bake chicken, Marian Anderson came to my rescue with this unusual one from her vast collection of recipes. A little complicated in the doing but after trying it out we both agreed it was worth including.

6 whole chicken breasts boned
⅔ cup butter
½ cup coarsely chopped walnuts
½ cup raisins
1 cup diced apples
½ cup pineapple chunks
½ teaspoon salt
1 teaspoon cinnamon
½ teaspoon nutmeg
¼ teaspoon ginger
¼ teaspoon ground cloves

Melt ⅓ cup butter in a frying pan and cook the chopped walnuts, raisins, and diced apples over a low heat for 5 minutes. Remove from the heat. Add the pineapple chunks, salt, cinnamon, nutmeg, ginger, and ground cloves. Spoon the fruit stuffing on the inside of each chicken breast. Fold the sides over and secure with string or toothpicks. Place the chicken breasts in a shallow baking pan and pour over the rest of the butter. Bake in a 400° oven for 50 minutes or until the chicken is tender and browned. Serve with fruit sauce.

Fruit sauce
1 tablespoon sugar
1 tablespoon cornstarch

⅛ teaspoon salt
½ teaspoon allspice
⅛ teaspoon cinnamon
⅛ teaspoon nutmeg
⅛ teaspoon ginger
1 cup orange juice
½ cup pineapple juice
½ cup crushed pineapple
1 tablespoon butter
1 tablespoon orange peel
1 tablespoon lemon peel

Combine sugar, cornstarch, salt, allspice, cinnamon, nutmeg, ginger, and orange juice. Mix well and add the pineapple juice, crushed pineapple, butter, orange peel, and lemon peel. Cook, stirring constantly, over a medium heat until the mixture comes to a boil and thickens. Pour over the chicken breasts.

Serves 6

Baked Herb Glazed Chicken
A glaze gives a beautiful shiny gloss to a chicken.

4-pound chicken fryer cut into pieces
¼ cup butter melted
1 teaspoon salt
¼ teaspoon pepper
¼ teaspoon oregano
1 teaspoon grated orange rind
¼ cup orange juice
½ cup dark corn syrup
¼ cup lemon juice

Melt ¼ cup butter in a frying pan and brown the chicken well on both sides. When browned transfer to a shallow baking pan. Sprinkle with salt, pepper, and oregano. Pour over the butter in the frying pan. Mix together the grated orange rind, orange juice, dark corn syrup, and lemon juice. Pour over the chicken in the baking pan and bake in a 400° oven for 50 minutes or until the chicken is tender.

Serves 4

Baked Broilers
So simple to prepare these delicious baked broilers.

2 1½-pound chicken broilers
3 tablespoons butter
½ teaspoon salt
1 teaspoon paprika
4 tablespoons chopped chives
½ cup butter

Rub the broilers well with the 3 tablespoons of butter. Sprinkle them with salt and paprika. Into the cavity of each broiler put ¼ cup butter and 2 tablespoons chopped chives. Truss the legs and wings close to the body and bake the broilers in a 400° oven 45 minutes to 1 hour or until the broilers are browned and tender. Baste frequently with the pan drippings.

Serves 2

Baked Broilers in Cream
Another fine way to bake broilers.

3 1½-pound broilers split in half
1 teaspoon salt
¼ teaspoon pepper
1 tablespoon flour
6 tablespoons butter
1 cup heavy cream

Season the broiler halves with salt and pepper and sprinkle them with the flour. Put 1 tablespoon butter on each half and place them in a baking pan. Pour over them the heavy cream and bake in a 400° oven for 45 minutes approximately or until they are browned and tender. Add more cream to the pan while baking if it becomes too dry.

Serves 6

Casserole Chicken

A casserole dish is a great boon to the modern cook. It can be made on the spur of the moment or it can be prepared well in advance and then popped into the oven at the last possible moment. It can be made up with whatever vegetables and herbs and seasonings you happen to have on hand. It can be something either simple or elaborate. It lends itself easily to both informal dinners and to buffet entertaining.

The chicken is usually sautéed in fat first to brown it. The fat can be butter, bacon fat, lard, salt pork, or olive oil, depending on the flavors wanted for the finished dish. Also depending on the type of ingredients that will be cooked with the dish. Heavy vegetables such as potatoes, turnips, carrots, go better with bacon fat or lard or salt pork. More delicate vegetables go better with butter.

The liquid for classic chicken casserole is hot chicken stock, wine, cream, sour cream, or a mixture of these liquids. Excessive fat should be strained from the sauce before serving the chicken. Often sweet or sour cream and egg yolks are added to a casserole to thicken the sauce. There is a wide range of herbs and spices to choose from to give the right accent to each dish. You can use either fresh chicken or leftover chicken, and it is a wonderful way to satisfy your family's appetite for a main meal dish.

Chicken Casserole
Little to do to prepare this delicious casserole dish.

4-pound chicken fryer
¼ cup butter melted
1 teaspoon salt

Truss the chicken. Melt the butter in a casserole large enough
to hold the chicken. When the butter is sizzling brown the
chicken on all sides on top of the stove. Sprinkle with salt.
Cover and place in a 375° oven. Cook for 1½ hours turning
the chicken once or twice during the cooking. Remove from
the casserole and place on a heated platter. Pour the juices
and butter from the casserole over the chicken.

Serves 4

Chicken Casserole I
This was my father's favorite casserole. He was an accom-
plished cook who delighted in turning out specialized dishes.

4-pound chicken fryer cut into pieces
1 teaspoon salt
¼ teaspoon pepper
½ cup flour
¼ cup butter
1 cup dry white wine
½ cup heavy cream
½ cup chicken stock
Bouquet garni
1 clove garlic minced
3 tablespoons chopped onion
1 cup scalded cream
2 egg yolks
2 tablespoons cream

Mix the salt and pepper with the flour and roll the chicken pieces in the seasoned flour. Melt the butter in a frying pan and brown the chicken well on both sides. Transfer the chicken to a casserole and pick up all the brown particles in the pan with the dry white wine. Add to the casserole. Add ½ cup heavy cream and ½ cup chicken stock. Cook on top of the stove over a high heat until the liquid has reduced to half. Then add a bouquet garni (parsley, thyme, bay leaf, peppercorns tied together in a cheesecloth bag so it can be removed before serving). Add the minced garlic, chopped onion, cover tightly, and bake in a 350° oven about 45 minutes or until chicken is tender. Transfer the chicken to a serving platter and keep hot. Strain the sauce from the casserole into a saucepan, bring to a boil, and add 1 cup scalded cream. Let simmer a few moments then add the egg yolks which have been beaten with 2 tablespoons cream. Cook for 1 minute over low heat stirring constantly. Pour the sauce over the chicken and serve.

Serves 4

Chicken Casserole II
This is a bit different but also good.

4-pound chicken fryer cut into pieces
1 teaspoon salt
¼ teaspoon pepper
½ cup flour
¼ cup butter melted
1 clove garlic minced
1 onion chopped fine
½ cup-carrots diced
½ cup celery diced
1½ cups chicken broth
1 cup mushrooms sliced
2 tablespoons butter
12 stuffed green olives cut in half

Mix the salt and pepper with the flour and roll the chicken pieces in the seasoned flour. Brown in hot melted butter until golden on both sides. Transfer the chicken to a casserole. Cook the garlic, onions, carrots, and celery in the pan the chicken was browned in until they are lightly colored. Add them to the chicken in the casserole along with the 1½ cups of chicken broth. Cover and bake in a 350° oven about 45 minutes or until the chicken is tender. In the meantime cook the sliced mushrooms in 2 tablespoons butter for 5 minutes. Add the stuffed green olives and cook 1 minute longer. Add to the chicken 10 minutes before the chicken is done. Serve from the casserole.

Serves 4

Chicken Casserole Hollandaise
This makes an excellent all-season dish.

4-pound chicken fryer cut into pieces
1 teaspoon salt
¼ teaspoon pepper
½ cup flour
¼ cup butter melted
2 tablespoons brandy
1½ cups sliced mushrooms
2 tablespoons flour
1½ cups chicken broth
¼ cup dry white wine
½ cup Hollandaise sauce

Mix the salt and pepper with the flour and roll the chicken pieces in the seasoned flour. Melt the butter in a frying pan and brown the chicken well on both sides. Pour over the brandy and ignite. When the flame has burned down remove the chicken from the pan and place in a casserole. Add the mushrooms to the frying pan and cook for 5 minutes. Add the mushrooms to the casserole with the chicken. Add 2 tablespoons flour to the frying pan and stir until smooth. Add the chicken broth and the white wine. Stir over medium heat until the sauce thickens. Pour the sauce over the chicken and mushrooms in the casserole. Cover tightly and cook in a 350° oven about 45 minutes or until the chicken is tender. Remove the cover and spread the Hollandaise sauce over the top. Brown quickly under the broiler and serve.

Serves 4

Chicken Casserole Bonne Femme

Rich brown gravy and vegetables make this chicken casserole more flavorful. Great as a meal in one for the family.

4-pound chicken cut into pieces
1 teaspoon salt
¼ teaspoon pepper
4 tablespoons butter melted
4 slices lean bacon cut into pieces
12 small white onions
12 small potato balls
12 small carrot balls
½ cup brown gravy or use a packaged brown gravy mix

Rub the chicken pieces well with the salt and pepper. Place the chicken in a large casserole and rub with 1 tablespoon melted butter. Add the lean bacon cut into pieces. In a skillet sauté the small white onions, potato balls, and carrot balls in the rest of the melted butter for 5 minutes. Add to the casserole with the chicken and cook in a preheated 350° oven for 1½ hours or until the chicken and vegetables are very tender. Remove the chicken to a serving platter and keep hot. Add the brown gravy to the casserole and cook on top of the stove over a medium low heat for several minutes, stirring constantly to mix in all the juices from the bottom. Pour the sauce and vegetables over the chicken and serve.

Serves 4

Tart Chicken Casserole
The good flavor of chicken is enhanced in this unique casserole by the tartness of apple cider and vinegar. Don't hesitate to try it.

4-pound chicken fryer cut into pieces
4 tablespoons butter
1 teaspoon salt
¼ teaspoon pepper
½ cup cider vinegar
½ cup apple cider

Melt the butter in a skillet and brown the chicken pieces well on both sides. Remove the chicken to a buttered casserole and season with salt and pepper. Pour over it the cider vinegar. Add the apple cider, cover the casserole, and cook in a 350° oven for 50 minutes or until the chicken is tender. Remove the cover and turn heat up to 450°. Cook just long enough for the juices in the bottom of the casserole to evaporate.

Serves 4

Chicken Casserole Jerusalem
A casserole dish to usher in the springtime.

4-pound chicken cut into pieces
½ cup flour
1 teaspoon salt
¼ teaspoon pepper
4 tablespoons butter melted
½ teaspoon allspice

¼ teaspoon powdered cloves
1 teaspoon grated orange peel
½ cup sliced mushrooms
6 artichoke bottoms quartered
½ cup sherry wine
2 cups cream scalded
Chopped chives and parsley

Add the salt and pepper to the flour and dredge the chicken pieces in the seasoned flour. Melt the butter in a skillet and brown the chicken well on both sides. Transfer the chicken to a greased casserole and season with the allspice, powdered cloves, and grated orange peel. Add the sliced mushrooms and quartered artichoke bottoms. Add the sherry and bake covered in a 350° oven for 40 minutes or until the chicken is tender. The sherry should be almost evaporated. Place the chicken pieces on a hot serving platter and keep warm. Add 2 cups scalded cream to the sauce in the casserole, stir well, and cook over low heat until thoroughly blended. Pour the sauce and vegetables over the chicken and serve with a sprinkling of parsley and chives.

Serves 4

Hearty Chicken Casserole
This casserole dish is a robust meal in itself.

4-pound chicken fryer cut into pieces
½ cup flour
1 teaspoon salt
⅛ teaspoon pepper
¼ cup butter melted
1 cup red wine
12 small potatoballs
12 small carrot balls
6 artichoke bottoms quartered

12 small white onions
3 tablespoons butter
1 tablespoon grated lemon peel

Add the salt and pepper to the flour and roll the chicken pieces in the seasoned flour. Melt $\frac{1}{4}$ cup butter in a skillet and brown the chicken pieces well on both sides. Transfer the chicken to a buttered casserole. Pick up all the brown from the skillet with 1 cup red wine and add to the casserole. Melt 3 tablespoons butter in another skillet and sauté the potato balls, carrot balls, artichoke bottoms, and small white onions for 5 minutes. Add them to the casserole. Cover and cook in a 350° oven for 40 minutes or until the chicken and vegetables are tender. Add more red wine if necessary. Serve from the casserole.

Serves 4

Casserole of Chicken and Broccoli
A terrific casserole dish to serve for a supper or a luncheon party.

6 chicken breasts boned
$\frac{1}{4}$ pound thin sliced cooked ham
1 egg
$\frac{1}{4}$ teaspoon salt
$\frac{1}{8}$ teaspoon pepper
$\frac{3}{4}$ cup cracker crumbs
$\frac{1}{4}$ cup butter melted
1 package frozen chopped broccoli

Sauce
3 tablespoons butter
3 tablespoons flour
1 cup milk
1 cup cream

1 teaspoon salt
⅛ teaspoon pepper
1 tablespoon chopped chives
¾ cup grated Parmesan cheese

Bone the chicken breasts. Beat the egg in a bowl with the salt and pepper. Dip the chicken breasts in the egg mixture, then roll in cracker crumbs. Let dry out for 10 minutes. Put in a pan with ¼ cup hot melted butter and brown until golden on both sides, turning frequently until the chicken is tender. Meanwhile cook the broccoli according to directions on the package until just tender. Drain and arrange in the bottom of a buttered casserole. Cover with the thin sliced ham. Top with the chicken breasts.

Make the sauce by melting 3 tablespoons butter and blending in the flour. Slowly add the milk and cream. Cook over a medium low heat until thickened, stirring constantly. Add salt, pepper, chopped chives, and ½ cup of the grated Parmesan cheese. Pour the sauce over the chicken and sprinkle the remaining ¼ cup Parmesan cheese over the top. Place in the oven and brown until the cheese is bubbly and hot. Serve from the casserole.

Serves 6

Sesame Chicken Casserole
Sesame seeds add a certain something to this chicken casserole.

4-pound chicken fryer cut into pieces
½ cup flour
1 teaspoon salt
1 cup sesame seeds
1 tablespoon paprika
1 teaspoon poultry seasoning
1 egg

1 cup milk
¼ cup butter melted

Mix the flour, salt, sesame seeds, paprika, poultry seasoning, together. Beat the egg with the cup of milk. Roll the chicken pieces in the seasoned flour, then dip in the egg-milk mixture and roll again in the seasoned flour until well-coated all over. Let dry out for 10 minutes. Melt the butter in a skillet and brown the chicken pieces well on both sides. Put them in a greased casserole, cover, and bake 40 minutes in a 350° oven. Uncover and bake 10 minutes longer to crisp the chicken.

Serves 4

Chicken Casserole with Peaches
Delightful! Enough said.

4-pound chicken fryer cut into pieces
1 teaspoon salt
⅛ teaspoon white pepper
4 tablespoons butter melted
4 tablespoons peach brandy
1 large onion chopped fine
¾ cup chicken stock
¼ cup peach brandy
4 large peaches peeled and sliced
2 tablespoons butter melted
Pinch of powdered cloves
3 tablespoons flour
¾ cup chicken stock
¼ cup peach brandy
¼ cup slivered toasted almonds

Sprinkle the chicken pieces with salt and white pepper and brown well on both sides in 4 tablespoons melted butter. Add the 4 tablespoons peach brandy and ignite. When the

flame has burned down transfer the chicken to a casserole.
In the same pan sauté the onions until soft. Add ¾ cup
chicken stock and ¼ cup peach brandy. Cook over low heat
for 1 minute scraping all the brown particles up from the
bottom of the pan. Pour over the chicken in the casserole.
Cover the casserole and cook in a 350° oven for 20 minutes.
Melt 2 tablespoons butter in a pan and brown the sliced
peaches over a medium heat. When browned, sprinkle with
the powdered cloves and flour. Blend thoroughly into the
peaches and juice. Gradually add ¾ cup chicken stock and the
final ¼ cup peach brandy. Cook over a low heat, stirring
constantly, until the sauce is thick and smooth. Pour the
sauce over the chicken in the casserole, recover the casserole,
and continue cooking for 20 minutes longer. Sprinkle the
top of the chicken with the slivered toasted almonds and serve
from the casserole.

Chicken Casserole with White Wine
Especially good—chicken casserole married to a respectable
white wine.

4-pound chicken fryer cut into pieces
½ cup flour
1 teaspoon salt
¼ teaspoon pepper
¼ cup butter melted
2 onions chopped fine
½ teaspoon paprika
1 teaspoon chervil
1½ cups dry white wine
1 teaspoon tomato paste
1 cup chicken stock
1 tablespoon flour
1 clove garlic crushed
12 small white cooked onions
12 small cooked baby carrots

Add the salt and pepper to the flour and roll the chicken pieces in the seasoned flour. Melt ¼ cup butter in a pan and brown the chicken pieces well on both sides. When browned place them in a casserole which has been lined with the finely chopped onions. Sprinkle with paprika and chervil and add the dry white wine. Cover and cook in a 350° oven for 20 minutes.

In the meantime mix the tomato paste with the chicken stock, 1 tablespoon flour, and the crushed clove of garlic. Pour over the chicken. Continue cooking for 30 minutes longer or until the chicken is tender. Uncover the casserole during the last 10 minutes and add the cooked onions and carrots. Serve in the casserole.

Serves 4–6

Chicken and Oyster Casserole

Oysters and cream give this casserole dish a new texture. As for flavor—m'm!

4-pound chicken fryer cut into pieces
½ cup flour
1 teaspoon salt
⅛ teaspoon pepper
4 tablespoons butter
1 cup chicken stock
1 cup heavy warmed cream
3 dozen fresh oysters

Add the salt and pepper to the flour and roll the chicken pieces in the seasoned flour. Melt 4 tablespoons butter in a skillet and brown the chicken pieces well on both sides. Transfer the chicken to a buttered casserole and add 1 cup chicken stock. Cover the casserole and cook in a 350° oven for 40 minutes or until the chicken is tender. Add the heavy warm cream and the 3 dozen fresh oysters. Cook 10 minutes longer. Serve from the casserole.

Serves 6

Chicken Noodle Casserole
An old favorite. It won't let you down.

1 large fowl cut up
3 cups boiling water
2 teaspoons salt
2 onions sliced
2 bay leaves
¼ cup butter melted
¼ cup flour
1½ cups cream
¼ teaspoon pepper
1 8-ounce package noodles
1½ cups Parmesan cheese

Place the chicken pieces in a large heavy kettle. Add 3 cups boiling water, 1 teaspoon salt, the sliced onions, and the bay leaves. Cover and cook over a low heat 1½ to 2 hours or until the chicken is tender. Cool the chicken, then remove the meat from the bones and cut into small pieces. Melt the butter in another pan, blend in the flour, and add 1½ cups of the chicken stock strained. Stir until smooth and thickened over a low heat. Add the cream, 1 teaspoon salt, and continue cooking until thickened. Cook the noodles in boiling salted water until tender. Arrange the chicken and noodles in alternate layers in a buttered casserole. Add 1 cup grated Parmesan cheese to the sauce and pour the sauce over the chicken and noodles. Cover with the remaining ½ cup Parmesan cheese and bake in a 350° oven until the cheese is melted and browned.

Serves 6

Chicken Casserole with Vegetables
This chicken casserole dish is a tantalizing meal.

1 large fowl
1 cup shell macaroni
12 small baby carrots cooked
12 small whole onions cooked
12 small potato balls cooked
1 cup fresh or frozen peas cooked
1½ cups chicken stock
Salt and pepper to taste

Put the chicken in a large heavy kettle and cover with boiling water. Simmer about 1½ to 2 hours or until the chicken is tender. Remove from the stock and cut the meat from the bones in small pieces. Cook the shell macaroni in boiling salted water until tender. Drain. Place a layer of the macaroni shells in the bottom of a buttered casserole. Sprinkle lightly with salt and pepper. Place the chicken pieces in a mound in the center and surround with the precooked vegetables. Pour over 1½ cups chicken stock and cook in a 325° oven for 30 minutes. Serve from the casserole.

Serves 4

Casserole of Chicken with Cranberries
Cranberries and dry vermouth create a superb flavor for this chicken dish.

4-pound chicken fryer cut into pieces
1 teaspoon salt
⅛ teaspoon pepper
½ cup flour
2 tablespoons butter
½ cup cranberry juice
½ cup dry vermouth
½ cup whole cranberry sauce

Add salt and pepper to the flour and roll the chicken pieces in the seasoned flour. Brown quickly on both sides in the butter and transfer the chicken to a casserole. Add the cranberry juice and dry vermouth to the drippings in the pan and cook over a medium heat for 1 minute, scraping up all the browned particles from the bottom. Pour the cranberry-vermouth sauce over the chicken in the casserole. Cover the casserole and cook in a 350° oven for 35 minutes or until the chicken is tender. Add the whole cranberry sauce and cook 5 minutes longer. Serve from the casserole.

Serves 4

Chicken with Coconut in Casserole
Wonderfully exotic is this chicken with coconut in a casserole.

4-pound chicken fryer cut into pieces
1 teaspoon salt
1/8 teaspoon pepper
1/2 teaspoon paprika
1/4 cup butter melted
1 tablespoon brown sugar
1/4 teaspoon salt
1 large Bermuda onion chopped fine
1/2 cup crushed pineapple
1 tablespoon lemon juice
1 cup shredded packaged sweetened coconut
1/4 cup butter melted
Juice of 1/2 lemon

Mix the salt, pepper, and paprika together and rub well into the chicken pieces. Melt 1/4 cup butter in a skillet and brown the chicken well on both sides. Remove the chicken from the pan. Stir into the drippings in the pan the brown sugar, salt, and chopped Bermuda onion. Cook stirring constantly until the onion is soft. Stir in the crushed pineapple and cook 1 minute longer. Put half the onion pineapple mixture in the bottom of a buttered casserole. Place the chicken pieces on top and cover with the remaining onion pineapple mixture. Sprinkle 1 tablespoon lemon juice over the top, cover, and cook in a 350° oven for 30 minutes. Mix the coconut with ¼ cup melted butter, add the juice of ½ lemon, and spread over the top of the chicken. Continue cooking uncovered for 20 minutes longer. Serve from the casserole.

Serves 4

The Capon

The capon, that royal bird, pride of the barnyard, is bigger, heavier, more tender-fleshed than the average chicken. It is meatier, fuller breasted, so that it is possible to get more white meat from the breast pound for pound. In fact, there is more flesh on the capon than on any other fowl. It is exquisitely flavored and should be prepared with great care so that nothing detracts from its delicate flavor.

The capon is a male chicken with sex privileges removed to improve the flesh and increase the growth. Not as large as the turkey nor as small as a roasting chicken, the capon is a compromise between the two. The capon weighs from 6 to 8 pounds and is usually from 7 to 10 months old. It is easily identified by the "capon prick" from which only part of the feathers have been removed.

The capon came into being in the days when Rome was at the peak of its glory and immense wealth and a corrupt court led to lavish expenditures on food and drink. The citizens of Rome spent unbelievable sums on the pleasures of the table and gorged themselves on such delicacies as the tongues of peacocks and nightingales, fat orioles, the bellies of virgin pigs, thrushes' entrails, sow ovaries, and other rare and costly dishes. The Senators, the chosen leaders, in the cause of virtue and restraint passed laws at various times to enforce moderation. One such law was a law not only restricting the consumption of chicken but further forbidding the eating of any fowl except a hen which could not be fattened for that specific purpose. The Romans, who had a real passion for chicken, applied themselves energetically to finding devious ways out of the dilemma. The problem was solved by a poor rooster who came into the limelight unexpectedly when a surgeon experimenting with a knife transformed him into a gelding. The ex-rooster grew plump and full breasted and thus was the capon created. Needless to say he was a huge success and the capon became one of the triumphs of gastronomy.

Galantine of Capon

A galantine is one of the great masterpieces of French cuisine and certainly no chicken cookbook worthy of its name should be without a recipe for it. Never having prepared one, I called on Marian Anderson for help, since besides being one of the best cooks I know she is also one of the most daring. We went into conference, bought the necessary ingredients, and starting from scratch by boning the capon, we bravely tackled it. The preparation took time and patience but the resulting royal dish gave us a real feeling of accomplishment. A galantine is a cold party dish and it is elegant both to look at and to eat.

5-pound capon
½ pound leg of veal
½ pound fresh pork loin
1½ pounds fat pork
½ pound lean cooked ham
½ pound cooked tongue
2 tablespoons shallot or onion finely chopped
1 teaspoon salt
3 sprigs parsley
1 bay leaf
⅛ teaspoon nutmeg
4 tablespoons cognac
1 teaspoon salt
Pinch of nutmeg

2 eggs well beaten
3 quarts hot chicken stock

Ask your butcher to bone the capon for you. Or if you wish
to do it yourself begin by cutting down the center of the skin
over the backbone with a small sharp knife. Working very
carefully cut away all the meat from the bones as shown in
my directions for boning chicken. Make sure you do not tear
the skin. This done, remove all of the meat from the capon
until the skin is quite clean. Set the skin aside.

Cut the breast and thigh meat from the capon into 12 strips
of uniform size. Cut one half of the leg of veal meat and one
half of the fresh pork loin into strips the size of the capon
meat strips. Cut one half the cooked ham and tongue into
similar strips. Cut 12 strips from the fat pork. Place all of the
strips in a shallow bowl with 2 tablespoons finely chopped
shallot or onion, 1 teaspoon salt, the sprigs of parsley, bay
leaf, nutmeg, and cognac. Cover the bowl and marinate in
the refrigerator overnight.

Cut 4 thin slices from the remaining fat pork and set them
aside. Combine the remainder of the fat pork with the rest
of the leg of veal meat, the fresh pork loin, lean cooked ham,
and cooked tongue. Add all of the remaining meat from the
capon. Cut into small pieces and run all together twice
through the finest blade of a food grinder. Add to the ground
meat 1 teaspoon salt, a pinch of nutmeg, and 2 well beaten
eggs. Drain the marinade from the meat strips and strain it
into the ground meat. Mix all together.

Spread a clean cloth on a table and lay on top of it the 4
slices of fat pork. Place the skin from the capon flat on top of
the fat pork with the outside of the skin on top of the slices
of fat pork. Spread a layer of the ground meat mixture evenly
over the skin and on top of this lay strips of meat, alternating

the different kinds so they form a pattern. On top of the meat strips spread another layer of ground meat and then another layer of meat strips. Repeat with the ground meat, and then the meat strips, finishing with the ground meat. There should be four layers of the ground meat and three of the meat strips.

Form into a roll, drawing the capon skin tightly together, and sew the skin securely the length of the roll. Roll the galantine in the cloth and tie the ends to keep the filling firmly packed. Lower the galantine into a kettle containing 3 quarts boiling chicken stock. Cook slowly for 1¾ hours. Remove the galantine from the stock and let stand until cool enough to handle. Remove the cloth in which it was cooked and roll the galantine in a clean cloth, tightening and tieing it again securely at both ends. Place a weight on top, not over 5 pounds, but just enough to press the galantine a little but not enough to squeeze out the juices. When cold remove the weight and the cloth and put the galantine in the refrigerator. Cover with creamy aspic coating.

Aspic for Galantine of Capon
1½ cups chicken stock
¼ cup chopped onion
¼ cup chopped carrots
¼ teaspoon dried tarragon
1¼ cups heavy whipping cream
1 envelope gelatin
3 tablespoons cognac

Bring the chicken stock to a boil and add the chopped onion, chopped carrots, and dried tarragon. Turn heat to low, cover, and simmer for 20 minutes. Strain and add the heavy whipping cream. Continue cooking until the sauce has reduced to about 2 cups. Soften 1 envelope of gelatin in 3 tablespoons cognac and add to the cream sauce. Stir over low heat until the gelatin has dissolved completely. Cool in the refrigerator until the mixture has thickened slightly.

Spoon a layer of the sauce over the chilled galantine and refrigerate until the aspic has set. Then spoon another layer of aspic over the galantine and let it set. Then another until all of the aspic is used up. If at any time the aspic becomes too thick to spread over the galantine smoothly reheat it and let it chill again until of the desired consistency. Allow plenty of time for each layer to set before applying the next layer of aspic. When finished, garnish the galantine with tarragon leaves, black truffle slices, pimiento strips, mushroom caps, or any other decoration you may fancy. To serve cut into slices.

Capon Virginia

This is a version of a very special party dish. While it may sound a little complicated, the finished product, I assure you, is well worth the effort.

1 capon about 6 or 7 pounds
2 quarts water
1 large onion
1 carrot
3 sprigs parsley
3 stalks celery and leaves
1 tablespoon salt
Ham mousse
Truffle slices
Clear aspic
Virginia ham slices
½ cup whipped cream
3 teaspoons horseradish
1 teaspoon water
¼ teaspoon salt

Truss the legs and wings of the capon close to the body. Place in a large kettle with 2 quarts water, onion, carrot, parsley, celery and leaves, and 1 tablespoon salt. Cover and cook slowly for 1½ to 2 hours or until capon is tender. Cool the capon in the stock. When cool remove the capon and place on a board on its back. Cut the breast meat from the bones in slices and set aside. Then cut away the bones under the breast leaving a bowl-like cavity. Fill the cavity with the Ham Mousse, rounding and patting it to reshape the bird. Arrange the breast meat on each side of the rounded surface of the Ham Mousse. Decorate with slices of truffles and chill the capon thoroughly. Pour ½ inch layer of clear aspic in a cold serving dish. Place the chilled capon in it and let it congeal. Then coat the decorated capon with more clear aspic. Garnish with rolled slices of Virginia ham stuffed with whipped cream to which 3 teaspoons horseradish soaked in 1 teaspoon water with ¼ teaspoon salt has been added.

Serves 8–10

Ham Mousse for Capon Virginia
This may be prepared a day ahead of time if you wish.

2 cups lean ground cooked Virginia ham
½ cup boiling water
1 tablespoon gelatin soaked in a little cold water to soften
Pinch of nutmeg, white pepper, and cayenne
½ cup whipped cream

Soak gelatin in cold water and add to ½ cup boiling water. Put the ham through a food chopper three times. Then to insure fineness rub through a sieve. Add to the gelatin and hot water. Season with nutmeg, white pepper, and cayenne. Add the whipped cream. Chill in the refrigerator until set or until ready to use.

Braised Capon with Lemon Compote
A dish for a festive dinner.

6-pound capon
1 teaspoon salt
3 sprigs fresh rosemary
4 tablespoons soft butter
Cold water
1 cup dry white wine

Lemon Compote
6 large lemons
Boiling water
6 tablespoons sugar
½ cup water

Sprinkle the capon inside and out with salt and tuck the 3 sprigs of rosemary into the cavity. Rub the outside well with the soft butter and truss. Place the capon in a braising kettle and brown over a medium high heat on all sides. Add enough cold water to barely cover and the dry white wine. Turn the heat to high and boil rapidly for 10 minutes. Reduce heat to low and simmer for 10 minutes longer. Transfer the kettle to a 350° oven and roast the capon for 1 hour, basting frequently with the pan drippings. Let the capon stand at room temperature for 10 minutes before carving it. Serve with the Lemon Compote.

To make the Lemon Compote cut the peel and all the white membrane from the lemons. Slice enough of the peel into thin strips to make ½ cup. Cover the strips with boiling water and let them stand for 10 minutes. Drain. Remove all the seeds from the lemon pulp and cut into very thin slices. Add the lemon pulp to the strips of lemon peel. Bring the 6 tablespoons sugar and ½ cup water to a boil. Let simmer for 10 minutes. Pour over the lemon mixture. Chill thoroughly before serving.

Serves 6

Truffled Capon
The delicacy of the capon is enhanced in this truffled delight.

8-pound capon
10 large truffle slices
Salt and pepper
¼ cup brandy
¼ cup soft butter
Foil
¾ pound lean fresh pork ground fine
¾ pound lean fresh veal ground fine
1½ teaspoons salt
½ teaspoon poultry seasoning
2 truffles chopped fine
⅓ cup brandy
⅓ cup sherry
3 tablespoons juice from truffle can
2 eggs well beaten
1 slice pork fat
1 teaspoon salt
½ cup water

Sprinkle the truffle slices with salt and pepper and marinate them in a bowl with the ¼ cup brandy for one hour. Carefully loosen the skin from the breast of the capon and lay 4 of the marinated truffle slices on each breast on each side. Loosen the skin from the legs in the same way and lay 1 truffle slice over the leg meat on each side. Rub the capon well with ¼ cup soft butter and wrap tightly in foil. Place the capon in the refrigerator overnight so the flavor of the truffles will go through the bird.

Mix the ground pork and ground veal together in a bowl. Add 1½ teaspoons salt and the poultry seasoning. Add the finely chopped truffles, ⅓ cup brandy, ⅓ cup of sherry, juice from the truffle can, and 2 well-beaten eggs. Stuff the neck and body cavities of the capon with this mixture and sew the openings closed. Truss. Tie a slice of pork fat over the breast, sprinkle with salt, and place the capon in a deep roasting pan. Roast for 20 minutes in a 425° oven, then reduce the heat to 350° and continue roasting for 1¼ hours or until the capon is tender, basting frequently. Remove the capon to a platter and keep hot. Skim the fat from the pan juices and add ½ cup water. Stir well over a medium heat scraping in all the brown particles. Serve the capon with the pan juices.

Serves 10

Capon with Caper Sauce

There are any number of excellent recipes for capon with Caper Sauce. This is a variation of one I consider especially good.

6-pound capon
¼ cup brandy
6 cups chicken stock
3 tablespoons butter
2½ tablespoons flour
2 cups cream
1 egg yolk beaten with 1 tablespoon water
¼ cup chopped capers
1 tablespoon lemon juice
Coarse salt
Chopped dill pickles

Truss the capon. Place in an open roasting pan and pour ¼ cup brandy over the bird. Ignite. When the flame burns down add 6 cups chicken stock. Roast for 20 minutes in a hot 425 oven. Lower heat to 325° and continue roasting for 1½ hours longer or until the capon is tender. Baste frequently with the juices. Remove from the oven and keep hot while preparing the sauce.

Melt the butter in a saucepan and blend in the flour. Add the gravy from the roasting pan and stir steadily over a low heat until smooth and creamy. Add the 2 cups cream and continue stirring over low heat until thoroughly blended and thickened. Add the egg yolk which has been beaten with 1 tablespoon water and continue cooking a few minutes longer. Add the chopped capers and the lemon juice. Carve the capon and serve in the caper sauce. Serve with side dishes of coarse salt and chopped dill pickles.

Serves 6

Stuffed Capon with Pistachio Nuts

Whenever Charles Samson gave a special party in his apartment on Telegraph Hill you could be assured of a fabulous dinner. This elegant capon dish was one of the most outstanding and while he was not one for using exact measurements I believe we managed to piece the ingredients back together quite accurately.

6-pound capon
1 teaspoon salt
⅛ teaspoon white pepper
⅛ teaspoon powdered ginger
3 cups breadcrumbs
½ cup rosé wine
Capon liver and heart chopped fine
3 tablespoons chives chopped fine
2 tablespoons parsley chopped fine
1 cup chopped pistachio nuts
Pinch of thyme, sweet basil, and powdered cloves

Salt and pepper to taste
¼ cup heavy cream
1 cup rosé wine

Sauce
4 tablespoons butter melted
1 onion chopped fine
2 whole cloves
2 tablespoons chopped parsley
1 tablespoon flour
1 cup chicken broth
2 egg yolks well beaten
2 tablespoons sherry
1 cup pistachio nuts

Rub the capon inside and out with the salt, white pepper, and ginger. Soak the breadcrumbs in ½ cup rosé wine and squeeze out the excess moisture. Add the chopped capon liver and heart, chopped chives, chopped parsley, and 1 cup chopped pistachio nuts. Season with the thyme, sweet basil, powdered cloves, and salt and pepper to taste. Mix thoroughly and add the heavy cream. Stuff the capon cavities with this mixture, sew the openings closed, and truss. Place the capon in an open roasting pan with the 1 cup of rosé wine. Roast in a hot 425° oven for 20 minutes. Reduce heat to 325° and continue roasting for 1½ hours, basting frequently with the drippings in the pan, until the capon is tender.

For the sauce melt 4 tablespoons butter in a pan and cook the chopped onions, cloves, and chopped parsley for 5 minutes. Add the flour and blend in well. Add the chicken broth and cook over a medium high heat until the sauce is reduced to less than half. Strain through a sieve and set aside until the capon is done.

When the capon is done place it on a hot platter. Skim off

the fat from the liquid in the pan. Add the sauce to the pan and cook over a low heat until thoroughly blended. Add the 2 egg yolks which have been well beaten with the 2 table-spoons sherry. Pour into a gravy boat and serve with the capon with a dish of chopped pistachio nuts on the side.

Serves 6

Roast Curried Capon
A succulent dish which adds zest to the capon.

5-pound capon
2½ teaspoons salt
3 teaspoons curry powder
2 tart apples peeled and sliced
1 onion sliced
1 clove garlic
1 sprig parsley
4 tablespoons butter
2½ teaspoons ginger
2 tablespoons orange peel
1 cup hot giblet gravy
½ cup heavy cream
2 tablespoons chopped chutney
1 onion chopped very fine
½ cup seedless raisins

Put capon neck and giblets in water to cover. Add a pinch of salt and simmer covered ½ hour. Strain and save the broth for gravy. Mix 1 teaspoon salt, 1 teaspoon curry, and 1 tea-spoon ginger together. Rub the inside of the capon with this. Place 1 sliced tart apple, 1 sliced onion, 1 clove garlic, and a sprig of parsley inside the cavity. Sew up the capon and truss. Melt 4 tablespoons butter in a pan and stir in ½ teaspoon salt, 1 teaspoon curry, ½ teaspoon ginger, and 1 tablespoon orange peel. Brush the capon well with this spiced butter mix-

ture. Place in an open roasting pan and roast in a 425° oven
for 20 minutes. Turn heat to 325° and roast 1½ hours longer
or until the capon is done, basting frequently with the drippings in the pan. When done remove the capon to a serving
platter and keep hot.

Make the gravy by adding 1 cup hot giblet gravy to the drippings in the pan, ½ cup heavy cream, ½ teaspoon salt, 2
teaspoons curry, 2 tablespoons chopped chutney, 1 sliced tart
apple, ½ cup seedless raisins, and 1 teaspoon grated orange
peel. Cover and simmer over low heat for 20 minutes. Serve
this sauce with the capon.

Serves 6

Braised Capon with Truffle Sauce
The succulent quality of the capon is enhanced in this aristocratic dish.

6-pound capon
1 teaspoon salt
⅛ teaspoon pepper
¼ cup flour
3 tablespoons butter
1 large sliced onion
1 sliced carrot
Water
2 cups burgundy wine
½ cup rum
1 stalk celery
2 sprigs parsley
1 bay leaf
3 truffles cut in thin slices
1 tablespoon butter
1 tablespoon flour
1½ cups capon broth

2 egg yolks
2 tablespoons heavy cream

Add the salt and pepper to the ¼ cup flour and rub the capon well with the seasoned flour. Melt 3 tablespoons butter in a heavy kettle and brown the capon well on all sides. Add the large sliced onion, sliced carrot, and when the onion begins to brown enough water to barely cover. Add 1 cup burgundy wine, 1 stalk of celery, 2 sprigs parsley, and 1 bay leaf. Cover the kettle and simmer the capon about 1½ hours or until it is tender. Add more burgundy wine if the kettle gets too dry.

Cut the truffles in thin slices. Mix 1 cup burgundy wine with ½ cup rum and soak the truffles in this for 1 hour. When the capon is done place it on a serving platter and keep hot while making the sauce.

For the sauce, in a small saucepan melt 1 tablespoon butter and blend in 1 tablespoon flour. Gradually add 1½ cups of the broth in which the capon was cooked. Simmer over low heat, stirring constantly, until the sauce is smooth and thickened. Add the truffles in their wine sauce. Boil up once stirring vigorously. Remove from the heat and stir in 2 egg yolks beaten with 2 tablespoons heavy cream and a little of the hot sauce. Serve with the capon.

Poached Capon with Gold Sauce
Another gala recipe for the royal capon.

5-pound capon
1 teaspoon salt
⅛ teaspoon pepper
Capon giblets plus five extra chicken livers
1 cup finely chopped cooked ham
4 cups dry breadcrumbs
1 onion chopped fine

6 tablespoons butter melted
2 tablespoons chopped parsley
Pinch of thyme
Salt and pepper
½ cup cognac
Chicken stock
1 tablespoon butter
1 tablespoon flour
½ cup heavy cream
4 egg yolks
2 ounces cognac

Rub the capon well with salt and pepper. Chop the giblets and livers into tiny pieces and sauté them along with the chopped onion in the 6 tablespoons melted butter. When the onions are soft and the livers browned, add the chopped cooked ham, dry breadcrumbs, chopped parsley, thyme, and salt and pepper to taste. Moisten with ½ cup cognac and mix in well. Stuff the capon with this mixture, sew up the openings, and truss. Place the capon in a large kettle with enough chicken stock to cover and poach covered for 1½ hours or until the capon is tender.

In a small saucepan melt 1 tablespoon butter and blend in 1 tablespoon flour. Slowly add 1½ cups of the stock the capon was cooked in and stir over low heat until thickened. Add ½ cup heavy cream and bring to a boil, stirring constantly. Remove from the heat and beat in 4 egg yolks one by one. Finally add 2 ounces cognac and mix in vigorously. Carve the capon and serve a generous helping of stuffing on each plate. Pour over the sauce.

Serves 6

Roast Capon Alexandre Dumas

"The individual delicacy of the capon is frequently passed over too lightly in gastronomic literature, and instructions for its use too often comment briefly on capon's resemblance to chicken, and recommend the same methods of preparation. There is at least one famous exception to this rule of general neglect, for Alexandre Dumas, gourmet author of the *Grand Dictionnaire de la Cuisine*, whose lyric tributes to fine viands are as honored in the history of literature as they are in the annals of gastronomy, created one formula for the preparation of capon which is worthy of this exquisitely flavored bird. The recipe was modernized by the chef at the Hotel du Pavillon, at Cannes, where it was among the most cherished and most famous specialties of the house."

This recipe is from Louis P. DeGouy's *Gold Cookbook*, used with permission from Chilton Book Company, Philadelphia.

1 5- or 6-pound capon
1 tablespoon kneaded butter
1 cup scalded heavy cream
1 small onion
1 whole clove
Flour
Pepper
Brandy

Clean and singe a 5- or 6-pound capon. Turn back the head and the neck of the capon into the breast cavity, and sew up the neck skin, thus closing the opening. Rub the lower cavity with brandy and with salt and pepper, and stuff it with the capon's liver, coarsely chopped, 1 tablespoon kneaded butter (equal parts of butter and flour, kneaded together), and a small onion, peeled and stuck with a whole clove. Close this opening with a skewer, and brush the bird with melted sweet butter. Roast for 15 minutes in a hot oven (425° F.); then reduce the temperature to 350° F., and continue to roast for 1½ hours, basting frequently with the drippings in the pan, to which has been added 1 cup scalded heavy cream. When the bird is done, it will have a thick golden, crusty skin. Arrange on a hot platter, and serve with a sauce boat of the pan gravy *au natural*, which has been strained and allowed to come to a boil once or twice.

Capon Au Gros Sel

This is the recipe from Alexandre Dumas' "Grand Dictionnaire de la Cuisine," from which the above recipe was probably taken:

"Capon au Gros Sel. Eviscerate, pluck, and clean. Truss with feet tucked inside. Cover with slices of bacon. Cook in consommé. Drain, salt, sauce with reduced beef gravy, and serve with a separate dish of coarse salt."

This recipe is from Alexandre Dumas' Dictionary of Cuisine, Edited, Abridged and Translated by Louis Colman, from Le Grand Dictionnaire de Cuisine, Simon and Schuster, 1958.

Leftover Chicken

Our chicken is the most versatile of birds. It appears at one mealtime roasted, broiled, sautéed, fried—and the next day it reappears again as an elegant dish in a wide variety of interesting and delectable ways. The art of using leftovers, as the French housewife knows, is limited only by the imagination of the cook, and when the leftovers happen to be chicken they can be the basis of any number of new and delightful dishes. Leftover chicken is featured in many gourmet recipes. They are in crepes, souffles, turnovers, fritters, croquettes, patties, burgers, savory omelets. Cubes of tender cooked leftover chicken can be served in numerous sauces: cream sauce, wine sauce, tomato sauce, cheese sauce, herbed sauce, Hollandaise sauce; and the sauces can be served over biscuits, cornbread, waffles, in patty shells, on toast or with noodles or rice. Some of the dishes have been immortalized by famous chefs such as Chicken à la Ritz, which is as succulent a dish ever devised; but there are many excellent dishes that make use of cooked chicken and they are all well worth trying.

Chicken Hash à la Ritz
This is my version of the famous Chicken Hash à la Ritz created by Louis Diat, the chef of the old Ritz-Carlton in New York.

3 cups diced cooked chicken
1½ cups cream
2 tablespoons butter

2 tablespoons flour
1 teaspoon salt
½ cup chicken stock or leftover gravy
1½ cups milk
½ cup cream
2 egg yolks beaten with 4 tablespoons whipped cream
4 tablespoons grated Parmesan cheese

Put the chicken meat in a saucepan with 1½ cups cream and cook over a low heat until the cream is reduced to about ½ of its original quantity. Melt 2 tablespoons butter in another saucepan and blend in the flour and salt. Slowly add ½ cup chicken stock or gravy and the 1½ cups milk. Cook over a low heat, stirring constantly, until the sauce is smooth and thickened. Add ½ cup cream and let the sauce reduce to about ⅓ of its original quantity. Add 1 cup of this sauce to the chicken mixture, mix well, and pour into a shallow baking dish. To the remaining sauce add the 2 egg yolks beaten with 4 tablespoons whipped cream and the grated Parmesan cheese. Spread over the chicken and broil under the broiler until the top is golden.

Serves 4

Curried Leftover Chicken
A chicken dish redolent of the East.

3 Bermuda onions chopped
1 clove garlic minced
3 tablespoons butter melted
1 tablespoon butter
1 tablespoon flour
1½ teaspoons curry powder
1 cup hot chicken broth
3 bananas sliced
1 tart apple sliced

½ cup white seedless raisins soaked ½ hour in
    ½ cup water
2 cups diced cooked chicken
½ teaspoon each powdered ginger and salt
½ cup heavy cream
1 egg yolk beaten with 1 tablespoon cream
1 teaspoon lemon juice
Rice
Chutney
Condiments

Sauté the chopped Bermuda onions and the minced clove of garlic in 3 tablespoons melted butter until golden. Melt 1 tablespoon butter in a saucepan and blend in the flour and curry powder. Gradually stir in the hot chicken broth and cook over a medium heat until thickened and smooth. Add the sliced bananas, apple slices, white seedless raisins, diced cooked chicken, and the powdered ginger and salt. Add the sautéed onions and garlic. Cover and simmer for 30 minutes. Add the heavy cream and cook 1 minute longer stirring constantly. Remove from heat and blend in the egg yolk which has been beaten with 1 tablespoon cream. Add the lemon juice and serve over fluffy white rice accompanied by chutney and other condiments.

Serves 4

Chicken and Oyster Hash
This makes a supreme main dish.

1 pint oysters
3 tablespoons butter
3 tablespoons flour
1 cup cream
2 cups diced cooked chicken
Salt and pepper to taste
Dash of cayenne

Sauce
1 teaspoon butter melted
1 teaspoon flour
½ cup thin cream
⅓ cup dry white wine
1 tablespoon grated Swiss cheese
1 tablespoon whipped cream

Poach the oysters in their own liquid until the edges curl. Drain the oysters and reserve the liquid. Melt 3 tablespoons butter in a saucepan, add 3 tablespoons flour, and blend in well. Slowly add the oyster liquid and cook, stirring constantly, until the sauce boils. Slowly stir in 1 cup cream and cook over low heat until the sauce is thick and smooth. Coarsely chop the oysters and add them to the sauce along with the 2 cups diced cooked chicken. Season to taste with salt and pepper and a dash of cayenne. Pour the hash into a baking dish and make the sauce.

For the sauce blend the butter and flour together. Add the thin cream and stir over low heat until smooth and thickened. Add the dry white wine and let the sauce reduce about ⅓ over a medium high heat, stirring constantly. Add the grated Swiss cheese and mix in 1 tablespoon whipped cream. Pour this sauce over the hash and glaze it under the broiler.

Serves 4

Chicken Imperial
The sherry and Cheddar cheese give this dish a special distinction.

½ cup butter
½ cup flour
2 cups thin cream
2 cups chicken stock

1 cup mushrooms sliced
2 tablespoons butter
3 cups diced cooked chicken
½ cup sherry
1½ cups grated Cheddar cheese
2 teaspoons minced onion
Salt and pepper to taste
½ cup slivered toasted almonds

Melt ½ cup butter in a saucepan. Blend in ½ cup flour. Slowly add the cream and chicken stock, stirring constantly over a medium low heat until smooth and thickened. Sauté the sliced mushrooms for 5 minutes in 2 tablespoons butter and add them to the sauce. Add the diced cooked chicken, the sherry, grated Cheddar cheese, minced onion, and salt and pepper to taste. Stir continually over the heat until the cheese has melted. Serve over crisp toast with slivered toasted almonds sprinkled over the top.

Serves 6

Almond Chicken
To me, this is one of the most delightful of chicken dishes.

½ cup sliced mushrooms
¼ cup butter melted
¼ cup chopped pimiento
2 cups diced cooked chicken
½ cup sherry
1 cup heavy cream
2 egg yolks
¼ teaspoon nutmeg
Salt and pepper to taste
1 cup slivered toasted almonds

Melt the butter in a large heavy frying pan and sauté the

sliced mushrooms for 5 minutes. Add the chopped pimiento, diced cooked chicken, and ½ cup sherry. Cook over a medium high heat until the sherry has been absorbed, stirring constantly. Add 1 cup heavy cream and simmer for 10 minutes. Add the 2 egg yolks mixed with a little of the hot sauce and cook over a low heat for 5 minutes. Add the nutmeg and salt and pepper to taste. Pour the sauce into a serving dish and sprinkle the top with the slivered toasted almonds. Serve immediately.

Serves 4

Chicken Soufflé
A very special luncheon dish.

2 cups cooked ground chicken
2 cups cream sauce
¼ teaspoon nutmeg
1 tablespoon minced parsley
1 tablespoon grated onion
3 egg yolks slightly beaten
3 egg whites stiffly beaten
Salt and pepper to taste
6 individual unbaked pie shells

Make the cream sauce very thick and combine with the cooked ground chicken. Season with nutmeg, parsley, and onion. Mix well and stir in the 3 slightly beaten egg yolks. Beat the egg whites very stiff and fold them into the mixture. Taste for seasoning and pour into the 6 individual unbaked pie shells. Arrange on a baking sheet and bake about 25 minutes in a hot 400° oven or until the crust is golden brown and the soufflé well puffed. Serve immediately as soufflés cannot wait.

Serves 6

Baked Chicken Loaf
A tasty baked chicken loaf with a wonderful mushroom sauce.

3 cups ground cooked chicken
1 cup dry bread crumbs
2 tablespoons minced parsley
1 tablespoon grated onion
1 tablespoon celery salt
1 teaspoon thyme
½ cup chopped green pepper
3 eggs well beaten

Combine the ground cooked chicken and breadcrumbs together in a bowl. Add the minced parsley, grated onion, celery salt, thyme, and chopped green pepper. Mix well and add the 3 well-beaten eggs. Mix thoroughly and pour into a greased loaf pan. Set in a pan of hot water and bake in a 350° oven about 1½ hours or until an inserted knife comes out clean. Serve hot with mushroom sauce.

Mushroom sauce
1 cup sliced mushrooms
2 tablespoons butter melted
2 tablespoons flour
2 tablespoons butter
¾ cup chicken broth
¾ cup cream
Few drops onion juice
1 teaspoon Worcestershire sauce
1 teaspoon salt
⅛ teaspoon white pepper

Sauté the sliced mushrooms in 2 tablespoons melted butter for 5 minutes. Melt another 2 tablespoons butter in a saucepan and blend in the flour. Slowly add the chicken broth and cream, stirring constantly over a medium low heat until thickened. Season with onion juice, Worcestershire sauce, salt, and white pepper. Add the sautéed mushrooms and mix in well. Serve hot poured over the chicken loaf.

Serves 4

Chicken au Gratin
Another delightful leftover dish flavored with Swiss cheese for added zest.

1 tablespoon butter
1 tablespoon flour
1 cup thin cream
1 cup grated Swiss cheese
1 teaspoon salt
⅛ teaspoon white pepper
½ cup sliced mushrooms
1 tablespoon butter
3 cups diced cooked chicken
1 cup cooked rice

Melt 1 tablespoon butter in a saucepan and blend in the flour. Slowly add 1 cup thin cream and stir over a low heat until thickened. Add the grated Swiss cheese and continue cooking until the cheese has melted stirring constantly. Sauté the sliced mushrooms for 5 minutes in 1 tablespoon butter. Add them to the cheese sauce along with the diced cooked chicken. Season to taste with salt and white pepper. Put a layer of the cooked rice in a buttered casserole. Cover the rice with a layer of the chicken mixture. Repeat until all of the rice and chicken has been used up finishing with a layer of the chicken. Bake in a 400° oven for 15 minutes. Serve from the casserole.

Serves 4

Chicken Turnovers
Chicken turnovers filled with a savory filling and enclosed in

a flaky golden brown crust are always welcome. Covered with a delightful cheese sauce they are doubly so.

4 tablespoons butter
4 tablespoons flour
1 cup chicken stock
1 cup cream
1 teaspoon salt
½ teaspoon white pepper
½ teaspoon Worcestershire sauce
⅛ teaspoon mustard
1½ cups diced cooked chicken
2 hard-cooked eggs chopped
½ cup chopped canned mushrooms
Pie pastry or package of pie-crust mix
½ cup grated Swiss cheese
1 tablespoon sherry

Melt the butter and blend in the flour. Add the chicken stock and cream. Cook over a medium heat, stirring constantly until sauce is thickened and smooth. Add salt, white pepper, Worcestershire sauce, and mustard. To half of this sauce add the diced cooked chicken, chopped hard-cooked eggs, and chopped canned mushrooms.

Roll out the pastry dough into a large square. Cut the square into 8 6-inch squares. Place some of the chicken mixture in the center of each square, fold over to form a triangle, and press the edges together sealing them wtih a fork. Make a slit in the tops so the steam will escape and bake in a preheated 450° oven for 15 minutes or until the crust is golden brown.

Add the grated Swiss cheese to the rest of the sauce and heat until the cheese has melted. Add the sherry and serve over the turnovers.

Serves 4

Chicken Croquettes
An excellent way to use up chicken from the previous dinner.

6 tablespoons flour
6 tablespoons butter
2 cups thin cream
1 teaspoon salt
¼ teaspoon pepper
¼ cup finely chopped onion
3 cups finely chopped cooked chicken
¼ pound finely chopped cooked ham
2 egg yolks well beaten
¼ cup grated Parmesan cheese
2 cups breadcrumbs
Deep frying fat

Melt the butter in a saucepan and blend in the flour. Slowly add the 2 cups thin cream and stir over a low heat until the sauce is very thick. Season with salt and pepper and the finely chopped onion. Mix in the chicken and ham. Add the well-beaten egg yolks and the grated Parmesan cheese. Chill in the refrigerator for several hours or overnight. Shape into croquettes—about 8—and roll in the breadcrumbs. Fry in deep hot fat until golden brown. Drain on absorbent paper and serve hot.

Serves 4

Almond Crusted Chicken Croquettes
Angostura Bitters gives this delicious chicken dish a piquant taste.

3 tablespoons butter
3 tablespoons flour
¾ cup milk
1 teaspoon salt

Dash of pepper
½ teaspoon Angostura Bitters
½ teaspoon mustard
1 egg yolk
2 cups chopped cooked chicken
1 egg white slightly beaten
1 cup ground almonds

Make a thick cream sauce by melting the butter in a saucepan, blending in the flour, and adding the milk. Stir over a
medium heat until thickened. Add the salt, pepper, Angostura
Bitters, mustard, egg yolk, and chicken. Pour the mixture into
a platter and chill in the refrigerator until firm enough to
handle. Shape into 12 croquettes. Brush each croquette with
egg white on all sides, then with the ground almonds. Allow
them to dry out for 30 minutes. Melt ¼ cup butter in a heavy
skillet and fry the croquettes until golden brown on all sides,
adding more butter if needed.

Serves 4

Chicken Fritters
Another excellent way to use up leftovers.

1 cup flour
1½ teaspoons salt
½ teaspoon nutmeg
2 tablespoons chopped parsley
2 egg yolks well beaten
⅓ cup milk
2 tablespoons sherry
2 egg whites beaten stiff
1 cup diced cooked chicken
Deep frying fat

Sift together the flour, salt, and nutmeg. Add the chopped

parsley. Beat the egg yolks until thick, then beat in the milk and sherry. Add to the seasoned flour mixing until smooth. Add the diced cooked chicken and fold in the stiffly beaten egg whites. Heat the fat to 375° and drop the fritters in by spoonfuls, a few at a time. Fry until they are golden brown on all sides. Drain on absorbent paper and serve hot.

Serves 4

Scalloped Chicken
A tasty dish with leftover chicken.

2 cups diced cooked chicken
2 cups breadcrumbs
6 tablespoons butter
1 tablespoon minced onion
½ teaspoon thyme
1 tablespoon chopped parsley
1 teaspoon salt
4 tablespoons flour
3 cups hot chicken broth
2 egg yolks slightly beaten

Melt 2 tablespoons of the butter in a pan and add the bread crumbs, stirring until they are well coated with the butter. Add the minced onion, thyme, chopped parsley, and ½ teaspoon salt. In another pan melt 4 tablespoons butter and blend in the flour. Slowly add the hot chicken broth and cook over a medium heat, stirring constantly, until thickened. Add ½ teaspoon salt. Stir in the slightly beaten egg yolks and cook over a very low heat stirring constantly. Put a layer of the buttered crumbs in the bottom of a casserole. On top of this put a layer of the diced cooked chicken and on top of the chicken a layer of the gravy. Repeat and sprinkle the last of the buttered crumbs over the top. Bake in a 350° oven for 30 minutes.

Serves 4

Chicken Newburg
Chicken Newburg makes a very tasty dish.

3 tablespoons butter melted
3 tablespoons flour
1 cup chicken broth
1 cup cream
½ cup sliced mushrooms
2 tablespoons butter
3 cups diced cooked chicken
½ teaspoon salt
⅛ teaspoon white pepper
2 egg yolks
2 tablespoons cream
¼ cup sherry
Dash of nutmeg

Melt 3 tablespoons butter in a saucepan and blend in the flour.
Slowly add the chicken broth and cream. Cook over a medium
low heat, stirring constantly, until smooth and thickened.
Sauté the mushrooms in 2 tablespoons butter for 5 minutes.
Add to the sauce along with the diced cooked chicken. Season
with salt and white pepper. Beat the egg yolks with 2 tablespoons cream and blend into the sauce. Cook over low heat
for 3 minutes, stirring constantly. Add the sherry and the nutmeg and serve over toast.

Serves 4

Chicken in Tomatoes
Chicken in tomatoes is a pleasing nuance.

4 large tomatoes
1 teaspoon salt
1 medium onion chopped fine

2 tablespoons butter
½ cup diced cooked chicken
¾ cup dry breadcrumbs
Salt and pepper to taste
1 tablespoon chopped parsley
1 egg

Cut the tops from the stem ends of the tomatoes. Scoop out the seeds and pulp and reserve. Sprinkle the inside of the tomatoes with the teaspoon of salt. Let them set for 15 minutes. Melt the butter in a skillet and sauté the onion until a light golden in color. Add the diced cooked chicken, bread crumbs, tomato pulp chopped, salt, pepper, and chopped parsley. Cook over a medium low heat stirring constantly for 5 minutes. Remove from heat, add the egg, and mix into the mixture thoroughly. Stuff the tomatoes with this mixture, replace the tops, and place in a greased baking pan. Bake in a 300° oven for 30 minutes.

Serves 4

Chicken in Avocados
So easy to make and yet so good.

1 cup diced cooked chicken
2 tablespoons butter
2 tablespoons flour
1 cup cream
½ teaspoon salt
⅛ teaspoon white pepper
¼ teaspoon celery salt
Dash cayenne
Few drops onion juice
1 tablespoon Madeira wine
2 large avocados

Melt the butter in a saucepan and blend in the flour. Slowly add 1 cup cream and cook over a medium low heat until thickened, stirring constantly. Add the chicken, salt, white pepper, celery salt, cayenne, onion juice. Cook 2 minutes longer and add the Madeira. Cut the avocados in half, peel, and remove the seeds. Fill the avocados with the chicken mixture and brown under the broiler.

Serves 4

Sautéed Chicken Leftovers

Chicken sautéed with mushrooms and green peppers with the tang of sour cream and dill.

1 cup sour cream
1 tablespoon dill
¼ cup butter
1 cup sliced mushrooms
½ cup chopped green pepper
2 tablespoons flour
1 cup chicken stock or broth
½ teaspoon salt
2 cups cooked chicken cut into large pieces

Add 1 tablespoon dill to the sour cream and set in the refrigerator for the flavors to penetrate. Melt the butter in a heavy frying pan and sauté the sliced mushrooms and chopped green pepper until soft. Blend in the flour and slowly add the chicken stock or broth, mixing in well. Cook and stir over a medium heat until the sauce has thickened. Add the salt and the chicken and cook over a low heat for 5 minutes. Add the dill flavored sour cream and cook 1 minute longer. Serve immediately.

Serves 4

Chicken and Spinach Casserole
This casserole is extremely good.

2 pounds fresh spinach
4 tablespoons butter
1½ cups diced cooked chicken
1½ cups Béchamel sauce
1 cup grated Parmesan cheese
Salt and pepper

Wash and trim the spinach. Place it in boiling salted water and cook uncovered for 5 minutes. Drain and cool. Squeeze the spinach with your hands to get out all the excess water. Reheat in 2 tablespoons butter and season with salt and pepper. Mix the diced cooked chicken with the Béchamel sauce and add ¾ cup of the grated Parmesan cheese. Salt and pepper to taste. Put a layer of the spinach in the bottom of a buttered casserole and cover with the chicken mixture. Sprinkle the rest of the grated Parmesan cheese over the top and dot with 2 tablespoons butter. Brown in a 400° oven until the cheese is bubbling and browned.

Serves 4

Chicken Remoulade Casserole
A quick and easy dish to make.

2 cups cooked chicken cut into pieces
½ cup chopped pimientos
½ cup toasted almonds chopped
1 teaspoon salt
⅛ teaspoon pepper
1 tablespoon prepared mustard
1 tablespoon chopped parsley
1 tablespoon capers
1 tablespoon grated onion
3 tablespoons pickle relish

1 cup mayonnaise
½ cup grated Cheddar cheese
½ cup dry bread crumbs
2 tablespoons butter

Combine all the ingredients together except the Cheddar cheese and the breadcrumbs. Pour into a buttered casserole. Sprinkle the top with the grated Cheddar cheese and breadcrumbs. Dot with the butter. Bake at 375° until the cheese has melted and the breadcrumbs browned.

Serves 4

Chicken and Sweet Potatoe Casserole
A chicken casserole that is utterly delightful.

¼ cup chopped onions
3 tablespoons butter
2 tablespoons flour
½ teaspoon salt
⅛ teaspoon thyme
⅛ teaspoon nutmeg
1 cup hot chicken gravy
1 cup hot milk
4 cups sliced cooked sweet potatoes
3 cups diced cooked chicken
6 slices raw bacon

Melt the butter in a skillet and sauté the chopped onion for 3 minutes. Blend in the flour, season with salt, thyme, and nutmeg. Gradually stir in the hot chicken gravy and hot milk. Cook stirring constantly until mixture thickens. Add the sliced cooked sweet potatoes and the diced cooked chicken. Pour into a buttered casserole and lay the slices of raw bacon over the top. Bake in a 375° oven for 35 minutes and serve at once.

Serves 6

Chicken Leftovers Fricasseed
A leftover dish for the epicurean palate.

2 cups diced cooked chicken
2 tablespoons butter
2 tablespoons flour
2 cups hot chicken stock or broth
2 cups sliced mushrooms
12 small white onions peeled
2 egg yolks
2 tablespoons water
Juice of ½ lemon

Melt 2 tablespoons butter in a saucepan and blend in the flour. Gradually add the hot chicken stock or broth and cook over a medium low heat until the sauce has thickened slightly. Add the mushrooms and small white onions and simmer over a low heat about 30 minutes or until the onions are tender. Add the diced cooked chicken and simmer 10 minutes longer. Add the egg yolks beaten with 2 tablespoons water to the sauce and continue cooking over low heat until the sauce has thickened, stirring constantly. Remove from heat and add the juice of ½ lemon. Blend in well and serve immediately.

Serves 4

Chicken Rice Ring with Mushroom Sauce
This leftover dish will make a hit.

2 cups diced cooked chicken
1 cup rice cooked
1 cup dry breadcrumbs
½ teaspoon salt
¼ teaspoon paprika
⅛ teaspoon dry mustard
1 teaspoon Worcestershire sauce

4 eggs well beaten
1 green pepper finely chopped
¼ cup butter melted
1½ cups chicken stock
1 cup thin cream
Cooked rice

Combine the ingredients in order given except for the last item. Mix well and pack into a greased ring mold. Bake in a 325° oven for 1 hour. Let stand for 15 minutes before unmolding into a warm platter. Serve with plain cooked rice in the center and mushroom sauce poured over the top.

Mushroom sauce
1 cup sliced mushrooms
4 tablespoons butter
2 tablespoons flour
¼ teaspoon salt
Dash of pepper
2 cups chicken stock
2 egg yolks slightly beaten
Juice of ½ lemon
1 tablespoon minced parsley

Melt 2 tablespoons butter in a pan and sauté the sliced mushrooms for 5 minutes. In another pan melt the remaining 2 tablespoons butter and blend in the flour and salt. Gradually add the chicken stock and cook, stirring constantly over a low heat, until the sauce comes to a boil and thickens. Combine the egg yolks with the cream and stir into the hot sauce. Cook a few moments longer. Remove from heat and stir in the mushrooms, lemon juice and parsley. Mix well and serve hot over the chicken rice ring.

Serves 4

Italian Style Chicken
This is an interesting and spicy chicken dish that was donated to me by a friend some time ago.

3 tablespoons butter
½ cup chopped onions
1 clove garlic minced
½ cup mushrooms sliced
2 cups tomato hot sauce
1 tablespoon tomato puree
1 teaspoon salt
½ teaspoon oregano
½ teaspoon basil
3 cups diced cooked chicken

Melt the butter in a large skillet. Add the onions, garlic, and sliced mushrooms. Sauté for 5 minutes. Add the tomato hot sauce, tomato puree, salt, oregano, and basil. Cover and simmer for 30 minutes. Add the diced cooked chicken, recover, and simmer an additional 15 minutes.

While the sauce simmers prepare the cornmeal mush ring.

Cornmeal Mush Ring
1 cup cornmeal
½ teaspoon salt
1 cup cold water
3 cups hot chicken broth

Mix the cornmeal and salt with the cold water. Add the hot chicken broth, stirring vigorously. Cook over a medium heat until thickened, stirring constantly. Turn heat to low, cover, and continue cooking 10 minutes longer. Pour into a ring mold which has been rinsed in cold water. Keep hot until the sauce is ready.

Turn the cornmeal ring onto a serving platter and fill the center of the ring with the hot chicken sauce. Serve immediately.

Serves 6

Savory Chicken Patties
Crusty browned chicken patties make a satisfying dish.

1 4-ounce can mushroom pieces
3 cups diced cooked chicken
2 cooked medium potatoes diced
1 medium onion chopped
1 teaspoon nutmeg
1 teaspoon salt
½ teaspoon paprika
1 egg well beaten
1 cup fine breadcrumbs
¼ cup butter melted
2 tablespoons flour
½ teaspoon salt
Pinch of nutmeg
¾ cup chicken broth
¾ cup cream

Drain the mushroom pieces and reserve half of them. Combine the other half with the diced chicken, potatoes, onion, nutmeg, salt, and paprika. Put through the medium blade of a food chopper or blend in an electric blender. Mix with the well-beaten egg and the fine breadcrumbs. Form into 8 patties. Melt the butter in a heavy frying pan and cook the patties over a medium heat until they are crusty and browned on both sides. Remove to a serving platter and keep hot. Add the flour to the pan with ½ teaspoon salt and a pinch of nutmeg. Stir until the flour has browned slightly. Then add the chicken broth and cook over a medium heat until thickened and smooth. Add the cream and reserved mushrooms and continue to cook until just heated through. Pour the sauce over the patties and serve.

Serves 4

Chickenburgers

We have hamburgers so why not chickenburgers? And these are delicious.

3 cups cooked ground chicken
2 eggs well beaten
2 stalks celery finely chopped
2 tablespoons onion finely chopped
1 tablespoon Worcestershire sauce
1 teaspoon salt
1/8 teaspoon pepper
4 tablespoons butter melted

Put the chicken meat through the finest blade of a meat grinder. Combine the ground chicken with the 2 well-beaten eggs, chopped celery, chopped onion, Worcestershire sauce, salt, and pepper. Shape the mixture into patties. Melt the butter in a heavy frying pan and cook the patties over a medium heat until they are firm and browned on both sides. Serve with the pan juices.

Serves 4

Chicken Pancakes

This chicken pancake recipe is extraordinary.

1½ cups ground cooked chicken
1 tablespoon baking powder
1 teaspoon salt
Pinch of cayenne

⅛ teaspoon thyme, mace, and nutmeg
½ cup flour
1 small onion grated
¾ cup milk
1 egg
2 tablespoons butter melted
1 can condensed cream of chicken soup
1 6-ounce can Hollandaise sauce

Place the ground cooked chicken in a bowl and add the baking powder, salt, cayenne, thyme, mace, nutmeg, and flour. Mix well and add the grated onion and milk which has been beaten with the egg. Mix thoroughly and add the melted butter. Spread with a spoon over a greased medium hot griddle and fry until browned on both sides like regular pancakes. Combine the condensed cream of chicken soup with the canned Hollandaise sauce. Heat through and pour hot over the chicken pancakes.

Serves 4

Chicken Crêpes Versailles
This gourmet dish is always a treat.

3 tablespoons butter
3 tablespoons flour
½ cup warm chicken stock
½ cup warm heavy cream
2 egg yolks
2 tablespoons heavy cream
1½ cups finely chopped cooked chicken
¼ cup chopped cooked mushrooms
2 green onions chopped fine
8 crêpes
¼ cup whipped cream
1 tablespoon sherry

Melt 3 tablespoons butter in a saucepan and blend in the
3 tablespoons flour. Gradually add the warm chicken stock
mixed with the ½ cup warm heavy cream and cook over low
heat, stirring constantly, until the sauce is thick and smooth.
Stir in the 2 egg yolks beaten with 2 tablespoons heavy cream
and a little of the hot sauce. Cook, stirring constantly for 2
minutes, being careful not to let the mixture boil. Add the
finely chopped cooked chicken, chopped cooked mushrooms,
and chopped green onions.

Spread the crêpes generously with the chicken filling and roll
up. Arrange close together in a shallow baking dish. Add the
sherry to the whipped cream and mix with the remainder of
the chicken filling. Pour this sauce over the top of the rolled
pancakes and put under the broiler just long enough to glaze
the top. Serve immediately.

Serves 4

Crêpes
3 eggs
¾ cup flour
½ teaspoon salt
Pinch of sugar
½ cup milk

Beat 3 whole eggs until they are thick and lemon colored.
Add the flour, salt, and pinch of sugar. Continue beating for 1
minute longer. Or if you are lucky enough to have an electric
blender blend until smooth which is much easier. Add ½ cup
milk and continue beating or blending until the mixture is of
an eggnog consistency. Spread with a spoon over a greased
medium hot griddle. The pancakes should be very thin. Brown
them lightly on both sides, stack on a platter, and keep warm
until ready to use.

Crêpes with Chicken
This is a fabulous dish to whip up in a hurry.

8 pancakes
4 thick slices leftover roast chicken
8 tablespoons butter melted
2 cups sour cream
2 tablespoons dill weed
1 teaspoon salt

Add the dill weed and salt to the sour cream ahead of time and let chill in the refrigerator an hour or so for the flavors to develop.

Make your own pancakes or if you prefer use a mix. The pancakes should be about ¼ inch thick and rather large. Stack them on a platter and keep warm. When ready to serve place a thick slice of leftover roast chicken on 4 of the pancakes and cover the chicken with another pancake. Pour 2 tablespoons hot melted butter over each pancake sandwich and cover with ½ cup of the dill-flavored sour cream. Serve immediately.

Serves 4

Chicken Livers

Herbs and spices and wines contribute greatly to the delicious flavor of chicken livers. Sherry and sour cream enhance the flavor of chicken livers in a Strogonoff. The addition of sherry or Madeira or burgundy will make a chicken liver dish outstanding. The spicy flavors of cloves, ginger, thyme, or chervil will make chicken livers a special treat. There are many unusual dishes that fall in this category which should please the most discriminating palate.

Broiled Chicken Livers
Broiled chicken livers with a spicy sauce that gives them a delightful flavor.

1 pound chicken livers
1 cup dry white wine
½ cup brandy
Dash of Tabasco
2 tablespoons Worcestershire sauce
8 whole cloves
1 teaspoon caraway seeds
1 teaspoon ginger
4 bay leaves
8 peppercorns
½ cup butter
Salt and pepper to taste
1 tablespoon flour

Combine all the ingredients except the livers and flour in a saucepan with the ½ cup butter melted. Let come to a boil and cook for 4 minutes. Pour over the chicken livers and place in the refrigerator to marinate for at least 6 hours. Remove the chicken livers from the marinade and drain. Reserve the marinade. Broil the chicken livers under the broiler until golden brown on both sides. Make a thin paste with some of the marinade and the 1 tablespoon flour. Bring the marinade to a boil and stir in the paste gradually. Cook until thickened. Pour over the livers.

Serves 4

Chicken Livers with Pineapple
Soy sauce and pineapple do something special for the livers. Do try them.

1 pound chicken livers
Soy sauce
¼ cup peanut oil
4 slices pineapple cut into chunks
½ cup sliced blanched almonds

Sauce
1¼ cups pineapple juice
¼ cup vinegar
¼ teaspoon salt
¼ cup sugar
2 tablespoons cornstarch

Cut the chicken livers in half. Dip them in soy sauce and brown them quickly in the peanut oil. Add the chunks of pineapple and the sliced blanched almonds. Cook over a medium low heat for several minutes. Mix the pineapple juice, vinegar, and sugar together in another pan. Add the salt and cook over a medium heat until the mixture just comes to a boil.

Add a little of the hot mixture to the cornstarch and stir into the rest of the sauce. Cook until thickened and combine with the chicken livers. Cook 1 minute longer and serve over rice.

Serves 4

Chicken Livers with Sherry
Sherry brings this chicken-liver dish to life.

1 pound chicken livers
½ teaspoon salt
1 teaspoon paprika
4 tablespoons butter
1 clove garlic minced
1 small onion minced
½ cup sherry

Cut the chicken livers in half. Dust them with salt and paprika. Melt the butter in a skillet and cook the livers until browned on both sides. Remove them from the skillet. Add the minced garlic and onion to the pan and cook until soft. Return the livers to the pan. Add the sherry, cover, and simmer over low heat for 5 minutes. Serve at once.

Serves 4

Chicken Livers in Madeira
The rich flavor of Madeira enhances this chicken-liver dish.

1 pound chicken livers
3 tablespoons butter
1 tablespoon flour
1 cup Madeira
Salt and pepper to taste

Melt the butter in a skillet and cook the chicken livers for 5 minutes. Remove them from the pan. Stir the flour into the pan over a low heat and when thoroughly blended slowly add the cup of Madeira. Turn heat to medium and let the wine come to a boil, stirring constantly. Add salt and pepper to taste and return the chicken livers to the pan. Heat through and serve at once on crisp buttered toast.

Serves 4

Chicken Livers in Cream

Chicken livers in cream with the pungent flavor of vermouth creates an intriguing nuance.

1 pound chicken livers
4 tablespoons butter melted
3 tablespoons flour
1½ cups warm heavy cream
¼ cup dry vermouth
Salt and pepper to taste

Cut the chicken livers in half and cook them for 5 minutes in the melted butter. Remove them from the pan. Blend in the flour and when blended slowly stir in the warm heavy cream. Cook, stirring constantly, over a medium heat until the sauce is thick and smooth. Add the dry vermouth and cook 1 minute longer stirring until blended thoroughly. Season with salt and pepper and return the chicken livers to the pan. Cook until they are heated through and serve over crisp buttered toast.

Serves 4

Fried Chicken Livers

A most delicious chicken liver dish.

1 slice bacon
2 tablespoons butter
1 onion chopped

6 chicken livers
2 tablespoons flour
½ cup brown gravy
½ cup Madeira
¼ cup sliced mushrooms
Chopped parsley

Fry the bacon in a skillet until crisp. Remove from the pan and set aside. Pour out the bacon fat and add the 2 tablespoons butter to the skillet. Add the chopped onion and cook until lightly colored. Add the chicken livers and brown on both sides. Blend in the flour and add the brown gravy and the Madeira. Mix in well and add the sliced mushrooms. Continue cooking until the mushrooms are soft and the sauce thickened and smooth. Stir occasionally. Crumble up the bacon and sprinkle the crumbled bacon and chopped parsley over the livers. Serve on a hot platter.

Serves 3

Chicken Livers Flambé
This excellent concoction will be a favorite.

1 pound chicken livers
¼ cup butter melted
¼ cup flour
¼ pound sliced mushrooms
4 green onions chopped fine
½ clove garlic minced
¼ cup brandy
1 cup white wine
1 cup heavy cream
¼ cup finely chopped parsley

Dredge the chicken livers with the ¼ cup flour. Melt the butter in a skillet and brown on both sides. Add the sliced mushrooms, green onions, and garlic. Cook 3 minutes. Add the brandy, ignite, and let the flame burn down. Add the white wine and let cook until the liquid is reduced to half its original quantity. Add the heavy cream and cook 1 minute longer, stirring constantly. Serve over crisp buttered toast and sprinkle the finely chopped parsley over the top.

Serves 4

Gascony Chicken Livers

As you will discover when you try this, the flavor of coffee gives the livers a remarkably piquant flavor.

1 pound chicken livers
Salt and pepper
4 ounces fat salt pork
12 small white onions
½ clove minced garlic
1 tablespoon flour
¾ cup burgundy wine
½ cup strong black coffee
French bread
1 clove garlic
Butter

Cut the chicken livers in half and season with salt and pepper. Dice the salt pork and fry out the fat in a heavy skillet. Add the chicken livers and brown on both sides. Remove them from the pan and set aside. Add the small white onions to the pan and let them brown lightly. Add the minced garlic and sprinkle over them the flour. Stir in well. Add the wine and strong black coffee. Stir until sauce is blended and slightly thickened. Cover the pan and simmer for 15 minutes. Return the chicken livers to the pan and simmer for 5 minutes longer.

Slice the French bread thin and rub well with the clove of

garlic. Spread one side with butter and place in an oven until heated and the butter melted. Serve the chicken livers and sauce with the toasted French bread.

Serves 4

Chicken Livers Strogonoff

Chicken livers in sherry and sour cream are a special treat.

1 pound chicken livers
¼ cup butter melted
3 tablespoons minced onion
¼ cup canned sliced mushrooms
2 teaspoons flour
½ cup chicken broth
1 cup sour cream
1 tablespoon sherry
1 tablespoon chopped parsley

Cut the chicken livers in half. Melt the butter in a heavy frying pan and cook the chicken livers and minced onion together over a low heat for 5 minutes being careful not to let the onions brown. Add the sliced mushrooms and stir in the flour. Add the chicken broth and cook until thickened. Add the sour cream and mix in well. Add the sherry and chopped parsley and cook 1 minute longer over low heat.

Serves 4

Chicken Livers en Brochette

En brochette is a good method with chicken livers.

1 pound chicken livers cut in 4 pieces
¾ pound bacon cut into squares
Salt and pepper

Cut the chicken livers into 4 pieces and sprinkle with salt

and pepper. Cut the bacon slices into squares. Alternate the pieces of bacon and liver on metal skewers placing 4 pieces of liver and 5 pieces of bacon on each skewer. Arrange skewers upright on the rack of a broiling pan and bake in a 425° oven until the bacon is crisp. Serve on the skewers.

Serves 4

Chicken Liver Loaf
This Chicken Liver Loaf makes a hearty buffet dish. Also it can be made a day ahead and reheated.

1 pound chicken livers
½ cup dry breadcrumbs
1 onion chopped fine
6 tablespoons soft butter
3 egg yolks well beaten
3 stiffly beaten egg whites
Salt and pepper to taste

Grind the chicken livers in a meat grinder or blend them in an electric blender. Add the dry breadcrumbs, the soft butter, chopped onion, and the 3 well-beaten egg yolks. Mix together and when thoroughly blended add 3 stiffly beaten egg whites. Fold in gently and pour the mixture into a greased loaf pan. Place in a pan of hot water and bake in a 350° oven for 45 minutes or until set. Serve hot.

Serves 4

Chicken Liver Omelet
A perfect omelet filled with flavorful chicken livers will always make a hit.

½ pound chicken livers
1 medium onion chopped
5 tablespoons butter

5 eggs
5 tablespoons water
1 teaspoon salt
⅛ teaspoon pepper
1 tablespoon Madeira

Cut the chicken livers into small pieces. Melt 2 tablespoons butter in a skillet and brown the chicken livers and chopped onions for 10 minutes. Melt the remaining 3 tablespoons butter in another skillet. Beat the eggs lightly with the 5 table-spoons water and the salt and pepper. Pour into the skillet when the butter is sizzling and cook the omelet over a medium heat until it has become set. Tilt the pan several times while cooking to allow all the moisture to run to the sides. Add the Madeira to the chicken livers and onions and when the omelet has become set and shiny pour the chicken livers and onions down the center. Set under a preheated broiler a few seconds to firm up the top. Roll the omelet off the pan onto a warm platter and serve at once.

Serves 3

Chicken Livers with Noodles
A delightful variation of an old favorite.

8-ounce package noodles
2 quarts boiling salted water
2 tablespoons butter
1 pound chicken livers cut into small pieces
1 pound mushrooms sliced
Salt and pepper
¼ teaspoon minced onion
1 tablespoon chopped parsley
Pinch of thyme
1 tablespoon flour
1 tablespoon brandy

3 tablespoons heavy cream
Breadcrumbs

Cook the noodles in 2 quarts boiling salted water about 10 minutes or until tender. Drain them and place them in a buttered baking dish. Melt the butter in a skillet and cook the chicken livers and sliced mushrooms over a medium heat for 5 minutes. Turn heat to low, sprinkle with salt, pepper, minced onion, chopped parsley, and a pinch of thyme. Add the flour and stir in well. Add the brandy and the heavy cream. Stir until smooth over a low heat. Remove from the heat, cover, and let stand a few moments. Put them on top of the noodles in the casserole and sprinkle bread crumbs over the top. Brown in a hot 400° oven. Serve immediately.

Serves 4

Chicken Livers with Rice
Chicken livers with an Italian flavor are very good too.

6 chicken livers
5 tablespoons butter
2 onions chopped fine
½ clove minced garlic
½ cup sliced mushrooms
¾ cup uncooked rice
2 teaspoons tomato paste
2 cups chicken stock
¼ teaspoon oregano
6 tablespoons grated Parmesan cheese

Brown the chicken livers in 4 tablespoons melted butter. When browned remove the chicken livers and brown the onions and garlic in the same pan. Add the mushrooms and cook 2 minutes longer. Add the uncooked rice, the tomato paste, the chicken stock, and oregano. Stir well, cover, and cook until the rice has absorbed the liquid. Add more chicken stock if necessary and stir frequently. Cut the chicken livers into bite-size pieces and mix into the rice. Sprinkle the grated Parmesan cheese over the top and dot with the remaining tablespoon of butter. Place under the broiler just long enough to melt and brown the cheese.

Serves 4

Spaghetti and Chicken Liver Sauce
A delicious and different sauce for spaghetti that does not require long cooking.

12 chicken livers
3 tablespoons butter
2 cloves garlic minced fine
2 onions chopped fine
12 mushrooms chopped fine
1 teaspoon salt
1/8 teaspoon pepper
1/2 teaspoon oregano, basil, thyme
1 tablespoon flour
2 cups tomato hot sauce
3 tablespoons tomato paste
1/4 cup chicken stock
Grated Parmesan cheese
Spaghetti

Brown the chicken livers on both sides in 3 tablespoons melted butter. Remove them from the pan and chop them fine. Add the minced cloves of garlic to the pan along with the chopped onions and cook until the onions begin to brown. Add the chopped mushrooms and cook for 3 minutes longer. Add the salt, pepper, oregano, basil, and thyme. Mix in well. Add the flour and stir into the pan. Stir in the tomato hot sauce, tomato paste, and chicken stock. Stir over the heat until the mixture comes to a boil, then simmer for 10 minutes. Add the chopped chicken livers and simmer 5 minutes longer. Serve over spaghetti with a bowl of grated Parmesan cheese on the side.

Serves 4–6

Chicken Liver Hors d'Oeuvres
Chicken livers as hors d'oeuvres and appetizers add zest to party occasions.

Chicken Livers Sauté
1 cup dry vermouth
½ cup soy sauce
2 tablespoons sugar
1 pound chicken livers cut into pieces
Olive oil

In a saucepan put 1 cup dry vermouth, ½ cup soy sauce, and the sugar. Simmer over a low heat for 3 minutes. Pour the hot sauce over the chicken livers which have been cut into bite-size pieces. Let them marinate for 1 hour at room temperature. Place the chicken livers on a cooky sheet and let them broil for 5 minutes under the broiler heat. Brush well with olive oil several times while broiling. Turn and broil the other side brushing several times with olive oil. Spear with tooth-picks and serve as hors d'oeuvres.

Chicken Liver Spread
½ pound chicken livers
¼ cup butter melted
2 tablespoons brandy
1 medium onion minced fine
4 slices crisp cooked bacon crumbled
1 hard-cooked egg chopped
Salt and pepper to taste

Mayonnaise
Finely ground almonds optional

Melt the butter in a skillet and cook the chicken livers until
they are tender. Pour the brandy over them and set aflame.
When the flame has burned down remove the livers and chop
them fine. Mix them with the minced onion, crumbled bacon,
and chopped hard-cooked egg. Season with salt and pepper to
taste. Add enough mayonnaise to make a smooth paste and
spread on Melba toast rounds. Or keep the mixture firm
enough to shape into small balls, roll them in finely ground
almonds and spear with toothpicks.

Chicken Livers in Bacon
Chicken livers
Bacon slices
Melted butter

Cook the chicken livers in melted butter until tender. Wrap
them in half slices of bacon and fasten them with toothpicks.
Broil under the broiler heat until the bacon is crisp. Serve
very hot, replacing the burnt toothpicks with fresh ones if
necessary.

Chicken Liver and Whiskey Balls
1 cup ground cooked chicken livers
1 tablespoon minced onion
6 hard-cooked egg yolks mashed fine
1 jigger bourbon or Scotch whiskey
Salt to taste
1 cup ground walnuts

Combine the ground chicken livers, minced onion, mashed
egg yolks, and whiskey. Mix to a smooth paste and add salt
to taste. Shape into small balls and roll in the ground walnuts.
Spear with toothpicks to serve.

Chicken Soups

Chicken soup might well be called an international favorite since chickens no longer young from time immemorial have ended up in a soup kettle. A good homemade chicken soup with a savory aroma quite often simmered on the back of the stove in an old-fashioned kitchen. Today homemade chicken soup is still popular. Soup chickens are referred to as stewing chickens and take several hours of cooking time. The soup can also be made with younger and more tender chickens, or with backs, necks, and wings. The cooking time will be much shorter and the tender meat from the younger chicken much tastier. If you don't want to start from scratch there are canned, dehydrated, or frozen soups to choose from with your own personal garnishes and seasonings added to enhance the flavor. Even cream of chicken soup or bisque can be made easily with the help of an electric blender.

Cooks from almost every country in the world have invented ways of utilizing the aging birds of the barnyards and many fabulous recipes have been devised for the soup chicken. There is the *poule au pot* of French fame, the classic borsch of Russia made with beef or chicken stock, Greece with its lemon and egg avgolemone, the Spanish cocido. There is the creamy chicken soup of the Dutch, the Austrian chicken giblet soup with liver dumplings, the refreshing Egyptian sherbah be tarbaya, all the delicately flavored Oriental soups, not to mention our own chicken chowders and gumbos and creamy chicken and corn soups. Then we have our delicious tasty chicken broths to which garnishes of rice, noodles, dumplings, can be added if you wish. There are so many versions of chicken soup and the soups can be hearty or thin, hot or cold, creamy or clear. I have included some of the best known under the various regional and international sections of this book. Therefore, in this chapter I will give you only the basic and interesting soups not included elsewhere.

Chicken Broth
This basic chicken broth can be made into chicken rice soup, chicken noodle soup, or enhanced with small dumplings or chicken meat or any other garnish you wish.

5-pound stewing chicken
3 quarts cold water
1 small onion
1 bay leaf
1 tablespoon chopped parsley
½ teaspoon salt
¼ teaspoon pepper

Put the chicken in a kettle and add the cold water, onion, bay leaf, chopped parsley, and salt and pepper. Bring to a rolling boil and skim off any froth that gathers on the top. Turn heat to low and simmer covered for 3 hours or until the chicken is very tender. Strain the broth if you wish a clear soup. Add a veal knuckle if you want a thick soup that will jell when cold.

Serves 6

Cream of Chicken Soup
A creamy delicious chicken soup may get you a medal.

5-pound stewing chicken cut into pieces
2 tablespoons butter
1 small onion minced

3 carrots scraped and cut into thin rounds
Cold water to barely cover
1 teaspoon salt
1 cup heavy cream
3 egg yolks beaten with 3 tablespoons cream

Melt the butter in a skillet and brown the chicken pieces well on both sides. Remove the chicken to a kettle and add the onion, carrots, cold water to barely cover, and salt. Bring to a boil and remove any skum that may have formed on the top. Lower heat, cover, and simmer for 3 hours or until the chicken is very tender. Add more water if the kettle gets too dry. There should be about a quart and a half of the broth. Remove the chicken and let it cool. Strain the broth. Remove all the chicken meat from the bones and return it to the soup. Add the cup of heavy cream and the egg yolks beaten with cream. Cook over a low heat, stirring constantly, until the soup has thickened slightly. Serve hot.

Serves 6

Chicken Corn Chowder
A tasty and filling chicken chowder.

5-pound stewing chicken
6 cups cold water
1 teaspoon salt
2 packages frozen corn kernels
Pinch of saffron or tumeric if saffron is unavailable
Minced parsley

Place the chicken in a kettle with the cold water and the salt. Bring to a rolling boil and skim off any foam that may have gathered on the top. Reduce heat to low, cover, and simmer for 3 hours or until the chicken is very tender. Remove the chicken and strain the broth. Cut the chicken into small pieces and discard the skin and bones. Return the chicken meat to the broth. Add the corn kernels and cook over a low heat for 15 minutes longer. Stir in the saffron and serve at once with parsley sprinkled over the top.

Serves 6

Chicken Ginger Soup

This is a delicate soup with an enchanting ginger flavor. It can also be made quickly by using canned chicken broth.

5-pound stewing chicken cut into pieces
6 cups cold water
1 teaspoon salt
2 thin slices onion
1 tablespoon grated ginger root
1 tablespoon sherry

Put the chicken in a kettle with the cold water. Bring to a rolling boil, skim off any foam that may have gathered on the top, and turn heat to low. Add the salt and onion slices. Cover and simmer for 3 hours or until the chicken is very tender. Remove the chicken and cut the meat from the bones into small pieces. Strain the broth and return the chicken to the kettle. Add the grated ginger root and sherry. Cook 1 minute longer. Serve at once.

Serves 6

Chicken Mushroom Soup

Always a popular soup.

6 cups chicken broth
¼ cup diced celery
½ small onion diced
½ cup sliced mushrooms

½ cup diced cooked chicken meat
1 egg well beaten
Salt and pepper to taste

Add the diced celery and onion to the chicken broth and cook until tender. Then add the sliced mushrooms and diced cooked chicken meat. Cook over a medium heat for 5 minutes longer. Stir the egg into the soup, mixing steadily, and cook until firm. Serve at once.

Serves 6

Chicken Walnut Soup

A delightful variation—chicken soup for a special occasion.

4 cups chicken broth
¼ cup diced celery
¼ cup chopped parsley
1 egg well beaten
1 tablespoon flour
1 cup heavy cream
Salt and pepper to taste
½ cup ground walnut meats
Whipped cream

Cook the celery and parsley in the chicken broth until the celery is tender. Beat the cream, flour, and egg together until they are smoothly blended. Mix about ½ cup of the hot soup into the egg cream mixture and then slowly add the mixture to the rest of the soup. Cook for 5 minutes stirring continually. Season to taste with salt and pepper. Serve in soup bowls garnished with the whipped cream and sprinkled with the ground walnut meats.

Serves 6

Chicken Curry Soup

After tasting the Pepperidge Farms delightful Chicken Curry Soup, I spent many hours testing and tasting and finally came up with this version which I think is equally good.

3½-pound chicken fryer cut into pieces
Water to barely cover
2 teaspoons salt
1½ cups coarsely diced raw potatoes
½ cup chopped leeks
½ cup chopped white onions
2 teaspoons Schilling's Indian Curry Powder
½ cup chopped red pimientos
2½ cups chicken broth
2 cups heavy cream
½ cup white wine
2 cups chicken meat cut into tiny pieces
Chopped chives

Place the chicken in a kettle with cold water to barely cover. Bring to a rolling boil, skim off any foam that may have gathered on the top, and turn heat to low. Add the salt, cover, and simmer for 3 hours or until the chicken is very tender. Remove the chicken and cut the meat into tiny pieces. Set aside. Put the potatoes, leeks, white onions, curry powder, chopped pimientos, and chicken broth in a saucepan and bring to a boil. Cover and cook until potatoes and onions are tender. Place the cooked vegetables in the container of an electric blender and blend until smooth or press the cooked vegetables through a fine sieve. Add the heavy cream, white wine, 2 cups chicken meat, and salt to taste. Serve either hot or very cold in previously chilled soup bowls. Sprinkle chopped chives on the top of each serving.

Serves 6

Quick Chicken Curry Soup
An exotic soup that is simple to prepare.

1 can condensed cream of chicken soup
1 soup can thin cream
1 teaspoon Schilling's Indian Curry powder
2 tablespoons toasted coconut

In a saucepan combine the condensed cream of chicken soup and the thin cream. Heat just until the boiling point is reached then turn heat to low, add curry powder, and simmer for 5 minutes. Pour into bowls and sprinkle the top of each one with toasted coconut. This is also good served very cold.

Serves 4

Chicken and Wild Rice Soup
As there are several commercial canned Chicken and Wild Rice Soups on the market, it seemed to me in a complete book on cooking chicken that expensive grain, wild rice, most certainly should not be overlooked. After some experimenting, and with the help of my friend Marian Anderson, we eventually came up with one of my favorite recipes for chicken soup.

3-pound chicken cut into pieces
3 quarts chicken stock
1 onion sliced
½ cup chopped celery
1 teaspoon salt
⅛ teaspoon pepper
1 cup wild rice
½ teaspoon thyme
½ teaspoon sweet basil
¼ cup pimientos finely chopped
½ cup sherry
Salt to taste

Place the chicken pieces in a kettle and cover with 3 quarts of cold chicken stock. Add the sliced onion, chopped celery, salt, and pepper. Bring to a rolling boil, skim off any scum that may have gathered on the top, lower heat, and simmer covered for 1½ hours. Remove chicken and cut enough meat from the bones into tiny pieces to make 1 cup. Save the rest for a leftover dish. Bring the kettle of chicken stock again to a boil and add the wild rice, thyme, sweet basil, and chopped pimientos. Lower the heat, cover the kettle, and simmer covered for 35 minutes. Add the 1 cup chicken and the ½ cup sherry. Heat through, salt to taste, and serve.

Serves 6–8

Chicken and Avocado Soup
For a delightfully refreshing summer soup, try this chilled.

1 can extra rich chicken broth
1 soft avocado
Juice of ½ lemon
Thin lemon slices

Peel the avocado and cut into small pieces. Place in an electric blender with the can of chicken broth and blend until smooth. Add the juice of ½ lemon and blend for 1 second longer. Chill in the refrigerator. Serve very cold garnished with thin lemon slices.

Serves 3

Chicken Salads

Salads play an important role in our busy everyday lives. There's a salad to fit every brunch, luncheon, dinner, or buffet. They can be an appetizer, go with a main course, be a meal in themselves, or they can fit in just about anywhere. They can be as simple or as complicated as you want to make them but whatever your choice make absolutely sure the ingredients are strictly fresh and thoroughly chilled, the greens crisp, and the plates cold.

There are so many different types of salads. The tossed salad bowl of greens, delicious when the greens are crisp and fresh and the dressing properly seasoned. There is the appetizer salad served as a first course to whet the appetite without satisfying it. The platter salad served most often at lunch is a complete meal, with individual foods decoratively arranged such as thin-sliced meat or chicken, a mound of crabmeat or shrimp, slivers of cucumber or radishes, thin disks of green pepper, and little rings of green onion with possibly a helping of potato salad on the side. There are the creamy chicken and seafood salads heaped high on tender lettuce leaves, colorful fruit and vegetable salads, molds of aspic or mousse or gelatin on crisp greens.

All these salads should be crisp and fresh, and the dressing, which is the final touch, should be carefully prepared. Most dressings combine oil, vinegar, and seasonings, but the proportions are a matter of individual taste. Just make sure that the vinegar is bland and the oil of the best quality. Herbs are important and they should be used carefully to bring out the flavors in the salad. A wide variety of greens can be used: head lettuce, iceberg lettuce, Belgian endive, romaine, escarole, chickory, spinach, watercress, dandelion greens. Always buy greens that look freshest and wash them thoroughly, separating the leaves with your fingers. Dry them lightly in paper toweling and store them in the refrigerator in a covered plastic bowl until ready to use.

Remember, appearance and texture are very important to the success of a salad and the ingredients should appeal both to the palate and to the eye. They should always be cold, contain an appropriate dressing, and look appetizing. The little extra effort it takes is well worth the trouble.

A chicken salad properly prepared is superb. Serve plump tender chunks of chicken, crisp chopped celery, and well-seasoned mayonnaise on a bed of lettuce with hot rolls or a crunchy bread, and it is a complete meal. Add out-of-the-ordinary ingredients for an unusual touch. A chicken mousse or an aspic served as the main dish at luncheon or supper can become an elegant dish with extra attention. For a more perfect chicken flavor the meat from a roasted chicken is far superior to that of a boiled one because in the roasting no flavor is lost from the chicken into the broth. Another hint is to use lots of chunky chicken pieces and to bind them with a good mayonnaise, preferably a homemade one that has been thinned down with a small amount of chicken broth.

Chicken Salad
Chunky chicken salad is a popular luncheon and supper dish, and when festively decorated it is all the more so.

4-pound roasted chicken cut into pieces
1 cup celery chopped
1 cup green pepper minced
2 teaspoons grated onion
1 cup mayonnaise
¼ cup whipped cream

2 tablespoons chicken broth
1 teaspoon salt
⅛ teaspoon pepper
Pineapple chunks, avocado slices, asparagus tips, stuffed olives,
    hard-cooked egg slices as garnishes
Finely chopped walnuts

Cut the meat from a roasted chicken into large chunks. Chill thoroughly. Combine the chicken chunks, chopped celery, minced green pepper, and grated onion. Mix the mayonnaise and whipped cream with the chicken broth. Blend into the chicken mixture all but ¼ cup of the mayonnaise dressing and chill until serving time. Arrange crisp lettuce on salad plates and place a mound of the chicken mixture on top of the lettuce. Circle with pineapple chunks, avocado slices, asparagus tips, stuffed olives, and hard-cooked egg slices. Spoon on mayonnaise and sprinkle the top with finely chopped walnuts.

Serves 6

De Luxe Chicken Salad
This molded chicken salad makes a wonderful buffet dish.

1 package lemon Jello
1 cup hot water
1 can tomato soup
2 tablespoons red wine
2 6-ounce packages cream cheese
¾ cup mayonnaise
2 cups diced cooked chicken
¼ cup finely chopped celery
½ cup sliced stuffed olives
Crisp lettuce, stuffed olives, tomato wedges

Empty the lemon Jello into a bowl and pour over 1 cup hot

water. Stir until dissolved and place in the refrigerator to cool until partially jelled. Add the tomato soup, red wine, cream cheese, and mayonnaise. Beat until thoroughly blended. Cool in the refrigerator until partially jelled. Add the diced cooked chicken, chopped celery, and sliced stuffed olives. Mix in well and pour the mixture into a mold. Place in the refrigerator until firm. When firm unmold onto a platter and garnish with crisp lettuce, stuffed olives, and tomato wedges.

Serves 6

Chicken Salad Bowl

A tasty chicken salad served in a bowl lined with crisp lettuce leaves and moistened with a flavorful Vinaigrette Sauce will whet anyone's appetite.

2 pounds cooked white chicken meat
Shredded lettuce
Vinaigrette Sauce
Lettuce leaves
Chopped parsley
Chopped green onions
Hard-cooked egg slices
Tomato wedges

Cut the white chicken meat into julienne strips and combine the strips with an equal amount of shredded lettuce. Add enough Vinaigrette Sauce to moisten the salad well. Toss it lightly. Line a salad bowl with crisp lettuce leaves. Place the chicken mixture on top of the lettuce leaves and sprinkle with the chopped parsley and chopped green onions. Garnish with hard-cooked egg slices and tomato wedges.

Vinaigrette Sauce
¼ teaspoon paprika
3 tablespoons tarragon vinegar

6 tablespoons olive oil
1 tablespoon grated onion
1 teaspoon finely chopped chives
1 teaspoon finely chopped parsley
1 teaspoon chopped capers
1 tablespoon cucumber pickle
Salt and pepper to taste

Put the paprika, tarragon vinegar, olive oil, grated onion, chopped chives, parsley, capers, cucumber pickle together in a saucepan and heat thoroughly. Place in the refrigerator and chill. Just before serving add salt and pepper to taste.

Serves 4

Chicken Almond Salad

A chicken salad with slivered almonds and seedless grapes and a tangy orange flavored mayonnaise makes a refreshing change.

4-pound cold roast chicken
1 cup seedless grapes
1 small head lettuce
3 stalks celery chopped
¼ cup slivered toasted almonds
½ orange
1½ cups mayonnaise
Salt and pepper

Cut the chicken meat from the bones into chunks. Shred the lettuce and put it in a bowl with the chopped celery, chicken chunks, seedless grapes, and slivered toasted almonds. Season with salt and pepper. Mix the juice of ½ orange with the mayonnaise and add to the chicken mixture. Mix well and serve very cold.

Serves 6

Chinese Chicken Salad
A chicken salad with the flavor of the East.

½ cup mayonnnaise
Pinch of ginger
2 tablespoons heavy cream
2 cups cooked chicken cut into chunks
½ cup diced celery
½ cup diced green pepper
½ cup chopped green onions
¼ cup diced pimiento
1 5-ounce can water chestnuts sliced
1 tablespoon preserved ginger minced fine
1 3-ounce can Chinese noodles
Crisp lettuce leaves

Combine the mayonnaise with the ginger and heavy cream. In another bowl combine the chicken, celery, green pepper, green onions, diced pimiento, water chestnuts, and preserved ginger. Mix together well and add the mayonnaise. Mix until all the ingredients are well coated. Chill thoroughly. Just before serving add the Chinese noodles and mix in quickly. Serve on crisp lettuce leaves.

Serves 6

Russian Chicken Salad
A flavorful chicken salad with a Russian dressing.

2 cups chicken chunks
1 2-ounce can anchovies chopped
2 hard-cooked eggs chopped
¼ cup chopped green onions
½ cup pickle relish
Shredded lettuce
1 tablespoon lemon juice

1 cup mayonnaise
¼ cup tomato catsup
¼ cup pickle relish
Few drops Worcestershire sauce
Pinch of dry mustard
Crisp lettuce leaves

Mix the chicken chunks, chopped anchovies, chopped hard-cooked eggs, chopped green onions, pickle relish, and shredded lettuce together in a bowl. Add the lemon juice and mix in well. Chill thoroughly. Mix the mayonnaise with the tomato catsup, ¼ cup pickle relish, Worcestershire sauce, and dry mustard. When ready to serve arrange the chicken mixture on crisp lettuce leaves and spoon the Russian dressing over the top.

Serves 6

Chicken Avocado Salad
Avocados stuffed with a luscious chicken mixture are a true delicacy.

3 avocados
Juice of 1 lemon
1 cup diced cooked chicken
3 teaspoons chopped celery
3 teaspoons chopped green pepper
3 teaspoons chopped cucumber
¼ cup whipped cream
¼ cup mayonnaise
3 teaspoons toasted slivered almonds
Paprika

Halve the avocados and remove the seeds. Remove the avocado flesh leaving a thin layer in the shells. Sprinkle with lemon juice to keep the flesh from darkening. Combine the avocado flesh diced with the diced cooked chicken, chopped celery, green pepper, and cucumber. Mix the whipped cream with the mayonnaise and add to the mixture. Stir in the slivered almonds and fill the avocado shells. Sprinkle with paprika. Serve very cold.

Serves 6

Chicken and Fruit Salad
Chicken even in a salad is versatile and it goes beautifully with fruit.

1 orange peeled
15 large grapes
1 apple diced
1 banana sliced
3 pineapple slices cut into small pieces
½ cup toasted slivered almonds
3 cups diced cooked chicken
1 cup mayonnaise thinned with 2 tablespoons pineapple juice
Crisp lettuce

Remove the seeds and membrane from the orange segments and cut them into wedges. Cut the grapes in half and remove the seeds. In a large bowl mix the orange wedges, sliced grapes, diced apple, sliced banana, pineapple pieces, slivered almonds, and diced chicken. Mix well with the mayonnaise thinned with pineapple juice. Chill thoroughly and serve on crisp lettuce leaves.

Serves 6

Chicken and Asparagus Salad
A chicken and asparagus salad is a titillating summer dish.

1½ cups diced cooked chicken
1 cup asparagus tips cut into ½ inch pieces

2 tablespoons minced green pepper
¼ cup shredded cabbage
¾ cup mayonnaise

Mix the diced cooked chicken, asparagus tips, minced green pepper, shredded cabbage, together in a bowl. Add ¾ cup mayonnaise and mix in well. Chill thoroughly and serve on crisp lettuce leaves.

Serves 4

Chicken Salad with Horseradish
This is a chicken salad with a real tang.

3 cups diced cooked chicken
5 hard-cooked eggs coarsely chopped
1 cup sour cream
1 tablespoon lemon juice
½ teaspoon salt
3 tablespoons horseradish
1 tablespoon cold water
Crisp lettuce

Mix the diced cooked chicken with the chopped hard-cooked eggs. Chill. Soak the horseradish in 1 tablespoon cold water. Mix with the sour cream, lemon juice, and salt. Add to the chicken mixture and blend together thoroughly. Serve on crisp lettuce leaves garnished with green onions and radishes.

Serves 6

Curried Chicken Salad
The flavor of curry adds zest to a chicken salad.

3 cups diced cooked chicken
½ cup diced celery
1 cup diced unpeeled tart apples

½ cup coarsely chopped green pepper
3 teaspoons grated onion
¼ cup mayonnaise
¼ cup whipped cream
2 teaspoons curry powder
¼ teaspoon white pepper
½ teaspoon salt
Crisp lettuce leaves

In a large bowl combine the diced cooked chicken, celery, tart apples, green peppers, and grated onion. In another bowl mix the mayonnaise with the whipped cream, curry powder, white pepper, and salt. Mix well and add to the chicken mixture. Stir until well coated. Chill thoroughly in the refrigerator and serve on crisp lettuce leaves.

Serves 6

Curried Chicken Salad in Tomatoes
This is a dish for a special occasion.

3 cups chicken cut into chunks
1 cup diced tart apples
2 teaspoons grated onion
2 teaspoons curry powder
1 cup mayonnaise
¼ cup whipped cream
1½ teaspoons salt
Dash of pepper
½ cup toasted slivered almonds
6 large tomatoes
Lettuce leaves

Mix the chicken chunks, diced apples, grated onion in a bowl. Season with salt and pepper. Blend the curry powder with the mayonnaise and whipped cream. Add to the chicken mixture. Add the toasted slivered almonds and mix in well. Chill thoroughly in the refrigerator. Peel the tomatoes, cut a slice off the stem end, and scoop out most of the tomato pulp leaving a thin shell. Place the tomatoes on lettuce leaves and fill with the curried chicken mixture. Serve very cold.

Serves 6

Chicken Salad in Curried Ring
Another party-type chicken salad.

1 envelope unflavored gelatin
1½ cups chicken broth
1 tablespoon curry powder
½ cup mayonnaise
1 tablespoon minced onion
½ teaspoon salt
½ cup finely chopped celery
¼ cup finely diced pimiento
½ cup mayonnaise
1 tablespoon minced onion
1 tablespoon lemon juice
½ teaspoon salt
Dash of pepper
2 cups diced cooked chicken
½ cup slivered toasted almonds
Crisp lettuce leaves

Soften the gelatin in ½ cup of the chicken broth. Add the curry powder and cook over low heat, stirring constantly until the gelatin is dissolved. Remove from the heat and add the remaining chicken broth, the mayonnaise, minced onion, salt, and chill in the refrigerator until partially set. Fold in the celery, pimiento, and pour into a ring mold. Chill until firm. Combine the ½ cup mayonnaise with the minced onion, lemon juice, salt, pepper, diced cooked chicken, and slivered toasted almonds. Unmold the curry ring onto a serving platter and fill the center with the chicken salad. Garnish with crisp lettuce leaves.

Serves 4

Chicken and Cucumber Aspic
During the hot days of summer what could be more refreshing?

4-pound chicken roasted
1 package lemon Jello
2 cups chicken broth
1 teaspoon Worcestershire sauce
1 teaspoon grated onion
3 large cucumbers
Crisp lettuce
2 hard-cooked eggs

Remove the skin from the chicken and slice the meat from the bones. Dissolve the lemon Jello in the chicken broth and stir until thoroughly dissolved. Add the Worcestershire sauce and grated onion. Chill in the refrigerator until the aspic is partially set. Then pour a thin layer in a long rectangular dish and let it chill in the refrigerator until firm. Place a layer of chicken slices on top of the aspic and cover with a layer of sliced cucumber. Pour on another layer of the aspic and let it jell until firm in the refrigerator. Place another layer of chicken slices over that and a layer of cucumber slices on top. Finish with a top layer of aspic and chill until set in the refrigerator. Unmold on a bed of lettuce and garnish with hard-cooked egg slices.

Serves 6

Chicken Mousse I
This delightful chicken mousse is an ideal buffet dish.

3 egg yolks well beaten
1½ cups milk
1½ tablespoons gelatin
¼ cup cold water
½ cup hot chicken broth
1½ cups cooked ground chicken
Salt and pepper to taste
Dash of cayenne
1 cup heavy whipped cream

Beat the egg yolks until thick and yellow. Gradually add the milk while beating steadily. Place in a saucepan over very low heat and cook, stirring constantly, until the mixture coats a spoon. Soak the gelatin in ¼ cup cold water, then add the hot chicken broth and stir until the gelatin is dissolved. Add the ground cooked chicken and mix in until thoroughly blended. Add to the egg-milk mixture and heat through but do not let it boil. Season with salt, pepper, and a dash of cayenne. Chill and when cold fold in the cup of heavy whipped cream. Turn mixture into a mold and let it set in the refrigerator until firm.

Serves 6

Chicken Mousse II
The flavor of dry vermouth gives this chicken mousse a zingy touch.

2 tablespoons gelatin
2 tablespoons dry vermouth
1 teaspoon lemon juice
½ cup hot chicken broth
2 egg yolks
½ cup mayonnaise

Few drops Tabasco
2 cups cooked diced chicken
¼ cup heavy cream
2 egg whites
Chopped toasted almonds

Put the gelatin, dry vermouth, lemon juice, and hot chicken broth into the container of an electric blender. Cover and blend at high speed for 1 minute. Add the egg yolks, mayonnaise, Tabasco, and diced cooked chicken. Cover and blend at low speed until the chicken is thoroughly blended. Add the heavy cream and blend for 30 seconds more. Beat the egg whites until stiff in a bowl and fold the chicken mixture in gently. Pour into a mold and chill until set. Serve sprinkled with chopped toasted almonds.

Serves 6

Chicken and Almond Mousse
Tarragon and toasted almonds give this chicken mousse a delicate and delightful flavor.

2 envelopes gelatin
¼ cup chicken broth
¼ cup white wine
2 teaspoons tarragon
2 teaspoons parsley
¾ teaspoon white pepper
1 teaspoon salt
½ cup slivered toasted almonds
2 eggs
1 cup chicken broth
2 cups diced cooked chicken
1 cup heavy cream

Put the gelatin, ¼ cup hot chicken broth, white wine, tarragon, parsley, and white pepper into the container of an electric blender. Cover and blend at high speed for 30 seconds. Add salt, slivered toasted almonds, and the 2 eggs. Cover and blend at high speed for 30 seconds longer. Add the chicken broth and the diced cooked chicken. Blend at low speed until thoroughly blended in. Add the heavy cream and blend at low speed until blended in. Pour into a loaf pan and chill until set. Garnish with crisp lettuce and sliced cucumbers.

Serves 6

Salad Dressings

The basic salad dressings are: French dressing, sour cream dressing, mayonnaise dressing, and cooked dressing. All other dressings are variations with the use of herbs, spices, wine, liqueurs, cheeses, sauces, and so on.

Basic French Dressing
¾ cup olive oil
¼ cup vinegar
1 teaspoon salt
½ teaspoon pepper

Combine ingredients in a jar and shake vigorously before using. This basic dressing can be varied with tarragon vinegar, red wine vinegar, wine, spirits, chili sauce, catsup, condensed tomato soup. Herbs, spices, garlic, onions, anchovies or other fish, chutney, grated cheese may be added for extra flavor.

Sour Cream Dressing
1 cup dairy sour cream
2 tablespoons vinegar or lemon juice
1 teaspoon salt
⅛ teaspoon white pepper or dash of cayenne
½ teaspoon sugar

Combine ingredients and serve at once. Tarragon or red wine vinegar may be used. Chopped chives, pickle relish, capers, chili sauce, catsup, Roquefort or bleu cheese may be added for variation.

Mayonnaise
2 egg yolks
½ teaspoon salt
½ teaspoon dry mustard
2 tablespoons vinegar or lemon juice
1 cup olive oil

Put the egg yolks, salt, dry mustard, and vinegar or lemon juice in the glass container of an electric blender. Cover and blend for 5 seconds. Then very slowly, without stopping the blending, pour in the olive oil drop by drop. Don't stop blending until all of the oil has been added and the sauce has become very thick. Correct the seasoning with vinegar or lemon juice and salt.

Variations: Besides varying the mayonnaise with either vinegar or lemon juice you can add anchovies, pickles, chives, herbs, heavy cream, fruit juices, chili sauce, catsup, or any other flavoring you desire.

Cooked Dressing
½ cup vinegar
¼ cup water
¼ cup butter melted
½ teaspoon dry mustard
1 teaspoon salt
1 tablespoon lemon juice
1 teaspoon sugar
4 egg yolks beaten lightly

In a saucepan combine the vinegar, water, melted butter, dry mustard, salt, lemon juice, and sugar. Bring to a boil, then remove from heat and let the mixture cool slightly. Add the 4 beaten egg yolks and place in the top of a double boiler. Cook over a medium heat, stirring constantly, until the sauce thickens. This basic dressing is used with vegetables, meat, fish, or poultry salads. It can be varied as you wish.

Chicken Sandwiches

Sandwiches are always good—easy to fix, easy to eat—whether they are hot or cold. They can be a snack, a main dish, or a party treat, according to how you prepare them. There are savory chicken sandwiches to tempt the appetite at midday, and chicken and other goodies between slices of toast topped with creamy sauces to hit the spot for a Sunday-night supper. There is the classic chicken sandwich smothered with lettuce and lots of mayonnaise; the club sandwich with layers of chicken delicately flavored and bacon, tomatoes, lettuce, mayonnaise; the hot chicken sandwich topped with good chicken gravy. There are many delightful variations of the chicken sandwich and all kinds of tempting spreads and fillings to choose from. You can use any kind of bread for sandwiches—white, whole wheat, rye, pumpernickel, French bread which is delicious, incidentally, with a chicken salad filling as are hard-crusted rolls or buns.

Be sure that the butter is softened—it makes so much easier spreading that way. Butter creamed with mashed anchovies, olives, onion, shrimp, smoked salmon, sardines, is used to fill party sandwiches or as a base for canapés—the butter keeps the base from getting soggy. They can also be used in place of plain butter for extra flavor in making cheese, meat, or chicken sandwiches. Choose fillings to create interesting contrasts in color and texture. Don't skimp on the fillings. Use several thin slices of meat or chicken rather than one thick one. In making a salad-type filling make sure it is not too runny or it is liable to make the sandwich soggy. Use a little

314

minced green onion for extra flavor. Add a finishing touch: olives, pickles, radishes, potato chips—these make a sandwich look so much more appealing.

Both open-faced and closed sandwiches may be made with a rich-flavored sauce poured over the top. An open-faced sandwich may be baked in the oven or toasted or grilled under the broiler. Closed sandwiches may be browned on an electric sandwich grill or in a skillet. French toasted sandwiches are dipped into a batter of milk and egg and fried quickly in hot melted butter. Incidentally, they are delicious.

Sandwiches may be prepared well in advance. They can be wrapped in wax paper or sandwich bags and stored in the refrigerator until wanted. For longer storage, sandwiches may be wrapped in foil or freezer bags and frozen. They may be wrapped together with several pieces of freezer paper separating them to prevent them from sticking. Avoid freezing fillings that contain mayonnaise, cream cheese, or hard-cooked eggs, for none of these freeze well.

Chicken Sandwich

An all-time favorite with everybody is a plain chicken sandwich filled with good slices of white chicken meat and smothered with mayonnaise.

2 slices fresh white bread
Softened butter
Sliced roast chicken breast
Mayonnaise
Lettuce

Spread the bread with softened butter to the very edge. Cover one piece with slices of the roast chicken breast and spread liberally with the mayonnaise. Top with the lettuce and cover with the second piece of bread. Cut diagonally and serve with a garnish of pickles, olives, and potato chips.

Serves 1

Chicken Salad Sandwich
One of the most delicious of sandwiches when the chicken salad is made properly.

1½ cups chopped cooked chicken
⅓ cup finely diced celery
2 teaspoons lemon juice
2 teaspoons minced onion
½ teaspoon salt
Dash of pepper
½ cup mayonnaise
12 slices sandwich bread
Softened butter

Combine the chopped cooked chicken, diced celery, lemon juice, minced onion, salt and pepper. Bind with the mayonnaise, pouring off the excess liquid if it seems too soupy. Chill in the refrigerator until ready to use. Butter the bread generously with the softened butter. Spoon the filling onto 6 slices of the buttered bread and top with the other 6 slices of bread.

Serves 6

Club Sandwich
The classic club sandwich is always a happy choice.

3 slices bread for each sandwich
Softened butter
Lettuce
Sliced cooked chicken
Mayonnaise
3 slices cooked bacon
2 slices tomato

Toast the 3 slices bread for each sandwich. Spread each slice with soft butter right to the edge. Place the sliced cooked chicken on one slice, spread with mayonnaise, and cover with the lettuce. Add the second slice of toast spread side up. Spread with mayonnaise, cover with the cooked bacon and the tomato slices, and top with the third slice of toast spread side down. Fasten at corners with toothpicks and cut diagonally into triangles. Garnish with olives, pickles, and potato chips. Serve at once.

Serves 1

Dagwood Chicken Sandwich

A sandwich filled with chicken, tomato and avocado slices, and with crisp bacon makes a delightful snack at any time.

2 slices bread for each sandwich
Softened butter
Sliced cooked chicken
Sliced tomato
Sliced avocado
Lettuce
Crisp bacon
French dressing

Toast 2 slices of bread for each sandwich. Spread with softened butter right to the edge. Place the chicken meat on one slice, top with the tomato, avocado, and spread with French dressing. Place the crisp bacon on top of that, then the lettuce, and cover with the second slice of toast. Cut diagonally and serve at once.

Serves 1

Open-Face Chicken Sandwich

Another good way to make a chicken sandwich. Roquefort and cream cheese give an extra zest.

2 slices bread
Softened butter
Sliced cooked chicken
Sliced tomato
Mayonnaise
Lettuce
Sliced hard-cooked egg
Roquefort and cream cheese mixture

Spread both slices of bread with softened butter. Cover both slices of bread with lettuce. Place chicken slices on top of the lettuce and spread with mayonnaise. Lay sliced tomato on top of that, then the sliced hard-cooked egg, and spread liberally with Roquefort and cream cheese mixed. This is best eaten with a fork.

Serves 1

French-Toasted Chicken Sandwich
A chicken sandwich French-fried quickly in hot melted butter is delicious.

2 eggs well beaten
1 cup milk
½ teaspoon Worcestershire sauce
⅛ teaspoon salt
8 slices white bread
Softened butter
Chopped cooked chicken moistened with chicken gravy
3 tablespoons butter melted

In a flat bowl combine the well-beaten eggs, milk, Worcestershire sauce, and salt. Spread the bread generously with butter and cover 4 slices with the chopped cooked chicken that has been moistened with chicken gravy. Top with the other 4 slices of bread and dip each sandwich on both sides in the egg-milk mixture. Brown quickly on both sides in hot melted butter in a frying pan.

Serves 4

Monte Cristo Sandwich

The Monte Cristo Sandwich originated in San Francisco. It contains sliced chicken and cheese, which can be Swiss or Cheddar or Monterey jack, and it is dipped in an egg-milk mixture and fried golden brown in butter.

2 eggs well beaten
1 cup milk
1/8 teaspoon salt
6 slices white bread
Softened butter
Sliced roast chicken
Sliced Swiss or Cheddar or Monterey jack cheese
3 tablespoons melted butter

In a flat bowl combine the well-beaten eggs, milk, and salt. Spread the bread generously with softened butter with two of the slices buttered on both sides. Lay the chicken meat on one slice of buttered bread and top with a slice of bread buttered on both sides. On top of this place the cheese and cover with the remaining slice of bread. Repeat for the other sandwich. Dip the sandwiches in the egg-milk mixture and fry in butter to a golden brown on both sides.

Serves 2

Hot Chicken Sandwich

A hot chicken sandwich topped with good chicken gravy is a meal-in-itself sandwich.

2 slices white bread
Softened butter

Thinly sliced roast chicken
Chicken gravy

Spread the 2 slices of white bread generously with butter and place on a serving plate. Heat the thinly sliced roast chicken in the gravy and when hot put the chicken slices on top of the bread and pour over the hot gravy. Good as a main dish served with mashed potatoes and tart jelly.

Serves 1

Hot Puffy Chicken Sandwich
This hot puffy chicken sandwich makes a wonderful change for a luncheon or late supper.

12 slices white bread toasted
Softened butter
Sliced cooked chicken
Sliced Swiss cheese
2 egg whites beaten stiff
¾ cup mayonnaise
Pinch of salt

Spread the toast generously with softened butter. On each slice of toast lay sliced cooked chicken topped by a slice of Swiss cheese. Combine the stiffly beaten egg whites with the mayonnaise and salt. Spoon thickly over each slice of toast. Put under the broiler until the top is puffy and browned.

Serves 6

Hot Swiss Chicken Sandwich
This is a delightful sauce to serve with a chicken sandwich.

4 slices white bread toasted
Softened butter
Slices of hot cooked chicken

½ pound Swiss cheese grated
½ cup dry white wine
½ teaspoon dry mustard
Paprika

Spread the toast with softened butter and put a slice of cooked chicken on top of each one. Place them in the oven to keep warm while making the sauce. Melt the Swiss cheese in the top of a double boiler. Gradually add the wine while stirring constantly. Add the mustard and continue stirring until the sauce just reaches the boiling point. Pour the cheese sauce over the open-faced sandwiches, sprinkle with paprika, and serve at once.

Serves 4

Hot Deviled Chicken Sandwich
Deviled ham gives this sandwich a piquant flavor.

4 slices white or brown bread toasted
Softened butter
1 small can deviled ham
Sliced cooked chicken
1 can condensed mushroom soup
3 tablespoons mayonnaise
¼ cup sherry
Paprika

Spread the toast with softened butter. Over the butter evenly spread the deviled ham. Place a slice of cooked chicken on top of the deviled ham and put the toast slices in a shallow baking pan. Combine the condensed mushroom soup, mayonnaise, and sherry in a saucepan and heat just to the boiling point. Spoon the sauce over the toast and bake in a preheated 400° oven until bubbly about 10 minutes. Sprinkle with paprika and serve at once.

Serves 4

Chicken Sandwich Fillings

There are many sandwich fillings with chicken that are excellent.

Chopped chicken mixed with crumbled crisp bacon and moistened with mayonnaise.

Chopped chicken mixed with chutney.

Minced chicken mixed with cream cheese, mayonnaise or cream, and finely chopped toasted almonds or walnuts.

Chicken and ham slices with cucumber pickle.

Chicken and cucumber slices.

Chopped chicken mixed with pâté de foie gras.

Chicken and cheese slices.

Finely chopped chicken and walnuts moistened with a little mayonnaise and lemon juice.

Chopped chicken mixed with finely chopped toasted almonds, minced onion, and mayonnaise flavored with curry.

Chicken mixed with Roquefort or bleu cheese.

Chicken, tongue, and tomato slices.

Chopped chicken mixed with finely chopped stuffed green olives, green pepper, and hard-cooked egg: moistened with mayonnaise and a few drops Worcestershire sauce.

Chicken and pineapple slices with lettuce and mayonnaise.

Sautéed sliced fresh mushrooms between slices of cooked chicken.

European Chicken

The tour of America draws to a close and now that our chicken has become a seasoned traveler she crosses the Atlantic to travel through the countries of Europe where in each land she finds that chicken has developed a new and exciting personality. She makes France her first stopping point where the chicken has gained immortality in such dishes as Coq au Vin, Poulet Chasseur, and Poulet Vallée d'Auge. On to Spain and the rich strong flavors of Arroz con Pollo and Paella. Italy where the chicken is enriched by the masterpieces of Italian cookery in such dishes as cacciatore, the southern version with tomatoes, garlic, oil, and white wine; the northern with anchovies, garlic, oil, and rosemary. Back across the continent on a gastronomic journey through England, Switzerland, and Holland. Then to Germany, Austria, and Hungary, with the pungent flavor of Chicken Paprika tinted with the scarlet condiment paprika. Scandinavia and the smorgasbord and chickens stuffed with butter and parsley and pot-roasted. On to Russia and that great creation Breast of Chicken Kiev. Thence back across Europe towards the blue Mediterranean and the aromatic flavors of Greece with Chicken Pilaf and Domades, both renowned, and where even a young American chicken should be impressed at the number of masterly creations that Europeans have devised for that most versatile bird, the chicken.

French Chicken

France has an unchallenged superiority in cooking. Classic French cuisine, the Haute Cuisine, is still celebrated and acknowledged as the finest in the world. The great tradition of the chefs in the best restaurants may be above the means of the average family in France today but the French have an inborn appreciation of good food and they still eat marvelously well no matter what income bracket they are in. The cuisine bourgeoise which is the traditional daily fare of the average Frenchman may be modest in comparison to the epicurean dishes cooked with truffles, mushrooms, cream, and fine wines, but some of them have become classics in themselves and they constitute the solid foundation upon which the Haute Cuisine of France was built.

The provinces too have their traditions of cooking. Brittany with its famous coastline offers the widest variety of fish in the world. Brittany is noted for its crêpes—pancakes, almond paste cakes, and the famous candied Angelica. The province of Champagne is known for its great champagne wines but it has never managed to develop a proper cuisine to go along with its wines. The one famous champagne dish is Poulet à la Champagne—chicken cooked in champagne sauce—and chicken is as delightful in champagne as it is in every other sauce.

Normandy, the scene of many a bloody battle, has a cuisine in which cream is lavishly used. The Norman breed of cattle are the best in France and the rich heavy cream is used in cooking in the form of a sauce Normande. Normandy is also the most important apple growing area in France and from

Normandy comes the well-known Calvados. Many dishes are made in Normandy with cider or Calvados which in the other provinces are made with wine.

There are the provinces of Poitou and Vendée and the Charante. There is Anjou, Gascony, and Byronne which is famous for its chocolate. There are Ile de France, Orléans, and Bercy with their rolling hills and fertile valleys. There is Tourlaine where the cuisine of France was developed with its beautiful chateaux, plentiful game, and the famed Loire Valley. And there is Bordeaux with its fabulous wines and wealth. It is a wonderful eating and drinking area and its city of Bordeaux is the second largest in all of France.

Burgundy is a gastronomic paradise with its superb cattle, plentiful game, exquisite fruits and vegetables, abundant fish, and the renowned wines of Burgundy. Its bourgeoise cuisine is equaled by few. Coq au Vin is a Burgundian dish. Beef Bourgogne, which is equally famous, is a beef cooked in red wine sauce accompanied by mushrooms, tiny onions, and small pieces of salt pork. Almost as well known a dish from Burgundy is Escargots de Bourgogne. The snails are considered the best in France, the most favored snails being the ones that feed on grape leaves waxing fat and luscious. And of course from Burgundy too comes the zestful Burgundy wines.

The number of superb chicken recipes in France is overwhelming. Some of the most delicious dishes of French cuisine have been created for chicken. Coq au Vin, Le Poulet Braise Financière, Poulet Chasseur, Poulet Marengo, to name just a few. Chicken Marengo was supposedly invented by a desperate chef in the field the night before the battle of Marengo. Napoleon had a great hunger for chicken, so the story goes, and during his campaigns he ate chicken every night. In fact, in order to have one ready for his master whenever he came in from the field, the chef would put a chicken on to cook at 20-minute intervals. But alas, the night before the Battle of Marengo there were no chickens because for some reason the supplies had been delayed. The desperate chef scoured the countryside until he came up with a tough old rooster which he proceeded to prepare with garlic, wine, mushrooms, tomatoes, and thereafter named in honor of the battle.

The average French housewife often mixes fresh pork or pure pork sausage with eggs and delicate herbs to stuff a big fat fowl. She poaches it with vegetables and a bouquet garni and the result is that Poule au Pot which good King Henri IV promised his subjects that they would enjoy on every Sunday throughout the year. "I want there to be no peasant so poor that he is unable to have a chicken in his pot every Sunday," King Henri declared. The promise, alas, never came true but for some time to come every peasant's mouth watered in anticipation. This Pot au Feu of historic fame is still made quite regularly in France and provides the basis for a whole week of good meals. Or if the French housewife cooks her chicken without a stuffing she will simmer it slowly with rice—le Poule au Riz—and serve it with a Hollandaise sauce. If it happens to be a plump young bird she will simply roast it plain in butter with the buttery juices served separately in a sauce boat.

Bouquet garni is commonly used in French cooking. It consists of 3 or 4 sprigs of parsley, a sprig of thyme, a small bay leaf, and several peppercorns tied together in a cheesecloth bag. Powdered thyme and parsley flakes may be substituted for the fresh sprigs if they are available. The bouquet garni is always discarded before serving.

Coq au Vin
Coq au Vin is that famous French dish served in a wine-dark sauce surrounded by little glazed white onions, mushrooms, and cubes of salt pork. The essential ingredient for Coq au Vin is the chicken's blood, and for that it is almost necessary to buy your chicken alive so you can catch the fresh blood in a bowl the moment it is killed; and to add to it quickly, to prevent the blood from congealing, a few spoonfuls of wine or

vinegar or lemon juice. The blood provides the rich binding for the sauce. The difficulty of obtaining chicken's blood may discourage many people from using this particular recipe. There are, of course, many variations without the blood but the purists, of which I am one, state staunchly that it is the blood that gives the sauce that particular flavor so distinctive in a true Coq au Vin.

1 fat young rooster freshly killed
Blood from the rooster
1½ tablespoons wine vinegar
3 tablespoons brandy
1 teaspoon salt
⅛ teaspoon pepper
4 slices salt pork diced
12 small white onions peeled
2 ounces brandy
1 tablespoon sugar
Bouquet garni
2 cloves garlic mashed
12 small fresh mushrooms
2 tablespoons butter
Burgundy wine

Collect the blood of a freshly killed rooster into a bowl in which you have mixed 3 tablespoons brandy with 1½ tablespoons wine vinegar. Keep stirring so that the blood will not curdle. Set aside. Clean the rooster and cut into serving pieces. Rub the pieces well with salt and pepper and set aside a few hours.

Sauté the diced salt pork with the small white onions until lightly browned in a large heavy pan. Add the chicken pieces and brown well on both sides. When browned add 2 ounces brandy and ignite. When the flame has burned down add a bouquet garni (composed of parsley, thyme, bay leaf, peppercorns, all tied together in a cheesecloth bag so they can be removed before serving). Add a mashed clove of garlic, the small fresh mushrooms, and enough red wine to just cover the chicken. Cover and simmer gently for about 1 hour or until chicken is tender. Arrange the chicken pieces on a hot serving platter along with the onions, salt pork, and mushrooms; keep warm. Discard the bouquet garni. Strain the sauce into another pan and gradually add 2 tablespoons butter. Add the blood mixture to the sauce very slowly, stirring continually over a low heat to prevent curdling. Do not boil. Pour over the chicken and serve at once.

Serves 4

Poulet Marengo
Chicken Marengo—the dish supposedly invented for Napoleon Bonaparte in the field the night before the Battle of Marengo (June, 1800).

2 broilers cut up, each weighing about 2½ pounds
½ cup flour
1 teaspoon salt
⅛ teaspoon pepper
4 tablespoons butter
2 large cloves garlic minced
Bouquet garni
½ cup dry white wine
1 jigger of brandy
6 medium tomatoes cut into pieces
1½ cups sliced fresh mushrooms
Chopped parsley

Add the salt and pepper to the flour and dredge the chicken pieces in the seasoned flour. Brown the chicken in a heavy pan in 4 tablespoons butter turning several times so both sides brown evenly. Add the minced garlic and the bouquet garni.

Add the dry white wine, the brandy, and the tomatoes cut into pieces. Cover the pan tightly and cook over low heat about 45 minutes or until the chicken is tender. Turn the chicken several times during the cooking. After 30 minutes taste for seasoning and add 1½ cups sliced fresh mushrooms. Continue cooking until chicken is tender. Serve on a hot platter sprinkled with chopped parsley.

Serves 6

Poulet Homard Marengo

A variation of Chicken Marengo with lobster—beautiful to behold and *trés harmonieux*.

¼ cup butter melted
4 chicken breasts skinned and split in half
3 finely sliced onions
2 tablespoons flour
½ cup dry white wine
2 tablespoons tomato paste
1 teaspoon salt
¼ teaspoon pepper
½ pound sliced mushrooms
1 pound lobster meat or 2 (10-oz. packages) frozen lobster
    tails
3 ripe tomatoes cut into pieces

Melt ¼ cup butter in a heavy pan. Add the chicken breasts and sauté them with the sliced onions until they are a light golden in color. Sprinkle with 2 tablespoons flour and blend in well. Add ½ cup dry white wine and stir until smooth. Add the tomato paste, salt, pepper, and cook covered for 30 minutes. Add ½ pound sliced mushrooms and cook 15 minutes longer. Meanwhile cook the lobster and remove the meat from the shell. Add the lobster meat to the chicken along with the tomatoes. Simmer 5 minutes longer or until lobster meat and tomatoes are just heated through. Arrange the chicken breasts, lobster, and tomatoes on a large hot platter and top with the sauce.

Serves 6

Poulet Chasseur
Poulet Chasseur (Hunters' Chicken) has many variations.

4-pound chicken fryer cut into pieces
½ cup flour
1 teaspoon salt
⅛ teaspoon pepper
¼ cup butter melted
½ cup dry white wine
2 onions minced fine
1 cup rich brown sauce or gravy
1 pound sliced mushrooms
2 tablespoons butter
2 tablespoons fines herbes

Add the salt and pepper to the flour and roll the chicken pieces in the seasoned flour. Melt ¼ cup butter in a heavy pan and brown the chicken pieces well on both sides. Remove the chicken from the pan and stir in ½ cup dry white wine, scraping up from the bottom to pick up all the browned particles. Add the minced onion and the rich brown sauce or gravy. Simmer a few moments, then return the chicken to the pan. Cover and simmer 45 minutes. Add the sliced mushrooms and simmer another 10 minutes. Remove the chicken to a hot platter and add 2 tablespoons butter to the sauce a little at a time and stirring until smooth. Pour the sauce over the chicken and sprinkle with fines herbes.

Serves 4

Poulet Sauté

A dish typical of the delightful food of the French countryside.

4-pound chicken fryer cut into pieces
½ teaspoon salt
⅛ teaspoon pepper
¼ cup butter melted
4 green onions chopped fine
½ cup canned sliced mushrooms
½ teaspoon flour
½ cup dry white wine
Chopped parsley

Sprinkle the chicken pieces with salt and pepper and place in a frying pan. Cook over a medium heat until they are nicely browned on one side. Turn them over, partially cover the pan, and continue cooking about 40 minutes or until they are tender. Turn once during the cooking. When the chicken is done remove to a platter and keep hot. Add the chopped green onions and the sliced canned mushrooms to the pan. Cook for 2 minutes then blend in the flour. Add the dry white wine and let it boil up, stirring in all the browned particles at the bottom of the pan. Pour over the chicken and sprinkle with chopped parsley.

Serves 4

Poule au Pot

This is as good a variation as any of Henri IV's famous Chicken in the Pot of historic fame.

5-pound roasting chicken
1½ pounds boneless beef roast
1 small knuckle of veal
6 cups cold water
1 onion sliced

2 carrots sliced
2 turnips sliced
2 leeks sliced
1 whole clove garlic
3 whole cloves
6 peppercorns
1 teaspoon salt
1 small head cabbage

Stuffing
Gizzard and heart of chicken
1 cup lean cooked ham
1 cup bread crumbs
2 tablespoons chopped parsley
1 clove garlic minced fine
1 onion minced fine
Salt and pepper to taste
Pinch each of thyme, mace, sage, nutmeg
1 well-beaten egg

Cook the gizzards and heart in water to cover until they are tender. Drain and put through a food chopper along with the lean cooked ham. Add the bread crumbs, chopped parsley, minced garlic, minced onion, salt, pepper, and a pinch each of thyme, mace, sage, and nutmeg. Mix well, then blend in the well-beaten egg. Fill the cavities of the chicken with this stuffing, or sew the openings tightly, and truss.

Place the stuffed chicken in a large kettle with the boneless beef and the knuckle of veal. Add 6 cups cold water and bring slowly to a boil. Simmer for 1½ hours over a very low heat. Add the onion, carrots, turnips, leeks, garlic, cloves, peppercorns, salt, and small head of cabbage. Bring quickly to a boil again then let simmer 2 hours longer adding more water if necessary.

Place the chicken and meat in a large deep platter with the vegetables. Pour over some of the broth, serving the rest in a gravy boat on the side. Serve with mayonnaise, prepared mustard, horseradish mixed with sour cream, and pickles.

Serves 6

Poule au Riz

When a French housewife cooks her chicken without a stuffing she simmers it slowly with rice—the Chicken with Rice of Louis Philippe—and it is also an excellent dish. Be sure to serve Hollandaise with this.

4-pound chicken cut into pieces
Chicken stock to cover
2 onions coarsely chopped
2 cloves garlic finely minced
1 teaspoon salt
⅛ teaspoon pepper
Bouquet garni
1 cup white rice
Flour
Hollandaise sauce

Put the chicken pieces in a kettle and cover with the chicken stock. Add 2 onions coarsely chopped, the finely minced garlic, salt, and pepper. Add a bouquet garni composed of parsley, thyme, bay leaf, peppercorns, all tied together in a cheesecloth bag so they can be removed before serving. Simmer covered over low heat for 1 hour. Then add 1 cup rice slowly so as not to stop the boiling. Recover and when the chicken is tender and the rice done, drain the liquid into another saucepan to thicken it. Allow 1 tablespoon flour for each cup of liquid, adding some of the lot liquid to the flour and mixing it to a thin paste, then pouring it back into the sauce. Bring to a boil and stir until smooth. Arrange the rice on a hot serving platter with the chicken on top. Pour over the sauce. Serve with a side dish of Hollandaise.

Serves 6

Poulet Poche
This is a great favorite in France.

4-pound roasting chicken
Neck and giblets
3 carrots sliced
2 onions halved
2 leeks halved
3 sprigs green celery leaves
Bouquet garni
1½ teaspoons salt
12 peppercorns
2 quarts water

Sauce
2 tablespoons butter
1½ tablespoons flour
1½ cups chicken stock
Salt and pepper to taste
Dash of nutmeg
1 egg yolk
¼ cup heavy cream
Juice of ½ lemon

Truss the chicken and put it in a large kettle with the neck and giblets, sliced carrots, halved onions, halved leeks, green celery leaves, and a bouquet garni. Add the salt, peppercorns, and 2 quarts cold water. Bring to a boil quickly, lower the heat, and simmer for 1½ hours or until the chicken is tender. Remove the chicken and keep hot while preparing the sauce.

Sauce: Melt 2 tablespoons butter in a saucepan and blend in the flour. Gradually add the hot chicken stock and stir over low heat until the sauce is smooth and thick. Season to taste with salt and pepper and a dash of nutmeg. Continue cooking over low heat for 10 minutes longer. Beat the egg yolk with the cream and add a little of the hot sauce. Stir slowly into the rest of the sauce. Add the juice of ½ lemon and cook 1 minute longer being careful not to let the sauce boil. Serve the sauce with the chicken.

Serves 4

Poule au Pot Béarnaise
Chicken in the Pot Béarnaise is another delicious way with chicken.

4-pound chicken fryer cut into pieces
¼ cup butter melted
½ clove garlic minced fine
½ pound bacon diced
2 ounces brandy
3 carrots sliced thin
12 small white onions
3 tomatoes cut into pieces
Bouquet garni
1½ cups red wine
1 teaspoon salt
⅛ teaspoon pepper

Melt the butter in a heavy Dutch oven. Add the chicken pieces, minced garlic, and diced bacon. Cook until the chicken is well browned on both sides and the bacon is crisp. Add the brandy and ignite. When the flame has burned down add the sliced carrots, small white onions, tomatoes, and bouquet garni. Add the red wine and the salt and pepper. Cover and simmer for 2 hours or until the chicken and vegetables are tender. Serve from the casserole.

Serves 4

Poule au Pot Farcie

This Poule au Pot Farcie, which is a stuffed boiled chicken, is typically French. The recipe was given to me by a French ski instructor who instructed at Mt. Shasta Ski Bowl several years ago.

5-pound roasting chicken
¼ cup butter melted
½ onion chopped fine
4 slices finely ground ham
2 tablespoons chopped parsley
1 teaspoon salt
¼ teaspoon pepper
½ teaspoon thyme
1 cup toasted breadcrumbs
1 egg well beaten
2 tablespoons Madeira
¾ cup ground toasted almonds
2 large cabbage leaves
Boiling salted water
3 carrots sliced
6 leeks cut into pieces
3 turnips sliced

Sauté the finely chopped onion in the melted butter and when they begin to get colored add the finely ground ham, chopped parsley, salt, pepper, thyme, and toasted breadcrumbs. Remove from the heat and mix with the well beaten egg, Madeira, and ground toasted almonds. Put half of this stuffing in the chicken cavity and sew the opening tightly closed. Make a ball of the rest of the stuffing and roll it up tightly in the cabbage leaves. Roll the cabbage leaves in a piece of cheesecloth and sew it tightly. Place it in a large kettle with the chicken and cover with boiling salted water. Add the carrots, leeks, and turnips and simmer covered for 1½ hours or until the chicken is tender.

Serve the chicken on a platter surrounded by the vegetables. Remove the cabbage balls from the cheesecloth and cut into slices. Serve on the platter with the chicken and vegetables.

Serves 4

Poulet à la Vallée D'Auge

Chicken à la Vallée D'Auge is the classic chicken dish from Normandy. It is a wonderful dish and the apples and Calvados for which Normandy is famous give it its unique flavor. If Calvados is not available, good applejack may be substituted.

4-pound chicken fryer cut into pieces
¼ cup butter melted
¼ cup Calvados
2 small onions minced
1 tablespoon chopped parsley
2 tart apples, peeled, cored, and chopped
¼ teaspoon thyme
½ cup Calvados
½ cup heavy cream
Salt and pepper to taste

Melt the butter in a heavy skillet and brown the chicken pieces well on both sides. Pour ¼ cup Calvados over the chicken and ignite. When the flame has burned down add the minced onion, chopped parsley, chopped tart apples, thyme, and remaining ½ cup Calvados. Blend in well, cover the pan, and cook over a low heat about 40 minutes or until the chicken is tender. Remove the chicken to a heated platter. Add the heavy cream to the sauce in the pan and blend in well. Heat the sauce but do not let it boil. Season to taste with salt and pepper. Pour the sauce over the chicken and serve at once.

Serves 4

Poulet au Riesling
Another example of the sublime artistry of the French.

4-pound chicken fryer
1/4 cup butter melted
3 tablespoons chopped chives
1/2 cup mushrooms sliced
1 cup Riesling wine
1 small can pâté de foie gras
1/2 cup heavy cream
1 egg yolk well beaten
Salt and pepper to taste

Melt 1/4 cup butter in a heavy skillet and brown the chicken pieces well on both sides. Add the chopped chives, sliced mushrooms, and Riesling wine. Let the wine come to a boil then add the can of pâté de foie gras. Stir continually until the pâté de foie gras melts. Cover and simmer over a low heat for 40 minutes or until the chicken is tender. Remove the chicken to a serving platter and keep hot. Add the heavy cream wthich has been beaten with the egg yolk to the sauce and cook until it is just heated through, stirring constantly. Salt and pepper to taste and pour the sauce over the chicken.

Serves 4

Poulet au Claret
The French have a knack for subtly flavoring with wine.

4-pound chicken fryer cut into pieces
1 teaspoon salt
1/8 teaspoon pepper
1/2 cup flour
1/4 cup butter melted
12 small white onions
12 small mushroom caps

½ pound diced Canadian bacon
1½ cups claret wine
Bouquet garni
1 tablespoon flour
½ cup hot chicken stock

Add the salt and pepper to the flour and roll the chicken pieces in the seasoned flour. Melt ¼ cup butter in a heavy pan and brown the chicken pieces well on both sides. Add the mushroom caps, small white onions, and diced Canadian bason. Continue cooking for 5 minutes, stirring frequently. Add the claret wine and a bouquet garni. Simmer covered over a low heat for 40 minutes or until the chicken is tender. Remove the chicken, mushroom caps, small white onions, and diced Canadian bacon to a platter and keep hot. Turn heat to high and let sauce reduce to about ½ cup. Blend the flour into the sauce and mix until smooth. Slowly add the chicken stock and stir over a low heat until thickened. Remove the bouquet garni and pour the sauce over the chicken and vegetables. Serve at once.

Serves 4

Poulet au Porto
An extravagant dish but perfectly delightful.

4-pound chicken fryer cut into pieces
½ cup flour
1 teaspoon salt
⅛ teaspoon pepper
¼ cup butter melted
2 tablespoons minced onion
½ clove garlic minced
½ cup port wine
½ cup dry white wine
2 ounces brandy
2 ounces kirsch

1 cup heavy cream
2 egg yolks

Add salt and pepper to the flour and roll the chicken pieces in the seasoned flour. Melt ¼ cup butter in a heavy pan and add the minced onion and garlic. When lightly colored add the chicken pieces and brown quickly on both sides. Add the port wine, dry white wine, brandy, and kirsch. Ignite and let the flame burn down. Continue cooking over a low heat, turning the chicken pieces frequently, about 40 minutes longer or until the chicken is tender. Remove the chicken to a serving platter and keep hot. Mix the heavy cream with the 2 egg yolks and add to the sauce in the pan. Stir over a low heat until the sauce is thickened and smooth being careful not to let it boil. Pour the sauce over the chicken and serve immediately.

Serves 4

Poulet au Porto II

Years ago my father first tasted this dish in a charming little restaurant in the famed Loire Valley and brought the recipe back with him. This is the recipe, or at least this is the way my father always prepared it.

4-pound chicken fryer cut into pieces
1 teaspoon salt
⅛ teaspoon pepper
¼ cup butter melted
1 cup sliced mushrooms sautéed in 2 tablespoons butter
1 cup port wine
1½ cups heavy cream
2 egg yolks

Rub the chicken pieces well with the salt and pepper. Melt the butter in a heavy Dutch oven and when it is hot add the chicken pieces. Turn each piece over as it begins to brown and then place the Dutch oven in a preheated 375° oven, basting frequently with the butter in the bottom of the pan. Cook for 30 minutes, then add the sliced mushrooms which have been sautéed in 2 tablespoons butter. Add the port wine, cover, and continue cooking for 15 miutes or until the chicken is tender. Remove the chicken to a serving platter and keep hot. Blend the heavy cream with the egg yolks and add to the sauce. Cook over a low heat, stirring constantly, until the sauce has thickened. Pour over the chicken and serve.

Serves 4

Poulet en Feuilleté

Several years ago my husband and I were invited to an unforgettably delicious dinner by Lucille Cammarier who is a typical French housewife. The main course dish was poulet en feuilleté, which is a stuffed chicken roasted in a blanket of pastry. Lucille told me that French cooks often roast a chicken this way to keep in the juices and flavor. Anyway the result was pretty impressive. Here is the recipe.

Pastry dough large enough to cover a chicken completely
4-pound roasting chicken
½ cup ground sausage meat
2 tablespoons brandy
1 can pâté de foie gras
1 teaspoon fines herbes
Salt and pepper
Soft butter
2 ounces warm brandy

Mix the ground sausage meat, 2 tablespoons brandy, pâté de foie gras, together and stuff into the cavity of the chicken. Sew up the openings and truss. Rub the chicken well with salt and pepper and the soft butter. Place in an open roasting pan and brown in a 425° oven for 20 minutes. Roll out the pastry dough very thin and lay the chicken on top of it. Then wrap the rest of the pastry around the chicken so that it is completely covered. Crimp the edges firmly and cut a vent hole in the top to let the steam escape. Insert a roll of foil in the hole to serve as a chimney. Place the pastry covered chicken back in the oven and let it continue cooking for 1 hour longer, pouring a tablespoon of brandy through the chimney every 15 minutes as it cooks.

Serves 4

Poulet Sauté aux Champignons
A French dish of herb-flavored chicken and fresh mushrooms.

4-pound chicken fryer cut into pieces
1 teaspoon salt
¼ teaspoon pepper
¼ cup butter melted
½ pound fresh mushrooms sliced
½ onion chopped fine
1 teaspoon thyme
1 tablespoon flour
1 cup white wine
¼ cup cream
1 egg yolk
Chopped parsley

Sprinkle the chicken pieces with salt and pepper. Melt the butter in a heavy pan and brown the chicken slowly until it has turned a deep golden color on both sides. Remove the chicken and keep hot. Add the fresh sliced mushrooms and the chopped onion to the pan and cook until soft but not browned. Add the thyme and flour and when blended return the chicken to the pan. Add the white wine, cover the pan, and cook over a low heat for 40 minutes or until the chicken is tender. Remove the chicken to a serving platter and keep hot. Add the cream and egg yolk to the pan and cook over a low heat a few minutes. Pour the sauce over the chicken and sprinkle with parsley.

Serves 4

Poularde Devil
A variation of another famous French specialty.

4-pound roasting chicken
4 slices fat salt pork diced
4 artichoke bottoms diced
2 tablespoons butter

Fry out the diced salt pork in a heavy braising kettle. Truss the chicken and brown it in the kettle well on all sides. Add a small amount of water, cover, and let the chicken braise about 40 minutes or until tender. Add more water if necessary. Sauté the diced artichoke bottoms in butter until they are tender. Place the artichoke bottoms in the bottom of a serving platter and pour a little of the chicken liquor over them. Carve the chicken and place on top. Serve what remains of the chicken liquor separately in a sauceboat.

Serves 4

Poulet à la Champagne
From the province of Champagne comes this most elegant chicken dish.

4-pound chicken fryer
1 teaspoon salt
⅛ teaspoon white pepper
4 tablespoons soft butter
1 pint champagne
2 pints heavy cream

1 medium onion chopped fine
½ clove garlic minced fine
¼ cup mushrooms minced fine
2 tablespoons minced parsley
1 bay leaf crushed
Pinch of thyme
1 cup champagne
2 tablespoons butter

Rub the chicken well with the salt and white pepper. Then rub the chicken well all over with the 4 tablespoons soft butter. Truss and place in an open roasting pan. Pour over the pint of champagne and roast in a 350° preheated oven allowing 25 minutes to the pound or until the chicken is tender. Baste often with the drippings and turn the chicken frequently so that all sides are well browned. When the chicken is done remove it to a serving platter and keep hot. To the drippings in the pan add the 2 pints of heavy cream, chopped onion, minced garlic, minced mushrooms, minced parsley, crushed bay leaf, and thyme. Cook over a medium low heat until the sauce has reduced to one third of its original quantity. Strain the sauce through a fine sieve and add the 1 cup champagne. Cook over a low heat, adding the 2 tablespoons of butter a little at a time and stirring constantly until all the butter has been blended in. Pour over the chicken and serve at once.

Chicken Cynthia à la Champagne
Ernie's is one of the great restaurants of San Francisco and one of their best dishes I think is chicken Cynthia à la champagne. This is not the exact recipe but in my estimation it comes pretty close.

4-pound chicken fryer cut into pieces
1 teaspoon salt
⅛ teaspoon pepper

¼ cup butter melted
1 cup champagne
1 ounce orange bitters
¼ cup orange juice
1 cup chicken broth
½ cup heavy cream
2 oranges peeled and separated into wedges
1 cup seedless white grapes skinned
2 egg yolks
2 tablespoons heavy cream

Add the salt and pepper to the flour and roll the chicken pieces in the seasoned flour. Melt ¼ cup butter in a heavy pan and brown the chicken pieces well on both sides. Add the cup of champagne, orange bitters, and orange juice to the pan. Cook over a medium low heat until the sauce has reduced to half. Add the chicken stock, cover, and simmer over low heat for 30 minutes or until the chicken is tender. Remove the chicken to a serving platter and keep hot. Add ½ cup heavy cream to the sauce in the pan along with the orange wedges and the seedless white skinned grapes. Stir over a low heat until heated through. Add 2 egg yolks which have been beaten with 2 tablespoons heavy cream and cook over low heat, stirring constantly, 1 minute longer. Pour the sauce over the chicken and serve at once.

Serves 4

Poulet Bonne Femme
A typical French recipe.

4-pound chicken fryer cut into pieces
1 teaspoon salt
¼ teaspoon pepper
½ teaspoon poultry seasoning
½ cup flour

6 slices bacon minced
4 tablespoons butter
3 medium onions chopped
2 cups hot chicken stock
2 cloves garlic minced
2 tablespoons chopped parsley
3 potatoes cooked and diced

Add the salt, pepper, and poultry seasoning to the flour and roll the chicken pieces in the seasoned flour. In a heavy frying pan combine the minced bacon and the butter and cook until the butter has melted. Add the chicken pieces and brown them well on both sides. Remove the chicken and add to the drippings in the pan the chopped onions. Sauté them until they are golden in color. Return the chicken to the pan and add 2 cups hot chicken stock, the minced garlic, and the chopped parsley. Cover and simmer for 40 minutes or until the chicken is tender. Add the diced cooked potatoes and cook 5 minutes longer. Serve immediately.

Serves 4

Poulet en Papillote
There are many variations of this dish but I think you will agree that this version is a very good one.

4 large chicken breasts
½ teaspoon salt
⅛ teaspoon white pepper
¼ cup flour
4 tablespoons butter melted
4 thin slices Swiss cheese
4 large mushroom caps
1 cup Marsala
1 teaspoon butter
1 cup rich brown sauce

4 thin truffle slices
4 large sheets foil or parchment paper

Season the chicken breasts with salt and pepper and dredge with the flour. Brown them well on one side in the melted butter. Turn over, lay one thin slice of Swiss cheese on top of each breast, and let them cook over a medium heat for about 25 minutes longer or until they are tender. Remove them from the pan and keep hot. In another pan sauté the mushroom caps in 1 teaspoon butter for 5 minutes. Set aside. Add the Marsala to the pan the chicken was cooked in. Stir up all the brown particles from the bottom and cook over a medium heat until the sauce has reduced to half. Add the rich brown sauce, blend in well, and continue cooking until the sauce is reduced to about 1 cup. Place each chicken breast on a square of parchment or foil, cheese side up. Top with a slice of truffle and a mushroom cap. Spread over each breast 2 tablespoons of the sauce. Bring the edges of the foil together and make a double fold, tucking in the edges securely. Just before serving time place them in a hot 400° oven and allow them to heat through—about 10 minutes. Serve the breasts in the foil.

Serves 4

Poulet Flambé
Another French triumph.

4-pound chicken fryer cut into pieces
6 tablespoons butter
¼ cup cognac
½ cup heavy cream
2 egg yolks
Salt and pepper to taste

Melt 4 tablespoons butter in a heavy pan and brown the

chicken well on both sides. Lower the heat and continue cooking the chicken for 30 minutes longer or until it is tender, turning frequently during the cooking. Pour over the cognac and ignite. When the flame has burned down add the heavy cream which has been beaten with the 2 egg yolks. Scrape from the bottom to blend in all the brown particles at the bottom of the pan. Add the 2 remaining tablespoons of butter bit by bit, stirring constantly, and cooking over a medium low heat until the sauce is thickened and smooth. Season to taste with salt and pepper. Remove the chicken to a hot serving platter and pour the sauce over it.

Serves 4

Poulet au Veronique
A delicious dish with herbs, white wine, and seedless white grapes.

4-pound chicken fryer cut into pieces
1 teaspoon salt
⅛ teaspoon pepper
½ cup flour
¼ cup butter melted
½ cup dry white wine
½ cup chicken broth
1 teaspoon fines herbes
½ bay leaf crushed
1 egg yolk
1 tablespoon cream
2 cups seedless white grapes skinned

Add the salt and pepper to the flour and roll the chicken pieces in the seasoned flour. Melt the butter in a heavy pan and brown the chicken well on both sides. Add the dry white wine, chicken broth, fines herbes, and crushed bay leaf. Cover the pan and simmer over low heat about 40 minutes or until the chicken is tender. Add the egg yolk which has been beaten with the cream and blend in well. Add the skinned seedless white grapes and cook over a low heat until just heated through, stirring constantly. Serve the chicken in a hot platter with the sauce poured over it.

Serves 4

Chaud-Froid de Poulet
Try this dish with the chicken served cold with the sauce. It's different.

4-pound roasting chicken
1 quart chicken stock
½ teaspoon salt
½ cup butter
4 egg yolks
¼ cup lemon juice
¼ cup heavy cream
Salt and white pepper

Truss the chicken and place it in a kettle with the chicken stock and ½ teaspoon salt. Cook covered over a low heat for 1½ hours or until the chicken is tender. Meanwhile make the sauce. Melt the butter in the top of a double boiler; beat the egg yolks with the lemon juice until thick and yellow; add to the melted butter beating constantly with a wire whisk over a low heat until thick and smooth. Add the cream and beat constantly over a low heat for 5 minutes. Cool to lukewarm.

When the chicken is done cut it into serving pieces. Dip each piece of chicken twice in the sauce to coat it thoroughly and place it on a rack to cool. Serve the chicken cold with the extra sauce on the side in a bowl.

Serves 4

Poulet en Gelée

This chicken dish with its syrupy jellied aspic is a French masterpiece. It should be served very cold.

4-pound chicken fryer
2 quarts chicken stock
¼ cup tarragon vinegar
2 tablespoons chopped fresh tarragon or 1 teaspoon dried
Salt to taste
Tarragon leaves

Truss the chicken and place it in a kettle with the chicken stock, tarragon vinegar, and chopped fresh or dried tarragon. Cover the kettle and cook over a low heat for 1 hour or until the chicken is tender. Remove the chicken and let it cool. Cut into serving pieces. Strain the broth through a piece of cheesecloth and season to taste with salt. Chill in the refrigerator until it has reached a syrupy jellied consistency. Spoon over the chicken pieces until they are well coated. Decorate each piece of chicken with tarragon leaves and pour the rest of the syrupy aspic around the chicken. Chill thoroughly in the refrigerator before serving.

Serves 4

Spanish Chicken

Spain, the home of the brave bulls, of Flamenco, of high-walled turreted castles seen dimly across arid plains like the scenes in an El Greco painting. Spain, a country of violent contrasts with the wet-green hills of Galicia, the high snow-capped peaks of the Pyrenees, the sun-scorched plains of Andalusia, the arid grandeur of Castile, and an infinite variety in its savory distinctive cuisine.

Many peoples have conquered Spain throughout its history and they have contributed to its culture, customs, and traditions. The Phoenicians in 600 B.C. landed on Spanish soil and planted the first olive trees. The olive trees flourished and grew; by the time Rome was at the height of its glory Spain was already famed for both olive oil and sherry. The heritage from the Moors gave Spanish cooking distinctive characteristics. The Moors brought the spices of the Orient—saffron, cumin, cinnamon; they planted orange, lemon, peach, and almond trees. The contribution from the Spanish conquistadors should not be overlooked either. They brought back from the New World tomatoes, pimientos, chocolate, and vanilla which were all adopted into Spanish cooking with enthusiasm.

The food in various parts of Spain varies greatly. The Basques who live in a forested mountainous region have a cuisine that is very Celtic in character. The Basques have claimed residence in Spain longer than any other people and their language is like no other known tongue. Catalonia, in the northeastern part of Spain, has a cuisine that very much resembles that of southern France. The Catalonians have remained more independent throughout their history than any other region of Spain. The Moors were only there for a very short time and consequently there is very little Moorish influence to be seen in Catalonia.

Castile, in central Spain and the furthest removed from the sea, uses very little seafood and specializes in meat dishes. The arid, harsh Castilian country was the birthplace of most of the conquistadors as well as the birthplace of the noblemen who plotted with Queen Isabella to overthrow the Moors. The Castilians cuisine is simple and hearty, strong of garlic and onions with the embellishment of few sauces and little subtlety.

It is Andulusia which was influenced the most by the Moors and the food even today has an almost Oriental flavor. Seville, that highly romantic city with its Moorish overtones, is the stronghold of the bullfight and of Flamenco, that hot-cold, passionate, rhythmic music, the high-pitched singing with Arabic overtones so much like the muezzin calling the faithful to prayer across the desert. There is Granada, the last city lost to the Moors, and the place most beloved by them in all of Spain. It is in Granada that the startlingly beautiful Alhambra stands and there the Moorish influence is so strong one can almost imagine turbaned Moorish ghosts lurking in its lovely courtyards.

Most Spanish dishes are savory and satisfying and they are not hot and spicy like most South American food. There is Arroz con Pollo, and the famed Paella, originally named for the pan in which it was cooked; Gazpacho, an icy summer soup; Tortilla, the name of a peasant omelet which is a fat little cake filled with potatoes and onions and chopped meat or chicken. There are provocative little appetizers served with sherry; wonderful seafood stews, delectable almond and sherry flavored desserts; intricate rice dishes first introduced by the Moors. Olive oil and garlic are used profusely in Spanish cooking as well as tomatoes and onions which form the foundation for many sauces. Sherry is used often for flavoring and saffron, considered the world's most expensive spice, with its intriguing Oriental flavor plays an important role in Spanish food. It is saffron that gives Arroz con Pollo its subtle flavor. Chickens are very popular in Spain and incidentally, pollo refers to a young tender chicken whereas gallina is the name for a more mature stewing hen.

Arroz con Pollo

The famous Spanish Arroz con Pollo with all its subtle and piquant blending of flavors.

2 tablespoons olive oil
1 clove garlic crushed
1 large onion diced fine
4-pound chicken fryer cut into pieces
½ cup flour
1 teaspoon salt
¼ teaspoon pepper
2 large tomatoes diced
1 green chili pepper diced fine
1 bay leaf
2 whole cloves
2 tablespoons minced parsley
¼ teaspoon powdered saffron
2 cups hot chicken broth
1 cup rice
1 cup Madeira

Heat 2 tablespoons olive oil in a large frying pan and when hot add the crushed clove garlic and the finely diced onion. Cook until the onion is a light golden color. Add the chicken pieces which have been seasoned with salt and pepper and dredged with flour. Brown them well on both sides. Add the diced tomatoes, the diced green chili pepper, bay leaf, whole cloves, parsley, and ¼ teaspoon powdered saffron dissolved in 2 cups hot chicken broth. Cover the pan closely and let the chicken simmer gently for 15 minutes. Add 1 cup rice slowly so as not to stop the boiling. Cook about 25 minutes or until the chicken and rice are tender. Add the Madeira and blend in lightly. Serve the golden chicken and rice on a large hot platter.

Serves 4

Paella

Paella is probably the best known of all Spanish dishes outside of Spain. The word paella originally referred to the special metal pan traditionally used for making rice dishes in the area around Valencia.

1 pound shrimps shelled and deveined
1 medium lobster
12 little-neck clams
2 onions chopped
2 cloves garlic minced
3 tablespoons olive oil
4-pound chicken fryer cut into pieces
1 cup canned tomatoes
Salt
3 tablespoons chopped parsley
1 chorizo (highly seasoned Spanish pork sausage) cut into
     pieces
½ cup diced pimiento
½ teaspoon saffron dissolved in ⅓ cup hot chicken broth
½ teaspoon oregano
1 package frozen green peas
1½ cups uncooked rice
2 cups hot chicken broth
Pimiento strips

Cut the lobster meat into chunks. Shell and devein the shrimps. Wash the clams. Set aside. Heat the olive oil in a heavy Dutch oven or paella pan and sauté the onions and garlic for 1 minute. Add the pieces of chicken and cook until browned on both sides. Add the tomatoes, salt, chopped parsley, and cook until the chicken is tender about 30 minutes. Add the chorizo, diced pimientos, saffron dissolved in ⅓ cup hot chicken broth, oregano, clams, and shrimp. Simmer for 2 minutes and add the rice along with 2 cups hot chicken broth. Bring to a boil, cover, turn heat to low, and cook for 15 minutes. Uncover, stir the rice well into the mixture, and add the lobster chunks and peas. Cook about 10 minutes longer or until peas are tender. Season with salt to taste and serve from the casserole garnished with strips of pimiento.

Serves 6

Chicken Valenciana
Pollo el Valenciana—this is a very delightfully flavored chicken rice dish from Valencia.

¼ cup olive oil
1 minced clove garlic
4-pound chicken fryer cut into pieces
½ cup flour
1 teaspoon salt
¼ teaspoon pepper
1 cup minced ham
3 tablespoons minced onion
½ cup pimientos cut into strips
1 tablespoon paprika
1 tablespoon parsley
⅛ teaspoon saffron
2 cups uncooked rice
1 cup white wine
2 cups hot chicken broth
1 can tomato hot sauce
¼ cup slivered toasted almonds

Heat the olive oil in a heavy frying pan and when hot add the minced clove of garlic. Cook for 1 minute. Add the salt and pepper to the flour and roll the chicken pieces in the seasoned flour, then put the chicken pieces in the pan with the garlic and brown well on both sides. Remove the chicken and set aside. Add the minced ham to the pan along with the minced onion, pimiento strips, paprika, parsley, saffron, and uncooked rice. Cook over low heat letting the rice heat up slowly, stirring constantly, until the rice is well coated and shows a yellowish tinge. Combine the white wine with the hot chicken broth and the tomato sauce. Pour it slowly over the rice, mix in well, and transfer the mixture to an ovenproof casserole. Return the chicken to the pan and add the slivered toasted almonds. Cover tightly and bake in a preheated 350° oven for 40 minutes or until the chicken is tender and the rice has absorbed all the liquid. Serve from the casserole.

Serves 4

Chicken in Wine Sauce
My mother who was part Spanish had a real flair for Spanish cooking. This is one of her specialties.

¼ cup olive oil
4-pound chicken fryer cut into pieces
1 large onion chopped
1 clove garlic minced
¼ teaspoon saffron
1 bay leaf crushed
¼ teaspoon thyme
1 heaping tablespoon flour
1 cup dry white wine
1 package frozen peas
½ cup chopped pimiento
1 teaspoon salt
¼ teaspoon pepper

Heat the olive oil in a heavy frying pan and when hot add the chicken pieces, chopped onion, minced garlic, saffron, bay leaf, and thyme. Cook over a medium heat until the chicken is well browned on both sides. Blend in a heaping tablespoon flour and when well mixed add the dry white wine. Cook until the sauce has thickened slightly, stirring constantly. Add the package of peas, chopped pimiento, salt, and pepper. Cover and cook over a low heat for 30 minutes or until the chicken is tender.

Serves 4

Catalan Chicken

Pollo Catalan—a chicken dish from the region of Catalonia that is more like the cuisine of southern France than of Spain.

4-pound chicken fryer cut into pieces
¼ cup butter melted
1 teaspoon salt
¼ teaspoon pepper
12 small white onions
½ cup chicken stock
4 medium tomatoes peeled and diced
½ cup sliced mushrooms which have been sautéed in
2 tablespoons butter
¼ cup sliced green olives
¼ cup chopped pimientos
1 heaping tablespoon flour
½ cup dry white wine

Melt the butter in a heavy frying pan and brown the chicken well on both sides. Add salt, pepper, the small white onions, chicken stock, and the diced tomatoes. Cover and cook over a low heat for 30 minutes or until the chicken is tender. Add the mushrooms which have been sautéed in butter, the sliced green olives, and chopped pimientos. Cook 5 minutes longer.

Remove the chicken and white onions and keep hot. Add the flour to the sauce and cook until thickened. Add the white wine and cook 5 minutes longer, stirring constantly. Pour the sauce over the chicken and white onions and serve immediately.

Serves 4

Spicy Chicken Fricassee
Pepitoria de Gallina—spicy chicken fricassee—is a tantalizingly flavored chicken fricassee.

1 stewing chicken cut into pieces
½ cup flour
1 teaspoon salt
¼ teaspoon pepper
3 tablespoons olive oil
1 large onion chopped fine
¾ cup almonds blanched
2 cloves garlic
¼ teaspoon saffron
½ teaspoon salt
2 hard-cooked egg yolks mashed
1 cup chicken stock
½ cup green stuffed olives sliced

Add the salt and pepper to the flour and roll the chicken pieces in the seasoned flour. Heat the olive oil in a skillet and when hot add the chicken pieces. Brown well on both sides. Remove the chicken to a casserole. Add the chopped onion to the skillet and cook until tender but not browned. Add the onion to the chicken in the casserole. Grind the almonds in a mortar with the garlic and when they are reduced to a paste add the saffron, salt, and mashed egg yolks. Gradually stir in the chicken stock and add this mixture to the chicken in the casserole. Cover and cook in a preheated 350° oven for 1½ hours or until the chicken is tender. The last 5 minutes of cooking time add the sliced green stuffed olives.

Serves 4

Chicken Aragon Style
Pollo à la Argonesa—chicken Aragon style—is a delicately spiced Spanish chicken. The cumin gives it a faint Oriental flavor.

4-pound chicken fryer cut into pieces
3 Spanish onions sliced
1 clove garlic minced
¼ cup olive oil
½ cup chicken broth
½ cup sherry wine
½ teaspoon salt
¼ teaspoon cumin
4 tablespoons heavy cream
1 tablespoon chopped parsley

Heat the olive oil in a heavy frying pan and when hot add the chicken pieces. Brown well on both sides. Add the sliced onions and the minced clove of garlic. Cook until lightly colored, then add the chicken broth, sherry wine, salt, and cumin. Cover and cook over low heat 40 minutes or until the chicken is tender. Remove the chicken to a serving platter and keep hot. Pour the sauce and onions into an electric blender and blend until the sauce is smooth. Return to the pan and cook until heated through. Add the cream and mix in well. Pour the sauce over the chicken and sprinkle with the chopped parsley.

Serves 4

Chicken Fricassee Seville Style

Gallina à la Sevillana—tomatoes, olives, and sherry keep this a Spanish dish.

4-pound chicken fryer cut into pieces
1 teaspoon salt
1/8 teaspoon pepper
1/4 cup olive oil
1/2 cup pimientos chopped
1 medium onion chopped
2 cloves garlic minced
2 tomatoes peeled and chopped
1/2 cup chicken stock
1/4 cup sherry
12 large green olives sliced

Add the salt and pepper to the flour and roll the chicken pieces in the seasoned flour. Heat the olive oil in a large frying pan and brown the chicken well on both sides. When browned remove the chicken to a casserole. Pour off all but 2 tablespoons olive oil from the frying pan. Add the pimientos, onion, and garlic. Cook until soft. Add the chopped tomatoes, chicken stock, and sherry. Cook for 10 minutes over a medium heat. Add the sliced green olives and pour the sauce over the chicken in the casserole. Cover and bake in a preheated 350° oven for 40 minutes or until the chicken is tender.

Serves 4

Fried Chicken Marinated in Sherry Sauce

Pollo Frito al Jerez—the Moorish influence is very pronounced in this delightful fried chicken marinated in Spanish sherry.

4-pound chicken fryer cut into pieces
1/3 cup good Spanish sherry
1/4 cup olive oil

1 teaspoon lemon juice
1 teaspoon cumin
¼ teaspoon coriander
2 cloves garlic crushed
1 teaspoon honey
1 teaspoon salt
¼ cup flour
4 tablespoons olive oil

Place the chicken pieces in a deep bowl and cover with a mixture of the sherry, olive oil, lemon juice, cumin, coriander, crushed garlic, honey, and salt. Marinate for 24 hours, turning the chicken several times. When ready to cook dredge the chicken with flour and fry in 4 tablespoons hot olive oil. Cook over a medium heat turning the chicken frequently, until it is crisp and tender about 40 minutes.

Serves 4

Chicken Casserole in Sherry
Gallina en Cazuela al Jerez—this Spanish favorite makes an excellent casserole dish.

4-pound chicken fryer cut into pieces
½ teaspoon salt
¼ cup flour
3 tablespoons olive oil
¼ cup blanched almonds
1 onion minced
2 cloves garlic crushed
1 chorizo (hot Spanish pork sausage) cut in pieces
¼ cup pimiento diced fine
1 teaspoon tomato puree
½ cup sherry
¾ cup chicken stock

Sprinkle the chicken pieces with the salt and roll in the flour.

Heat the olive oil in a heavy frying pan and when hot brown the chicken pieces well on both sides. Remove the chicken from the pan and place in a greased casserole. Add the blanched almonds to the frying pan and toast lightly. Add them to the chicken in the casserole. Add the onion, garlic, chorizo, and pimiento to the frying pan and cook until the onion is soft. Add the tomato puree, sherry, and chicken stock. Stir in well and cook over a low heat for 3 minutes. Pour the sauce over the chicken in the casserole. Bake uncovered in a preheated 350° oven for 30 minutes or until the chicken is tender. Serve from the casserole.

Serves 4

Chicken with Garlic Sauce
Gallina en Pebre—a chicken roasted in garlic sauce is very Spanish and the garlic gives this chicken an enticing flavor.

5-pound roasting chicken
½ cup butter
1½ teaspoons salt
½ teaspoon white pepper
3 cloves garlic minced
2 tablespoons lemon juice
1 bay leaf
2 tablespoons minced parsley
1 cup chicken broth
1 egg yolk beaten lightly with 1 tablespoon cream

Make a paste of the butter, salt, white pepper, minced garlic, and lemon juice. Spread thickly over the chicken. Truss. Place the chicken in a shallow roasting pan and roast in a preheated 375° oven allowing 20 minutes to the pound until the chicken is tender. Baste frequently. After the first 30 minutes add the bay leaf, minced parsley, and chicken broth. Continue roasting, basting frequently with the sauce. When the chicken is done remove it to a heated platter and keep hot. Strain the gravy into a pan. Add the egg yolk which has been beaten lightly with 1 tablespoon cream and cook over a low heat a few moments, stirring constantly, until the sauce is slightly thickened. Pour into a gravy boat and serve with the chicken.

Serves 6

Chicken in Madeira
Another great Spanish dish is Pollo al Madeira.

4-pound chicken fryer cut into pieces
¼ cup butter melted
1 medium onion chopped
1 bay leaf
½ stick cinnamon
Pinch of powdered cloves
½ teaspoon salt
⅛ teaspoon pepper
¼ cup Madeira
½ cup chicken stock
½ cup chopped pimientos

Melt the butter in a heavy frying pan and add the chicken pieces. Brown well on both sides. When well browned add the chopped onion, bay leaf, stick cinnamon, powdered cloves, salt, pepper, Madeira, and chicken stock. Cook uncovered over a medium low heat for 10 minutes. Add the chopped pimientos and continue cooking 30 minutes longer or until the chicken is tender. If sauce is too liquid turn heat to high and reduce the sauce. Serve chicken in the sauce.

Serves 4

Pepitoria of Chicken
Gallina en Pepitoria—a typical sherried saffroned casserole.

4-pound chicken fryer cut into pieces
3 tablespoons olive oil
1 large onion chopped fine
1/4 cup blanched almonds
3 cloves garlic
1 tablespoon minced parsley
1/2 teaspoon salt
2 hard-cooked egg yolks
1/2 cup chicken stock
1/2 cup sherry
1/4 teaspoon saffron
15 pimientos stuffed green olives sliced

Heat the olive oil in a heavy frying pan and when hot add the chicken pieces. Brown well on both sides. Remove to a greased casserole. Add the onion to the frying pan and cook until soft but not browned. Add to the chicken in the casserole. Brown the blanched almonds in the frying pan. Remove them and blend them in an electric blender until fine. Add the garlic and parsley to the blender and blend until fine. Add the hard-cooked egg yolks, chicken stock, sherry, and saffron. Blend until thoroughly mixed. Salt to taste and add to the chicken in the casserole. Cover and bake in a preheated 350° oven for 40 minutes or until the chicken is tender. Add the sliced pimientos stuffed green olives the last 15 minutes of cooking time.

Serves 4

Italian Chicken

The Italian cuisine is extensive and varied and Italy has had a great gastronomic history from the ancient days of Rome, with all of its extravagances of rich living and excesses in gluttony, to the rise of the Renaissance out of the Dark Ages when Italy became a leader in music, painting, sculpture, architecture, and literature. It was then that the art of fine cooking was developed in Italy and the Italians gave the same glowing enthusiasm to their cookery as they did to their other achievements. Italian cooking rose to such a degree of perfection that it became renowned throughout Europe. It was not, in fact, until 1533 when Catharine DeMedici arrived at the court of Henri II bringing her own special army of Florentine chefs along that French culinary history began.

Italy is one of the largest countries in Europe and its boot-shaped peninsula stretches southward to the Mediterranean at one end and northward to the high mountain peaks of the Alps at the other. From one region to the other there is a marked difference in the cooking style. There is a difference in the geography which leads to differences in dress, in mode of life, and in eating habits as well. There is a wealth of raw materials of every kind in Italy but each region has its own specialties in foods and its own eating habits. Rome with its ancient buildings and historic background has a varied and sophisticated style of food which contrasts with Sicily's fondness for sweet desserts. The northern plains with its level land and rich fertile soil features rich pasta sauces, famous Parmesan cheese, and butter. The Adriatic seacoast supplies Venice with superb seafood. The blue bay of Naples with Vesuvius in its background teems with fish. Lombardy's Milanese style of cooking is completely different. In southern Italy one finds more garlic and tomatoes used. In the district around Bologna where herds of cattle graze in the fertile fields, milk and cream and butter are used in almost every dish.

Despite the variety in Italian dishes from region to region spaghetti in one of its various forms has been the daily bread of Italians for centuries except in parts of northern Italy where palenta and risette are popular. There is almost no end to the type of sauces that have been devised to accompany it. Boiled and stewed meats, tomatoes and herbs such as marjoram, thyme, bay leaf, oregano, basil, rosemary are used in almost every Italian recipe. Cheese too is used extensively: Gorgonzola, which is very pungent and flavorful, Incastrate, a Sicilian grating cheese from cow's and ewe's milk combined; Mazzarella, a moist, white, unsalted cheese; Fortina, a nippy white Cheddar; Romano, an off-white grating cheese; Parmesan, a mild yellow cheese usually grated as seasoning; and Ricotta, a fresh unsalted cottage cheese.

Italy possesses a rich heritage of traditional dishes which are purely national. In fact Italy shows less trace of any outside influence in their cooking than any other country in Europe. Italians like good food and they like good wine to accompany it. Wine, usually a mild burgundy or chianti, almost takes the place of drinking water in many Italian households. Most Italians believe that in order to get the full enjoyment out of eating pastas and sphaghetti, with their accompanying spicy flavorful sauces, a tart red wine is a necessity.

Chicken also plays a leading part in many Italian dishes. It appears in many forms, one of the most well-known dishes being, of course, Chicken Cacciatore (hunter style) which is the classic chicken dish of Italy. There are two types of cacciatore. The southern Chicken Cacciatore in which tomatoes are always added; and the northern and central Chicken Cacciatore in which rosemary, anchovies, vinegar, oil, and herbs are used. Chicken Cacciatore is one of Italy's most famous and most traditional dishes. It is both colorful and appetizing and it is also one of the best known to most Americans.

Chicken Cacciatore

Pollo alla Cacciatore—Chicken, Hunter Style—one of the best known Italian dishes. This is the northern and central regions traditional Cacciatore in which rosemary, anchovies, vinegar, oil, and other herbs are used.

3 tablespoons olive oil
3 cloves garlic chopped fine
4-pound chicken fryer cut into pieces
½ cup flour
½ teaspoon salt
⅛ teaspoon pepper
½ cup dry white wine
2 tablespoons vinegar
½ teaspoon rosemary
½ teaspoon sweet basil
Pinch of thyme
Pinch of oregano
½ teaspoon chopped parsley
4 anchovy fillets chopped fine
3 or 4 tablespoons white wine

Add the salt and pepper to the flour and roll the chicken pieces in the seasoned flour. Heat the olive oil in a heavy pan with the garlic and when hot add the chicken pieces. Brown the chicken over a medium high heat and when well browned on both sides add the white wine and the vinegar. Add the rosemary, sweet basil, thyme, oregano, and chopped parsley. Mix in well and turn heat to low. Add the chopped anchovies and 3 or 4 more tablespoons white wine. Mix in well, cover, and simmer about 45 minutes or until the chicken is tender and the sauce is thick and rich.

Serves 4

Chicken Cacciatore II

Pollo alla Cacciatore—Chicken, Hunter Style—this is the cacciatore from the southern region in which tomatoes are always added. A favorite of southern Italians this dish has many variations.

4-pound chicken fryer cut into pieces
1 teaspoon salt
¼ teaspoon pepper
½ cup flour
½ cup olive oil
1 large onion chopped
1 large clove garlic chopped fine
¼ cup chopped carrot
2 cups tomatoes fresh or canned
½ cup green pepper chopped
Bouquet garni
½ cup dry white wine

Add the salt and pepper to the flour and roll the chicken pieces in the seasoned flour. Heat the olive oil in a heavy pan and when hot add the chicken pieces. Brown well on both sides. Add the onion, garlic, carrot, tomatoes, green pepper, and the bouquet garni. Cover tightly and simmer the chicken and vegetables together over a low heat for 30 minutes. Add the dry white wine to the liquid in the pan. Recover and continue cooking 15 minutes longer or until the chicken is tender. Remove the bouquet garni and serve the chicken hot with the sauce.

Serves 4

Chicken Cacciatore Maddalena

Pollo alla Cacciatore Maddalena—another version of cacciatore with celery and mushrooms, and the addition of Marsala to give an enticing flavor.

4-pound chicken fryer cut into pieces
2 tablespoons olive oil
1 teaspoon chopped parsley
½ clove garlic chopped fine
½ cup chopped celery
½ cup chopped mushrooms
1 teaspoon salt
⅛ teaspoon pepper
2 bay leaves crushed
½ cup Marsala
2 tablespoons Marsala

Heat the olive oil in a heavy frying pan and add the chicken pieces. When well browned on both sides add the parsley, garlic, celery, mushrooms, salt, and pepper. Cook for 2 minutes over medium heat and then add the bay leaves and the Marsala. Cook over a medium low heat until the wine has almost evaporated about 30 minutes approximately. Add 2 more tablespoons Marsala, cover, and cook over a low heat for 10 minutes longer or until the chicken is tender.

Serves 4

Chicken Cacciatori Alla Martinotti

According to my friend Joe Martinotti, who was born in Italy, his wife makes the best chicken cacciatore of all. Here is the recipe he wrote out for me.

4-pound chicken fryer cut into pieces
1 teaspoon salt
¼ teaspoon pepper
½ cup flour
¼ cup butter melted
¼ cup ham cut into thin strips
1 cup fresh mushrooms sliced
½ cup chicken broth
½ cup dry white wine

Add the salt and pepper to the flour and roll the chicken pieces in the seasoned flour. Melt ¼ cup butter in a heavy frying pan and brown the chicken pieces well on both sides. When well browned add the ham cut into thin strips, the sliced mushrooms, and ½ cup chicken broth. Turn heat to low, cover, and simmer for 40 minutes or until the chicken is tender. Turn heat to high, uncover, and add the dry white wine. Cook on high heat until the sauce is almost evaporated, stirring constantly. Serve at once.

Serves 4

Chicken alla Diavola

You will find this one very delicately flavored.

4-pound chicken fryer cut into pieces
½ teaspoon salt
⅛ teaspoon pepper
¼ cup butter melted
½ cup dry white wine
¼ cup brandy

Rub the chicken pieces with the salt and pepper. Melt the butter in a large heavy frying pan and when hot add the chicken. Brown well on both sides. Add the dry white wine and cook over a medium heat about 40 minutes or until the wine has absorbed. Turn the chicken frequently while cooking. When the wine has absorbed and the chicken is tender pour the brandy over the chicken. Turn heat to high and cook 1 minute longer.

Serves 4

Chicken Rizotto alla Piemontaise

Pollo Rizotto alla Piemontaise—In the northern part of Italy a Rizotto is as essentially Italian as spaghetti and pasta. And a Rizotto properly made is indeed a delightful accompaniment to chicken.

1 medium onion chopped fine
½ cup butter
½ pound white rice
3 cups chicken stock
Salt and pepper to taste
1 can tomato paste
½ cup grated Parmesan cheese
Pinch of saffron
4-pound chicken fryer cut into pieces
1 teaspoon salt
¼ teaspoon pepper
½ cup flour
¼ cup butter melted
Grated Parmesan cheese
Grated Swiss cheese
Italian style tomato sauce

Fry the chopped onion in ½ cup melted butter and when soft add to it the ½ pound of white rice. Turn heat to low and let the rice heat up slowly, stirring constantly until it is well saturated with butter. Add more butter if necessary to keep it moist. Then moisten the rice with the chicken stock, adding more each time it becomes absorbed, about 7 or 8 times approximately. Salt and pepper to taste. Add the tomato paste, grated Parmesan cheese, and a pinch of saffron. Transfer the Rizotto to a casserole, cover, and cook 30 minutes in a preheated 350° oven.

For the chicken—add the salt and pepper to the flour and roll the chicken pieces in the seasoned flour. Brown well on both sides in ¼ cup melted butter. Then cook over a medium heat about 40 minutes or until the chicken is tender, turning frequently while cooking. When tender drain on absorbent paper and arrange the chicken pieces around the Rizotto. Serve grated Parmesan and Swiss cheese on the side along with an Italian style tomato sauce.

Serves 4

Chicken alla Tetrazzini
This great Italian dish with chicken and spaghetti was created expressly for the opera singer Luisa Tetrazzini.

5-pound roasting chicken cut into pieces
Boiling water
1 teaspoon salt
1 pound mushrooms sliced thin
3 tablespoons butter
3/4 pound spaghetti
4 tablespoons butter
2 cloves garlic minced
4 tablespoons flour
1 2/3 cups heavy cream
1/3 cup sherry
3/4 cup grated Parmesan cheese
Salt to taste

Place the chicken pieces in a kettle with boiling water to cover. Add salt and simmer covered 1 1/2 hours or until the chicken is tender. Allow the chicken to cool in the broth. Then remove the skin and bones and cut the meat into large pieces. Put the skin and bones back in the broth and let them cook until the broth has reduced to 2 cups. Strain.

Sauté the thinly sliced mushrooms in 3 tablespoons butter for 5 minutes. At the same time cook the spaghetti in salted boiling water until barely tender.

Melt 4 tablespoons butter with the minced garlic. Blend in the flour and add the hot strained reduced chicken broth a little at a time. Cook, stirring constantly, until the sauce is smooth and thick. Add the heavy cream and the sherry. Cook over a low heat until the cream and sherry are well blended into the sauce. Put a layer of spaghetti in the bottom of a buttered casserole. On top of that put a layer of the chicken meat and cover that with a layer of the mushrooms. Sprinkle heavily with grated Parmesan cheese and cover with some of the cream sauce. Repeat until the casserole is full, ending with the cream sauce and a final coating of grated Parmesan cheese over the top. Bake in a hot 450° oven until the cheese is bubbling and browned.

Serves 8–10

Chicken with Mushrooms

Pollo con Funghi—Chicken with Mushrooms—the combination of chicken with mushrooms and garlic and onions and wine is very popular in northern Italy.

4-pound chicken fryer cut into pieces
1 pound fresh mushrooms sliced
2 cloves garlic minced
1 large onion sliced
1 teaspoon salt
¼ teaspoon white pepper
6 tablespoons olive oil
1 tablespoon butter melted
½ cup sherry

Sprinkle the chicken with salt and pepper. Melt the butter in a skillet and add 4 tablespoons olive oil and the minced garlic. Cook 1 minute then add the chicken and brown well on both sides. Turn heat to low and continue cooking for 30 minutes, turning the chicken once. In another saucepan sauté the sliced onion in 2 tablespoons olive oil until soft. Add the sliced mushrooms and continue cooking over low heat for 5 minutes. Add the onion and mushrooms to the chicken, cover, and cook over low heat 10 minutes longer or until the chicken is tender. Add the sherry. Boil up quickly and serve at once.

Serves 4

Chicken Oregano
Pollo Oreganato—parsley, oregano, and lemon juice give this dish a satisfying Italian flavor.

2 broilers split in half
1 teaspoon salt
¼ teaspoon pepper
1 teaspoon chopped parsley
2 teaspoons oregano
⅓ cup olive oil
¼ cup lemon juice
1 clove garlic minced

Rub the salt and pepper well into the broiler halves. Mix the olive oil, parsley, oregano, lemon juice, and garlic together. Brush the chicken generously with this mixture. Put the broilers on a broiler pan 6 inches from the heat skin side down. Broil about 20 minutes basting often with the marinade. Turn and broil skin side up 20 minutes longer or until the chicken is brown and tender. Baste often with the marinade. When done pour the remainder of the marinade over the chicken and serve hot.

Serves 4

Chicken Florentina
Pollo alla Florentina—Chicken as prepared in Florence—this dish is simple and beautiful.

4-pound chicken fryer cut into pieces
¾ cup olive oil

4 tablespoons lemon juice
1¼ teaspoons salt
½ teaspoon black pepper
1 cup flour
2 eggs beaten lightly
2 tablespoons minced parsley

Mix together ¼ cup of the olive oil, the lemon juice, salt, and pepper. Marinate the chicken in this mixture for several hours, turning occasionally. Drain. Roll the chicken in flour, dip in the beaten eggs, and then roll in the flour again. Heat the remaining ½ cup olive oil in a frying pan and brown the chicken well on both sides over a medium high heat. Turn heat to medium, continue cooking about 40 minutes longer or until the chicken is tender, turning frequently while cooking. Drain on absorbent paper and serve at once.

Serves 4

Chicken alla Romano
A Roman specialty is this chicken dish with its zestful, robust flavor.

4-pound chicken fryer cut into pieces
½ teaspoon salt
⅛ teaspoon pepper
2 tablespoons olive oil
3 slices prosciutto cut into small pieces
1 clove garlic minced fine
1 teaspoon rosemary
1 cup red wine
2 cups canned tomatoes
¼ cup red wine

Heat the olive oil in a large heavy frying pan and when hot add the prosciutto and the chicken. Sprinkle with salt and pepper and brown the chicken and prosciutto well on both sides. Add the garlic, rosemary, and 1 cup red wine. Cook over a medium heat until the wine has evaporated. Add the tomatoes. Continue cooking until the sauce has cooked down to about one third and the chicken is tender. Add ¼ cup red wine, stir in well, and turn heat to high. Cook on high heat until the sauce has cooked down to a very small amount. The sauce should be thick, dark, and rich.

Serves 4

Breast of Chicken Bolognese Style
Filetti di Pollo Bolognese—this is a chicken dish for the gods.

4 chicken breasts
1 teaspoon salt
¼ teaspoon pepper
½ cup flour
4 tablespoons butter melted
4 slices cooked ham
½ cup sliced mushrooms sautéed in 1 tablespoon butter
½ cup grated Parmesan cheese
¼ cup chicken broth

Remove the skin from the chicken breasts and pound them to flatten them. Add the salt and pepper to the flour and roll the chicken breasts in the seasoned flour. Melt the butter in a heavy frying pan and brown the chicken well on both sides. Cut 4 slices cooked ham the same size as the chicken breasts and place 1 slice on each breast. Arrange the sautéed mushrooms on top of the ham and sprinkle with the Parmesan cheese. Add the chicken broth, cover, and simmer about 30 minutes or until the chicken is tender. Place under the broiler a few moments to brown the cheese.

Serves 4

Breast of Chicken alla Ravieri

Filetti di Pollo alla Ravieri—Breast of Chicken in Cheese Sauce. Parmesan and Fontinella make a delightful sauce for a chicken dish. The Fontinella is a sharp white Cheddar cheese produced in Wisconsin. My butcher, George Theobolt, claims that it is better than the Fontina cheese imported from Italy, and from which Fontinella is derived. If it is not available use any strong white Cheddar.

4 chicken breasts
½ teaspoon salt
⅛ teaspoon pepper
3 tablespoons butter
1 tablespoon flour
½ cup milk
¼ cup grated Parmesan cheese
¼ cup grated Fontinella cheese

Pound the chicken breasts with a mallet to flatten them like a cutlet. Rub them well with salt and pepper. Melt 2 tablespoons butter in a frying pan and add the chicken breasts. Brown them well on both sides. Set aside. Melt 1 tablespoon butter in another pan, blend in the flour, and slowly add the milk. Cook over a medium heat, stirring constantly, until the sauce is thickened and smooth. Add the grated Parmesan and the grated Fontinella and stir until melted. Place the chicken breasts in a shallow baking pan and spread each piece with the cheese sauce. Brown in the oven and serve immediately. Serves 4

Buttered Chicken

Pollo al Burro is a truly splendid chicken dish.

5-pound roasting chicken
2 tablespoons olive oil
3 cloves garlic

½ cup butter
4 sprigs parsley
1 teaspoon salt
⅛ teaspoon pepper

Rub the cavity of the chicken with ¼ cup butter. Insert the sprigs of parsley and 2 cloves garlic. Truss. Rub the outside of the chicken well with the remaining ¼ cup butter and the salt and pepper. Place the chicken in a shallow roasting pan and add the olive oil and 1 clove of garlic to the pan. Roast in a preheated 375° oven allowing 20 minutes for each pound until the chicken is tender. Baste frequently with the juices in the pan. The last 20 minutes of cooking time turn the chicken over so the underside will brown nicely too.

Serves 4

Stuffed Chicken
Pollo Imbottite—a savory Italian stuffing makes this a zestful and satisfying dish.

5-pound roasting chicken
1 teaspoon salt
¼ teaspoon pepper
3 tablespoons brandy
1 gizzard and liver
½ cup prosciutto slices chopped fine
2 tablespoons olive oil
Pinch of thyme
2 cloves garlic minced
2 teaspoons chopped parsley
1½ cups soft brown bread crumbs
2 egg yolks well beaten
2 egg whites stiffly beaten
¼ cup butter

Rub the chicken well with the salt and pepper. Then rub the

inside of the cavity as well as the outside of the chicken with the brandy and let it soak in. Chop the gizzard and liver fine and mix with the chopped prosciutto slices. Brown in 2 tablespoons hot olive oil. Add a pinch of thyme, 1 clove garlic minced, and the chopped parsley. Add the brown bread crumbs and mix in well. Remove from the heat and stir in the 2 well-beaten egg yolks. Cool. Then add the stiffly beaten egg whites. Stuff the chicken lightly with this mixture and sew or skewer the openings closed. Truss. Rub the chicken well with butter and place in an open roasting pan. Roast in a preheated 375° oven allowing 20 minutes to the pound until the chicken is tender. Baste frequently with the pan juices. The chicken is done when the meaty portion feels tender and the drumsticks move up and down easily. The last 20 minutes of roasting time turn the chicken over to brown the underside.

Serves 4

English Chicken

England brings to mind Shakespeare, Marlowe, Thackeray, and Dickens . . . the storybook thatched cottages and gardens, the stately country houses, the picturesque churches; the pastoral green rolling landscape, the woodlands, the well-kept fields, the white cliffs of Dover have all made the English countryside famous for its beauty.

Tradition lives long in England and the old ways change slowly. The English people have always had a great love for the royal family and the pomp and ceremony which goes with it holds a very special place in their hearts. So too do the landed gentry and the English country life of the squires who molded four centuries of English history; the country gentlemen with their passion for hunting, shooting, racing, for breeding fine horses, and for growing prize gardens.

England too has its culinary traditions and some of the old traditional dishes are well worth trying—Yorkshire pudding, which goes back to the days when great joints of meat were roasted over an open fire; there are game pies which are renowned; there is the York ham, the Trifle, the Christmas pudding which dates back for many centuries; the famous steak-and-kidney pie. Tea time has always been one of England's special traditions with its thinly sliced bread and butter sandwiches, its coconut cakes, seed cakes, and crumpets; its scones served hot, split, buttered, and spread with homemade jam.

The English have always excelled at roasting and grilling meat. Our own popular outdoor barbecue was once the ritual of the feudal castle's courtyard, and before that the ancient

Saxons roasted their meat on live coal fires under the open sky. The Norman conquerors were the first to introduce a refinement to English cooking. The English also excel in game cookery; pheasants, partridge, and woodcocks are cooked with skill. Salmon and trout from the rivers and the matchless Dover sole—all enhance England's cookery.

The chicken takes an important place on the English table too. It is prepared in many ways, but like meat it is at its best in England when grilled or roasted. The roast chicken usually comes to the table on Saturday night and then on Sunday it is finished up cold. Potatoes roasted in the drippings and green peas are the usual accompaniment. The chicken is stuffed with a standard bread stuffing to which sausage is quite often added. The chicken's breast is covered with bacon, which is removed towards the end of the roasting time in order to let the breast brown. The basting is done with bacon fat. The English roast chicken is always served with a Bread Sauce. The Bread Sauce is traditional, and while it is not very popular outside of England, as an accompaniment to roast chicken it is considered essential.

English Roast Chicken

This is the standard way a roast chicken is cooked in England. Potatoes roasted in the drippings and fresh green peas go with it. And of course a Bread Sauce is a must.

5-pound roasting chicken
4 slices fat bacon
2 tablespoons bacon fat
Salt and pepper to taste
½ pound pork sausage meat
½ teaspoon poultry seasoning
Grated rind of ½ lemon
2 tablespoons breadcrumbs
1 egg or a little chicken stock
Salt and pepper to taste

Make the stuffing by mixing the pork sausage, poultry seasoning, lemon rind, and bread crumbs together in a bowl. Add a well-beaten egg and stir well into the mixture. Stuff the chicken with this and sew or skewer the openings closed. Truss. Melt 2 tablespoons bacon fat in a roasting pan and place the chicken in it. Brown the chicken on all sides over a medium high heat and then place it in a preheated 375° oven and roast, allowing 20 minutes to the pound, until the chicken is tender. Be sure to place 4 slices of fat bacon over the breast of the chicken before placing it in the oven. Remove the bacon the last 30 minutes so the breast will brown. When breast has browned turn the chicken over so that the underside will brown too. When the chicken is done remove the chicken to a hot platter and serve with the Bread Sauce.

Serves 4–6

English Bread Sauce
This English Bread Sauce is a rather mild sauce but it is good. The onion and the seasonings gives it its flavor. It should be of the consistency of a medium thick white sauce, smooth, and free from lumps.

3 cloves
1 medium onion
1 bay leaf
2 cups milk
4 tablespoons stale breadcrumbs
Salt and pepper to taste
1/4 teaspoon nutmeg
1 tablespoon butter
1 tablespoon cream

Stick cloves into the onion and put it with the bay leaf and milk into a saucepan. Cover and barely simmer over a very low heat for 15 or 20 minutes or until the milk is well flavored. Remove the onion and bay leaf and stir the breadcrumbs into

the milk. Simmer over low heat for 5 minutes or until the
sauce is thickened and creamy, stirring constantly. Remove
from heat and season with salt and pepper and nutmeg. Add
the butter and cream. Reheat gently to serve hot with the
roast chicken.

Chicken Casserole Metropole
Recipe of the Hotel Metropole, London, England—reprinted
by permission from Louis P. de Gouy's *Gold Cook Book*,
Chilton Company, Philadelphia.

3-pound roasting chicken cut into pieces
Salt, pepper, marjoram, thyme to taste
½ cup olive oil
Scalded thin cream
⅓ cup minced onion
1 tablespoon curry powder
2 tablespoons flour
2 cups thin cream
1 large bay leaf
1 clove garlic
1 sprig fennel top
1 clove
2 egg yolks
Salt to taste

Roll the chicken pieces in a mixture of salt, pepper, marjoram,
and thyme to taste. Brown on all sides in ½ cup olive oil
over a bright flame, stirring frequently with a wooden spoon.
Transfer the chicken to a well-oiled earthenware baking dish;
pour over enough scalded thin cream to barely cover, and
bake in a 375° oven until the chicken is tender and the cream
almost evaporated.

Meanwhile cook ⅓ cup minced onions until tender but not
browned in the oil left in the pan, stirring frequently with

a wooden spoon; then stir in 1 tablespoon curry powder sifted with 2 tablespoons flour, until thoroughly blended. Gradually add 2 cups thin cream scalded with 1 large bay leaf, 1 whole clove garlic, 1 sprig fennel top, and 1 whole clove. Bring to a boil, stirring frequently. Simmer gently for 5 minutes, remove from the fire, and stir in 1 at a time 2 egg yolks, stirring briskly after each addition. Season to taste with salt, bring to the boiling point; pour over the chicken and glaze under the flame of the broiler oven. Serve right in the casserole or in individual heated casseroles.

Serves 4

English Chicken Casserole
This English casserole dish makes a soul-satisfying meal.

4-pound chicken fryer cut into pieces
1 teaspoon salt
¼ teaspoon pepper
2 medium onions chopped fine
4 tablespoons bacon fat
1 cup fresh peas
1 tablespoon flour
Chicken stock

Rub the salt and pepper well into the chicken pieces. Heat the bacon fat in a heavy frying pan and add the chicken pieces and the chopped onions. Brown the chicken well on both sides. Add the fresh peas and let them turn brown along with the onions. Add 1 tablespoon flour and mix in well. Add just enough chicken stock to moisten the gravy so that the pan is not too dry. Reduce the heat, cover the pan, and cook for 30 minutes or until the chicken is tender. Check from time to time to make sure the pan is not too dry and add more chicken stock if necessary.

Serves 4

Brown Chicken Fricassee
This chicken recipe was given to me by a friend who lived in London for several years.

3½-pound chicken fryer cut into pieces
3 slices fat bacon
3 carrots cut in slices
2 medium onions chopped
1 teaspoon salt
1 tablespoon chopped parsley
½ bay leaf crumbled
½ cup rich brown gravy

Cut the bacon in small pieces and fry them out in a heavy frying pan. When they begin to turn brown add the chicken pieces and brown well on both sides. Add the sliced carrots, chopped onions, salt, parsley, and crumbled bay leaf. Cook over a medium heat for 15 minutes. Add the ½ cup rich brown gravy, mix in well, cover the pan, and simmer over a low heat for 20 minutes or until the chicken and vegetables are tender. Serve the chicken with the brown gravy and the vegetables.

Serves 4

Chicken Pudding
Chicken Pudding is typically English.

2 cups flour
4 teaspoons baking powder
1 teaspoon salt
2 tablespoons shortening
¾ cup milk
3-pound chicken fryer cut into small pieces
3 slices ham cut into strips
2 tablespoons chopped parsley
½ teaspoon salt

⅛ teaspoon pepper
½ cup mushrooms sliced
1 thin slice fresh veal

Mix the flour, baking powder, and salt together in a bowl. Work in the shortening and add the milk. Turn out on a floured board, knead several times, and roll out the dough. In the center place the chicken pieces, ham strips, chopped parsley, salt, pepper, sliced mushrooms, and thin slice of fresh veal. Bring the dough up carefully around the stuffing and lift it into a buttered mold with a tight cover. A 5-pound lard tin or coffee can may be used for this purpose. Place the mold on a trivet in a kettle containing boiling water. The water should come up halfway around the mold. Steam for 1 hour and 20 minutes keeping the water at boiling point constantly. Add more boiling water if necessary. Unmold and serve hot.

Serves 4

Chicken Edward VII
It is the custom in some of the best restaurants in England to name dishes after members of the royal family.

5-pound roasting chicken
3 cups cooked rice
½ cup sliced mushrooms
2 tablespoons butter melted
1 can pâté de foie gras
2 tablespoons meat glaze
2 tablespoons heavy cream
Chicken stock
1 tablespoon butter
1 onion chopped fine
½ bay leaf
⅛ teaspoon ginger
1 tablespoon curry powder
½ teaspoon salt

1 tablespoon flour
1 cup chicken stock
1 cup heavy cream

Sauté the sliced mushrooms in 2 tablespoons melted butter for 5 minutes. Add them to the cooked rice along with the can of pâté de foie gras, meat glaze, and the 2 tablespoons of heavy cream. Mix well and stuff the chicken with this mixture. Sew or skewer the opening closed and truss the chicken. Poach the chicken in chicken stock to cover for 1½ hours or until the chicken is tender.

In the meantime make a curry sauce by melting 1 tablespoon butter in a saucepan and sautéing the chopped onion until soft but not browned. Add the bay leaf, ginger, curry powder, and salt. Mix well and blend in the flour. Slowly add 1 cup chicken stock and cook until smooth and thickened. Add the heavy cream and cook over a low heat, stirring constantly, until heated through. Serve separately with the chicken.

Serves 6

Breast of Chicken Queen Elizabeth
A variation of another famous dish, named for the reigning Queen.

6 chicken breasts
6 thin slices cooked ham
6 thin slices Swiss cheese
1 egg well beaten
¼ cup flour
3 tablespoons butter melted
½ pound mushrooms sliced
⅓ cup dry white wine
1 teaspoon tomato puree
1 cup heavy cream
1 cup white sauce

Salt to taste
Chopped parsley

Separate the chicken breasts in half so there are two filet sections for each breast. Flatten them with a mallet. Lay a slice of ham and a slice of Swiss cheese on 6 of the filets and cover them with the remaining filets like a sandwich. Dip the breasts in the well-beaten egg then roll them in the flour. Melt 3 tablespoons butter in a frying pan and brown the breasts for 15 minutes on one side. Turn and cook 15 minutes on the other side or until they are tender. Remove them to a serving platter and keep hot. Add the sliced mushrooms to the pan along with ⅓ cup dry white wine. Cook until the liquid is reduced to half. Add the tomato puree and the heavy cream and continue to cook until the cream has reduced to half. Add 1 cup white sauce and season to taste with salt. Pour the sauce over the chicken breasts and sprinkle with chopped parsley.

Serves 6

Chicken Croquettes
The English are fond of croquettes; this recipe is among the best.

3 tablespoons butter
4 tablespoons flour
1¾ cups milk
1 cup diced cooked chicken meat
½ cup diced cooked tongue
1 tablespoon chopped parsley
½ teaspoon salt
⅛ teaspoon white pepper
¼ teaspoon nutmeg
2 egg yolks beaten lightly
½ cup flour
1 cup breadcrumbs
Deep fat for frying

Melt the butter in a saucepan and blend in the flour. Slowly add the milk and stir over a medium heat until the sauce is smooth and thick. Add the diced chicken, diced smoked tongue, chopped parsley, salt, white pepper, and nutmeg. Let the mixture come to a boil then remove from heat and cool. The mixture should be thick and firm. Shape into individual croquettes. Roll the croquettes in flour, dip them in the beaten egg yolks, and then roll them in breadcrumbs. Let them set about 30 minutes for the coating to dry. Heat the fat in a deep fry pan until it is very hot. Deep-fry the croquettes until they are golden brown all over. Drain on absorbent paper and serve hot.

Serves 4

Chicken Turnovers

The English are traditionally fond of pie and pastry meat dishes. This chicken turnover dish is a delicious one.

1½ cups ground cooked chicken
1 tablespoon minced parsley
1 tablespoon minced chives
6 slices bacon cooked until crisp then crumbled
Salt and pepper to taste
Whipped cream
Rich pie dough cut in rounds

Combine the ground cooked chicken, chopped parsley, chopped chives, crumbled bacon, and salt and pepper to taste in a bowl. Add just enough whipped cream to bind the filling. Place a tablespoon of the filling on each round of pie dough. Fold the dough in half over the filling and seal the edges securely. Prick the turnovers with the tines of a fork and bake in a 375° oven for 20 minutes or until the crust is browned.

Serves 4

Irish Chicken

Ireland is often called the Emerald Isle because the bright
green countryside is as pure a green as an emerald. A mild
climate with much rain accounts for the deep greenness of
the grass, the fertile soil, the rich pastureland where millions
of cattle graze and wax fat. Ireland is well known for the excellence of her beef cattle and they are exported all over Europe. Oats and barley grow well in the Irish soil. Barley malt
is used in making the famous Irish whiskey, and as far as the
oats are concerned—like the Scots, most Irish families eat oatmeal porridge every day of the year.

It is the potato that is the most essential part of the diet of
the Irish. When a blight destroyed the potato crop in the mid-
nineteenth century it brought about the worst disaster in Irish
history. Not only did thousands of people starve to death in
Ireland but during the black years famine drove hundreds of
thousands of Irish to take refuge in other lands. Potatoes have
been an important part of their diet for centuries; the Irish
have always eaten potatoes every way: boiled, fried, mashed,
in their famous stew, in soups, in breads, and in pancakes.

Much poultry is raised in Ireland too. I have heard several
staunch Irishmen say that the Irish chicken tastes much better
than its feathered counterparts on this side of the ocean. I
rather think that this is a bit of Celtic blarney, because most
chicken recipes in Ireland are much like those of England,
with several notable exceptions. A unique method devised by
wandering tinkers was to capture any straying chicken, quickly
kill it, and plaster it—feathers, guts, and all—in a thick coating
of soft mud. This is similar to the clay-baked chickens of the

Southwest except that the bird was cooked in a hole in the Ould Sod with a bonfire burning over the top instead of flamboyantly in the embers of the fire itself. The Polynesians also cooked chickens in a hole in the ground, with the difference that they lined the hole with porous stones and wrapped their chickens in tara or banana leaves instead of soft mud.

In this section I have included several unusual Irish chicken recipes given to me by Coras Trachtala—the Irish Export Board: Chicken and Cabbage, Hen with Golden Eggs, and Chicken Pascal with Mountain Dew—and what could be more Irish than the famous Irish whiskey, Mountain Dew? These recipes were first printed in a little Irish recipe book by the Mount Salus Press Limited, Dublin, and they are as Irish as the brogue and wit and lore of the land. Another Irish chicken recipe worth mentioning, and one I have included in this section, is Chicken and Irish Stout, that black yeasty noble brew, which in Ireland is an even more popular drink than is whiskey.

Chicken and Cabbage

Corned Beef and Cabbage may be one of the most famous of all Irish dishes but you will also find cabbage served in many other forms in Ireland. Chicken and Cabbage is one of them. This recipe is with the compliments of Coras Trachtala —the Irish Export Board, from an Irish recipe book printed by the Mount Salus Press, Dublin.

3½-pound chicken cut into pieces
1 cup white wine
1½ teaspoons salt
1 onion finely chopped
½ medium head cabbage shredded
3 tablespoons bacon fat
½ teaspoon fresh ground pepper
1 tablespoon lemon juice
½ lemon

Rub the chicken well with the ½ lemon. Place it in a pan with the white wine and salt. Cover the pan and cook for about 1 hour or until the chicken is tender. It is important to keep the pan covered. Brown the finely chopped onion and shredded cabbage in the bacon fat. Add pepper, the lemon juice, and cooked chicken. Cover the pan tightly and steam for 15 minutes.

Serves 4

Hen with Golden Eggs

This Irish chicken dish with its delightful name is from the Irish recipe book printed by the Mount Salus Press, Dublin, and was given to me with the compliments of Coras Trachtala —Irish Export Board.

1 large whole chicken
1 pint half glaze
½ cup butter
9 eggs
½ pint white sauce
2 egg yolks slightly beaten
1 egg beaten
Breadcrumbs
1 pound short paste
Straw potatoes
Watercress

Melt the butter in a pan and add the chicken. Turn the chicken in the melted butter until golden brown all over. Add the half glaze, cover, and cook for 40 minutes or until tender. In the meantime cook 9 eggs until hard, mince, and mix over the heat with the 2 slightly beaten egg yolks and enough of the white sauce to make a very thick sauce. Divide into 12 pieces and shape each piece like an egg. Coat with beaten egg and breadcrumbs and fry until golden brown. Make 24 half spheres out of the short pastry dough and bake. Then join them together in twos to make egg cups. Arrange the cooked chicken on a large dish. Pour around the rest of the white sauce. Place the fried eggs in the pastry cups and stand them around the chicken. Garnish with straw potatoes and watercress.

Serves 6

Chicken Pascal

What could be more Irish than Chicken Pascal cooked with Irish whiskey—Mountain Dew. This recipe is with the compliments of Coras Trachtala—the Irish Export Board, from the Irish recipe book printed by the Mount Salus Press, Dublin.

$2\frac{1}{2}$-pound spring chicken
6 mushrooms sliced
1 onion finely chopped
3 tablespoons butter
$\frac{1}{2}$ pound mashed potatoes
1 egg
Salt and pepper to taste
4 slices bacon
1 glass Mountain Dew (Irish whiskey)

Have your butcher bone the chicken leaving the filets intact— or do it yourself. Melt the butter in a pan and add the sliced mushrooms and finely chopped onion. Sauté in the butter for 3 or 4 minutes. Add the mashed potatoes and salt and pepper to taste. Bind with the egg. Roll out the chicken filets as thin as possible without tearing them. Place the stuffing mixture in the center of the filets, roll over, wrap them in bacon, and braise them in the oven for 30 to 35 minutes. Place on a silver platter—an ovenproof platter will do—and pour over the glass of Mountain Dew. Set aflame and serve immediately.

Serves 2

Chicken and Irish Stout

As Irish as the Blarney Stone is this chicken dish made with good sturdy Irish stout. Guinness is the only brand you would ask for in an Irish pub.

4-pound chicken cut into pieces
½ cup flour
1 teaspoon salt
⅛ teaspoon fresh ground black pepper
¼ cup butter melted
½ pound bacon diced
4 small yellow onions chopped
1 clove garlic minced
1 teaspoon thyme
1⅓ cups Irish stout
½ cup heavy cream

Add the salt and pepper to the flour and roll the chicken pieces in the seasoned flour. Melt the butter in a heavy frying pan and brown the chicken pieces well on both sides. When browned remove the chicken and drain off all but 1 tablespoon of the butter. Add the diced bacon, chopped onions, and minced garlic. Cook until bacon is crisp and onions browned. Return the chicken to the pan and add the Irish stout. Add the thyme, cover the pan, and cook over low heat for 40 minutes or until the chicken is tender. Add the heavy cream, heat through without letting the sauce boil, and serve immediately.

Serves 4

Scottish Chicken

Scotland is a small rugged mountainous country, the land of the Rowan tree, the loch, the heather; the hardy clansmen with their tartans, their famous kilts, the stirring bagpipes, the magic of Roberts Burns. There are barren rocky peaks, deep glens, heather-covered plateaus in the highlands. Low rolling hills and wide fields of fertile soil make up much of the lowlands. Sleek herds of Aberdeen-Angus cattle fatten in the fields. The fishing is excellent and there are always salmon in the rushing rivers and trout in the lakes and streams. The long 2300 mile coastline is a fisherman's dream and with large catches of whitefish, herring, crab, and lobster to choose from the Scots have developed many tasty fish dishes.

Scottish cooking is delightful and there are many traditional dishes that are as well known to us as the poems of Robert Burns: haggis, the renowned blood-pudding cooked in the lining of a sheep's stomach; Highland Briddies, little meat cakes which are served customarily at wedding feasts; scones, crumpets, shortbread, Dundee cake are all teatime favorites. The wonderful marmalades and jams. Mention should be made here too of that world-famous distillery product which is known in Scotland simply as whiskey.

The staff of life to the Scotsman for generations has been oatmeal. Besides the well-known porridge the Scottish cooks have used oatmeal in many other ways. There is a mixture with boiling water and butter called brose; a dessert with toasted oatmeal mixed with whipped cream; dumplings made with oatmeal and suet and onions. There is oatmeal pudding, oatmeal cakes, and a famous drink called Athol brose (whiskey, honey, and oatmeal). Also Scottish cooks quite often thicken their soups with oatmeal, roll their fish in oatmeal prior to cooking it, and use it frequently with onions as a stuffing for chicken. In fact, the Scots are as nostalgic about their oatmeal as they are about Bonnie Prince Charlie and the gathering of the clans.

Chickens have always been popular in Scotland and the Scots have given their chicken dishes many intriguing names. There is Friar's Chicken, supposedly the favorite dish of King James VI; Chicken Pot-Posy, which takes its name from the bouquet of fresh herbs with which it is cooked; Smoored Pullets, a dish that came to the Carolinas from Scotland with the fleeing supporters of Bonnie Prince Charlie in the 1700's; Chicken Stovies, an old Scottish dish made with potatoes which has been a staple food in Scotland almost as long as it has in Ireland. These are famous Scottish dishes and they are typical of the cuisine of the rugged and canny Scotch character.

Friar's Chicken
Friar's Chicken, an old Scottish dish, was supposedly the favorite of King James VI.

4-pound chicken fryer cut into pieces
3 cups chicken stock
2 whole cloves
3 egg yolks
¼ cup heavy cream
Finely chopped parsley

Put the chicken pieces in a kettle with the chicken stock and the whole cloves. Bring to a boil, skim, cover the kettle tightly and cook over a low heat for 40 minutes or until the chicken is tender. Beat the egg yolks and heavy cream together and add to the stock. Cook over a low heat, stirring constantly, until the sauce has thickened slightly. Serve the chicken in deep bowls with the sauce and parsley sprinkled over the top.

Serves 4

Chicken Pot-Posy

A dish with a homey-sounding name: the pot-posy meaning, of course, the bouquet of fresh herbs the chicken is cooked with. The stuffing is made with oatmeal.

5-pound roasting chicken
2 tablespoons butter
2 cups oatmeal
1 teaspoon salt
¼ teaspoon pepper
1 large onion chopped fine
2 stalks celery with tops
4 carrots
1 onion sliced
6 peppercorns
Bouquet garni (fresh sprigs of thyme, parsley, rosemary, chives) tied together with string
1 teaspoon salt
Water to cover
½ cup butter melted
½ cup chopped parsley

Make a stuffing by mixing the 2 tablespoons butter, oatmeal, salt, pepper, and chopped onion together. Stuff the chicken with this mixture and sew the opening closed. Truss. Put the chicken in a kettle with the celery and tops, carrots, sliced onion, peppercorns, and bouquet garni. Cover the chicken with water and cook covered over a low heat about 1½ hours or until the chicken is tender. When the chicken is done add the chopped parsley to ½ cup melted butter and serve on the side with the chicken.

Serves 6

Chicken Stovies

"Stovies" or stoved potatoes made with potatoes and onions in a heavy pan is an old Scottish dish. The same dish with chicken added is just as often encountered.

4-pound frying chicken cut into pieces
4 large potatoes sliced thin
Salt and pepper
½ cup butter
Chicken stock 1 cup approximately

Arrange chicken, potatoes, and onions in layers in a large heavy pan. Dot each layer with butter and sprinkle with salt and pepper. Add just enough water to keep the chicken and potatoes from burning, about 1 cup. Cover tightly, and simmer over a low heat for 1 hour or until the chicken and potatoes are tender.

Serves 4

Smoored Pullets

This is an old Scottish dish that came with the supporters of Bonnie Prince Charlie when they first settled in the Carolinas.

2 broiler chickens split in half
½ cup flour
1 teaspoon salt
¼ teaspoon pepper
½ cup butter
2 tablespoons flour
1 cup heavy cream
½ cup chopped parsley

Add the salt and pepper to the flour and roll the chicken pieces in the seasoned flour. Melt the butter in a heavy frying pan and brown each chicken half on both sides. When all the pieces are browned, cover the pan, and cook over a low heat for about 30 minutes or until the chicken is tender. Turn the chicken several times while it is cooking. Remove the chicken to a hot serving platter. Blend the flour into the pan and slowly add the heavy cream. Cook, stirring constantly, until the sauce has thickened. Add the chopped parsley and pour over the chicken.

Serves 4

German Chicken

Few countries in Europe can boast a landscape more varied than that of Germany. It is not a large country but it has almost every kind of terrain there is. In southern Swabia there is the Black Forest that takes its name from the heavy forests of dark fir trees that cover its mountain slopes. There are orchards and vineyards, chalets and spas, and well-managed game forests. Bavaria, the largest state in West Germany, has always been a travel-poster image with its Tyrolean overtones, its Alpine ski slopes, and its famous resorts.

The story of Germany is a story of war but it is also a story of philosophers, scholars, scientists, and some of the world's greatest musicians. Germany too has contributed to the art of cooking with intriguing flavors of sweet and spicy and sour. German cusine is substantial and hearty with the aroma of roasting game and Huhn im Topf, of smells sweet and spicy, of tender cutlets simmering about Steinpilze, of red cabbage and sauerkraut, sausage, beer, and fine soups.

The Germans have always leaned towards robust foods and their cuisine was slow in developing. Even as late as the mid-eighteenth century the German diet was limited in range; vegetables were scarce with only cabbage and root crops available in the market place. Even potatoes, which were later to play an important role in the German diet, were not cultivated until the late 1700's. Most of the meat eaten was pork and the principal fats used in cooking were lard and bacon fat. German sausages are excellent, the soups outstanding, as are the black and rye and pumpernickel breads; the sauerkraut, dumplings, the cabbage dishes; and the delicious cakes and pastries. Germans are great meat eaters and they want their meat served in enormous portions. The southern Germans have a great fondness for dumplings and the northern Germans for potatoes, but today the food of Germany, like most of Europe, has become international. The interest in food is enormous and new ideas have been adopted from all over the world and adjusted to the German palate.

The most varied and interesting of the German cuisine is found in Bavaria. Traditional dishes such as Sauerbraten, Pfeffernüsse, Flammeris, Wiener Schnitzel are well known to all of us. But delicious as these dishes are they do not represent the whole of German cooking. The Rhineland, being wine country, features a cuisine that is lighter, less spiced with vinegar, and which put a German accent on many dishes that were originally French.

Because of game management and reforestation programs the game is plentiful in Germany and the game dishes are superb. German cuisine also includes some excellent poultry specialties, and while chicken is not featured very often on restaurant menus it is a very popular dish in private homes. In fact, the German Hausfrau has displayed real genius in developing wonderful stuffings for chicken.

Chicken in Beer
Huhn im Bier—a typically German dish. Beer adds a refreshing tang.

$3\frac{1}{2}$-pound chicken fryer cut into pieces
$\frac{1}{2}$ cup flour
1 teaspoon salt
$\frac{1}{4}$ teaspoon pepper
3 tablespoons butter
1 onion sliced thin
$1\frac{1}{3}$ cups beer
$\frac{1}{2}$ cup heavy cream
2 tablespoons minced parsley

Add the salt and pepper to the flour and roll the chicken pieces in the seasoned flour. Melt the butter in a heavy frying pan and brown the chicken and onions in it. When well browned add the beer. Cover and cook over low heat for 40 minutes or until the chicken is tender. Add the heavy cream and minced parsley. Heat through but do not let boil.

Serves 4

Chicken in Beer Batter

Huhn im Bierteig—another beer recipe. Just as beer drinking is the custom of Germany, beer often replaces wine in the cookery.

3½-pound chicken fryer cut into pieces
1 teaspoon salt
¼ teaspoon black pepper
1 cup flour
2 eggs
½ to 1 cup beer
2 tablespoons melted butter
2 tablespoons minced parsley
Fat for deep frying

Season the chicken pieces with the salt and pepper. Make a smooth mixture of the flour, eggs, and melted butter. Then add as much beer as necessary to make a smooth rather thick batter. Add the minced parsley. Coat the chicken pieces with the batter heavily and let chill 1 hour in the refrigerator. Heat the fat to 375° and deep fry the chicken until golden brown. Drain and place in a shallow baking pan. Bake in a preheated 350° oven for 30 minutes or until tender.

Serves 4

Chicken in Sour Cream Sauce

This German chicken in sour cream sauce accompanied by

potato pancakes and a crisp salad makes a most delightful meal.

4-pound chicken fryer cut into pieces
1 teaspoon salt
¼ teaspoon pepper
½ cup flour
6 tablespoons butter
½ pound mushrooms sliced
4 tablespoons flour
2 cups chicken stock
1 cup beer
1 cup sour cream
Salt to taste

Add the salt and pepper to the flour and roll the chicken pieces in the seasoned flour. Melt 2 tablespoons butter in a heavy skillet and brown the chicken well on both sides. Remove the chicken and place in a buttered casserole. Add 2 tablespoons butter to the skillet and sauté the mushrooms in it for 5 minutes. Add to the chicken in the casserole. Add 2 more tablespoons butter to the skillet and when hot add the flour. Blend until smooth and slowly add the 2 cups chicken stock, stirring constantly. Add the 1 cup beer and cook over a low heat stirring constantly until thickened and smooth. Remove from heat and stir in the sour cream. Taste for seasoning and pour the sauce over the chicken. Bake in a 350° oven for 40 minutes or until the chicken is tender.

Serves 4

Crisp Cockerel

Gebratener Huhn is a chicken braised the way the Germans prefer it. It is simple, good, and flavorful.

5-pound roasting chicken
1 teaspoon salt

Juice of ½ lemon
4 tablespoons butter
3 sprigs parsley
3 tablespoons flour
1 large onion chopped
½ cup water

Rub the chicken inside and out with the salt and the lemon
juice. Rub the inside with 1 tablespoon butter and stuff
the cavity with the parsley. Dust the chicken with the flour.
Melt 3 tablespoons butter in a heavy Dutch oven and brown
the chicken well on all sides. Add the chopped onions and
the ½ cup water. Cover and braise over low heat for 1½ hours
or until the chicken is tender. The onions and chicken braise
down to a deep golden brown.

Serves 6

Munich Grilled Chicken
Münchner Wiesenhähndel—Grilled Chicken—is very popular.
This is a specialty served during the October Beer Festival
in Munich.

2 1-pound broilers whole
1 teaspoon salt
8 sprigs parsley
¼ cup butter melted

Sprinkle the inside of the broilers with the salt and stuff
with the parsley. Tie the legs together. Brush well with melted
butter and grill in 400° preheated oven about 45 minutes to
1 hour or until broilers are tender. Baste frequently with the
melted butter. To serve split in half.

Serves 2

Chicken Fricassee

Hühner Frikassee—Chicken Fricassee—is a wonderful dish and typical of German cuisine.

5-pound roasting chicken cut in pieces
1 large onion sliced
2 carrots scraped and cut into pieces
3 stalks celery diced
3 sprigs parsley
6 peppercorns
1 teaspoon salt
2 bay leaves
1½ quarts chicken broth
3 tablespoons butter
3 tablespoons flour
1 egg yolk
¼ cup heavy cream
Juice of ½ lemon
½ pound sliced mushrooms sautéed in 2 tablespoons butter
3 cups hot cooked rice

Put the chicken pieces in a heavy Dutch oven with the onion, carrots, celery, parsley, peppercorns, salt, and bay leaves. Cover with the chicken broth. Bring to a boil, turn heat to low, and simmer for 1½ hours or until chicken is tender. Melt the butter in a saucepan and blend in the flour. Slowly add 1 cup of the chicken broth, stirring over low heat until smooth and thickened. Stir the thickened sauce into the Dutch oven with the chicken. Simmer for 5 minutes. Beat the egg yolks with the heavy cream and add to the sauce. Add the juice of ½ lemon. Add the sliced mushrooms which have been sautéed in 2 tablespoons butter. Serve hot with rice.

Serves 6

Chicken in Casserole with Vegetables and Noodles

Huhn im Topp Gemüse Nudeln—chicken in casserole with

vegetables and noodles—is another example of good substantial German cooking.

3-pound chicken fryer cut into pieces
2 cups chicken stock
4 carrots scraped and sliced
1 large onion sliced
3 stalks celery chopped
1 bay leaf
6 peppercorns
2 teaspoons salt
½ pound noodles
½ cup beer

Place the chicken in a large heavy kettle. Add the carrots, onion, celery, bay leaf, peppercorns, and salt. Add the chicken stock with enough water to cover. Cover kettle, bring to a boil, lower heat and simmer about 40 minutes or until chicken is tender. Remove chicken and vegetables to a casserole and keep hot. Strain the broth and cook the noodles in the broth until tender. Add the noodles to the chicken and vegetables. Pour over some of the broth and ½ cup beer. Cook 5 minutes in a preheated 350° oven. Serve from the casserole.

Serves 4

Chicken in Anchovy Sauce
Huhn mit Sardellensauce—Chicken in Anchovy Sauce—the flavor of anchovies gives it an enticing flavor.

4-pound chicken fryer cut into pieces
Boiling salted water to cover
1 onion stuck with 2 cloves
Anchovy paste
2 tablespoons butter
2 tablespoons flour

1 cup heavy cream
½ cup chicken stock

Place the chicken in a kettle with boiling salted water to cover. Add the onion stuck with the cloves and simmer covered over low heat for 45 minutes or until the chicken is tender. Remove chicken from the broth, skin, and cut the meat from the bones into large pieces. Arrange in a buttered baking dish and spread the chicken with a thin layer of the anchovy paste. Melt the butter in a saucepan and blend in the flour. Add the heavy cream and ½ cup of the chicken stock strained. Cook over a low heat until thickened slightly and pour over the chicken. Bake in a preheated 350° oven for 20 minutes. Serve in the baking dish.

Serves 4

Chicken Soufflé
Hühner Soufflé—Chicken Soufflé—is a very simple, tasty German dish.

3 tablespoons butter
3 tablespoons flour
1 cup milk
1 cup cream
½ teaspoon salt
⅛ teaspoon pepper
½ cup breadcrumbs
2 cups diced cooked chicken
3 egg yolks well beaten
3 stiffly beaten egg whites

Melt the butter in a saucepan and blend in the flour. Add slowly the milk and cream and salt and pepper, stirring over a low heat until thickened. Remove from the heat and add the chicken and the well-beaten egg yolks. Fold in the stiffly beaten egg whites. Butter a baking dish and pour in the mixture. Bake in a 350° oven for 35 minutes. Serve at once.

Serves 4

Sautéed Chicken with Apple and Onion Rings
This is a delicious German dish with chicken, apples, onions, and beer.

4-pound chicken fryer cut into pieces
1 teaspoon salt
⅛ teaspoon pepper
2 tablespoons bacon fat
1 large onion sliced in rings
4 tart apples sliced in rings
1 tablespoon flour
1½ cups beer
1 bay leaf
2 tablespoons grated lemon rind

Rub the salt and pepper well into the chicken pieces. Melt the bacon fat in a large heavy frying pan and fry the onion rings until they are soft but not browned. Add the sliced apple rings and continue to fry until they are tender. Remove the onions and apple rings to a greased casserole and place the chicken pieces on top. To the fat left in the pan blend in 1 tablespoon flour and slowly add the beer over a medium heat, stirring constantly. Cook until the mixture thickens. Pour over the chicken and apple and onion rings in the casserole. Add the bay leaf and grated lemon rind. Cover and cook in a 350° oven for 1 hour or until the chicken is tender. Serve from the casserole.

Serves 4

Chicken with Wine and Vinegar
A spicy and deliciously tart German chicken dish.

3½-pound chicken fryer cut into pieces
6 tablespoons butter
2 cloves garlic unpeeled
3 tablespoons dry mustard
4 teaspoons tomato puree
5 teaspoons white wine
4 teaspoons wine vinegar
4 teaspoons heavy cream
1 teaspoon Worcestershire sauce
Salt and pepper to taste

Melt 6 tablespoons butter in a heavy frying pan and add the chicken pieces and the unpeeled cloves of garlic. Cook over medium low heat for 40 minutes, turning the chicken frequently until chicken is tender. Meanwhile mix in a bowl the dry mustard, tomato puree, and white wine. When the chicken is almost tender add 4 tablespoons wine vinegar to the pan and cook until the chicken is almost dry. Remove the chicken and keep hot on a serving platter. Add the mustard-wine mixture to the pan and cook, stirring constantly, for 1 minute. Add 4 tablespoons heavy cream and the Worcestershire sauce. Stir well and pour over the chicken. Serve with potato pancakes.

Serves 4

Ragout of Spring Chicken

Feines Ragout von Hühnchen—Ragout of Spring Chicken—the combination of lemon and dill and pâté de foie gras makes this a superb dish.

2 1½-pound broiler chickens split in half
¼ cup butter melted
½ teaspoon salt
1 lemon unpeeled and sliced thin
½ cup chicken stock

1 tablespoon flour
1 bay leaf crushed
1 teaspoon dill
3-ounce can pâté de foie gras
½ pound mushrooms sliced

Split the boilers in half and brown well on both sides in ¼ cup melted butter. When well browned, add the salt, lemon slices, and ½ cup chicken stock. Cover the pan and simmer over low heat 20 minutes or until the chicken is tender. Remove the chicken and lemon slices from the pan and keep hot. Mix enough of the sauce in the pan with the flour to make a smooth paste. Add the crushed bay leaf, dill, and the can of pâté de foie gras. Mix well with the sauce in the pan and stir over the heat until thickened and smooth. Return the chicken and lemon slices to the pan along with the sliced mushrooms and simmer over low heat for 10 minutes. Serve the chicken in the sauce.

Serves 4

Broiler Chickens Fried in the South German Style
Backhähndel nach Suddeutscher Art—this dish from southern Germany consists of broilers or very young chickens fried and served in a spicy sour sweet mushroom sauce.

2 1-pound broilers split in half
1 teaspoon salt
¼ teaspoon pepper
¼ cup butter melted
½ cup thinly sliced mushrooms
2 tablespoons butter
1 heaping tablespoon flour
½ cup heavy cream
½ cup dry white wine
1 tablespoon vinegar

Juice of ½ lemon
2 egg yolks beaten lightly with 2 tablespoons heavy cream

Season the broiler halves with salt and pepper and fry in ¼ cup melted butter until browned and tender. Remove to a serving platter and keep hot. Melt 2 tablespoons butter in a skillet and sauté the mushrooms for 3 minutes. Sprinkle over them the flour and blend in well. Slowly add the heavy cream and dry white wine. Cook over a medium low heat until thickened, stirring constantly. Add the vinegar and lemon juice. Blend in well. Add the egg yolks beaten with the cream and cook 1 minute longer. Serve 1 broiler half per person with some of the mushroom sauce poured over it.

Serves 4

Weiner Backhuhn

Weiner Backhuhn—Fried Chicken the Viennese way—has long been a favorite throughout Germany.

4-pound chicken fryer cut into pieces
Juice of 1 lemon
1 teaspoon salt
¼ cup flour
3 eggs well beaten
Breadcrumbs
½ cup lard or vegetable shortening
½ cup butter melted

Sprinkle the chicken pieces liberally with the juice of 1 lemon. Add the salt to the flour and dredge the chicken pieces in the seasoned flour. Dip each chicken piece in the beaten eggs and then roll in the breadcrumbs. Let the crumbs dry out for 15 minutes. Heat the lard or vegetable shortening in a deep pan and when it is hot add the chicken. Brown quickly on both sides over a medium heat. Turn heat to low and continue cooking for 30 minutes longer. Turn frequently so the chicken browns evenly on both sides. Remove the chicken to a flat baking pan and pour over the melted butter. Bake in a preheated 375° oven for 10 minutes or until the coating is dry and crisp.

Serves 4

Chicken Mayonnaise

Hühner Mayonnaise—Chicken Mayonnaise—a cold chicken dish with a spicy tang.

4-pound chicken fryer cut into pieces
Boiling salted water
1 cup mayonnaise
Juice of ½ lemon
1 tablespoon prepared mustard
2 tablespoons chopped gherkins
¼ cup sour cream
Dash of cayenne

Cook the chicken in boiling salted water to cover for 1 hour or until chicken is tender. Remove the chicken, cool, skin, and cut the meat from the bones into large pieces. Place in the refrigerator to chill. Combine the mayonnaise, lemon juice, prepared mustard, chopped gherkins, sour cream, and cayenne. Arrange the chicken on a serving platter and cover with the mayonnaise.

Serves 4

Hungarian Chicken

The Hungarians are a proud and independent people and they have always had a strong love for tradition and custom and for bright gay clothing. They have a way with food too, an indefinable something about their cooking that is as characteristic of them as their colorful and unforgettable gypsy music. Nine out of ten of the population of Hungary are Magyars, descendants of a nomad tribe that moved into Europe from Asia over a thousand years ago. The Magyars adopted much of the culture and religion of the West but they cling to many of their own traditions, their distinctive costumes, and their festive celebrations. Their well-known celebrations of a wedding is probably as gala as any wedding celebration in the world with its ceremonial banquet, with lavish feasting and drinking and dancing continuing until such time in the early dawn when all supplies of food and drink are finally exhausted.

Once Hungary was a powerful kingdom, but at the end of World War I it was divided into small pieces and today it is just a small country run by a communistic dictatorship. Much of it is a rolling plain with the Carpathian Mountains rising on the northern side and the Danube River flowing through it. It is one of the world's most fertile areas and millions of bushels of corn and wheat are grown in the rich black soil of its farmlands. The sleek herds of cattle that graze in the pastures produce fine beef, milk, and cheese. Hardy sheep roam the hills and furnish both mutton and wool. Livestock was the ancient Magyars' primary food, and they also raised some of the finest poultry in Europe including turkeys and geese. Even today livestock and poultry hold an important place in Hungarian tradition.

Although paprika is used extensively in Hungarian cooking, it did not actually reach Hungary until the Turkish invasion in the 1500's and was not widely used by the Hungarians until the second half of the nineteenth century. Now it is considered the most vital ingredient in Hungarian cooking. The Hungarian paprika has a much richer flavor than the American or Spanish paprika, and growing the sweet red peppers for use in making paprika is a very important farm occupation. Much of it is grown for export, but few other countries use paprika as generously as do the Hungarians. It is the special ingredient that gives Hungarian dishes their characteristic piquant flavor. Sour cream and onions are also used extensively in Hungarian dishes.

Hungarians are famous for their cooking and the food has managed to retain its originality. The way they cook a chicken for instance. Their boned stuffed chicken sliced cold is one of the choicest of chicken dishes. Their Chicken Paprika with sour cream, onions, and paprika is noted throughout the world. Breaded chicken is another specialty, and crêpes or palacinta with chicken in a rich Béchamel sauce or French-fried in deep hot fat until crisp. Holidays and festivals always find a large chicken or a capon stuffed and roasted on the festive board. Goose fats, chicken fats, and lard are used almost exclusively in Hungarian cooking. Butter is very rarely used.

Paprika Chicken
Paprikastcsirke—paprika chicken—This is the most famous of all Hungarian dishes.

3 tablespoons lard
2 Bermuda onions chopped fine
2 tablespoons paprika
1 tablespoon tarragon

1 teaspoon red wine vinegar
4-pound chicken fryer cut into pieces
½ cup flour
1 teaspoon salt
¼ teaspoon pepper
½ cup chicken broth
½ cup sherry
½ cup sour cream

Melt the lard in a heavy frying pan. Add the Bermuda onions and sauté them until soft but not browned. Add the paprika, tarragon, and red wine vinegar. Stir in well and add the chicken pieces which have been rolled in the flour mixed with salt and pepper. Brown lightly on both sides. Add the chicken broth and the sherry. Cover the pan and cook over low heat about 40 minutes or until the chicken is tender. Remove the chicken to a serving platter and keep hot. Add the sour cream to the sauce in the pan, blend in well, and heat thoroughly. Pour over the chicken and serve with freshly boiled soft noodles.

Serves 4

Chicken Paprika with Dumplings

Dumplings are perfect with this chicken paprika dish. Hungarians rarely use butter in cooking but being an American cook I much prefer using butter in place of lard in making the dumplings.

2 medium onions chopped
4 slices bacon chopped
4-pound chicken fryer cut into pieces
1 teaspoon flour
1 clove garlic minced
1½ cups white wine
1 cup chicken stock

2 teaspoons paprika
½ cup sour cream

Dumplings
4 eggs
4 tablespoons melted butter
4 cups all-purpose flour
1 teaspoon salt
½ cup milk or more
Boiling salted water

Cook the onions and bacon together in a heavy Dutch oven for 3 minutes. Add the chicken and cook until browned on both sides. Remove the chicken. Add the flour and minced garlic to the pan and cook for 2 minutes. Add the white wine, chicken stock, and paprika. Mix in well and return the chicken to the pan. Cover and cook over low heat about 40 minutes or until the chicken is tender. Add the sour cream and blend well into the sauce. Add the dumplings and spoon the sauce over the chicken and dumplings.

For the dumplings—beat the eggs with 4 tablespoons melted butter. Add the flour which has been sifted with 1 teaspoon salt. Add enough milk to make a very stiff batter. Drop by teaspoonfuls into boiling salted water and let boil for 10 minutes. Drain and add to the chicken.

Serves 4

Seared Chicken
Pörköltcsirke—Seared Chicken—another very delightful paprika chicken but this one is without sour cream.

4-pound chicken fryer cut into pieces
2 onions chopped fine
2 tablespoons lard

2 tablespoons paprika
1 teaspoon salt

Melt the lard in a heavy pan and when hot add the chopped onions and brown lightly. Add the paprika and the salt and mix in well. Add the chicken and cook over a medium low heat until tender and well browned on both sides about 45 minutes. Turn frequently while cooking.

Serves 4

Boned Stuffed Chicken
Boned Stuffed Chicken is one of the choicest of chicken dishes. It may be a little trouble to prepare but it is well worth the extra effort for it is utterly delicious. Serve it for a party or a buffet.

5-pound roasting chicken
2 teaspoons salt
1 onion chopped fine
2 tablespoons lard
1 pound ground veal
½ pound chicken livers ground fine
1 cup dry breadcrumbs
2 hard-cooked eggs
2 tablespoons paprika
1 egg well beaten
¼ cup white wine
¼ cup sour cream
1 teaspoon salt
2 cloves garlic
1 onion stuck with 2 cloves
Sprigs of parsley
Thin lemon slices

Ask your butcher to bone the chicken leaving bones in the wings and legs. Or if you are daring try doing it yourself. Rub the chicken well with salt. Melt the lard in a skillet and cook the onions until soft but not browned. Add the ground veal and chicken livers and brown them, separating the bits of meat with a fork while browning. Add the dry breadcrumbs. Force the hard-cooked eggs through a sieve and combine with the meat mixture. Add the paprika, well beaten egg, white wine, sour cream, and salt. The mixture should be a lovely pink color. Stuff the chicken with the mixture and sew the chicken back into shape. Tie the chicken up in a buttered napkin and place in a large kettle with water to cover. Add the garlic and the onion stuck with 2 cloves. Cook slowly for 1½ hours or until the chicken is tender. Remove the chicken carefully to a platter and chill it thoroughly in the refrigerator. Remove the wings and slice the chicken crosswise to serve so that some of the stuffing is included in each serving. Garnish with parsley and thin lemon slices.

Serves 6–8

Half Chicken Hungarian
Huhn Ungarische Art—Half Chicken Hungarian—a wonderful way to serve a young tender chicken.

2 2½-pound broiler chickens
1 teaspoon salt
3 tablespoons lard
1 large Bermuda onion chopped
2 teaspoons paprika
1 tablespoon flour
1 cup chicken stock
¼ cup heavy cream
Hot boiled rice
2 tablespoons chopped fresh dill

Split chickens in half and sprinkle with salt. Melt the lard in a heavy frying pan and cook the chopped onions for 2 minutes. Stir in the paprika. Add the chicken halves and brown evenly on both sides. Sprinkle with flour and add the chicken stock. Cover the pan and cook over low heat about 40 minutes or until the chicken is tender. Remove the chicken to a hot serving platter. Let the sauce reduce down over a high heat to about ½ cup. Add the heavy cream and cook 5 minutes longer. Serve the chicken garnished with hot boiled rice and pour the sauce over the top. Sprinkle with chopped fresh dill.

Serves 4

Chicken with Cabbage

Káposztas Csirke—Chicken with Cabbage combine to make a zesty chicken dish. A Hungarian lady is responsible for the recipe and she tells me this combination is very popular in Hungary.

4-pound chicken fryer cut into pieces
4 tablespoons lard
1 onion chopped fine
1 teaspoon salt
1 teaspoon paprika
½ cup white wine
½ cup cider vinegar
½ head cabbage chopped

Melt the lard in a large heavy frying pan and add the chicken pieces and the chopped onions. Cook until the chicken is well browned on both sides. Sprinkle with salt and blend in the paprika. Add the white wine and the vinegar. Cover the pan and cook over a low heat for 40 minutes or until the chicken is tender. Add the chopped cabbage and continue cooking over a medium high heat until the chicken is almost dry. Stir constantly. Serve at once piping hot.

Serves 4

Breaded Chicken

Rántotta Csirke—Breaded Chicken—this is a favorite Sunday night supper dish in Hungary.

4-pound chicken fryer cut into pieces
1 teaspoon salt
⅛ teaspoon pepper
½ cup flour
2 eggs slightly beaten
1 cup fine breadcrumbs
½ cup fat

Add the salt and pepper to the flour and roll the chicken pieces in the seasoned flour. Then dip the chicken pieces in the beaten eggs and roll in the fine bread crumbs. Let dry out for about ½ hour. Heat the fat in a large heavy kettle and fry the chicken slowly until golden brown on both sides and tender. Turn frequently to brown evenly.

Serves 4

Hungarian Chicken Sauté

Tangy paprika and white wine distinguishes this mouth-watering Hungarian dish.

4-pound chicken fryer cut into pieces
4 tablespoons melted lard or bacon fat
1 onion chopped fine
1 teaspoon salt
1 teaspoon paprika
1 cup dry white wine

Brown the chicken well on both sides in the melted lard or bacon fat. Remove from the pan and add the chopped onion, salt, and paprika. Mix together and cook until the onions are soft but not browned. Return the chicken to the pan and add the white wine. Cover the pan and cook over a low heat for 40 minutes or until the chicken is tender. Turn heat to high and cook uncovered until the sauce has reduced down to a tablespoon or two. Stir constantly. Serve at once.

Serves 4

Chicken Palacsinta

Palacsinta Scirke—Chicken Palacsinta—thin French pancakes or crêpes with chicken in a rich Mornay sauce.

4-pound roasting chicken cut into pieces
Boiling salted water
1 tablespoon butter melted
1 tablespoon flour
1 cup thin cream
1 tablespoon butter
Dash of paprika
2 tablespoons grated Parmesan cheese
2 tablespoons grated Swiss cheese
1 tablespoon whipped cream
French pancakes or crêpes

Place the chicken pieces in boiling salted water to cover and cook over low heat, covered, for 1 hour or until tender. Remove the chicken and cool. Discard skin and bones. Cut the meat into large pieces and set aside.

Melt 1 tablespoon butter in a pan and blend in the flour. Slowly add 1 cup thin cream, stirring constantly, and cook over low heat until thickened. Add 1 tablespoon butter, a dash of paprika, and the grated Parmesan and Swiss cheese. Mix ½ of the Mornay sauce with the chicken and taste for seasoning. Place 1 tablespoon of the chicken mixture on thin French pancakes and roll up. Arrange in a baking dish. Add 1 tablespoon whipped cream to the remaining Mornay sauce

and cover the tops of the crêpes with this sauce. Bake at 400°
until browned on top. Allow 2 or 3 pancakes for each person.

French Pancakes or Crêpes
2 cups sifted flour
1 teaspoon salt
4 eggs separated
3 cups milk

Combine flour, salt, egg yolks, and 1 cup of the milk, stirring
until smooth. Gradually stir in the rest of the milk to make
a batter the consistency of heavy cream. Beat the egg whites
until stiff and fold into the batter. Stir before dipping each
pancake.

Bake full size thin cakes on an 8-inch skillet, tipping to spread
the batter thin. Heat the skillet and when a few drops of
water will dance on it the skillet is hot enough for even
browning. Grease the skillet before cooking each pancake.
For an 8 inch pancake dip ¼ cup batter onto the hot greased
skillet. With a quick rotary motion, tip the skillet to spread
the batter thinly.

A batter with stiffly beaten egg whites added separately should
be stirred before each dipping. A fluffy batter will bake a
thicker pancake but once off the griddle it too will become
thin.

Brown the pancakes only very lightly. When browned ease the
pancake onto a warm baking dish. Spread filling on the baked
pancake while another one is cooking. Even spreading is not
important since the warmth of the pancake distributes the
filling. Roll or fold each pancake and when all are cooked
reheat in a 350° oven for about 15 minutes. Always serve
them hot.

Paprika Chicken Pancake Noodles

Paprikáscirkes Palacsinta—Paprika Chicken with Pancake Noodles—this dish is a great favorite with Hungarians.

French pancakes or crêpes
3½-pound chicken fryer cut into pieces
2 onions chopped fine
3 tablespoons fat
2 tablespoons paprika
1 teaspoon salt
1 cup sour cream

Brown the onions lightly in melted fat. Add the paprika and the chicken pieces. Sprinkle with salt. Cover and cook slowly about 40 minutes or until tender. Remove the chicken and cut the meat from the bones into small pieces. Cut the cooked crêpes into ½ inch strips to make the pancake noodles. Mix the chicken with the sour cream. Combine with the pancake noodles. Turn into a greased casserole and bake in a 350° oven for 30 minutes. Serve from the casserole.

Serves 6

Fried Chicken Pancakes

Kirantott Csirkespalacsinto—Fried Chicken Pancake—I first tasted these wonderful fried pancakes at a charming little Hungarian restaurant in San Francisco. This is as near an approximation of the crispy entrees as I was able to make.

French pancakes or crêpes
3 cups minced cooked chicken
2 egg yolks
1 cup sour cream
1 teaspoon salt
1 teaspoon paprika
½ teaspoon ginger

¼ cup grated Swiss cheese
1 whole egg
½ cup flour
1 cup dry breadcrumbs
Deep fat for frying

Make crêpes extra thin for rolling. Combine minced chicken,
egg yolks, sour cream, salt, paprika, ginger, and Swiss cheese.
Spread 1 tablespoon filling on each pancake. Roll up and
tuck in ends carefully. Beat egg slightly. Dip each rolled pancake first in egg, then in flour, then again in egg, and finally
roll in the breadcrumbs. Let dry out about ½ hour. Fry in
deep hot fat until browned. Drain on paper and serve hot,
allowing 2 or 3 pancakes for each person.

Layer Chicken Pancakes
Rakott Csirkespalacsinta—Layer Chicken Pancakes—another
wonderful way to serve French pancakes.

French pancakes or crêpes
3 cups minced cooked chicken
2 egg yolks
1 cup sour cream
1 teaspoon salt
1 teaspoon paprika
1 teaspoon ginger
¼ cup grated Swiss cheese

Combine minced chicken, egg yolks, sour cream, salt, paprika,
ginger, and Swiss cheese. Place a French pancake on a buttered
baking dish. Spread with 1 tablespoon of the chicken filling,
and lay another pancake over the top. Spread that with the
chicken filling and repeat until you have 12 or more layers
of pancakes and filling. Place in a 350° oven for 20 minutes
or until the filling is set. Cut pie fashion and serve hot.

Serves 4

Austrian Chicken

Snow-capped mountain peaks and Tyrolean Alpine slopes make up most of the scenery of Austria. There are thick wooded foothills, emerald-green meadows, and pasture lands on which Austria's fine herds of dairy cattle graze to furnish the cream the Austrians love so dearly. Fairy-tale villages are set deep in the high valleys while above, on lonely mountain ledges, nestle the houses of upland farmers.

Farming has always been difficult in the Austrian Tyrol because of the steep terrain, poor soil, and a very short growing season. Grass and alfalfa grow extremely well on the high meadowland and as a result most of the Alpine farmers have gone in for raising dairy cattle. They have developed unique dairy methods for the terrain and in some areas have built pipelines up to three miles long to carry the milk from their high farms to transfer points below in the valley.

In the north the blue Danube flows past the famous capital Vienna. Steeped in the tradition and culture of a colorful past, Vienna has been a great capital for two hundred years, and to epicures Viennese cooking has been considered the most refined in the civilized world. The seat of a mighty empire and the cultural center of Europe, Vienna drew people from many lands. The result has left a legacy of cooking which is both exciting and different; the soups and stews; the cakes and pastries; the fish and meat dishes; the wonderful breads. The Austrians gave something distinctive to every dish they borrowed, even the great French ones.

The Austrians are very fond of cream and use it quite lavishly in their cooking. Vienna, of course, is famed for her pastry concoctions and her pastry cooks rank among the finest in the world. They are past-masters in the art of making extravagant concoctions of meringue and whipped cream as well as making tortes and strudels and marvelous crescent rolls.

The Austrians have absorbed the food and cooking ideas from many peoples and adapted them to their own palate. The sour cream they use in so many dishes first came from the Slavs. The paprika they use so much of came from Hungary. The many noodle dishes from Italy. Their cooking is substantial and nourishing: the celebrated Wiener Schnitzel, the many veal dishes for which Austrian is renowned. Their rich soups with dumplings or noodles are wonderfully hearty and filling. And how the Austrians love sweets—and such rich sweets. No Austrian meal is complete without a rich sweet to top it off with.

The Austrians have many brilliant ways of cooking chicken. It does not play the important role in Austria that it plays in some of the other countries in Europe but it is still a very popular dish. Chicken is served in a variety of different ways and the Austrians have given many dishes, no matter what their origin, a national individuality. Paprika Chicken, that most famous dish which the Austrians claim the honor of inventing along with the Hungarians, has been given an extra sparkle of its own. The delightful Backhähdel—a fried chicken made as a Wiener Schnitzel—is another typically Austrian dish. Then there is Suppe mit Leberknudeln—Chicken Giblet Soup with Liver Dumplings—which is popular with the mountain folk and very substantial. All these chicken dishes reflect the vitality and gaiety of the Austrian people and whatever nationality the dishes may have been originally, the light and deft hand of the Austrian cook has transformed them into something individual and national.

Paprika Chicken

Paprika Huhn—Paprika Chicken—Austria's most famous chicken dish, even though Hungary has a claim on it.

4-pound chicken fryer cut into pieces
1 teaspoon salt
½ cup butter
1 large Bermuda onion diced
2 teaspoons paprika
½ tablespoon flour
1 cup chicken stock
1 tablespoon heavy cream
1 cup thick sour cream
2 tablespoons chopped fresh dill

Rub the chicken pieces well with salt. Melt the butter in a heavy Dutch oven and heat until a light brown. Add the diced Bermuda onion and cook until soft but not brown. Stir in the paprika. Add the chicken and cook until colored on both sides. Turn heat to low, cover, and cook 30 minutes longer. Add the flour and blend in well. Add the chicken stock and the heavy cream. Recover and simmer 10 minutes longer. Remove the chicken to a hot serving platter. Stir the sour cream into the pan and cook until heated through, stirring constantly. Pour over the chicken and sprinkle with fresh dill.

Serves 4

Paprika Chicken with Egg Barley
An interesting variation of Austria's famed Paprika Huhn.

¼ cup butter melted
1 Bermuda onion chopped fine
1 tablespoon paprika
1 teaspoon salt
1 teaspoon pepper
4-pound chicken fryer cut into pieces
¼ cup flour
1 cup hot chicken stock
1 cup heavy cream

1 cup sour cream
2 cups egg barley or finely chopped noodles
1 medium onion chopped
1 bay leaf
2 tablespoons chicken fat
1 quart chicken stock

Melt the butter in a heavy Dutch oven and add the Bermuda
onion. Cook until tender but not browned. Add the salt,
pepper, and paprika. Blend well into the melted butter and
onions. Dredge the chicken pieces with the flour and add them
to the pan. Brown well on both sides. Add the hot chicken
broth, cover and simmer for 40 minutes or until the chicken
is tender. Remove the chicken to a serving platter and keep
hot. Add the cup of heavy cream to the drippings in the pan
and let it reduce down over a medium high heat to ⅓ of its
original quantity. Add the sour cream, blend in well, and cook
1 minute longer. Pour the sauce over the chicken and serve
with the egg barley.

To Prepare Egg Barley
Place the egg barley or fine noodles in a baking pan. Add the
chicken fat, chopped onion, bay leaf, 1 quart chicken stock,
and bake in a 375° oven for 20 minutes. Serve with the Paprika Chicken.

Serves 4

Creamed Paprika Chicken
Another Paprika Chicken variation.

4-pound chicken fryer cut into pieces
¼ cup butter melted
½ cup sour cream
2 medium onions chopped
1 tablespoon paprika
3 teaspoons tomato puree

Melt the butter in a heavy Dutch oven and add the chopped
onions. Cook until they are soft but not browned. Add the
paprika and stir in well. Add the chicken and brown lightly
on both sides. Add the tomato puree, cover, and simmer over
a low heat about 40 minutes or until the chicken is tender.
Remove the chicken to a serving platter and keep hot. Add
the sour cream to the sauce, blend in well, and cook until just
heated through. Pour over the chicken.

Serves 4

Smothered Chicken with Sour Cream and Lemon
A dish that shows the sparkle of Austrian cooking. This one
with herbs, sour cream, and lemon is splendid.

4-pound chicken fryer cut into pieces
¼ cup butter melted
2 tablespoons flour
1½ cups sour cream
1 teaspoon salt
⅛ teaspoon pepper
1 cup sliced mushrooms
1 tablespoon chopped parsley
1 tablespoon fennel
1 tablespoon chopped chives
1 tablespoon lemon juice
Grated rind of 1 lemon

Melt the butter in a heavy frying pan and brown the chicken
well on both sides. Remove the chicken to a casserole. Stir the
flour into the pan juices and blend in the sour cream. Add the
salt and pepper and cook over a low heat, stirring constantly,
until thickened. Add the sliced mushrooms, parsley, fennel,
and chopped chives. Mix in well and pour the sour cream
sauce over the chicken in the casserole. Cover and cook over
a low heat for 40 minutes or until the chicken is tender. Re-

move from the heat and add the lemon juice and grated lemon rind. Serve at once.

Serves 4

Viennese Fried Chicken

Wiener Backhähdel—Viennese Fried Chicken—a fried chicken cooked as a Wiener Schnitzel is another delightful Austrian specialty.

4-pound chicken fryer cut into pieces
Salt and pepper
Flour
2 eggs slightly beaten
Fine cracker crumbs
3 tablespoons butter
Juice of 1 lemon
½ cup tomato puree
¼ cup thin cream
1 bay leaf crumbled
1 teaspoon celery salt
1 clove garlic mashed
1 small onion sliced
½ teaspoon salt
⅛ teaspoon pepper
Pinch baking soda
1 tablespoon flour
1 cup thin cream
½ cup heavy cream scalded
Finely chopped parsley
Lemon slices

Rub the chicken pieces well with salt and pepper. Dip each piece of chicken in flour, then in the beaten eggs, and last in the fine cracker crumbs. Brown well on both sides in 3 tablespoons melted butter. Turn heat to low, cover, and cook for 40 minutes or until the chicken is tender. In the meantime combine the tomato puree with ¼ cup thin cream, the bay leaf, celery salt, garlic, onion slices, salt, and pepper. Cook for 10 minutes. Blend in an electric blender or force through a fine sieve. Add a pinch of baking soda and set aside. When the chicken is tender sprinkle with lemon juice, arrange on a serving platter, and keep hot. Pour off all but 1 tablespoon of the drippings in the pan. Add 1 tablespoon flour and blend in well. Add a cup of thin cream and stir over a medium heat until thickened. Add the tomato mixture and the heavy cream scalded. Blend thoroughly and pour the sauce over the chicken. Sprinkle with finely chopped parsley and garnish with lemon slices.

Serves 4

Chicken with Egg Sauce

Hühn In Sasse—Chicken with Egg Sauce is a delightful Viennese dish with a distinctive touch.

4-pound chicken fryer cut into pieces
Beef stock to cover
2 tablespoons tarragon vinegar
6 egg yolks
¼ cup finely chopped chives
1 teaspoon salt
¾ cup butter
Thin lemon slices sprinkled with paprika

Place the chicken pieces in a kettle with beef stock to cover and simmer over a low heat about 45 minutes or until the chicken is tender. Remove the chicken from the stock and when cooled, skin the pieces, and set aside. Strain 1 cup of the cooking stock. Put the tarragon vinegar, egg yolks, finely chopped chives, salt, and butter in the container of an electric blender and blend until smooth, about 5 seconds. Remove the cover and as blending continues slowly add the cup of strained stock. Pour the mixture into the top of a double boiler and cook over hot water, stirring constantly, until the sauce is of the consistency of a soft custard. Remove from heat and pour the sauce over the skinned chicken pieces. Garnish with lemon slices sprinkled with paprika.

Serves 4

Chicken with Curry Sauce

Indische Hühner—Chicken with Curry Sauce—this is a very elegant Viennese dish.

1 cup rice
Salted water
2 goose livers chopped
½ cup truffles chopped
½ teaspoon salt
4-pound chicken fryer
4 slices bacon
1 quart hot chicken stock
3 teaspoons curry powder
2 egg yolks
½ cup heavy cream

Half cook the rice in salted water according to the directions on the package. Drain and cool. Add the chopped goose livers, the chopped truffles, and ½ teaspoon salt to the rice. Fill the cavity of the chicken with this mixture and sew or skewer the opening closed. Truss. Tie the bacon slices over the breast and thighs and place the chicken on a rack in a kettle with 1 quart of chicken stock. Cover and cook over a low heat for 1 hour or until the chicken is tender. Remove the chicken from the kettle, discard the bacon slices, and keep the chicken hot. Reduce the chicken stock over a high heat to 2 cups. Strain and stir in the curry powder that has been dissolved with some of the chicken stock. Beat the egg yolks with ½ cup heavy cream and add to the stock. Stir in well and cook over a low heat until slightly thickened. Carve the chicken and serve in the sauce with some of the stuffing on the side.

Serves 4

Mushroom Chicken

Eingemachtes Huhn mit pilve—Mushroom Chicken—this is another popular Austrian way of preparing a chicken.

3½-pound chicken fryer cut into pieces
1½ cups sliced mushrooms
¼ cup butter melted
2 tablespoons flour
1 cup heavy cream

Melt the butter in a heavy frying pan and brown the chicken well on both sides. Add the sliced mushrooms, cover, and cook over a low heat for 40 minutes or until the chicken is tender. Remove the chicken and keep hot. Sprinkle the flour over the drippings left in the pan and blend in well. Slowly add the heavy cream and cook over a low heat, stirring constantly, until thickened and smooth. Pour the sauce over the chicken and serve at once.

Serves 4

Chicken Villeroi

A brilliant Viennese specialty.

4-pound chicken fryer cut into pieces
3 sprigs parsley
2 bay leaves
2 celery stalks
1 carrot scraped
1 onion sliced

6 peppercorns
2 cups Villeroi Sauce
1 cup dry breadcrumbs
Deep fat for frying

Put the chicken in a large kettle with salted water to cover.
Add the parsley, bay leaves, celery stalks, carrot, sliced onion,
and peppercorns. Cover and cook over a low heat about 45
minutes or until the chicken is tender. Remove the chicken
from the stock and cool. When cooled discard the skin. Coat
the chicken well with the Villeroi Sauce and chill in the
refrigerator for 1 hour. Dip the chicken in more of the
Villeroi Sauce and roll in the dry breadcrumbs. Brown
quickly in hot deep fat. Drain on absorbent paper and
serve at once.

Villeroi Sauce
3 tablespoons butter
5 tablespoons flour
3 cups strained chicken stock
½ cup cream
3 egg yolks slightly beaten
½ teaspoon salt
⅛ teaspoon pepper
1 teaspoon Worcestershire sauce
1 package gelatin dissolved in ¼ cup cold water

Melt the butter and blend in the flour. Add the chicken
stock and stir over a medium heat until thickened and
smooth. Add the cream and the slightly beaten egg yolks.
Stir over the heat until well blended. Add the salt, pepper,
Worcestershire sauce, and gelatin which has been dissolved
in ¼ cup cold water. Continue cooking over the heat until
the sauce is thick enough to coat a spoon.

Serves 4

Hungarian Chicken Stew

Ungarisches Hühner Porkele—Hungarian Chicken Stew—this simple peasant dish, when adopted by the Austrians, took on an elegant air.

4-pound chicken fryer cut into pieces
2 onions chopped fine
2 tablespoons butter
2 tablespoons chopped parsley
½ teaspoon salt
2 teaspoons paprika
1 cup hot chicken stock
2 tablespoons tomato puree
1 cup heavy cream
2 egg yolks well beaten

Sauté the chopped onion and parsley in butter until the onions are soft but not browned. Sprinkle with salt and paprika and blend in well. Add the chicken and brown on both sides. When browned add the hot chicken stock, cover, and cook over a low heat 40 minutes or until tender. Remove the chicken to a serving platter and keep hot. Add the tomato puree to the sauce in the pan along with the heavy cream which has been mixed with the 2 well-beaten egg yolks. Cook, stirring constantly, over a low heat 5 minutes longer. Pour over the chicken and serve with noodles.

Serves 4

Chicken in Spinach Soup

Hühner in Spinat Suppe—Chicken in Spinach Soup—a wonderful dish on a winter night.

4-pound chicken fryer cut into pieces
2 stalks celery
2 carrots scraped

1 sprig parsley
6 peppercorns
3 cups boiling salted water
3 cups hot chicken stock
1 package frozen chopped spinach
3 tablespoons minced onion
3 tablespoons butter
¼ cup flour
Salt to taste
2 egg yolks
1 cup heavy cream

Put the chicken pieces in a kettle with the celery, carrots, parsley, peppercorns, and boiling salted water. Add the hot chicken stock, cover, and cook over a low heat for 40 minutes or until the chicken is tender. Remove the chicken from the broth, skin, and keep hot. Strain 4 cups of the chicken stock and set aside. Cook the spinach according to package directions. Sauté the minced onion in 3 tablespoons melted butter until soft but do not let it brown. Stir in the flour and blend in well. Add the 4 cups chicken stock gradually and cook, stirring constantly, until thickened. Add the cooked spinach and salt to taste. Beat the egg yolks into the heavy cream and add to the soup. Cook over a low heat until just heated through. Place a piece of chicken in each soup bowl and pour over it the hot spinach soup.

Serves 6

Chicken Giblet Soup with Liver Dumplings
Suppe mit Leberknudeln—Chicken Giblet Soup with Liver Dumplings—rich soup with the addition of noodles, dumplings —typically Austrian.

1 pound chicken giblets
1 quart salted cold water

1 carrot
1 rutabaga
3 tablespoons butter
Salt and pepper
1¼ cups flour
1 egg
½ cup water approximately
½ pound chicken livers
1 tablespoon butter
¼ cup sour cream

Put the giblets in 1 quart salted cold water, cover, and cook over a low heat for 1 hour. Chop the carrot and rutabaga fine. Melt 3 tablespoons butter in a kettle, add the chopped carrot and rutabaga, and cook over a low heat for 15 minutes. Sprinkle with salt and pepper and add ¼ cup of the flour. Blend in well and slowly add the water the giblets were cooked in. Cook over a low heat, stirring constantly, until thickened. Chop the giblets fine and add them to the soup. Continue cooking over a low heat.

Make the liver dumplings. In a bowl mix 1 cup flour with 1 egg. Add enough water to make a fairly thick dough about ½ cup. Chop the chicken livers very fine and fry them for 3 minutes in 1 tablespoon butter. Add them to the dough. Raise the heat under the soup to where it begins to boil and when it is boiling drop teaspoonfuls of the dumpling dough into the hot soup. Reduce the heat again, cover the kettle, and let the dumplings cook gently for 5 minutes. Remove the soup from the stove, stir in the sour cream, and serve at once.

Serves 4

Swiss Chicken

Switzerland is a small mountainous country high in the Alps. Its snow-capped peaks, its green valleys, its blue lakes, and its wonderful food have made it a great tourist attraction. It is a paradise for skiers and mountain climbers alike. It is also a land of breath-taking beauty with lush green meadows, clear sparkling lakes, and quaint fairy-tale villages nestled in deep emerald valleys and always in the background there is the majestic grandeur of the snow-capped Alps.

The Swiss are famed for their hotels, fine restaurants, and excellent restaurant schools. They have produced some of the world's greatest chefs. In the Italian, French, and German-speaking areas of Switzerland the cooking has been influenced by the cuisine of those countries but there are still Swiss regional dishes that are as ancient as Swiss history. Wines and spirits are an integral part of Swiss life and cooking—as is its favorite beverage, kirsch. It is kirsch that flavors that most famous of all Swiss dishes, the world-renowned Swiss Fondue.

Switzerland's most celebrated product is Swiss cheese and it is the most delicious of all cheeses. It is also called Emmentaler and it is produced in the Bernese Valley. Closely resembling Swiss cheese is the well-known Gruyère, which has smaller holes and is stronger in flavor. There are also many other fine cheeses produced in Switzerland and every mountain hamlet has its own special kind of cheese.

Chicken is cooked in many different ways in Switzerland. There may be subtle differences in the dishes of the various regions, the Italian, German, French, Swiss, but the skill of the Swiss cooks is evident in all of them. Nor could it be otherwise in a country that boasts the best restaurant schools in the world. There is Supreme de Volaille au Kirsch, one of the great specialties of Swiss cuisine; Chicken Casanova, Fricassee de Volaille Stockli, and Volaille de Neuchatel, a wonderful dish from Neuchatel made with Swiss cheese.

Supreme de Volaille au Kirsch
This is one of the great specialties of Swiss cuisine.

4 chicken breasts boned
6 tablespoons clarified butter
½ cup cognac
½ cup kirsch
3 egg yolks
1 cup heavy cream
Salt and pepper to taste
2 truffles minced

Have your butcher bone, skin, and halve the chicken breasts for you. Melt the butter in a large skillet and sauté the chicken breasts over a medium heat for 10 minutes on each side. Remove the chicken to a serving platter and keep hot. Add the cognac and the kirsch to the skillet and stir in well, scraping all the brown particles from the bottom of the pan. Beat the egg yolks with the heavy cream and add slowly to the skillet. Season with salt and pepper to taste. Heat through over a low heat being careful not to let the sauce boil. Pour the sauce over the chicken breasts and sprinkle with minced truffles.

Serves 4

Chicken in Curried Cream Sauce
Another delectable dish from Switzerland.

4-pound chicken fryer cut into pieces
1 teaspoon salt
1/8 teaspoon pepper
1/4 cup butter melted
1 teaspoon Indian curry powder
1 cup chopped onions
1 tablespoon flour
1 cup tomato sauce
2 tablespoons chutney
3 tablespoons cream
4 thin slices ham
4 pineapple slices
2 tablespoons butter

Season the chicken pieces with the salt and pepper. Melt
1/4 cup butter in a heavy frying pan and add the curry.
Stir in well and add the chicken pieces and the chopped
onions. Brown the chicken well on both sides. When browned
add 1 tablespoon flour and mix in well. Add the tomato
sauce and stir over a medium heat until the sauce is
thickened. Lower the heat, cover the pan, and simmer for
30 minutes or until the chicken is tender. Melt 2 tablespoons
butter in another pan and brown the ham and the pineapple
slices. Set aside. When the chicken is tender remove it to a
serving platter and keep hot. Add the chutney and the
cream to the sauce and stir over a low heat for 2 minutes.
Pour the sauce over the chicken and garnish with the ham
and pineapple slices.

Serves 4

Volaille de Neuchatel
A wonderful dish from Neuchatel.

4-pound chicken fryer cut into pieces
1 teaspoon salt

2 eggs lightly beaten
½ cup breadcrumbs
1 cup grated Swiss cheese
⅓ cup butter melted

Add the salt to the eggs and beat lightly. Combine the breadcrumbs and grated Swiss cheese together in a bowl. Dip the chicken pieces in the breadcrumbed Swiss cheese mixture, then in the beaten egg, and again in the bread-crumbed Swiss cheese mixture, making sure that they are well coated. Let them set and dry out for 30 minutes. Melt the butter in a heavy frying pan and when hot brown the chicken well on both sides. Turn heat to low, partially cover the pan, and cook over low heat for 40 minutes, turning the chicken over once during the cooking. The chicken should be tender and succulent on the inside and coated with a crisp golden brown crust.

Serves 4

Chicken Fricassee de Volaille
An example of the great skill of the Swiss chefs.

4-pound chicken boned and cut into pieces
4 tablespoons butter melted
½ teaspoon salt
¼ teaspoon thyme
½ teaspoon sweet basil
1 large onion chopped
½ cup carrots diced
½ cup celery chopped
¼ cup rich brown gravy
¼ cup chicken stock
1 cup raw potatoes diced
1 tablespoon tarragon
¼ cup heavy cream

Have your butcher bone the chicken and cut it into serving pieces. Melt the butter in a heavy Dutch oven and add the chicken pieces. When the chicken is well browned on both sides add the salt, thyme, sweet basil, and the chopped onions. Cook for 2 minutes, then add the chopped celery, diced carrots, and cook for 3 minutes. Add the rich brown gravy and mix in well. Add the chicken stock, cover, and cook over low heat for 10 minutes. Add the diced raw potatoes and continue cooking 20 minutes longer or until the chicken and vegetables are tender. Add the tarragon and the heavy cream. Cook over low heat until just heated through. Serve the chicken with the vegetables and gravy.

Serves 4

Crêpes de Volaille Mornay
The delicate and delightful Swiss version of Chicken Crêpes Mornay is one of the notable dishes of the Swiss cuisine.

4 crêpes
3 tablespoons butter
3 tablespoons flour
1 cup cream
½ cup mushrooms sliced
2 tablespoons butter
2 tablespoons chopped parsley
1 teaspoon salt
1½ cups diced cooked chicken
½ cup sherry

Mornay Sauce
1 cup Béchamel or cream sauce
¼ cup heavy cream
2 egg yolks beaten lightly with 2 tablespoons heavy cream
¼ cup grated Swiss cheese
1 tablespoon butter

Make the crêpes first and put them in an oven to keep warm. Melt 3 tablespoons butter in a saucepan and blend in the flour. Add the cream and cook over a medium heat until the sauce has thickened. Sauté the sliced mushrooms in 2 tablespoons butter for 3 minutes and add to the sauce. Add the chopped parsley, salt, and diced cooked chicken. Cook over a medium low heat for 5 minutes, stirring constantly. Add the sherry, blend in well, and keep hot while making the Mornay sauce.

Mornay Sauce. Add the ¼ cup heavy cream to the Béchamel sauce and cook over a medium low heat for 5 minutes, stirring constantly. Add the egg yolks which have been beaten lightly with the cream and the grated Swiss cheese. Continue cooking until the cheese has melted but do not let the sauce boil. Add the 1 tablespoon butter, bit by bit, beating briskly after each addition.

Fill the crêpes with the chicken mixture, roll them up, and put them in a buttered baking dish. Pour the Mornay sauce over them and put under the broiler until the top is lightly browned. Serve at once.

Serves 4

Dutch Chicken

The tranquil Dutch landscape is like a picture postcard with its dikes and windmills and many canals. The flat lowlands stretch for miles, with no sloping hills, and the blue channels cut across the land in winding meanders; quaint black-and-white-step-gabled houses stand along the banks and the Dutch windmills whirl day and night to help keep the water from the land.

Middle class life prospered in Holland after the overthrow of Spanish rule. By the 17th century the middle class burgher was well-fed and well-off. Meals were bountiful and the center of Dutch life was the spotlessly clean kitchen often tiled with colored porcelain and with pewter and copper utensils gleaming in the cupboards. Dairy cattle grazing along the channels gave the Dutch milk, butter, and cheese. The lowlands especially were rich in fruits and vegetables. The canals and the open sea furnished many varieties of fish. In the 14th century a zealous Dutchman discovered a way to preserve herring by curing it and pickling it in brine. From then on the herring industry became an important business in Holland. The beginning of the herring season is always a gala occasion. The herring fleet sails out from the various seaports with full sails and flags flying, to parade along the coast, while the Dutch come from all over Holland to watch from the dunes.

Holland is famous for its tulips and its Edam and Gouda cheeses. The national drink is called Genever or Dutch gin and is a distillation of grain flavored with juniper berries.

Herring is both cheap and plentiful in Holland and it is consumed in large quantities. It is not only eaten fresh but the surplus is pickled, smoked, or salted and eaten during the rest of the year. The Dutch method of salting and smoking herring is well known and some of their ways of cooking fish are delicious. Beefsteak is also very popular and the Dutch way of cooking makes it unusually tender. The beefsteak is cut against the grain to prevent a loss of blood during cooking. Their cooking has been much influenced by their colonies and rice and cinnamon are used extensively in Dutch dishes. In the cold dank climate soups play an important part too and hearty soups such as bean or pea are eaten frequently as a whole meal in themselves.

Chicken is well liked in Holland but it is still considered to be a Sunday treat. Chicken is not more expensive than beef, but the butter used in preparing it is; and it takes quite a bit of butter to make the necessary amount of gravy to go with the accompanying potatoes. So while they do eat chicken occasionally, the Dutch stick to their beefsteak and herring most of the time.

Roast Chicken

Gebraden Kip—Roast Chicken—the Dutch are not particularly imaginative in their preparation of chicken but this roast chicken is still a very tasty dish.

2 2-pound broiler chickens
½ cup butter
1 teaspoon salt

Pour boiling water over the inside and outside of the chickens. Dry well. Rub with salt and put a lump of butter inside the cavities of the chickens. Melt the remaining butter in a heavy frying pan. Place the chickens in the pan and brown well all over on a high heat, turning often so the chickens brown evenly. Reduce the heat to medium low and half cover the frying pan. Continue cooking about 20 minutes longer or until the chickens are tender. Serve with potatoes boiled or fried.

Serves 4

Chicken Waterzootjie

There are two kinds of Waterzootjie—one made with chicken and the other with fish. Both are popular in Holland.

5-pound roasting chicken cut into pieces
Juice of ½ lemon
¼ cup butter melted
2 onions sliced
4 carrots cut into pieces
3 leeks cut into pieces
4 sprigs parsley
½ teaspoon nutmeg
⅛ teaspoon powdered cloves
3 cups chicken stock
3 cups dry white wine
1 lemon sliced thin
4 egg yolks
⅓ cup heavy cream

Rub the chicken pieces well with the juice of ½ lemon. Melt the butter in a heavy pan and brown the chicken pieces well on both sides. When browned place the chicken in a heavy Dutch oven or casserole. Add the sliced onions, carrots, leeks, parsley, nutmeg, and powdered cloves. Add the chicken stock and bring to a boil. Reduce heat, add the dry white wine, cover, and simmer about 1 hour or until the chicken is tender. Remove the chicken and keep hot. Add the sliced lemon. Beat the egg yolks with the cream and stir into the sauce. Cook until thickened slightly but do not let the sauce boil. Pour the sauce over the chicken and serve with the vegetables.

Serves 6

Creamy Dutch Chicken Soup

Gebonden Hollandse Kippersoep—the Dutch dearly love a creamy chicken soup like this one.

5-pound hen
2 quarts cold water
2 medium onions sliced
1 carrot sliced
1 teaspoon salt
⅛ teaspoon mace
⅛ teaspoon thyme
½ cup rice
3 tablespoons butter melted
4 tablespoons flour
1 egg
¼ cup cream
Chopped parsley

Place the chicken in a kettle with 2 quarts cold water. Add the sliced onions, sliced carrot, salt, mace, and thyme. Cover and bring to a boil, then reduce heat to low and simmer for 2 hours or until the chicken is tender. Remove chicken and let it cool. Skin and cut the meat from the bones into strips. Set aside. Add the rice to the chicken broth and cook over low heat for 20 minutes. Blend the flour into the melted butter and add to the chicken broth and rice, stirring constantly over a low heat until thickened. Add the chicken strips and continue cooking 1 minute longer. Beat the cream and egg together and add to the soup. Beat in well and serve immediately sprinkled with chopped parsley.

Serves 6

Scandinavian Chicken

Scandinavia—Norway, Denmark, Sweden, Finland, Iceland—the name refers to the countries where these nationalities live. Their history is rich in folk tales, of sagas of Norse gods and heroes, some of them dating back a thousand years and more. The Scandinavian people share many similar foods and food customs but each country has certain regional specialties and methods of preparation that distinguishes one from another.

The Swedes take a keen interest in cookery and are very proud of their national dishes. They are noted for their Smorgasbord, a word that makes one's mouth water as one begins to visualize a huge table laden with all manner of delicacies, smoked salmon, pickled herring, salted fish, anchovies, delightful salads, assorted meats, and these are eaten with excellent Swedish bread and butter with a glass of spirits. The Swedes make wonderful breads, one of the best being the limpa. Sweden has great forests and is also noted for its superb game. There are many lakes and rivers in Sweden but the fishing is not as good in the seas around it as it is near Norway's long Atlantic coast. Consequently the Norwegians eat enormous amounts of fish, many of the people having meat only on special occasions as a luxury. Norwegian cooking on the whole is rather plain. They have a great liking for smoked meats and salted fish, and smoked salmon is a very popular dish. Salted herring, anchovies, and shell fish of every discription are served frequently with the delicious Norwegian rye bread.

Denmark, a narrow peninsula with nearby islands, is a

gently rolling countryside of small green farms, blue lakes, and white beaches. It is noted for its pork and dairy products. Danish cooking is very much like that of Norway and Sweden but the Danes are prodigious eaters and go in for heavy soups and other filling foods. Finland is noted for the Russian overtones of many of its dishes and its thirty varieties of mushrooms. While Iceland with most of the inhabitants settled along the seacoast, is best known for its fish and excellent fishing.

Scandinavia is far better known for its seafood than for its chicken. Chicken is regarded as a party dish actually and especially so when it is roasted. Scandinavians usually stuff a chicken with butter and parsley, brown it in butter, and afterwards pot-roast it. The chicken is always served with a cream gravy to which horseradish is sometimes added. Although this is not true in Norway, according to a Norwegian friend of mine, who told me that a clear sauce is customarily served with a roast chicken without any addition of flour at all. In a number of Scandinavian recipes the chicken is merely boiled and served with rice and a cream sauce. Scandinavians are fond of sweet-and-sour flavor contrasts and serve them in side dishes with their chicken, such as rhubarb in Denmark and cranberries in Norway and Sweden. Scandinavian chicken is very good but it is not original. The Scandinavians excel more in the cooking of wild game and fish, which are far more characteristic of Scandinavian cooking than is chicken.

Danish Chicken

This is how they usually cook a chicken in Denmark.

4-pound roasting chicken
1 teaspoon salt
¼ teaspoon pepper
1 large bunch parsley
4 tablespoons butter
¼ cup water

1 cup heavy cream
1 tablespoon flour

Season the cavity of the chicken well with salt and pepper. Wash the parsley, break off the coarse stems, and stuff the parsley into the chicken cavity. Melt 4 tablespoons butter in a heavy Dutch oven and brown the chicken well on all sides. Add ¼ cup water, cover, and simmer slowly about 2 hours or until the chicken is tender. The last 15 minutes of cooking time remove the cover and add 1 cup of heavy cream. Keep the heat very low to prevent the cream from curdling. Remove the cooked chicken to a platter. Thicken the drippings with flour blended with a little cold water. Season to taste with salt and pepper. Remove the cooked parsley from the cavity and serve a little with each plate of chicken. Put the sauce in a bowl to serve separately. Serve with a bowl of rhubarb sauce on the side.

Serves 4

Kylling (Chicken)
The typical way of roasting a chicken in Norway, according to a Norwegian friend; add a little hot water to juices in the pan to make the sauce thick and clear.

5-pound roasting chicken
1 teaspoon salt
¼ teaspoon pepper
1 large bunch parsley
4 tablespoons butter
½ cup water
Hot water

Season the cavity of the chicken well with salt and pepper. Wash the parsley, break off the stems, and stuff the parsley into the chicken cavity. Melt the butter in a heavy Dutch oven and brown the chicken well on all sides. When it is nicely browned add ½ cup water, cover the pan, and simmer very gently for 2 hours or until the chicken is tender. Remove the chicken from the pan and keep hot. Add just enough hot water to the pan to separate the thick part of the pan juices. Mix in well, scraping up all the browned particles with a spoon. The sauce should be thick and clear. Serve the sauce with the chicken.

Serves 6

Chicken in Horseradish Sauce

Hohne I Feberrodsauce—Chicken in Horseradish Sauce—a Norwegian friend gave me this recipe. Creamed sauces are apparently very popular in Norway.

4-pound chicken cut into pieces
Water to cover
1 onion
3 sprigs parsley
1 teaspoon salt
4 tablespoons butter
3 tablespoons flour
2 cups chicken stock
1 tablespoon lemon juice
2 tablespoons cream
4 tablespoons fresh grated horseradish
Salt and pepper to taste

Put the chicken pieces in a kettle with water to cover. Add the onion, parsley, and salt. Cover, bring to a boil, and let simmer 1 hour or until tender. Remove chicken and keep hot. Blend the flour with 4 tablespoons melted butter in a saucepan. Add the chicken stock and cook over a medium heat, stirring constantly, until thickened and smooth. Add the lemon juice, cream, fresh grated horseradish, and salt and pepper to taste. Pour over the chicken and serve.

Serves 4

Swedish Chicken

Chicken Breasts à la Ems Nielsen—this is a very special party dish in Sweden.

4 whole chicken breasts skinned and boned
4 cups hot chicken stock
10 tablespoons butter
4 tablespoons flour
Salt and pepper to taste
½ cup heavy cream
2 cups sliced mushrooms sautéed in 4 tablespoons butter
3 truffles sliced
Pimiento strips

Place the chicken breasts in a heavy Dutch oven. Cover with the hot chicken stock and add 6 tablespoons butter. Simmer, covered, over a low heat for 40 minutes or until the chicken is tender. Remove the chicken and keep hot. Skim fat off the stock and measure 3 cups. Melt 4 tablespoons butter in a pan and add the flour. Blend well and add the 3 cups chicken stock. Cook, stirring constantly, until the sauce is thickened and smooth. Season with salt and pepper to taste. Remove from heat and stir in heavy cream and the mushrooms. Heat through but do not allow to boil. Place chicken breasts on a large platter and pour over the sauce. Garnish with truffle slices and strips of pimiento.

Serves 4

Iceland Chicken Scrapple

Kvekling Polsa—Chicken Scrapple—this Iceland chicken is something like the chicken stuffing without the chicken.

4-pound chicken cut into pieces
Boiling salted water
2 carrots scraped and cut into slices
1 cup diced celery
1 onion sliced
1 cup barley
½ teaspoon paprika
1 teaspoon thyme
2 tablespoons butter

Place the chicken in a kettle and cover with boiling salted water. Add the carrots, celery, onion, and let simmer for 1 hour. Add the barley and let simmer slowly another hour. Stir occasionally. Remove the chicken and let it cool. Cut the meat from the bones and cube it. Return it to the barley mush and simmer another 15 minutes. Add paprika and thyme. It should be of the consistency of mush. Pour it into a loaf pan and let it harden. Cut into ½ inch slices and brown in butter. Serve hot.

Serves 6

Finnish Chicken
Stekt Kylickling—Roast Chicken with Gravy, Finnish Style—a chicken roasted this way is very juicy and the gravy is delicious.

4-pound roasting chicken
½ lemon
2 teaspoons salt
⅛ teaspoon pepper
1 bunch parsley
3 tablespoons butter
¼ cup water

Gravy
2 tablespoons fat from drippings

1 tablespoon flour
1⅓ cups cream and drippings mixture
Chicken livers chopped
½ teaspoon salt
⅛ teaspoon pepper
3 tablespoons horseradish
1 teaspoon fresh dill

Rub the inside of the chicken with lemon and sprinkle with salt and pepper. Put the parsley and 1 tablespoon butter into the cavity. Rub the outside of the chicken with 1 tablespoon butter. Truss. Melt remaining 1 tablespoon butter in a heavy Dutch oven and brown the chicken slowly on all sides. Add water, cover closely, and simmer for 1½ hours or until the chicken is tender. Remove the chicken to a platter and keep hot. Strain drippings into a pan and use for gravy. Let stand a few moments until the fat floats to the top.

Gravy. Pour the fat from the drippings into the Dutch oven. Blend in the flour. Stir over medium heat until it turns a light brown. Add cream mixed with the strained drippings to make 1⅓ cups liquid. Slowly stir into the flour mixture. Add the chopped chicken livers, salt, pepper, horseradish, and dill. Cook until smooth and thickened. Serve the gravy with the chicken.

Serves 4

Chicken with Tomato Sauce
Hons I Tomatsous—Chicken with Tomato Sauce—another specialty from Finland with the flavor of fresh dill to give it a zest.

4-pound chicken fryer cut into pieces
½ cup flour
1 teaspoon salt

⅛ teaspoon pepper
4 tablespoons butter melted
1 tablespoon grated fresh dill
Juice of 1 lemon
4 tablespoons tomato puree
4 tomatoes peeled and chopped
¼ cup water

Add the salt and pepper to the flour and roll the chicken pieces in the seasoned flour. Melt 4 tablespoons butter in a heavy frying pan and brown the chicken well on both sides. Add the fresh dill, the lemon juice, and tomato puree. Mix well and add the chopped tomatoes. Add ¼ cup water, cover, and simmer for 40 minutes or until the chicken is tender. If the sauce seems too thin reduce over a high heat before serving.

Serves 4

Russian Chicken

If there is one quality that distinguishes Russian cooking it is heartiness. Most Russian food is rich and substantial: robust beet and cabbage soups, blini, pirog, piroshki, Beef Strogonoff, meat pie, black bread. Through the centuries Russian food has been shaped by Asiatic and European influences. Russia had borrowed the pilafs and skewered meats of Turkey and Persia; the fancy pastries from Italy when Ivan the Terrible, Russia's first czar, imported Italian workers to build parts of the Kremlin; the cuisine of France introduced by Parisian chefs at the court of Catherine the Great. As a result of the Napoleonic Wars even Poland, England, and Germany have influenced the Russian cuisine. However, Russian cooking never became truly refined in a European sense and time transformed it in strange and exotic ways that are truly Russian in character. The Revolution may have destroyed many culinary traditions of the past but many native dishes and customs endured and Russia today still has a very definite cooking heritage.

Most Russians love to eat—four meals a day as a general rule—but they prefer to eat their own kinds of food: sour cream, beets, cabbage, Russian breads. Sour cream is one of the most pronounced features of Russian cooking and the Russians keep on hand a pail of sour cream (smetana) to use as needed. Extensive use is made of pickled beets, pickled cucumbers, dried mushrooms, and their favorite flavoring is dill.

The hors d'oeuvres or zakooska holds a prominent place in the Russian household. They consist of small portions of tempting dainties such as sliced sausage, dill pickles, cheeses,

456

and herring, the herring being the most important item, attractively laid out on a side table to whet the appetite. With them vodka is served. Vodka is the national beverage of Russia and good vodka is almost tasteless. Russia is renowned for many dishes. There is their wonderful black caviar, which is the salted roe of sturgeon; borsch, the classic soup made with beet and meat or poultry stock; dark pumpernickel bread is customarily served with this soup. There is blini, the popular Russian pancake; pirog and piroshki, which are delicious filled rich pastries; Beef Stroganoff, that justly famous dish named after a member of the Russian nobility, Count Paul Stroganoff, in the nineteenth century.

The average Russian family eats a lot of chicken too, usually roasted, broiled, or steamed. Fried chicken is rarely served. The Russians also eat chicken in special dishes that are unique and distinctly Russian in character. These are the recipes included in this section. There is the famous Breast of Chicken Kiev which is one of the greatest of Russian creations. There is Pojarski Cotletki, a culinary masterpiece which is famous all over Russia. There is the chicken-filled piroshki and the wonderful bite-and-a-half rolled-up piroshki. Chickens in Russia are lean and muscular since they forage for the most part for themselves. Capons are popular, also young spring chickens called tsiplyeta. They are smaller than the American broiler and are a very special delicacy served with green gooseberry sauce or in a deep-dish pie with a Russian crust.

Breast of Chicken Kiev

Breast of Chicken Kiev is one of the great Russian creations. Chicken Kiev is actually a half breast of chicken stuffed with butter and then rolled up and fried. But there is a trick to doing it properly. The dish is delicious and is deservedly famous.

3 chicken breasts boned and cut in half
½ pound butter ice cold and very hard

Salt
White pepper
Flour
1 egg beaten lightly
Fine dry white breadcrumbs
Deep fat for frying

Remove the bones and skin from the chicken breasts and separate the two halves of each breast so you have 6 half breasts. Allow two half breasts for each portion. Place each piece between two sheets of wax paper and flatten them to ¼ inch in thickness with a mallet. The breasts should be thin. Cut the hard butter into sticks about 2 inches long and ½ inch thick. Place one butter stick in the middle of each chicken breast. Season with salt and white pepper. Roll the breast up, tucking in the ends and the sides until the breast resembles a cigar. Make sure the butter is completely enclosed using a toothpick if ncessary. Dip in flour, then in the beaten egg, and roll in the fine breadcrumbs. Chill for 1 hour. Fry in deep hot fat until golden brown about 10 minutes in all. Drain on absorbent paper and serve very hot.

Serves 3

Spring Chicken with Gooseberry Sauce
A young spring chicken served with a green gooseberry sauce is a special delicacy in Russia.

2 spring chickens cut in half
1 onion sliced
1 cup green gooseberries
¼ cup sugar
1 tablespoon butter
1 tablespoon flour
2 cups chicken broth
¼ cup white wine
Salt and pepper

Place the spring chicken halves in a kettle with the sliced onion and water to cover. Bring to a boil, cover, and let simmer about 35 minutes or until the chicken is tender. Remove the chicken halves and keep them hot. Strain the broth. Add 1 cup of the broth to the gooseberries and the sugar. Simmer covered over a low heat for 10 minutes. In another pan melt 1 tablespoon butter and blend in the flour. Slowly add 1 cup chicken broth and stir over a low heat until thickened. Add the white wine and the gooseberries. Boil up once and pour over the chicken.

Serves 4

Pojarski Kotletki with Chicken

A culinary masterpiece created by a tavernkeeper in Torjok, a town on the old post road between Moscow and Leningrad. The dish was famous all over Russia—meat cakes originally made with game but now usually made with chicken or veal.

4-pound roasting chicken
2 cups stale breadcrumbs
½ cup milk
½ teaspoon salt
1 tablespoon vodka
2 tablespoons sour cream
2 tablespoons softened butter
1 whole egg
Flour
Breadcrumbs
1 egg yolk well beaten
½ cup butter melted
Sour cream

Remove the skin from the uncooked chicken. Cut away all the meat from the bones and put the chicken meat through a food grinder. Soak the 2 cups of breadcrumbs in milk for ½ hour and squeeze them dry. Add them to the ground chicken. Add the salt, vodka, sour cream, softened butter, and 1 whole egg. Mix well and form the mixture into 12 small thick oval cakes. Dip the cakes in flour, then in the beaten egg yolk, and roll in remaining breadcrumbs. Fry in hot melted butter until golden brown. Serve with sour cream.

Serves 4

Chicken Pudding
Chicken pudding with a hot shrimp sauce is a tremendous Russian favorite.

1 cup milk
1 cup soft breadcrumbs
1 cup ground cooked chicken
1/2 teaspoon nutmeg
2 tablespoons butter melted
3 egg yolks well beaten
2 egg whites beaten stiff

Scald the milk and add to the breadcrumbs. Cool slightly, then add the ground cooked chicken, nutmeg, melted butter, and egg yolks. Fold in the stiffly beaten egg whites, add salt and pepper to taste, and pour into a buttered baking dish. Bake in a preheated 350° oven for 30 to 45 minutes. Turn out onto a hot platter and serve with the shrimp sauce.

Shrimp Sauce
1 cup cooked shrimp chopped fine
2 tablespoons butter
1 1/2 tablespoons flour
3 tablespoons dried dill
3/4 cup chicken broth
3/4 cup sour cream
1 tablespoon lemon juice

Sauté the chopped cooked shrimp in 2 tablespoons melted butter for 2 minutes. Blend in the flour and the dill. Add the chicken broth and cook over a medium heat, stirring constantly until thickened. Add the sour cream and continue cooking until smooth. Add the lemon juice and serve over the chicken pudding.

Serves 4

Braised Chicken Moscow Style
Russians like the flavor of cinnamon in their gravy.

5-pound roasting chicken
1½ pounds chestnuts
2 cups stale breadcrumbs
½ onion chopped fine
¼ cup butter melted
4 tablespoons dried currants
3 tablespoons Madeira
1 teaspoon salt
½ teaspoon ground cinnamon
1 tablespoon lemon juice
4 sprigs parsley
1 celery stalk chopped
1 bay leaf crushed
6 peppercorns
1 tablespoon lemon juice
2 tablespoons Madeira
½ teaspoon ground cinnamon

Slit the chestnut shells and simmer the chestnuts in water to cover for 5 minutes. Drain and remove the shells and inner skin. Put the nuts in fresh boiling water and cook them over a low heat for 20 minutes or until they are tender. Rub them through a sieve and blend them thoroughly with the stale bread crumbs. Sauté the onions in the melted butter until they are soft. Add the dried currants and cook 1 minute longer. Add to the breadcrumbs and chestnuts along with 3 tablespoons Madeira, the salt, ground cinnamon, and the lemon juice. Mix well and stuff the chicken with this mixture. Sew up the cavities and truss. Sprinkle the chicken with flour and put it in a deep heavy pot. Add ¼ cup water, the parsley, chopped celery, bay leaf, peppercorns. Cover tightly and cook over a medium high heat for 20 minutes turning the chicken once during this time. Lower the heat and continue cooking for 1½ hours or until the chicken is tender, turning the chicken several times during the cooking. Add more water if necessary. When the chicken is tender remove the cover and place the chicken in a hot 425° oven until it is browned. Remove to a hot serving platter, strain the gravy, and thicken it with flour. Add the lemon juice, the remaining 2 tablespoons Madeira, and cinnamon. Serve hot with the chicken.

Serves 6

Bitke of Chicken
Russians consider this a very tasty dish.

5-pound roasting chicken
1 teaspoon salt
¼ teaspoon pepper
¼ cup flour
¼ cup butter melted
1 cup hot chicken stock
¼ cup sour cream
2 tablespoons grated Gruyère cheese

Cut all the meat from the chicken into large pieces. Season them with salt and pepper and dredge with flour. Melt the butter in a large heavy pan and brown the chicken pieces until tender, turning frequently to brown both sides evenly. When done, remove the chicken to a serving dish and keep hot. Add the sour cream and grated Gruyère cheese to the hot chicken stock. Stir and cook a few moments over a low heat until the cheese has melted. Pour over the chicken and serve immediately.

Serves 6

Chicken Mushroom Pirog (Pie)

A genuine Russian Pirog filled with a mouth-watering chicken-mushroom filling is a most delicious dish, as any true Russian will tell you. These large oblong pastries are served traditionally as holiday dishes. They are also delicious cold.

2 cups diced cooked chicken
2 cups thinly sliced mushrooms
3 tablespoons parsley
4 tablespoons butter
6 small green onions chopped fine
1 tablespoon flour
¾ cup sour cream
Salt and pepper
1 egg yolk lightly beaten
4 hard-cooked eggs chopped
Sour cream pastry

Sauté the sliced mushrooms with the parsley in melted butter for 5 minutes. Add the chopped green onions and the flour and stir until smooth. Add the sour cream and cook over a medium low heat, stirring constantly, until thickened. Add salt and pepper to taste and the lightly beaten egg yolk. Cook over a low heat 5 minutes longer. Cool and add the chopped hard-cooked eggs.

Sour Cream Pastry
Sift 3½ cups flour with 1 teaspoon baking powder and 1 teaspoon salt. Work in ½ cup butter. Beat 2 eggs slightly and

mix with 1 cup sour cream. Add to the flour and stir until the dough is thoroughly mixed. It should be smooth but not too stiff to handle.

Roll out the dough to less than ¼ inch in thickness and to form a rectangular shape about 24 by 16 inches. Lay the chicken mushroom filling in the center of the dough at least 4 inches from the edges. Bring up the long sides of the dough and pinch them together at the center, then smooth the pinch marks out of the dough. Now bring the short sides up and pinch their edges together, making sure the dough is well sealed. Lightly grease a cookie sheet and gently ease the pirog onto it so the folded edges of the dough are on the bottom. Cut 2 slits in the top and brush over with the yolk of an egg diluted with a little cold water. Bake 15 minutes in a hot 425° oven then lower the heat to 350° and bake 30 minutes longer or until the pirogshka is browned.

Serves 6

Minced Chicken Piroshki
A platter of hot piroshki, those small bite-and-a-half pieces of rolled-up pie crust and filling, makes wonderfully good eating at any time.

1 medium onion chopped fine
2 tablespoons butter
1 tablespoon flour
¼ cup sour cream
2 cups minced cooked chicken
Salt and pepper to taste
¼ teaspoon nutmeg
Raised dough

Sauté the chopped onion in the butter until soft. Blend in the flour and then add the sour cream. Stir over a medium heat until thickened. Add the minced cooked chicken, salt and pepper to taste, and the nutmeg. Mix well and cool.

Raised Dough
1 cake yeast
1 cup lukewarm milk
5 cups sifted flour
4 eggs
½ cup butter
2 teaspoons sugar
1 extra egg yolk
1 teaspoon salt

Dissolve yeast in the lukewarm milk. Stir in 1 cup flour and let stand 1 hour in a warm place. Beat the eggs slightly and add salt and sugar. Melt butter and cool slightly before adding. Combine with the yeast mixture and add the rest of the flour. Knead with your hands and form the dough into a ball. Place it in a large slightly greased bowl and cover with a cloth. Place in a warm place to rise for 3 or 4 hours. Pinch off a small amount of dough for each piroshki and roll into an oval shape about ¼ inch thick. Place 1 tablespoon of the chicken filling in the center of the rolled dough and seal the edges together. Let rise for 15 minutes. Brush the top of each piroshka with egg yolk diluted with a little cold water. Bake on a greased cookie sheet in a 400° preheated oven. Then reduce the heat to 350° and bake 15 minutes longer.

Piroshki can also be fried in deep fat like doughnuts.

Chicken Pashtet
Chicken Pashtet, in case you don't know, is a Russian Chicken Pie and very popular for gala occasions.

5-pound roasting chicken cut into pieces
¼ cup butter melted

1 cup Madeira
1 onion sliced
2 tablespoons grated lemon peel
1 bay leaf
3 sprigs parsley
6 peppercorns
Salt to taste
1 pound ground veal
½ pound ground sausage meat
1 cup dry breadcrumbs
2 tablespoons minced green onion
3 hard-cooked eggs chopped
¼ cup sour cream
3 egg yolks
Short pastry
½ cup Madeira
Juice of ½ lemon

Brown the chicken pieces well on both sides in ¼ cup melted butter. When browned add the Madeira, sliced onion, lemon peel, bay leaf, parsley, peppercorns, and enough water to cover. Salt to taste and cook covered over a low heat for 1 hour or until the chicken is tender. Remove chicken, strain the broth, and set aside. Cut the chicken meat from the bones in large pieces.

Mix the ground veal and ground sausage with the dry bread-crumbs. Add the minced green onion, chopped hard-cooked eggs, sour cream, and egg yolks. Stir until blended and smooth.

Roll out the short pastry and line bottom of a deep dish. Put a layer of the forcemeat on top, then a layer of chicken, then a layer of forcemeat, then a layer of chicken, repeating until the dish is full. Cover the top with pastry, make several large slits for the steam to escape, and bake 1 hour in a 350° oven.

Make a gravy by thickening the chicken broth with a little

flour. Add ½ cup Madeira and season with salt and pepper. Add the juice of ½ lemon. Pour some of the sauce through the slits in the crust from time to time and serve the rest separately.

Serves 6

Old-Fashioned Karnik

A karnik is a deep-dish chicken pie and a great favorite in Russia.

4-pound chicken
1 large onion sliced
1 clove garlic
2 sprigs parsley
6 peppercorns
1 bay leaf
Chicken stock
1½ teaspoons salt
½ cup sour cream
1 teaspoon lemon juice
1 cup rice
1 cup mushrooms sliced
2 tablespoons butter
5 hard cooked eggs
Rich pie pastry top

Put the chicken in a large heavy kettle with the onion, garlic, parsley, peppercorns, and bay leaf. Add the chicken stock to cover the chicken and the salt. Simmer covered about 1½ hours or until the chicken is tender. Remove the chicken and slice the breastmeat in thin slices. Cut the rest of the meat into small pieces, discarding the skin and bones. Mix 1½ cups of the chicken stock with the sour cream and cook over a medium low heat until it has reduced to 1 cup. Add the lemon juice and the small pieces of chicken. Set aside.

Cook the rice until just barely tender according to the directions on the package. Drain. Then put the rice in the kettle with the chicken stock and continue cooking for 5 minutes longer. Drain. Sauté the sliced mushrooms in 2 tablespoons melted butter for 5 minutes.

Line a deep pie dish with half of the rice. On top of that place a layer of chopped hard-cooked eggs, over that a layer of mushrooms, and then a layer of the chicken mixture. Repeat. On top of this arrange the slices of chicken breastmeat and cover with the last of the chicken mixture. Cover the top with a rich pie pastry and cut slits for the steam to escape. Bake 15 minutes in a 400° oven. Reduce heat to 350° and continue cooking until the crust is browned and the pie is bubbling.

Serves 6

Greek Chicken

Greece, with its sun-drenched islands and mythological past of gods and heroes, was once the center of a glorious civilization. That golden age has faded but ancient buildings still stand, the temple of Nike Aptreros, the Parthenon on the Acropolis in Athens, the shrine of the oracle of Apollo at Delphi, as reminders of Greece's former grandeur.

The modern Greeks inherited a simple way of life from the ancients, making a living from the soil and from the sea as their ancestors did. Farming is limited by thinning soil and rocky hillsides but gray-green olive trees grow well in the rocky terrain, and grapes, citrus fruits, and figs thrive in the liquid sunshine. They supply the flavorful oil and wine, the citrus lemon for avgolemono, the delightful lemon-egg sauce that gives so many Greek dishes a tang. Lamb is the principal meat. For holidays they ceremoniously roast a whole carcass. For everyday meals the lamb is broiled on skewers or baked in casserole dishes. The Greeks have always been clever in the way they used herbs and their meat, fish, vegetables, and chickens are always aromatic with mountain grown herbs.

Greece is surrounded by water on three sides and the vivid blue Mediterranean supplies an abundance of fish and shellfish. Since the days of Greek mythology Greeks have been great fish-eaters and have enjoyed a marvelous variety of seafood. Chefaria Plaki—baked fish—is one of the great national dishes of Greece.

The Greeks have a zest for good food and wine. There are magnificent cheeses, pickled vegetables, bite-size meatballs, small pieces of octopus fried crisp in oil and served with lemon. There is skewered meat flavored with oregano and garlic, delicious vegetables bathed in the tart creamy avgolemono sauce with eggs and lemon juice, fish smothered in pungent garlic sauce called skordalia. There is the famous Easter soup, mageritsa, which is a traditional part of killing and cooking the pastoral lamb, the heart and liver being used for the soup and the carcass of the lamb roasted on Easter Sunday. There are cheese pastries delicately crusted and sweet, the baklava, a wonderful concoction rich with nuts and dripping with honey, the Greek Dolmades and pilafs of Turkish origin.

The staple meat dish of Greece is a lamb stew cooked with vegetables. Chicken is not too plentiful but it is one of the favorite dishes. It is usually sautéed, stewed, or pot-roasted in savory sauce or else the famous avgolemono sauce is poured over the cooked chicken. A popular dish is Kotopoulo Bamies —Chicken with Ladyfingers—which is a chicken cooked in a pot with butter and the bamies and seasoned with oregano and tomato puree. The bamies are a variety of okra that can be bought in cans in specialty shops around the country. Quite often a chicken is marinated in olive oil and lemon juice and oregano before it is cooked; when it is spit-roasted again lemon juice and olive oil are used for basting. Rarely are chickens roasted in the oven. In the rural districts, especially, cooking facilities are still quite primitive and most Greek cooking is done atop a kerosene stove or over an open charcoal fire. When baking needs to be done it is sent out to a local baker's oven.

Roast Chicken with Grapes

It is true that in Greece very few chickens are roasted but in this country we do use ovens. Kota Psiti me Stefili—Roast Chicken with Grapes—is a flavorful chicken and the ingredients are typically Greek.

4-pound chicken fryer
1 teaspoon salt

⅛ teaspoon pepper
1 teaspoon oregano
2 cloves garlic minced
4 tablespoons soft butter
1 tablespoon butter melted
2 cups seedless grapes
2 tablespoons honey
3 tablespoons dry white wine
3 tablespoons sherry

Mix the salt, pepper, oregano, minced garlic, with the soft butter and rub the chicken well both inside and outside with this butter mixture. Truss. Place the chicken in an open roasting pan and roast in a preheated 375° oven, allowing 20 minutes to the pound, until the chicken is tender. The last 20 minutes of cooking time turn the chicken over so the underside will brown nicely too. In the meantime melt 1 tablespoon butter in a pan, add the grapes, and shake the pan until they are well coated. Add the honey, white wine, and sherry. Cook just until blended, stirring constantly. Cover the pan and let stand a few minutes. Carve the chicken into serving pieces and serve the grape mixture spooned over the chicken.

Serves 4

Grecian Baked Chicken
The Greeks use citrus fruits in many of their dishes. This chicken baked in orange juice makes a delightful change.

5-pound roasting chicken
Juice of 2 oranges
Juice of ½ lemon
Grated rind of 1 orange
2 tablespoons soft butter
Salt to taste

Truss the legs and wings of the chicken. Place the chicken in a deep kettle. Add the juice of the oranges, the lemon juice, and the grated rind of 1 orange. Add water to just barely half cover the chicken. Bring to a boil and simmer covered for 10 minutes. Remove the chicken and place in an open roasting pan. Rub it well with the soft butter and roast in a 375° preheated oven for 1½ hours or until the chicken is tender. Baste frequently with the orange juice liquid. Add salt to taste.

Serves 6

Chicken with Dill Sauce

Kota me Anithe—Chicken with Dill Sauce—a chicken flavored with chopped scallions and dill with the famous Greek avgolemono sauce poured over it when it is cooked is a dish par excellence.

4-pound chicken cut into pieces
4 tablespoons butter
½ cup scallions chopped
4 tablespoons fresh chopped dill
1 teaspoon salt
1 cup boiling water

Avgolemono Sauce
3 eggs separated
Juice of 2 lemons

Melt the butter in a heavy frying pan and brown the chicken pieces well on both sides. When browned add the chopped scallions and fresh chopped dill. Cook until soft but not browned. Season with salt and add the boiling water. Cover the pan and cook on low heat about 40 minutes or until the chicken is tender. Remove the chicken from the pan and keep hot.

Make the avgolemono sauce by beating the egg whites until stiff. Add the egg yolks and the lemon juice and beat in vigorously. Gradually beat in the hot liquid from the chicken. Pour the hot avgolemono sauce over the chicken and serve immediately.

Serves 4

Chicken with Ladyfingers

Kotopoule Bamies—Chicken with Ladyfingers—this is a favorite Greek dish. The ladyfinger is a variety of okra cultivated in tropical countries and it is obtainable in specialty shops in the larger cities. Fresh okra may be used as a substitute.

4-pound chicken fryer
1 pound ladyfingers or okra
Juice of 1 lemon
¼ cup lemon juice
¼ cup olive oil
Salt and pepper
1 teaspoon oregano
1 6-ounce can tomato paste
½ cup hot water
4 tablespoons butter

Wash and cut the stems from the ladyfingers or okra. Place them in a flat dish and pour over the juice of 1 lemon. Mix the ¼ cup lemon juice with the ¼ cup olive oil and rub the chicken well with the mixture. Place in an open roasting pan and roast in a 375° oven until about half-cooked, basting frequently with the olive oil and lemon juice mixture. Remove the chicken from the oven and cut into serving pieces. Place the chicken in a buttered casserole and season with salt, pepper, and oregano. Add the tomato paste, hot water, the okra or ladyfingers in the lemon juice. Dot with butter, cover the casserole, and simmer over a low heat for 30 minutes or until the chicken and vegetable are tender.

Serves 4

Ketopoulo Pilaf

Ketopoulo Pilaf—Chicken Pilaf with Browned Butter—is one of the delightful dishes that Greece is famous for.

3½-pound chicken fryer cut into pieces
2 medium onions chopped fine
3 tablespoons butter melted
1 teaspoon salt
⅛ teaspoon pepper
1 cinnamon stick
2 tablespoons tomato paste
½ cup water
1 cup long-grained white rice
2 cups water
5 tablespoons butter melted
Yoghurt flavored with dill

Melt 3 tablespoons butter in a heavy frying pan and brown the chicken and onions in it. Add salt, pepper, cinnamon stick, tomato paste, and ½ cup water. Cover and cook over low heat 40 minutes or until chicken is tender. Remove the chicken from the pan and keep hot. Pour 2 cups water in the pan and bring to a boil. Add the rice, cover, and simmer 20 minutes or until the rice is tender. In a separate pan melt 5 tablespoons butter and heat until lightly browned. Pour over the rice and mix in well. Serve with the chicken and a side dish of yoghurt flavored with dill.

Serves 4

Chicken with Cheese

Kotopoulo me Tyri—Chicken with Cheese—if possible try to get hold of one of the magnificent Greek cheeses at one of the fancier grocery stores. Lacking that, use a good Italian cheese.

¼ cup butter melted
4-pound chicken fryer cut into pieces
1 medium onion chopped
1 teaspoon salt
⅛ teaspoon pepper
1 clove garlic minced
1 tomato peeled and cut into small pieces
1 cup chicken broth
¼ pound Greek or Italian cheese cut into cubes

Melt the butter in a heavy skillet and brown the chicken and chopped onion together until the chicken is well browned on both sides. Season with salt and pepper. Add the garlic, tomato, and chicken broth. Cover and cook over low heat for 40 minutes or until the chicken is tender. Add the cheese and cook until the cheese has melted, stirring constantly. Serve with a rice pilaf.

Serves 4

Greek Barbecued Chicken

Kotopoulo Kotta Stovarno is an interesting barbecue version of chicken basted in the Greek way with lemon juice and olive oil.

4-pound chicken fryer
2 tablespoons olive oil
2 tablespoons lemon juice
1 lemon unpeeled and sliced

Heat the olive oil and lemon juice together in a pan. Stuff the inside of the chicken with the unpeeled lemon slices.

Brush well with the hot olive oil and lemon juice mixture and roast in a preheated 425° oven until the chicken has begun to turn brown. Reduce the heat to 375° and continue roasting until the chicken is tender about 1 hour and 10 minutes in all. Baste frequently with the olive oil and lemon juice to keep the chicken from turning too brown.

Serves 4

Chicken with Noodles
Kotopoulo Hilopites is a savory Peloponnesian dish.

4-pound chicken fryer cut into pieces
1 teaspoon salt
⅛ teaspoon pepper
¼ cup butter melted
2 medium onions chopped
2 cloves garlic minced
1 cup dry white wine
1 cup canned tomatoes mashed
½ can tomato sauce
¼ cup celery
2 tablespoons chopped parsley
½ teaspoon cinnamon
1 pound noodles
Parmesan cheese grated

Sprinkle the chicken with salt and pepper and brown in ¼ cup melted butter until golden brown on both sides. Remove the chicken and keep hot. Add the onions and garlic to the pan and cook until soft. Return the chicken. Add the white wine and cook covered over low heat for 10 minutes. Add the tomatoes, tomato sauce, celery, parsley; cover and simmer for 30 minutes or until the chicken is tender. Add the cinnamon the last 10 minutes of cooking time. Cook the noodles in boiling salted water according to the directions on the package.

When tender drain well and add to the chicken and sauce. Arrange on a heated platter and serve sprinkled with grated Parmesan cheese.

Serves 4

Avgolemono
Avgolemono—Egg Lemon Soup—Greece's famed avgolemono is a refreshing classic chicken soup.

6 cups strong strained chicken broth
½ cup rice
Salt to taste
1 egg well beaten
2 egg yolks
½ cup lemon juice

Bring the chicken broth to the boiling point. Add the rice to the broth and cook until soft. Add salt to taste. Beat the egg well with the 2 egg yolks. Add the lemon juice, beating in thoroughly with a rotary beater. Dilute with a little of the hot soup, beating continually. Then add the remaining soup to the egg mixture, stirring constantly as you add it slowly. Bring just to the boiling point. Remove from the heat and let set a few moments before serving.

Serves 4–6

The Eastern Chicken

The tour of Europe draws to its close and it is time to leave our European chickens and continue down to the eastern end of the Mediterranean Sea. The first stop Turkey with its mosques and palaces and enchanting chicken served Circassian style or as a pilaf or a delicately spiced Chicken Dolma. Across to Egypt with the great tombs of the Pharaohs and a Mohammedan breaking the fast of Ramadan with a refreshing chicken soup and Khooba Kahleb, a staple bread since the process of leavening was discovered in the Nile Valley thousands of years before. Through the Moslem countries, over the sands of the Sahara by camel and caravan and the muezzin call across the desert summoning the faithful to prayer in praise of Allah. A pause in Syria where they stuff chicken with a mixture of cracked wheat, lamb, and pine nuts. A flight to India and the subtleties of Chicken Curry. The mysteries of the Orient and China where there is a great respect for fine foods, and chicken is held in high esteem. . . . Japan, where cooking is treated as an art and chicken is served in Sukiyaki or in Yakatori which is broiled over a charcoal gill. . . . The islands of Oceania where chicken is given exotic tropical flavors. . . . The Philippines and its most famous dish Chicken en Adobe. . . . And then by plane to South America. . . .

In Mexico there is Chicken Mole Poblano in a delicious dark brown sauce made with chili peppers and chocolate. There is Argentina with its classic national Cocido, Brazil with the Cuscuz, and in Peru a marvelous chicken and pepper dish called Aji de Pollo. And so our chicken finds itself in the limelight, a favorite everywhere, whether it be Cairo or Bombay or Tokyo or Buenos Aires. In every land, on every civilized island, and every corner of the earth we find that chicken is eaten with enjoyment.

Middle Eastern Chicken

The Middle East . . . the Moslem countries at the eastern end of the Mediterranean Sea . . . Turkey, Syria, Lebanon, Saudi Arabia, Iran, Algeria, Egypt. . . . In the Middle East the sky is sapphire blue, the domed mosques and minarets are dazzling white, and on a moonlight night the ghosts of turbaned sultans and harem dancing girls haunt the gleaming palaces like a tale from the Arabian Nights. Nomads still roam vast stretches of arid desert wastelands; from dark narrow mysterious streets comes the spicy smell of strange exotic perfumes.

The variety of foodstuffs that can be grown in the Middle East is limited. Sheep have always been the major source of meat and goats furnish milk and cheese while the nomads roaming the desert depend upon the camel for their basic diet. One of the most popular ways of cooking the lamb is on skewers, shiskebab, and it has been cooked that way ever since the first fierce Turkish warriors came out of central Asia in the eleventh century. These fierce warriors strung chunks of meat on their swords and cooked them over open fires. Besides lamb, the majority of Middle Eastern dishes are built around rice, beans, eggs, nuts, and vegetables, and to a lesser degree fish and chicken. Oil and yoghurt take the place of butter and cream. The cereal mainstay is burghul or bulgur which is usually cooked as a pilaf. Burghul has a slightly nutty flavor and is also used in desserts or as a porridge. Peaches, pears, figs, melons, and grapes are grown in abundance as are herbs and spices which are used with great skill. With the food that is available to them the cooks of the Middle East have created dishes that are culinary masterpieces. Savory stews and pilafs with rice or cracked wheat; eggplant, zucchini, tomatoes, grape and cabbage leaves stuffed with succulent fillings of lamb or chicken, delicately spiced. Desserts of rich honeyed sweetness and tissue thin pastries so that the smallest nibble is satisfying; and coffee so thick and syrupy, one cup is sufficient.

Circassian chicken is the most famous chicken dish. The dish originated in Circassia, a region on the coast of the Black Sea, where the women were famed for their beauty and prized as slaves by the Turks. It is a cold chicken dish with a ground walnut paste coating the chicken. Cooks in the Middle East often rub their chickens inside and out with spices and then stuff them with hashwa (a mixture of minced lamb, pine nuts, and lemon juice) or with a mixture of rice, minced giblets, and English walnuts. The chicken is then trussed and placed in a large kettle to simmer until it is almost tender. Lastly, it is roasted until golden brown in an oven.

Circassian Chicken

Circassian Chicken is a highly original dish which got its name from the handsome people who once inhabited Circassia, a region on the eastern coast of the Black Sea. The chicken is simply poached in this recipe but the sauce that goes with it is made from walnuts. The sauce is laborious to make if one does not have an electric blender, but in a blender the walnuts are quickly homogenized for the sauce.

2½ quarts boiling water
4-pound chicken fryer
1 large onion sliced
1 carrot cut in pieces
1 stalk celery chopped
4 tablespoons parsley minced
1 teaspoon salt
1 teaspoon cayenne
1½ cups walnuts

2 slices white bread
¼ teaspoon ginger

Place the chicken in a large kettle and pour over the boiling water. Add the carrot, onion slices, celery, parsley, salt, and cayenne. Simmer over low heat for 1 hour or until the chicken is tender. Cool chicken in the stock. Grind the walnuts and bread together in the electric blender on high speed. Remove from the blender. Add about ½ cup chicken stock to the blender along with a little of the cooked onion, carrot, and celery. Return 1 cup of the blended walnuts and bread mixture and blend until smooth. Add the rest of the walnut-bread mixture and blend until it is the consistency of a smooth paste. Add the ginger and stir until it is thoroughly mixed. Remove the chicken from the stock and drain. Carve the chicken into large pieces and spread each piece heavily with the walnut paste. Arrange on a serving platter and chill thoroughly in the refrigerator before serving.

Serves 4

Stuffed Tomatoes
Banadoora Migshee—Stuffed Tomatoes—are another delightful Turkish dish. The tomatoes are usually served cold but they are also good hot.

8 large firm tomatoes
2 teaspoons salt
⅛ teaspoon black pepper
½ cup olive oil
1 large onion chopped
2 cups chopped cooked chicken
½ cup raw rice
8 tablespoons dried currants
½ cup water
1 cup boiling water

2 tablespoons minced parsley
½ cup sliced almonds
¼ cup olive oil

Cut ½ inch off stem end of tomatoes and set aside. Scoop out the pulp from the tomatoes and chop fine. Sprinkle the inside of the tomatoes with 1 teaspoon salt and $\frac{1}{16}$ teaspoon pepper. Heat the ½ cup olive oil in a skillet and brown the chopped onion and chopped chicken in it. Stir in the raw rice and cook until well coated. Add the tomato pulp, the dried currants which have been soaked in ½ cup water for ½ hour, and the remaining salt and pepper. Add 1 cup boiling water, cover, and cook over low heat for 10 minutes. Mix in the parsley and sliced almonds and stuff the tomatoes with this mixture. Replace the tops. Arrange the tomatoes in an oiled baking dish and brush with ¼ cup olive oil. Bake in a preheated 350° oven for 45 minutes.

Serves 4

Stuffed Grape Leaves

Dolmeh Barg—Stuffed Grape Leaves—a delicately spiced Turkish dish. Grape leaves can be bought in specialty shops in the larger cities.

1 jar grape leaves
2 cups chicken broth
Juice of 2 lemons
1 tablespoon tomato paste

Chicken filling
3 cups ground cooked chicken
1 cup half-cooked rice
1½ teaspoon salt
½ teaspoon black pepper
½ teaspoon cinnamon

½ cup minced green onions
½ cup chopped parsley
2 tablespoons melted butter
Yoghurt

Drain the grape leaves and spread on a flat surface. Cut off the stems. Use half the leaves for stuffing and the rest for lining the pan and between the layers. Put 1 heaping tablespoon of chicken filling on each grape leaf. Arrange the rolls in tight layers, separating each layer with grape leaves. Add a mixture of the chicken broth, lemon juice, and tomato paste. Put a heavy plate on top to weigh it down, cover the pan, and cook over a low heat for 1½ hours. Serve either hot or cold with yoghurt as a topping.

Serves 6

Chicken Dolma

A chicken dolma is one of the most popular dishes in Turkey.

3 cups ground cooked chicken
1 large onion minced
1 cup uncooked Ala or cracked wheat
½ cup uncooked rice
1 can tomato paste
2 teaspoons salt
½ teaspoon pepper
1 teaspoon cinnamon
½ cup cold water
4 medium zucchini
4 medium tomatoes
Cabbage leaves
Grape leaves
3 cups chicken broth
Juice of 2 lemons
Yoghurt

Mix together in a large bowl the ground cooked chicken, chopped onion, Ala, and rice. Add ½ of the tomato paste and the salt and pepper. Add the cinnamon and the cold water and mix in well. Scoop out the zucchini and the tomatoes and mash the pulp. Add to the chicken mixture. Stuff the zucchini and the tomato shells with the chicken mixture. Scald the cabbage leaves until they are soft enough to roll without splitting. Lay them flat and put a heaping tablespoon of the chicken mixture in the center of about 10 of the leaves. Roll up tightly tucking in the ends. Lay out the grape leaves, cutting off the stems, and stuff and roll up in the same manner until all the chicken mixture is used up. Place the stuffed vegetables in a shallow pan close together. Add the rest of the can of tomato paste to the chicken broth along with the juice of 2 lemons. Cover the pan and bake in a preheated 350° oven for 1 hour. Serve with yoghurt as a topping.

Serves 6

Chicken in Walnut Sauce

Feissan Juan—Chicken in Walnut Sauce—this is an exotic Persian dish.

4-pound chicken fryer cut into pieces
¼ cup butter melted
1 teaspoon salt
⅛ teaspoon pepper
2 pounds walnuts
1½ cups apricot nectar

In a heavy frying pan melt the butter and brown the chicken pieces well on both sides. Season with salt and pepper. Blend the walnuts in an electric blender until of a fine consistency. Add them to the chicken and sauté them for 5 minutes, being careful not to let them scorch. Add the apricot nectar, cover the pan, and cook over low heat for 40 minutes or until the chicken is tender. The sauce should be cooked down to a thick walnut consistency. Serve with rice.

Serves 4

Chicken Pollo
This chicken dish from Persia has a very enticing flavor.

4-pound chicken fryer cut into pieces
¼ cup butter melted
Hot water
2 cups rice cooked partly tender
Cinnamon
½ teaspoon saffron
3 tablespoons butter
Yoghurt

Melt the butter in a heavy skillet and brown the chicken pieces well on both sides. Reduce heat, add hot water to barely cover, and simmer the chicken until it is almost tender. Butter a casserole and put a layer of the half cooked rice in it. Place several of the chicken pieces on top of that and sprinkle heavily with cinnamon. Repeat with layers of rice and chicken and cinnamon until all of the ingredients are used up, finishing with a layer of rice with cinnamon sprinkled on top. Add the saffron to the juices left in the frying pan, mix in well, and pour over the chicken and rice. Dot the top with 3 tablespoons butter. Make a few holes in the pollo so the steam can escape. Cover the pollo with a dish towel and steam it over boiling water for 1 hour. Turn it out onto a large platter and serve topped with yoghurt.

Serves 4

Syrian Chicken with Hashwa Stuffing
A chicken stuffed with a Hashwa stuffing is a typical Middle Eastern delicacy.

5-pound roasting chicken
3 tablespoons olive oil
1 pound ground lamb
1 cup slivered blanched almonds
½ cup rice half-cooked
1 teaspoon salt
1 teaspoon cinnamon
¼ teaspoon nutmeg
Juice of 1 lemon
Salted water to cover
4 tablespoons olive oil

Heat 3 tablespoons olive oil in a heavy skillet and brown the ground lamb for 10 minutes. Add the slivered almonds, rice, salt, cinnamon, nutmeg, and juice of 1 lemon. Cook a few moments and stuff the chicken with the mixture. Sew the opening tightly closed and truss. Place the chicken in a large kettle with salted water to cover. Cook over a low heat about 1½ hours or until tender. Remove the chicken from the kettle and drain. Brush the chicken with 4 tablespoons olive oil and roast it in a preheated 400° oven for 35 minutes or until the chicken is nicely browned.

Serves 6

Joojeh

Joojeh—Stuffed Chicken—This is another popular way to stuff Eastern chickens. Burghul, also called bulgur, is sold in this country as Ala and distributed by the Fisher Flouring Mills, Seattle, Washington. Burghul is the cereal mainstay of the Middle Eastern diet.

5-pound roasting chicken
¼ cup burghul (Ala)
3 teaspoons salt
4 tablespoons butter
1 cup water

1 cup canned chick peas drained
1 cup pine nuts
1 teaspoon cinnamon
1 teaspoon pepper

Put the cracked wheat or ala in the top of a double boiler with
1 teaspoon of the salt, 1 tablespoon butter, and 1 cup water.
Cover. Place over hot water and cook for 1½ hours or until
the water is absorbed by the wheat. Mix together the cooked
cracked wheat, chick peas, pine nuts, and ½ teaspoon pepper.
Cream the 3 remaining tablespoons butter with the remaining
salt, pepper, and cinnamon. Rub the butter paste on the outside and inside of the chicken. Stuff the chicken with the
cracked wheat mixture and sew the openings closed. Place the
chicken in a roasting pan and roast in a 375° preheated oven
allowing 20 minutes to the pound until tender. Baste frequently with the drippings in the pan. The last 20 minutes of
cooking time turn the chicken over to brown the underside.

Serves 6

Chicken and Chestnuts
Pile Yahnia—Chicken and Chestnuts—this chicken dish has a
deliciously sweet spicy flavor.

½ pound chestnuts
6 tablespoons butter
4-pound chicken fryer cut into pieces
1 cup chopped onions
2 teaspoons salt
¼ teaspoon pepper
1 teaspoon cinnamon
½ cup tomato sauce
1¼ cups hot chicken broth
Cut crisscrosses in the top of the chestnuts. Cover them with
water, bring to a boil, and cook over medium high heat for 10

minutes. Drain, cool slightly, and peel. Melt the butter in a Dutch oven and brown the chicken in it. Add the onions, cover, and cook over low heat until the onions are browned. Add salt, pepper, cinnamon, tomato sauce, and the broth. Cover and cook over low heat for 30 minutes. Add the chestnuts. Cover and cook 15 minutes longer or until the chicken and chestnuts are tender.

Serves 4

Chicken Pilaf

Morg Polou—Chicken Pilaf—pilaf is one of the principal foods of Turkey. This one makes a very satisfying dish.

1½ cups raw rice
4 tablespoons olive oil
4-pound chicken fryer cut into pieces
2 onions sliced thin
1½ cups light cream
Juice of ½ lemon
2 teaspoons salt
¼ teaspoon white pepper
1 teaspoon allspice
2 cups hot chicken broth
1 green pepper sliced thin

Wash the rice, cover with water, and bring to a boil. Remove from heat and let stand for 15 minutes. Drain. Heat the olive oil in a heavy skillet and brown the chicken and onion slices in it. When well browned add the cream, lemon juice, salt, white pepper, and allspice. Mix thoroughly and cook covered over a low heat for 10 minutes. Add the rice and the chicken broth and the sliced green pepper. Cover and continue cooking over low heat for 30 minutes. By that time the pilaf should be fairly dry and the chicken tender.

Serves 4

Turkish Chicken Soup

Tavuk Corbasi—Turkish Chicken Soup—is a delightfully piquant soup made with yoghurt.

5 cups rich chicken stock
2 tablespoons uncooked rice
2 tablespoons butter melted
2 tablespoons flour
1 cup yoghurt
Salt and pepper to taste
2 tablespoons chopped chives
1 cup diced cooked chicken meat
1 tablespoon lemon juice
1 teaspoon grated lemon rind

Add the uncooked rice to the chicken stock and simmer over a low heat for 20 minutes or until the rice is tender. Melt 2 tablespoons butter in another saucepan and blend in the flour. Add the yoghurt and cook over a low heat until the sauce is thick and smooth. Add the sauce to the chicken stock and cook over low heat until thickened. Add salt and pepper to taste, the diced cooked chicken meat, lemon juice, and lemon rind. Heat through and serve at once.

Serves 4

Egyptian Chicken Soup

Shorbah Be Tarbaya—Egyptian Chicken Soup—is a tantalizingly refreshing soup.

½ cup rice
6 cups chicken broth
3 egg yolks
3 tablespoons lemon juice
Lemon slices

Wash the rice and cover with hot water. Let soak 10 minutes.

Strain. Bring the broth to a boil, add the rice, and cook over low heat for 15 minutes. Beat the egg yolks with the lemon juice in a bowl. Gradually add 1 cup of the soup, beating constantly to prevent curdling. Add this mixture to the rest of the soup and stir over low heat until the soup is heated through. Do not let it boil. Serve with thin slices of lemon in each bowl.

Serves 6

Djedjad-Imur

A friend fetched me this recipe from a friend who spent a year teaching school in an ancient Arab land. I have changed the ingredients slightly to suit the American palate, but the flavor is exotic and the chicken is served dripping with honey, sweet syrup, and chopped pistachio nuts. My friend tells me it is favored by the Arabs.

5-pound roasting chicken
¼ cup honey
¼ cup butter melted
1 tablespoon orange-flower water
4 tablespoons chopped pistachio nuts
2 tablespoons preserved ginger chopped fine
2 teaspoons orange-flower water
4 tablespoons honey

Mix ¼ cup honey with ¼ cup melted butter and rub the chicken well with this mixture both inside and outside. Pour 1 tablespoon orange-flower water into the cavity and truss. Place the chicken in an open roasting pan and roast in a 375° oven until tender basting frequently with the butter-honey mixture. When the chicken is tender remove from the oven and cut in half. Sprinkle each half with chopped pistachio nuts and chopped preserved ginger. Pour over 2 teaspoonfuls of orange-flower water and a little honey over the top.

Serves 6

Indian Chicken

India with its teeming millions and violent contrasts of rich and poor is probably known more for its fiery curry than for any other Indian dish. However, authentic Indian dishes never use a prepared curry powder as we know it. The word curry was originally derived from the Hindustani *turkari,* meaning a meat or vegetable dish with sauce. The English took it up as a general term for any meat dish with gravy seasoned with hot Indian sauces and served with rice and condiments. In fact Major Grey, who became famous for his chutney, was partly responsible for the great misunderstanding in the use of curry. When he left India to return to the foggy mists of London he had his Indian cook prepare for him a special blend of many spices which he immortalized upon his return to England as a commercial curry powder.

In India a prepared curry powder is unknown to Indian cooking. Every individual dish is given its own individuality of flavors and no two dishes are made with the same spices. Nor is curry a specific dish. It is a way of cooking that is universal in India. Aromatic spices and condiments are the essence of Indian cooking. If possible, the spices should be freshly ground with mortar and pestle. The main spices used are: tumeric, coriander, cumin, fresh green ginger or ground ginger, cloves, cinnamon, cardamom, mustard seed, fennel, and poppy seed. The hot seasonings are: cayenne, dried red chili, chili powder, paprika, white and black pepper. The spices, onions, garlic, and all aromatics are cooked in ghee (clarified butter which has a higher smoking temperature than butter). Although it has been said about India that the climate is hot, the dishes are hotter, and the condiments are hottest of all; good curries as prepared by an Indian cook are usually more subtle and rich in flavor than they are fiery.

Besides the curry dishes, India offers a wide variety of excellent cooking. There are rich Kormas—spiced game—Koftas which are spiced meatballs and croquettes; special dishes such as Dhal, an onion and lentil combination; Solach, a fish dish made with eggs and vegetables; Goa, bass cooked with coconut and spices; Dolmas and Kabobs. There are delicious chicken dishes too: Chicken tandoori, Murghi Biryani; and Burdwan, which is a spiced chicken; Pulao, a chicken-and-rice dish containing more chicken than rice in proportion than any other rice dish in the Far East. The Pulao is very different from curry and it is sometimes savory and sometimes sweet.

India's tradition of cooking is thousands of years old—in fact, as old as the pre-Aryan Indus Empire, and from descriptions in the Veda the Aryan hearth was the center of importance in family communal life. Then as now, the people were extremely fond of milk, cream, yoghurt, curds, and ghee. Wild game was cooked on a spit over an open fire and in the Veda there are scenes depicting wild boar and other game sizzling over a fire. Indian cooking has had a long and colorful historical background, but India is primarily not a meat-eating country, owing to the religious prejudices of so many of the people. Chicken is eaten far more frequently than meat and in India it is both plentiful and good.

Chicken Curry

This special Indian Chicken Curry is one I serve to friends who enjoy a good curry dish.

4 tablespoons butter melted
1 large onion chopped fine
3 cloves garlic minced
Coconut meat from 1 coconut ground fine

2 teaspoons salt
½ teaspoon powdered ginger
2 teaspoons tumeric
4 teaspoons ground coriander
¼ teaspoon ground cloves
¼ teaspoon cinnamon
¼ teaspoon black pepper
4 bay leaves crumbled
4-pound chicken fryer cut into pieces
¼ cup chicken broth
1 cup yoghurt
Juice of ½ lemon

Melt the butter in a heavy frying pan and brown the chicken pieces well on both sides. When browned remove the chicken and add the chopped onions and minced garlic to the pan. Grind the meat from the coconut very fine and mix it with salt, ginger, tumeric, coriander, cloves, cinnamon, black pepper, and the crumbled bay leaves. Add this mixture to the pan and cook until the onions are soft. Add the chicken broth and mix in well scraping up all the browned particles from the bottom of the pan. Add the yoghurt and return the chicken to the pan. Cover and cook for 40 minutes over a low heat or until the chicken is tender. Before serving squeeze over the juice of ½ lemon. Serve with plain boiled rice and a tray of condiments on the side.

Serves 4

Chicken Mulligatunny
Chicken Mulligatunny—Murghi Shoorva—is a famous Indian dish which I felt should be included in this chapter on Indian Chicken. This recipe is from *The Complete Book of Oriental Cooking* by Myra Waldo, copyright 1960 by David McKay Company, Inc., and used by permission of David McKay Company, Inc.

4-pound pullet, disjointed
2 quarts water
6 peppercorns
1 tablespoon salt
1 teaspoon tumeric
½ teaspoon powdered ginger
2 teaspoons coriander, ground
1 teaspoon vinegar
1 tablespoon butter
½ cup thinly sliced onions
¼ teaspoon dried ground chili peppers

Wash the chicken and combine in a saucepan with the water, peppercorns, and salt. Bring to a boil, cover loosely, and cook over low heat 1½ hours or until tender. Skim the fat.

Pound together to a paste the tumeric, ginger, coriander, and vinegar. Melt the butter in a skillet; sauté the onions and chili peppers over very low heat for 10 minutes without browning. Stir the spices into the onions and cook for 5 minutes. Add to the soup and cook 10 minutes. Taste for seasoning. The chicken may be removed from the bones and served in the soup or served on the bones separately.

Serves 6

Baked Chicken Curry
A simple way to make a delicious chicken curry.

4-pound chicken fryer cut into pieces
1 large onion chopped
3 cloves garlic minced
1 bay leaf crushed
1 teaspoon salt
½ teaspoon cinnamon
⅛ teaspoon powdered cloves
1 teaspoon tumeric

1 tablespoon coriander
1 teaspoon cumin
½ teaspoon cayenne
¼ teaspoon black pepper
1 tablespoon paprika
½ teaspoon ginger
2 tablespoons vinegar
3 large onions sliced fine
1 cup hot chicken broth

Put in an electric blender the chopped onion, garlic, bay leaf, salt, cinnamon, powdered cloves, tumeric, coriander, cumin, cayenne, black pepper, paprika, ginger, and vinegar. Blend on high speed to a smooth paste. Rub the chicken pieces heavily with the spice paste and let set in the refrigerator for several hours. Grease a flat baking dish and place the chicken pieces in it. Cover with the sliced onions and pour over the top the hot chicken broth. Cover tightly and bake in a 375° oven for 1 hour. Uncover and cook about 5 minutes longer or until the onions are lightly browned. Serve with rice and condiments.

Serves 4

Chicken in Lime Juice
Moorgee Tanjore—a variation of an especially good Indian chicken dish that is pungently seasoned.

Juice of 2 limes
½ teaspoon salt
¼ teaspoon cayenne
½ teaspoon paprika
3 teaspoons coriander
½ teaspoon cardamom seeds
1 teaspoon cumin
1 teaspoon chopped fresh ginger root
8 small green onions chopped

6 chicken breasts
3 tablespoons butter

In an electric blender put the juice of 2 limes, salt, cayenne, paprika, coriander, cardamom, cumin, ginger root, and the chopped green onions. Blend on high speed until smooth. Pour over the chicken breasts and marinate them for 3 hours, turning over several times. Melt the butter in a heavy skillet and brown the chicken breasts well on both sides. When browned pour the marinade over the chicken, cover the skillet, and cook over low heat 40 minutes or until the chicken is tender.

Serves 6

Chicken and Apricots

Murgh Khoo Bani—chicken cooked with spices and apricots—is a delicately flavored curry dish that makes delightful eating.

4-pound chicken fryer cut into pieces
¼ cup butter melted
2 large onions chopped fine
3 cloves garlic minced
3 bay leaves crushed
¼ teaspoon cinnamon
1 teaspoon ginger
1 teaspoon tumeric
1 tablespoon coriander
1 teaspoon cumin
⅛ teaspoon cayenne
1 teaspoon grated orange peel
1 teaspoon salt
⅛ teaspoon black pepper
2 tablespoons tomato paste
1 cup brown gravy (packaged brown gravy mix may be used)
Water
1 cup dried apricots

Melt ¼ cup butter in a heavy skillet and brown the chicken well on both sides. When browned remove chicken and add the chopped onions and minced garlic to the pan. Cook until lightly colored. Add bay leaves, cinnamon, ginger, tumeric, coriander, cumin, cayenne, grated orange peel, salt, and black pepper. Cook for 5 minutes. Add the tomato paste, mix in well, and stir in the brown gravy. Return the chicken to the pan and add enough additional water to cover the chicken. Cover the pan and cook over low heat for 30 minutes. Add the dried apricots which have been soaked in cold water for ½ hour. Continue cooking until the chicken is tender and the apricots soft. Add more water if the apricots seem too dry. Serve with chutney and other condiments.

Serves 4

Chicken Tandoori
In northern India food is quite often cooked in a tandoori which is the primitive clay oven of the Punjab.

4-pound chicken fryer
2 cups yoghurt
1 teaspoon grated ginger root
2 teaspoons salt
4 bay leaves crushed
1 teaspoon cardamom
½ teaspoon cayenne
½ teaspoon black pepper
½ teaspoon cumin
1 teaspoon cinnamon
Water

Skin the chicken and make slits in the skin with a sharp knife. Place it in a pan and cover with the yoghurt. Marinate overnight in the refrigerator turning several times. Blend all the other ingredients together with enough water to make a thick paste. Remove the chicken from the yoghurt marinade and rub well with the spice mixture. Let set for several hours. Place the chicken on a spit, or, if you have one, a rotisserie, and cook over a hot bed of coals, brushing frequently with the spice paste until the chicken is tender.

Serves 4

Delicate Chicken Curry

A delightful chicken curry delicately flavored with fresh nectarine yoghurt. The recipe was given to me by a dear friend who has been experimenting for some time in Indian cooking. The use of ground cardamom in this dish cuts down the sweetness and also gives a piquant flavor.

3-pound chicken fryer cut into pieces
1 teaspoon salt
¼ teaspoon white pepper
¼ cup butter melted
1½ cups fresh fruit flavored nectarine yoghurt
½ teaspoon Schilling's Indian Curry Powder
½ teaspoon ground Ceylon cardamom
Juice of ½ lemon

Prick the chicken pieces with a fork and rub them well with the salt and pepper. Melt the butter in a heavy frying pan and add the nectarine yoghurt, Schilling's Indian Curry Powder, and the ground cardamom. Mix together well and add the chicken. Let the sauce come to a boil, then reduce the heat, cover the pan, and let the chicken simmer for 40 minutes or until tender. Baste frequently as the chicken cooks so that it will be well coated with the nectarine yoghurt sauce. Before serving pour over the juice of ½ lemon. Serve over rice.

Serves 3

Murghi Biryani

From Pakistan comes this traditional dish. The Biriani is a rich rice dish which calls for lamb and chicken with alternate layers of rice and rich curry sauce baked together and garnished with nuts, raisins, and fresh mint leaves.

2 large onions chopped
1/4 cup butter
1 teaspon grated ginger root
1/8 teaspoon cayenne
2 cloves garlic minced
1/2 cup almonds chopped fine
1 1/2 pounds lamb stew cubed
3-pound chicken fryer cut into pieces
1 teaspoon salt
1 1/2 cups raw rice
1 cup yoghurt
1/2 teaspoon powdered cloves
1/2 teaspoon ground cardamom
1/2 teaspoon cumin
1 teaspoon coriander
Juice of 1 lime
1/2 teaspoon saffron soaked in 1/2 cup water
1 cup yoghurt
Chopped fresh mint leaves
Nuts and raisins

Melt the butter in a large heavy pan and cook the onions until lightly colored. Add the grated ginger root, cayenne, garlic, and almonds. Stir and cook for 2 minutes. Add the cubed lamb stew and chicken pieces. Add the salt and cook until the meat is browned on both sides. Boil the rice according to directions on the package. Drain. Combine 1 cup yoghurt with the powdered cloves, cardamom, cumin, coriander, and juice of 1 lime. Stir into the frying pan with the chicken and lamb. Cook for 2 minutes. Butter a large casserole and place a layer of the chicken and lamb in the bottom of it. Pour over some of the sauce. Cover with a layer of the rice. Repeat until all of the lamb, chicken, sauce, and rice have been used up. The top layer should be rice. Pour the ½ cup saffron water and the 1 cup yoghurt over the mixture. Cover tightly and bake in a 350° oven for 1 hour. Garnish with fresh chopped mint leaves, nuts, and raisins.

Serves 4–6

Chicken Kabob

Murghi Kabob—a chicken roasted in yoghurt and pungently flavored with the spices of India that is yet not too fiery for the American palate.

4-pound chicken fryer
2 teaspoons salt
¼ teaspoon black pepper
1 tablespoon coriander
1 teaspoon powdered ginger
2½ cups chopped onions
1 tablespoon Indian curry powder
4 tablespoons butter melted
1 cup yoghurt

Mix the salt, black pepper, coriander, ginger with enough water to make a thick paste. Rub the chicken well with this mixture both inside and out. Place the chicken in a shallow roasting pan and roast for 10 minutes in a hot 425° oven. Turn heat to 375° and continue roasting allowing 20 minutes to the pound until the chicken is tender. Combine the chopped onions, tumeric, and butter. Pound to a paste and blend in the yoghurt. Pour over the chicken and baste with this sauce frequently while the chicken is roasting.

Serves 4

Lentils with Chicken
This is an excellent Indian dish that is not the least bit hot!

3 onions sliced
¼ cup butter
2 tablespoons Indian curry powder
1 teaspoon salt
4-pound chicken fryer cut into pieces
¼ cup chicken stock
2 bay leaves crushed
1½ cups coconut milk
2 cups lentils (soaked overnight)

Fry the onions in butter until soft. Add the curry, salt, and the chicken pieces. Cook until the chicken is well browned on both sides. Add enough chicken stock to just cover the chicken. Add the bay leaves, coconut milk, and lentils that have been soaked overnight in cold water. Cover the pan and cook for 1 hour or until the chicken and lentils are tender.

To make coconut milk—Grate the white meat from a good-sized coconut and place in several thicknesses of cheesecloth over a bowl. Add 1 or 2 cups boiling water and squeeze through the cheesecloth. The hot water softens the oil but the less water the richer the milk.

A substitute for fresh coconut milk may be prepared by covering 3 cups shredded packaged coconut with 1½ cups hot milk. Allow it to set ½ hour then simmer for 10 minutes. Strain through several pieces of cheesecloth, squeezing out as much liquid as possible.

Pulao
Pulao—a chicken and rice dish that is very different from curry. It is both savory and sweet and contains more chicken than rice in proportion than any other rice dish in the Far East.

½ cup blanched almonds
½ cup raisins
½ cup butter
2 onions sliced
4 cloves
1 inch stick cinnamon
1½ cups raw rice
2-pound cooked broiler chicken
3 cups chicken stock
4 hard-cooked eggs sliced

Cook the almonds and raisins in ½ cup melted butter for 5 minutes. Remove from the pan and set aside. Add the onions, cloves, and cinnamon stick to the pan and cook until the onions are soft. Stir in the rice and cook until all the butter is absorbed. Add the chicken stock, cover, and cook over a low heat for 15 minutes or until the rice is tender. Mix the almond raisin mixture into the rice and place the rice in a baking dish. Make a hollow in the center. Cut up the chicken and put the pieces into the hollow. Bake for 15 minutes in a 350° oven or until all the moisture is absorbed. Garnish with sliced hard-cooked eggs and serve.

Serves 4

Sambal Dressing

This savory dish is from *The Complete Book of Oriental Cooking* by Myra Waldo, copyright 1960 by David McKay Company, Inc., and used with their permission. Miss Waldo states in her book on Far Eastern cuisine: "Sambals are served as an accompaniment to curries and other Indian dishes in the same way we serve a relish. You can use any leftover cooked vegetable, sliced tomatoes, cucumbers, fish, or seafood in the dressing. Combine with the dressing 1 hour before serving and sprinkle with a little flaked coconut."

2 tablespoons oil
1 cup minced onions
1 minced garlic clove
1 teaspoon tumeric
½ teaspoon ground cumin
¼ teaspoon dried ground chili peppers
1 teaspoon salt

Heat the oil in a skillet; sauté the onions, garlic, tumeric, cumin, chili peppers, and salt over very low heat until soft but not brown.

Ghee
Indian cooks use ghee instead of butter for frying because ghee has a much higher smoking temperature.

To make ghee, place butter in a saucepan with high sides. Cook over a low heat from 30 to 40 minutes or until solid particles are formed. Be careful not to let the butter brown. Strain through cheesecloth. The finished ghee should be yellow.

Japanese Chicken

Possibly the greatest contribution the Japanese have made to the cuisine of cooking is in their presentation of foods. They will spend hours preparing a dish of food so that it not only looks appetizing but it is also a delicately designed work of art. In a clear consommé soup a Japanese will place a tiny sliver of carrot in the shape of a tree, or decorate a vegetable dish with exquisite leaves of spun sugar, or arrange small pieces of meat in a dish with almost mathematical precision. Color and form play an important part in Japanese cooking and the cook's aim is to seek admiration for his artistry of presentation as a prelude to the meal.

The way the Japanese set their tables is artistic too. The tables are usually low, oblong in size, and covered with mats like the floor upon which they sit. The food is served on trays in small bowls. One bowl is for tea, one bowl for rice which is scooped up continually from a larger bowl in the center of the table. The other bowls contain small portions of a wide variety of foods: pieces of dried, salted, raw, or boiled fish, bits of vegetables, fish tempura, soups with greens or bean curds, bean curd salad, fish balls, grated horseradish, and always soy sauce. Soy sauce, also called shoyu sauce, is a dark red-brown liquid made from wheat, soybeans, and salt. It is dearly loved by the Japanese for its piquant flavor and they use it in almost every dish of food they eat.

Most Japanese meals begin with the serving of saké. The saké is always served warm. Japanese etiquette has certain rules which are scrupulously followed even today, and the way saké is served is one of them. The saké is brought to the table in a small bottle and the guest holds a miniature cup in his right hand partly supported by the left, while the hostess fills his cup. After the cup is filled the guests will then pour for another person, as it is considered impolite to pour for oneself.

Sukiyaki and tempura are the two best known dishes to Westerners. Tempura is a deep-fried food and sukiyaki is, of course, the classic dish made with either chicken or beef with a soy-sauce base and then pan-fried with vegetables. The Japanese also enjoy a great variety of other foods, and through the centuries have evolved many tempting ways of serving them. The Japanese have always been great fishermen; they eat a lot of seafood, most typical of the dishes being Sashami (raw seafood). Vegetables also have long made up the major part of their diet. During the sixth century, when Buddhism came to Japan, the people were discouraged from touching meat of any kind so it was necessary for them to cultivate the soil intensely to maintain an adequate vegetarian diet. Even after the ban against meat was lifted, vegetables continued to be an important item in their diet. A little meat, fish, or chicken was stretched a long way by cooking it with several flavorful vegetables. The Japanese have always tended their tiny plots of well-fertilized and irrigated land with great care to produce a wide variety of fresh vegetables. Because it is the custom to cook foods only slightly the vegetables are picked when they are the most tender and flavorsome.

Sukiyaki

The classic Japanese dish with chicken in a soy sauce base. It can be cooked at the table in a hibachi, chafing dish, or electric skillet. And don't overcook the vegetables. They should be crisp.

2 tablespoons fat
4-pound chicken fryer cut into thin strips
½ cup soy sauce

½ cup chicken broth
¼ cup saké
3 tablespoons sugar
¼ teaspoon pepper
¾ teaspoon Ac'cent
2 onions sliced thin
1 cup sliced celery
1 cup sliced bamboo shoots
½ green pepper cut in thin rings
1 cup sliced mushrooms
4 green onions cut into tiny pieces

Melt the fat in a heavy skillet over a hot heat. Add the thin strips of chicken meat and brown quickly on both sides. Combine the soy sauce, chicken broth, saké, sugar, pepper, and Ac'cent. Pour over the chicken and cook 1 minute longer. Add the thin sliced onions, sliced celery, sliced bamboo shoots, green pepper rings, sliced mushrooms, and green onions. Cook over high heat, stirring constantly, for 6 minutes. The vegetables should be just barely tender and still crisp. Serve at once with boiled rice.

Serves 4

Yakitori
Yakitori, which is a broiled chicken, is a fine Japanese way to prepare a chicken.

2 broilers, 1½ pounds each, quartered
⅓ cup soy sauce
⅓ cup saké
3 tablespoons sugar
1½ teaspoon powdered ginger
2 tablespoons prepared horseradish
3 tablespoons chopped onion

Combine the soy sauce, saké, sugar, powdered ginger, horse-

radish, and onion in a saucepan. Simmer over a low heat for
10 minutes. Brush the broilers well with the mixture and let
them stand for 30 minutes. Place them on an oiled broiling
pan and broil 15 minutes on each side, brushing frequently
with the sauce. Serve hot.

Serves 4

Yakitori

Yakitori made with chicken and giblets shows another way
the Japanese broil their chicken.

1½-pound broiler chicken cut into bite-size pieces
¼ pound chicken gizzards cut into small pieces
¼ pound chicken livers cut into small pieces
8 scallions cut into 1½ inch lengths
⅓ cup saké
⅓ cup soy sauce
3 tablespoons sugar
½ teaspoon grated ginger root

Place the chicken gizzards in a pan, cover with water, and
cook over medium heat for 10 minutes. Drain. Use 8 small
skewers and thread the gizzards, livers, and chicken meat with
the scallions on them alternately. Arrange them on an oiled
broiling pan. Combine the saké, soy sauce, and sugar in a
saucepan. Bring to a boil and simmer for 5 minutes. Brush
heavily over the skewered chicken. Broil for 10 minutes, then
turn them over. Baste heavily with the sauce and broil until
they are crispy brown but still juicy. Sprinkle with grated
ginger root and serve with grated horseradish and the remaining sauce.

Serves 4

Mazutaki

Mazutaki is a chicken casserole and a very tempting dish.

5-pound chicken
2 quarts water
1 small bunch spinach
½ pound mushrooms sliced
1 head Chinese cabbage
½ cup chicken stock
½ cup soy sauce
¼ cup saké
3 tablespoons sugar
¼ teaspoon pepper
¾ teaspoon Ac'cent

Bring 2 quarts water to a boil. Add the chicken and cook un-covered until the chicken is just tender. Remove chicken from the broth and cool. Cut the meat from the bones in bite-size pieces. Boil the head of Chinese cabbage just long enough to soften the leaves. Boil the spinach until the leaves are tender. Drain. Prepare vegetable rolls by laying out the leaves of the cabbage. Cover with a few leaves of spinach and roll up neatly. There should be 12 rolls in all. Arrange the chicken pieces, vegetable rolls, and sliced mushrooms together in a casserole. Combine the chicken stock, saké, and soy sauce with the sugar, pepper, and Ac'cent. Pour over the chicken and vegetables in the casserole. Cover the casserole and bake in a 350° oven until just heated through about 30 minutes. Serve immediately.

Serves 6

Umani
Umani is an interesting dish with ground chicken cooked more or less like meatballs in sauce with vegetables.

3-pound chicken; cut meat into pieces
1 tablespoon water
1 tablespoon cornstarch

¼ cup water
½ cup chicken broth
¼ cup soy sauce
¼ cup saké
3 tablespoons sugar
¼ teaspoon pepper
¾ teaspoon Ac'cent
4 carrots cut lengthwise
½ pound string beans

Put the chicken meat through a meat grinder. Place in a bowl with 1 tablespoon water and the cornstarch. Form the chicken mixture into balls about the size of walnuts. Make a sauce by combining the ¼ cup water, chicken broth, soy sauce, saké, sugar, pepper, and Ac'cent. Boil for 1 minute then add the chicken balls. Cover and cook over a medium heat for 8 minutes. Cook the carrots in boiling salted water until tender. Drain and add to the chicken balls and sauce. Cook the string beans in boiling salted water until tender. Drain and add to the chicken balls and sauce. Serve the chicken balls, string beans, and carrots together in the sauce.

Serves 4

Japanese Chicken in the Pot
Even Japan has its own version of the famed Pot au Feu.

2 quarts chicken stock
4-pound chicken fryer cut into pieces
8 mushrooms
8 cabbage leaves rolled up
½ pound buckwheat noodles
Soy sauce
Chopped green onions
Grated fresh horseradish

Cook the chicken pieces in the chicken stock for 40 minutes

or until the chicken is tender. When the chicken is almost tender add the mushrooms, Chinese cabbage rolls, and the buckwheat noodles. Cook until the noodles are tender, about 7 minutes. Place the chicken and vegetables in deep bowls and pour over some of the broth. Serve soy sauce, chopped green onions, and grated fresh horseradish on the side.

Serves 4

Japanese Roast Chicken
This is not exactly a roast chicken but it is a delicious chicken dish.

1 pound chicken meat cut into 1/4 inch slices
1/2 cup Soy sauce
1/2 cup Saké
2 tablespoons sugar
1 tablespoon salad oil
1 lemon sliced very thin

Mix the soy sauce, saké, and sugar together. Marinate the chicken slices in this mixture for 3 hours. Heat the salad oil in a heavy skillet and fry the chicken until tender, brushing often with the marinade. Serve with a thin slice of lemon over the top.

Serves 2

Scrambled Chicken
In Japanese cooking eggs are quite often stirred into a dish for variety.

1/4 cup clam juice
1/4 cup beef broth
1/4 cup soy sauce
1/4 cup saké
1 tablespoon sugar

⅛ teaspoon pepper
½ teaspoon Ac'cent
1 chicken breast sliced very thin
¼ pound mushrooms sliced very thin
1 large onion sliced very thin
4 eggs well beaten

Combine the clam juice, beef broth, soy sauce, saké, sugar, pepper, and Ac'cent in a saucepan. Bring to a boil and add the thin chicken slices, mushroom slices, and onion slices. Cook over a medium heat for 6 minutes or until the chicken is cooked. Stir in the well-beaten eggs and cook until the eggs are set, stirring occasionally.

Serves 4

Chinese Chicken

Ancient records show that the Chinese first began using the chicken as food in 1400 B.C., and it was also considered important in Chinese cookery. In early times the chicken was looked upon as the symbol of the reincarnation of Yang and represented all the positive elements of universal life. Chicken was always served to dinner guests in China, and especially at wedding celebrations it was served in a special dish to insure a happy marriage. Besides its philosophical attributes the Chinese took pride in the superior flavor of their chickens. They were killed fresh to insure their natural flavor, and as one experienced Chinese restaurant owner said to me, the number of dishes devised for chicken is so vast in Chinese cookery its history reads almost like a bible.

The cooking of Chinese food takes great care and preparation. In fact, the preparation of many dishes takes almost as long as the actual cooking. The cutting and chopping of foods beforehand to the proper sizes and shapes is extremely important. Many dissimilar ingredients can be blended together when they are of uniform size and it is this skill in blending many flavors to complement each other upon which the culinary arts of China were built.

Cantonese cooking has always been the most popular style of cooking in the United States but there are actually four distinct regional types of cooking in China: Eastern, Western, Northern, Southern. The Eastern region takes in the area around Shanghai. Soy sauce is used very liberally in the cooking there and more sugar is added to the sauces than in the other regions. The Western region takes in the province of Szechuan where the climate is hotter than in the rest of China, and like all people who live in hot climates the food is highly seasoned and spicy hot to taste. In the Northern region is the province of Shantung, the native land of Confucius. The Peking Duck, of course, is the most famous dish, but the region is also known for its wine-cooked meats and soft-fried foods. The Northern Chinese also make great use of the Mongolian firepot. The Southern region is Cantonese and they have a wider range of dishes than any of the other regions. The flavors are more delicately blended, the foods more varied, and the chefs excel in all lines of cooking. In fact, Cantonese cooking is considered the best in all of China. Mention might be made here too of Fukien, the province just above Canton. The Fukienese, being close to the sea, are mostly sailors and much of their food is soup or soupy dishes and, of course, sea food.

Culinarily speaking, San Francisco's large Chinatown is Cantonese and has become renowned for its excellent Cantonese cuisine. The last few years, however, more and more Northern Chinese food is being served in the restaurants also. There are now several restaurants which specialize in the cooking of Northern China exclusively. One of them, The Mandarin, features a chicken dish called Beggar's Chicken, which is a bird covered with a salt clay and then baked. Another interesting dish featured there, as well as in several other Northern Chinese restaurants in San Francisco, is the Mongolian chafing pot. This is a firepot heated by a charcoal fire in a center funnel. A rich chicken broth is poured into the firepot and thinly sliced chicken meat or pork or beef is added to it and simmered until tender. The morsels of meat are dipped in a spicy sauce before eating.

As far as I know there is only one restaurant in San Francisco, possibly in the United States, that features the cooking of Western China. The restaurant is in the old Colony Hotel on Bush Street in San Francisco and the food served is the highly seasoned cuisine of Szechuan. They feature a fiery hot peppery chicken dish called Sweet-Sour Hot Chicken as well as several other highly spiced chicken dishes. They also serve a delicious sizzling soup with crisp fried rice that is a hearty rich soup very unlike the delicate clear soups of Cantonese cuisine. The proprietor told me they use stronger flavors to complement other flavors in Western China and then put them together to make an entirely new flavor. He considers Cantonese cooking too bland and prefers the more highly spiced foods of Western China.

Chinese food is distinctive and while many of the dishes are easy enough to prepare it is still an art that I have not yet wholly mastered. Since I have tried to keep this book on cooking chicken selective of the best chicken dishes as they are enjoyed around the world, I have gone to the experts on Chinese cooking for help and advice. They have chosen for me authentic and delightful chicken recipes that should not be too difficult for the average American housewife to prepare and which at the same time are the chicken dishes you will find in the finest Chinese restaurants in San Francisco.

The Empress of China is possibly the newest and most elegant Chinese restaurant in Chinatown. The owner, Kee Joon, is a restaurateur of many years' experience; he has owned many restaurants during his lifetime, most notable among them being a partnership in the well known Imperial Palace. Mr. Joon tells me that the Empress of China is his dream restaurant come true. The restaurant decor of the new six-story building was created by the nationally known firm of Campbell and Wong and reflects the classic architectural form and design of ancient China. There are four dining rooms on the top floor and one large one on the fifth called the Empress Ballroom which will serve 700 people at a time. Mr. Joon told me it is probably the most costly Chinese restaurant construction on the Western continent and that the interior of the restaurant cost $800,000 alone. The lovely carvings and chandeliers are priceless antiques and there is a rare teakwood screen in the entrance to one dining room that is an object of exquisite beauty.

The Empress of China features the distinctive cuisine of all China since the age of the Five Emperors (2674–2183 B.C.) including a number of rare and unusual dishes. Both Cantonese and North Chinese dishes are offered, and while Cantonese is known all over China as the best, Mr. Joon feels that both types of cooking have merit. As he quoted to me from an old Chinese saying, "Soo Chow is the place one would choose to be born because the men are so tall and handsome and the women so beautiful; Hang Chow the place to live because it has the most beautiful climate; Canton the place to eat because the food is the best in all of China."

The menu at the Empress of China offers a wondrous array of dishes, superb delicacies from many regions, each cooked to perfection. There are delightful soups—won ton, mustard greens, bean curd and mushroom, South Sea shark fin, bird's nest. . . . There are tangy meat, fish, and shellfish dishes. Chicken comes in a variety of ways. There is almond and cashew chicken; chicken with mushroom and oyster sauce; chicken with shrimps and spices and wine; chicken with lichees and water chestnuts; and a fascinating dish called Drunkard Chicken Li Po, named in honor of Li Po, a great poet and the most prodigious drunkard in ancient China.

Mr. Joon has kindly given me two chicken recipes to use in this chapter of my book. One is Chicken in Plum Sauce, which is a delicious dish with boneless cubes of chicken, and mushrooms, and water chestnuts sautéed in plum sauce. This is a North Chinese dish, and as Mr. Joon says, one that should be easy for an American housewife to duplicate. He has also given me the recipe for Lichee Chicken, which is both Cantonese and North China.

The Sun Hung Heung Restaurant is one of the oldest restaurants in San Francisco's Chinatown. In August of this year it will celebrate its 50th year in the same location. The restaurant was originally named Sun Hung Heung Jow Low after a

Chinese village known all over China for its celebration of food and drink. Jow Low means a house where liquor is served, but in the course of time Jow Low was dropped from the name. The restaurant still has a bar—in fact, a very comfortable and modern bar—but the restaurant has been known for many years now simply as Sun Hung Heung. There are a few priceless Chinese antiques in the background but the decor is mainly modern and the atmosphere very friendly.

The food served at Sun Hung Heung is Cantonese and the variety of dishes offered on the a la carte menu so many it is difficult to decide which mouth-watering specialty to try first because all of the food is superb. Leonard Wong, who is the chef and assistant manager at Sun Hung Heung now, learned to cook by training in the restaurant. He took me back to see the large modern stainless-steel kitchen. Along one wall was a large special gas range with several *woks* set into it, one filled with rice, one simmering soup, another chopped vegetables put there to cook a few moments. The *wok,* as Leonard explained to me, is the most basic utensil in Chinese cooking. Made of thin iron or stainless steel, it ranges in size from 12 inches in diameter for family use to 24 inches in diameter for restaurant use. The *wok* is used for boiling, frying, and steaming. The rounded bottom gives an even heat and its bowl shape is desirable for the quick-stir cooking used in so many Chinese dishes.

A necessary addition to the *wok* is a circular steel ring support for the bottom of the *wok.* The ring support is fitted over the gas burner to give the proper degree of heat for cooking Chinese foods. For this reason almost all Chinese kitchens use gas ranges, for the ring support cannot be fitted over an electric burner.

A large stainless-steel cabinet in the center of the kitchen provided cutting and chopping surfaces, shelves for serving dishes, and hangers for ducks and chickens to dry out. The chopping surfaces, cleavers, and cutting knives, Leonard explained to me, were the next most important items in a Chinese kitchen because it is a necessary part of Chinese cooking to have all the meats and vegetables cut to uniform size. In fact, the preparation and cutting and slicing of foods is as important to Chinese cooking as is the actual cooking itself.

Among the specialties served at Sun Hung Heung are several delectable chicken dishes. Chicken Wrapped in Paper is one of them; another is Chicken Salad—Sau Ghee Gui—which is a chicken steamed, hung to dry, deep fried until crisp, cut into strips, and then mixed with parsley, green onions, sesame oil, spices, and served warm. Leonard gave me the recipes for these two chicken dishes and they are included among the recipes in this section.

The Sai Yon is a Chinese family-style restaurant in San Francisco with a long-standing reputation for the excellence of its Chinese cuisine. The reputation is justly deserved, for not only does Sai Yon offer some of the best food in Chinatown but the food is authentically Chinese. There are any number of enticing dishes offered on the menu, one of the most delightful being fresh-water snails cooked to perfection in their shells with chili peppers, garlic, spices, and black-bean sauce. These are spicy and hot and wonderful to eat with wooden toothpicks right from the shells.

The present owner and manager, Mrs. Helen Jung, has had many years' experience in running the restaurant. This charming Chinese lady has been in complete charge since 1939 and is well versed in all phases of Chinese foods from the traditional and home-type to the most exotic. She has remodeled and enlarged her restaurant several times; the last renovation in 1966 saw the addition of a large banquet hall at the back of the building. Sai Yon now boasts two modern dining rooms as well as the new banquet hall. The dining room which you enter first is informal with a counter along one side, the second dining room is informal also, and the banquet hall quite impressive with stark red walls and a contemporary Chinese atmosphere.

Mrs. Jung has given me several delightful chicken recipes

to add to this chapter on Chinese chicken: Boneless Sweet Sour Chicken; Boned Chicken with Snow Peas; Boiled Chicken; Fried Chicken Crispy; Pot Chicken. Also, she has given me interesting bits of advice on the proper way of cooking these Chinese dishes. One bit of advice is to hang a whole chicken up after cooking it when you want the skin to be crisp. Another is when cooking a chicken Chinese style it is far better to undercook it and have the skin smooth than to overcook it and have a dish ruined by a coarse-textured chicken. Also she stressed the importance of careful organization with everything you need within easy reach, so that nothing can be overcooked or burned.

I am deeply grateful for the use of these delightful and authentic Chinese chicken recipes. I hope even those who have never cooked Chinese food before will find pleasure in trying out these selected recipes from the best restaurants in San Francisco's Chinatown. Most of the recipes will serve four people if you use them American-style as a main dish. They should not be too difficult to prepare and most of the ingredients are available in supermarkets or in any Chinese grocery store.

Chicken Salad (Sau Ghee Gui)

This is an unusual chicken dish from the Sun Hung Heung restaurant given to me by Leonard Wong, the chef. It is not a true chicken salad in the American style, since it is served warm as one of the main entrees in a Chinese dinner.

3-pound chicken
1 teaspoon salt
½ teaspoon pepper
1 tablespoon soy sauce
2 cloves garlic
2 ounces ginger root
1 cup tapioca flour
2 green onions

Handful of Chinese parsley
½ head lettuce
¼ pound crushed walnut meats
Fat for deep frying
1 teaspoon salt
½ teaspoon sugar
½ teaspoon monosodium glutamate
Dash of pepper
1 teaspoon sesame oil
Shredded lettuce

Rub the insides of the chicken with the salt, pepper, and soy sauce. Place the garlic cloves and ginger root inside the cavity and put the chicken in a deep pan. Lower the pan into a steamer, cover, and steam the chicken for 10 minutes. Remove the chicken from the steamer and dredge it with the tapioca flour. Return the chicken to the steamer and steam covered for 5 minutes longer. Remove the chicken and hang it up to dry out.

While the chicken is drying slice very fine 2 green onions and a handful of Chinese parsley. Chop ½ head lettuce very fine. Mix together in a bowl with ¼ pound crushed walnut meats. Set aside.

When the chicken has dried out sufficiently, deep-fry it whole in a deep fat fryer for 5 minutes to make the skin crisp. Drain and bone the chicken carefully. Cut the meat into strips of uniform size. Add 1 teaspoon salt, the sugar, monosodium glutamate, pepper, and sesame oil to the finely chopped vegetables and crushed walnut meats. Add the chicken strips and toss all together well. Line a platter with the shredded lettuce and place the chicken salad on top. Serve warm.

Serves 4

Chicken Wrapped in Paper

This delicious dish was given to me by Leonard Wong of Sun
Hung Heung.

4-pound chicken
3 cloves garlic
1 teaspoon grated ginger root
2 green onions
½ bunch Chinese parsley
1 tablespoon sugar
1 teaspoon soy sauce
3 tablespoons catsup or barbecue sauce
2 tablespoons oil (vegetable or peanut)
2 tablespoons cornstarch
Salt and pepper
1 package 6-x-6-inch squares of cooking parchment (or oiled
    browned butcher paper)
Kettle of fat for deep frying

Bone chicken and chop into little chunks. Chop the garlic,
ginger root, green onions, and parsley into fine pieces. Mix all
remaining ingredients together, add chicken and chopped
seasonings, then wrap in squares of cooking parchment. Lay
the paper with a corner point at the top, bottom, and each
side. Spoon a small amount of the mixture in the middle.
Fold the bottom up over it, the point coming to about 1½
inches below the top corner. Fold the left side over, the point
coming three inches from the right corner; then the right side
over, the same distance. You should now have a rectangle of
about four inches by three with a triangular piece across the
top. Fold the rectangle exactly in half, its bottom coming to
the base of the triangle flap. Tuck flap into this piece. Heat
the fat to 350° and deep fry the chicken envelopes for about
10 minutes. Serve in the paper and they will stay warm until
you open them to eat. Makes approximately 2 dozen packages.

Serves 4–6

White Chicken Dish

Adena Robinson, who is home economist at the high school in Marin County, California, gave me this recipe for White Chicken. She was born in the interior of China of missionary parents and lived there until she was almost a young lady. Consequently she is well versed in both Chinese cooking and customs. She told me everything in the dish should come out a pale delicate color—hence the name White Chicken.

White meat from a 5-pound roasting chicken
2½ quarts water
1 teaspoon salt
¼ cup flour
3 tablespoons peanut oil
½ teaspoon salt
1 clove minced garlic
1 teaspoon minced ginger root
1 cauliflower head
¼ cup white bamboo shoots
½ cup sliced mushrooms
Chopped chives

Bring 2½ quarts water to a boil with 1 teaspoon salt. Add the chicken, cover the pot, and simmer the chicken for fifteen minutes. Remove the chicken from the pot and cool by running cold water over it. Carefully remove the skin from the chicken and cut all of the white meat into bite-size pieces. Save the dark meat of the chicken for another dish. Dredge the chicken pieces with the flour. Heat the peanut oil in a skillet with ½ teaspoon salt. When hot add the floured chicken and cook over a medium high heat for 2 minutes being careful not to let the chicken brown. Add the minced garlic and ginger root, the buds of a cauliflower cut into bite-size pieces, the sliced mushrooms, and the bamboo shoots. Mix together well with the chicken, cover the pan, and simmer for 5 minutes or until the cauliflower is just barely tender. Serve with chopped chives sprinkled lightly over the top.

Serves 4

Antique Tangerine Peel Chicken

A friend of mine, Helen Stilz, who is taking a course in Chinese cooking at the YWCA in San Francisco's Chinatown, gave me this recipe for Antique Tangerine Peel Chicken which she learned to make through her cooking class. The tangerine peel can be bought in most Chinese grocery stores. It is fairly expensive but a little bit goes a long way.

3-pound chicken boned
½ ounce dried tangerine orange peel
¼ cup warm water
¼ cup soy sauce
¼ cup sherry
¼ teaspoon minced ginger root
2 green onions minced fine
½ teaspoon monosodium glutamate
1 tangerine cut into thin slices
1 tablespoon cornstarch
2 tablespoons water
Tangerine slices for garnish
Several sprigs of Chinese parsley

Have the chicken boned by your butcher. Cut it into bite-size pieces. Soak the dried tangerine orange peel in ¼ cup warm water for 30 minutes. Then pour it into a wok or skillet along with the soy sauce, sherry, minced ginger root, minced green onion, monosodium glutamate, and thin slices of tangerine. Bring to a boil and add the bite-size chicken pieces. Cook at high heat for 2 minutes tossing and stirring the chicken continually. Turn heat to low, cover the pan, and simmer for 30 minutes or until the chicken is just tender.

Remove the chicken to a hot serving platter and strain the juices into a saucepan. Add the cornstarch mixed with the cold water to the juices and cook over a medium heat until the sauce thickens, stirring constantly. Pour the sauce over the chicken and garnish with tangerine slices and sprigs of Chinese parsley.

Serves 4

Fried Chicken Crispy

This is a very special Chinese dish given to me by Mrs. Helen Jung of Sai Yon. Serve it at a party and your guests will be delightfully surprised at its elegance.

3-pound chicken
Hot water
1 teaspoon salt
1 tablespoon soy sauce
Oil for deep frying
Several thin slices ham
Several thin lemon slices

Clean a 3-pound chicken. Bring to a boil enough hot water to cover the chicken. Add 1 teaspoon salt and the chicken. Cover the pot and simmer for 15 minutes. The chicken should be just about half-cooked. Remove the chicken from the pot and hang up to dry out. This will make the skin crispy. Rub the inside of the chicken with the soy sauce then deep fry quickly in hot oil—about 5 minutes or just long enough for the skin to take on a crisp golden brown appearance.

Now comes the complicated part. You may not do too well the first time but this dish is well worth trying again. First the crisp golden brown skin is cut through and the meat separated from the bones. Then the meat is sliced thinly into small pieces and the meat and skin replaced in their original form. Now lay thin slices of ham on the bottom of a serving platter and carefully place the chicken on top. Cover the chicken with thin slices of lemon and serve with hot mustard and soy sauce or oyster sauce on the side.

Serves 4

Boiled Chicken

A classic Chinese recipe given to me by Mrs. Helen Jung of Sai Yon restaurant. The chicken keeps its delicate natural flavor by simmering and Mrs. Jung cautioned me against overcooking it. As she said, it would be far better to have the chicken undercooked and smooth-textured than over-cooked and coarse-textured.

3-pound chicken
2½ quarts water
1 teaspoon salt
Sesame oil
1 bunch green onions
2 tablespoons salt
3 tablespoons sesame oil

Clean the chicken. Bring the water to a boil with 1 teaspoon salt. Add the chicken, cover the pot, and simmer the chicken for ½ hour. Remove the chicken from the pot and cool by running cold water over it. The cold running water keeps the chicken from becoming soggy. Carefully remove the skin from the chicken and rub a little sesame oil all over it. Then chop the chicken, bones and all, into small pieces of uniform size. Make a sauce by combining 1 bunch green onions finely chopped with 2 tablespoons salt and 3 tablespoons sesame oil. Serve the chicken with the onion-salt-oil sauce as a dip.

Serves 4

Pot Chicken

An excellent Chinese home-style dish presented to me by Mrs. Helen Jung. It has a pleasing contrast of flavors.

3-pound chicken
2 tablespoons vegetable oil
½ cup dried Chinese mushrooms
½ cup dried Chinese vegetables
6 thin slices ginger root
4 tablespoons water
1 tablespoon cornstarch
2 tablespoons white wine
¼ teaspoon soy sauce

Clean a 3-pound chicken. Heat the vegetable oil in a heavy pan and brown the chicken on all sides. Soak the dried Chinese mushrooms and dried Chinese vegetables in warm water for 30 minutes. Drain and slice very thin. Add to the chicken along with the thin slices of ginger root. Cook 1 minute. Add the water, cover, and cook over low heat about 20 minutes or until the chicken and vegetables are just barely tender. Remove the chicken and cut into small pieces. Mix the cornstarch with the white wine and soy sauce. Add to the vegetables and liquid in the pan and toss and mix at high heat until the gravy thickens. Pour the gravy and vegetables into a warm serving dish and place the chicken pieces on top.

Serves 4

Boned Chicken with Snow Peas

Snow peas are used in many Chinese dishes to give texture. They must be cooked quickly with very little liquid to retain their flavor and color. They are also called pea pods. This recipe was given to me by Mrs. Helen Jung of Sai Yon restaurant.

3-pound chicken boned
2 tablespoons vegetable oil
¼ pound snow peas
4 water chestnuts sliced thin
½ cup canned mushrooms sliced thin
1 tablespoon water
1 tablespoon cornstarch mixed with 1 tablespoon water
1 tablespoon white wine
½ teaspoon sugar
¼ teaspoon salt
1 tablespoon soy sauce

Have a 3-pound chicken boned. Cut it into small pieces. In a preheated frying pan or Wok put 2 tablespoons vegetable oil and when the oil has heated up add the chicken pieces. Stir and cook the chicken at high heat for 2 minutes. Add the snow peas, water chestnuts, and canned mushrooms. Add 1 tablespoon water and stir and cook for 2 minutes longer. Mix the cornstarch and water together and add to the pan along with the white wine, sugar, salt, and soy sauce. Stir constantly over the heat until the sauce thickens. Serve immediately.

Serves 4

Boneless Sweet-Sour Chicken
Boneless Sweet-Sour Chicken always tastes delicious. This recipe, given to me by Mrs. Helen Jung of Sai Yon, is first-rate.

3-pound chicken, boned
1 egg slightly beaten
½ teaspoon salt
1 teaspoon soy sauce
¼ cup flour
Hot oil for deep frying
½ cup sugar
¼ cup vinegar

¼ cup tomato catsup
1 tablespoon soy sauce
2 tablespoons cornstarch
¼ cup water
1 cup pineapple chunks
½ cup green pepper sliced very thin
3 green onions chopped into tiny pieces

Have a 3-pound chicken boned. Cut it into small pieces. Mix
the slightly beaten egg with ½ teaspoon salt and 1 teaspoon
soy sauce. Dip the chicken pieces into this egg mixture and
then into the flour. Deep fry the chicken pieces quickly in
hot oil until they are browned. Drain and keep warm.

In a saucepan or a *wok* mix together the sugar, vinegar,
catsup, and soy sauce. Add the cornstarch mixed with ¼ cup
water and cook over a medium heat, stirring constantly, until
the sauce has thickened. Add the pineapple chunks, green
pepper slices, and chopped green onions. Add the browned
chicken pieces and mix thoroughly. Stir together over the
heat until the chicken and vegetables are heated through.

Serves 4

Chicken in Plum Sauce

Chicken in Plum Sauce is a delicious dish with boneless cubes
of chicken, mushrooms, and waterchestnuts sautéed in a wonderful Chinese Plum Sauce. The dish is featured on the menu
of the elegant Empress of China Restaurant and was given to
me by the owner, Mr. Kee Joon. Mr. Joon told me it should
be an easy dish for an American housewife to duplicate since
the Chinese Plum Sauce can be obtained in a jar in any
Chinese grocery store and the other ingredients purchased in
a local supermarket.

3½-pound chicken, boned
3 tablespoons Chinese Plum Sauce

1 medium onion, diced
½ teaspoon salt
1 small can button mushrooms cut in half
1 dozen whole water chestnuts, diced
¼ teaspoon Tabasco sauce

Sauté chicken in hot pan with oil until brown. Add onion, water chestnuts, and mustrooms and sauté together. Add Chinese Plum Sauce (obtained in a jar in Chinese grocery store). Stir together, adding the salt and hot Tabasco sauce. Stir until well mixed and serve immediately.

Serves 6

Lichee Chicken

Lichee Chicken is both a Cantonese and North China dish. It is another wonderful Chinese chicken dish featured on the menu of the elegant Empress of China Restaurant, the recipe given to me by the owner, Mr. Kee Joon.

3½-pound chicken, boned
½ cup tomato catsup
4 tablespoons sugar
4 tablespoons cornstarch
Waterchestnut flour
½ cup vinegar
½ teaspoon salt
1 No. 2 can lichee

Cut the boned chicken in slices and dip in dry waterchestnut flour. French-fry until the slices turn brown. Combine catsup, vinegar, sugar and salt and thicken with the cornstarch. Put chicken into this sauce and add the lichee. Mix together and serve immediately.

Serves 6

South Pacific Chicken

The tropical islands of the South Pacific lie like dots in the immense, teeming ocean. They are island worlds we are familiar with and yet unknown, steeped in ancient tradition, mysterious, romantic. They include the Hawaiian Island group and, further south, the myriads of islands of Oceania. The Polynesian, Melanesian, and Micronesian groups—including the Samoan, Gilbert, Caroline, Marshall, and Tonga chains of islands. Here the people live on whatever is available: fish, wild game, taro root, breadfruit, yams, or their own small crops. On the outer islands that are far from trading posts there are all the necessities for the support of human life as the Polynesians knew it when they journeyed from island to island in their great migration across the Pacific, carrying with them the foodstuffs needed for colonization.

How the Polynesians were able to find their way across the mighty Pacific to unknown islands so many centuries ago is still a mystery. That they were able to sail hundreds of miles across the open sea in wooden canoes held together by pegs and cords and only the naked eye and the stars to guide them stands among the great achievements of the human race. But it is a well-established fact that they pushed north and south in their population movements and managed to explore and colonize all the habitable islands of Polynesia.

On the long voyages to colonize strange islands the Polynesians stored useful plants and foodstuffs and animals in their canoes. They took breadfruit, coconut, taro, yam, sweet potatoes, sugar cane, as well as a number of the less important fruits. The foods were highly nutritious but lacking in flavor. Taro in particular was insipid, but the Hawaiians learned by accident to make pao out of it and thenceforth included it in their famous luaus. Breadfruit, which is not at all like bread, is more promising than taro. It is a waxy, chewy, meatlike substance but when baked it has a slightly chestnut flavor.

The domesticated animals the Polynesians carried with them were only three in number: the pig, the dog, and our chicken, which was then only a primitive jungle fowl. In their new homes these animals multiplied rapidly and were used for feast luxuries. The most important was the pig, and even to this day no Hawaiian luau is complete without a roasted pig. The dog was also used for feasting, also the chicken, a strikingly beautiful jungle cock, accompanied by his plain mate, both of them originally natives of Asia. The gorgeous gold and silver plumage of the cock was used for feather headdresses and ornamentation as well as the flesh for feasting.

The sea always provided an abundance of fish and shellfish to experienced fishermen and was utilized in every possible way. The Polynesians were usually short of high-grade proteins; they would eat anything edible they could catch and bring to shore.

The people of the South Pacific have always been able to utilize what they had on hand, and even though in recent times people of all races and cultures have added new ingredients to Polynesian cooking, it has still managed to keep its basic character. Curry cooking may have influenced Fuji, adapted from the descendants of laborers brought in from India to grow sugar cane over three generations ago. A Hawaiian influence is traceable in more subtle flavors. The imported Chinese laborers introduced soy sauce and ginger and the tradition of Cantonese cooking to Tahiti and Hawaii. The Japanese laborers came with their own special way of cooking. In spite of the influence of the other races and cultures, Polynesian cooking has managed to remain authentic.

The Polynesians eat whatever happens to appeal to them or whatever happens to be on hand. There are always island fruits, ripe and inviting and warmed by the tropical sunshine—pineapples, mangoes, bananas, papayas. Until recent times their cooking equipment was meager, and usually when they came across something edible they either ate it on the spot or baked it in a pit oven.

The pit was dug four feet deep and lined with porous stones. A fire was built on top of the stones, and when the fire was good and hot the embers were removed and the items to be cooked, such as fish, chicken, pig, taro, breadfruit, were wrapped in banana leaves and placed on the hot stones. In cooking a whole pig, hot stones were placed inside the pig's abdomen. All the food was covered with more banana leaves and dampened down with burlap sacks and earth. Then it was left for hours, the timing being a matter of judgment, for in the tropical islands there was always plenty of time.

Hawaiian Chicken

This chicken dish may have been influenced by the Orient but it has a definite Polynesian flavor.

5-pound roasting chicken cut into pieces
Water to cover
1 teaspoon salt
Juice of 1 lime
6 peppercorns
1 bay leaf
1 small fresh coconut or 1 cup packaged grated coconut
1 small fresh pineapple or 1 cup canned pineapple chunks
¼ cup butter
¼ cup flour
1¾ cups coconut milk and chicken stock combined
¼ cup sherry
1 tablespoon grated ginger root
½ cup chopped cashew nuts

Put the chicken pieces in a kettle with water to cover. Add salt, juice of 1 lime, peppercorns, and bay leaf. Cover and simmer 1 hour or until chicken is tender. Remove chicken from stock and cut the meat from the bones into strips. Strain the stock and reserve. Bore 2 large holes in the coconut, drain the milk, and combine with the chicken stock to make 1¾ cups. Grate the coconut meat. Slice the pineapple. Cut into wedges. Melt the butter in a pan and blend in the flour. Slowly add the coconut milk chicken stock mixture and cook over a medium low heat, stirring constantly, until thickened. Add the sherry and grated ginger root. Butter a baking dish and arrange layers of chicken, grated coconut, pineapple, cashew nuts, and sauce in the dish. Bake in a preheated 350° oven for 30 minutes. Serve at once.

Serves 6

* See recipe for coconut milk on page 543.

Hawaiian Chicken Luau
Moa Luau A Me Wai Niu—a typical chicken dish for a Hawaiian Chicken Luau.

2 coconuts
4-pound chicken fryer cut into pieces
Salt and pepper
2 cups taro leaves (spinach leaves can be used instead)

Grate the coconut meat and strain the liquid through a piece of cheesecloth. Add boiling water to the pulp and strain again. Reserve the liquid. Place the chicken in a kettle with water to cover and simmer for 40 minutes or until the chicken is tender. Wash the taro or spinach leaves and cook in water until tender. Drain. Combine the coconut mixture with the chicken and the leaves. Cook until just heated through and serve.

Serves 4

Pansit Guisado Hawaiian
A delicious Hawaiian dish with Chinese overtones.

5-pound roasting chicken
2 cloves garlic minced
6 peppercorns
1 teaspoon salt
Water to cover
1 pound lean pork
¼ cup soy sauce
¼ cup lime juice
2 tablespoons lard
2 packages long rice
2 tablespoons soy sauce
2 tablespoons sherry
1 teaspoon monosodium glutamate

Place the chicken in a large kettle with water to cover. Add the minced garlic, peppercorns, and salt. Cover and simmer about 1½ hours or until the chicken is barely tender. Do not overcook. Remove the chicken. Strain and reserve the stock. Cut the chicken from the bones into small pieces, discarding the skin and bones. Cut the pork meat into thin narrow strips. Combine the ¼ cup soy sauce with the ¼ cup lime juice and marinate the pork strips for 1 hour. Soak the long rice in cold water and when soft drain and cut into 2-inch lengths. Put it in the kettle with the reserved chicken stock and cook until tender adding more liquid if necessary. Add 2 tablespoons soy sauce, 2 tablespoons sherry, the chicken pieces, and the pork strips. Cook over a medium heat, stirring constantly, until the pork is tender—about 5 minutes. Add the monosodium glutamate and cook 2 minutes longer.

Serves 6

Polynesian Chicken Curry

This is a heavenly curry cooked with toasted almonds and coconut cream for a real taste teaser.

4-pound chicken fryer
Water to cover
1 teaspoon salt
2½ cups heavy cream
1 cup shredded packaged sweetened coconut
2 tablespoons butter
2 tablespoons flour
1½ tablespoons curry powder
½ cup toasted halved almonds
Salt to taste

Put the chicken in a pot and cover with water. Add the salt, and cook over a low heat for 45 minutes or until tender. Remove the chicken, and when cool cut the meat from the bones into small pieces. Combine the heavy cream and sweetened coconut in a saucepan and let the mixture just come to a boil. Cool slightly and squeeze through a piece of cheesecloth. This should make about 2 cups of coconut cream. Melt the butter in another pan and blend in the flour. Add the coconut cream and curry powder. Stir over a medium heat until thickened. Add the chicken and the toasted almonds. Cook over a low heat until heated through. Taste for seasoning and serve hot with boiled rice.

Serves 4

Tahitian Chicken

A succulent chicken dish from Tahiti.

4-pound chicken fryer cut into pieces
1 teaspoon salt
⅛ teaspoon pepper

Heavy aluminum foil
½ cup butter melted
2 tablespoons soy sauce
2 tablespoons pineapple juice
1 small onion minced fine
½ teaspoon ginger root grated fine
¼ teaspoon cardamom

Rub the chicken pieces well with the salt and pepper. Place each piece of chicken on a separate square of heavy aluminum foil. Melt the butter in a saucepan and add the soy sauce, pineapple juice, minced onion, grated ginger root, and cardamom. Mix together well and cook over a medium heat for 2 minutes, stirring constantly. Spoon this sauce over each chicken piece and fold the aluminum foil over the chicken pieces so that each piece is tightly sealed. Place the aluminum foil packets on a cookie sheet and bake for 1 hour in a preheated 425° oven.

Serves 4

Litchi Chicken

Litchi gives this chicken dish an exotic flavor. The litchis are a sweet tropical fruit about the size of a small plum and can be bought canned in specialty shops.

4-pound chicken fryer cut into pieces
Water to cover
2 egg yolks
½ teaspoon salt
1 teaspoon soy sauce
⅔ cup chicken broth
6 tablespoons flour
1 cup peanut oil
¼ cup chicken broth
1 teaspoon cornstarch

1 teaspoon soy sauce
½ teaspoon grated fresh ginger root
½ cup litchi juice from can
1 cup canned litchi fruit

Put the chicken in a kettle with water to cover and simmer for 45 minutes or until the chicken is tender. Combine the egg yolks, salt, soy sauce, ⅔ cup chicken broth, and flour to make a smooth paste. Dip the chicken pieces in the batter and fry them in hot peanut oil until they are golden brown on both sides. Drain on paper toweling. Mix the ¼ cup chicken broth and the cornstarch together until smooth. Add the grated ginger root, 1 teaspoon soy sauce, and the litchi juice. Cook over a medium heat, stirring constantly, until the sauce thickens. Add the litchi fruit and cook until just heated through. Pour the sauce over the chicken and serve at once.

Serves 4

Kanaka Chicken Stew

Bananas are used in many ways by the people of the South Pacific and this Kanaka Chicken Stew is a simple way of combining chicken with bananas.

4-pound chicken fryer cut into pieces
1 teaspoon salt
⅛ teaspoon pepper
4 tablespoons butter melted
1 cup onions chopped fine
½ cup water
1½ cups bananas cut into rounds

Rub the chicken pieces well with the salt and pepper. Melt the butter in a heavy frying pan and brown the chicken pieces well on both sides. When browned, remove the chicken and add the onions to the butter left in the pan. Cook until browned about 5 minutes. Return the chicken to the pan and add the water. Cover and cook over a low heat for 40 minutes. Add the bananas and cook 10 minutes longer.

Serves 4

Chicken Papaya Stew
A Tahitian chicken with the addition of papaya to give it a tropical flavor.

4-pound chicken fryer cut into pieces
2 cloves garlic mashed
2 tablespoons butter
2 tablespoons grated fresh ginger root
1 teaspoon salt
1 cup pineapple juice
1 cup hot water
2 green papayas peeled and diced

Melt the butter in a heavy skillet and add the mashed garlic. When it begins to color add the chicken pieces and the grated fresh ginger root. Cook until the chicken is well browned on both sides. Add the salt, pineapple juice, and hot water. Cover the pan and simmer for 40 minutes or until the chicken is tender. About 15 minutes before the chicken is done add the diced papaya and continue cooking covered for 15 minutes. Remove the chicken and papaya to a hot serving platter. Reduce the sauce to half over a high heat and pour over the chicken and papaya.

Serves 4

Chicken Oriental
The combination of pineapple, soy sauce, vinegar, brown sugar, and ginger gives this Polynesian dish a wonderful flavor.

4-pound chicken fryer cut into pieces
2 teaspoons powdered ginger
1 teaspoon salt
⅛ teaspoon pepper
½ cup flour
4 tablespoons butter
½ cup soy sauce
½ cup pineapple juice
2 tablespoons red wine vinegar
¼ cup brown sugar
1 cup crushed pineapple

Add the ginger, salt, and pepper to the flour and roll the chicken pieces in the seasoned flour. Melt the butter in a heavy frying pan and brown the chicken pieces well on both sides. Pour off any excess butter. Mix the soy sauce, pineapple juice, wine vinegar, and brown sugar. Pour over the chicken. Add 1 cup crushed pineapple. Cover and simmer over low heat 40 minutes or until the chicken is tender. Serve with boiled rice.

Serves 4

Polynesian Chicken with Nuts and Pineapple
An exotic and refreshing dish from Oceania.

4-pound chicken fryer cut into pieces
Water to cover
1 onion sliced
1 tablespoon salt
3 3 tablespoons butter melted
3 tablespoons soy sauce
2 tablespoons sherry
1 tablespoon chutney
2 cups pineapple juice
2 tablespoons grated ginger root

4-ounce can water chestnuts cut in half
1 cup cashew nuts
1 cup drained pineapple chunks
1 cup canned Chinese chow mein noodles

Put the chicken pieces in a kettle with water to cover. Add sliced onion, salt, and simmer over low heat for 40 minutes or until the chicken is tender. Remove the chicken and cut the meat into small pieces. Discard the skin and bones. Melt the butter in a skillet and add the soy sauce, sherry, chutney, pineapple juice, and grated ginger root. Cook over a medium low heat for 2 minutes, stirring constantly. Add the water chestnuts, cashew nuts, and chicken meat. Cook for 2 minutes then add the pineapple chunks and Chinese chow mein noodles. Cook 1 minute longer.

Serves 4

Chicken in Coconut Shells
A popular Polynesian way of cooking a chicken is to bake it in a ripe coconut.

4-pound chicken cut into pieces
Juice of 1 lime
1 teaspoon salt
1 bay leaf
Water to cover
2 small coconuts
1 cup coconut milk
Grated coconut
Biscuit dough

Place the chicken in a kettle with the juice of 1 lime, salt, and bay leaf. Add water to cover and cook over low heat, covered, for 1 hour or until chicken is tender. Remove chicken and cut into large pieces. Cut the coconuts in half with a saw. Pour off the coconut liquid and set aside. Score the inside of the coconuts with a fork. Divide the chicken meat, coconut liquid, and 1 cup of coconut milk among the 4 shells. Sprinkle grated coconut over the top and cover with biscuit dough. Bake in a preheated 350° oven for 1 hour. If the crust gets too brown cover the top with foil. Serve ½ coconut to each person and accompany with hot biscuits made from remaining dough.

Serves 4

Chicken in Pineapple Shells
Another popular Polynesian dish is chicken baked in pineapple shells.

4-pound chicken cut into pieces
Water to cover
Juice of 1 lime
1 teaspoon salt
1 bay leaf
¼ cup butter melted
1 onion chopped fine
1 teaspoon salt
1 tablespoon curry powder
4 tablespoons flour
1 cup chicken stock
4 tablespoons soy sauce
½ cup heavy cream
4 tablespoons sherry
2 fresh pineapples
Mint leaves, grape leaves, or any broad flat leaf that will give
a tropical appearance for garnish

Place the chicken in a kettle with water to cover along with the juice of 1 lime, salt, and bay leaf. Cover and simmer for 1 hour or until chicken is tender. Remove chicken and cut the meat into small pieces. Discard skin and bones. Melt the butter in a heavy frying pan and cook the onion until soft. Combine the salt, curry powder, and flour. Blend into the onion mixture. Add the chicken stock, soy sauce, heavy cream, and sherry. Cook over low heat, stirring constantly, until thickened and smooth. Add the chicken meat and cook 1 minute longer. Cut the pineapples in half, removing the hard core. Score the center and cut the pineapple meat loose from the shell. Fill with the chicken mixture, heaping it high on top. Wrap tightly in foil and bake in a preheated 375° oven for 40 minutes. Remove the foil and serve on plates garnished with mint leaves, grape leaves, or any broad flat green leaf that will give a tropical appearance.

Serves 4

Chinese Pot-Roasted Chicken Hawaiian
Chicken cooked in a pot with soy sauce, pineapple juice, ginger root, and sherry is authentically Polynesian even though it does have a Chinese touch.

4-pound chicken fryer cut into pieces
½ teaspoon salt
3 tablespoons butter
¼ cup soy sauce
2 tablespoons ginger root minced fine
½ cup pineapple juice
2 tablespoons sherry
½ cup Chinese snow peas
¼ cup sliced water chestnuts

Rub chicken pieces well with salt and brown well on both sides in 3 tablespoons butter. Combine the soy sauce, minced ginger root, pineapple juice, and sherry. Pour over the chicken, cover, and cook over low heat for 40 minutes or until the chicken is tender. Remove the chicken to a serving platter and keep hot. Add the Chinese snow peas and the sliced water chestnuts to the sauce in the pan. Cook until just heated through and pour the sauce and vegetables over the chicken.

Serves 4

Coconut Milk

To make coconut milk bore holes in the two eyes in the end of a coconut. Drain all the liquid from the inside. Crack open the coconut and grate all the meat. There should be about 3 cups of grated coconut meat. Add boiling water to the coconut liquid so that it makes 1 cup. Pour the hot liquid over the grated coconut and let it stand ½ hour. Strain through several pieces of cheesecloth, squeezing and pressing with your hands to extract all the liquid.

A substitute for fresh coconut milk may be prepared by covering 3 cups shredded packaged coconut with 1½ cups hot milk. Allow it to set for ½ hour then simmer for 10 minutes. Strain through several pieces of chesecloth squeezing out as much liquid as possible.

Filipino Chicken

I have placed the Filipino chicken in a separate chapter because while the Philippines may be a part of the South Pacific their cooking culture is far different from that of the Polynesians. For over three hundred years they were a part of the Spanish Empire and as a result their cuisine includes many dishes with a Spanish flavor. The early Spanish explorers and navigators brought cocoa, sweet potatoes, squash, eggplant, lima beans, and red chili peppers to the Philippines and the Filipinos quickly added them to their own diet of rice, coconuts, pineapple, mangoes, bananas, pork, and chicken. Rice is the staple food and appears usually at every meal. Sweet potatoes are consumed in great quantities in some sections of the country.

Hills and mountains cover much of the islands but there is enough lowland to let Filipinos raise most of their own food. They are farmers mostly and do almost all of their work by hand. They raise few animals besides pork. Their meat is mostly fish and chicken. In fact about half of their main dishes contain fish and the other half chicken. They are also fond of combinations of two or more ingredients such as chicken and shrimp, chicken and pork, chicken and fish, and the contrast in flavors is very interesting. Adabong Manok—Chicken en Adobe—is their most famous dish and it very definitely shows its Spanish background.

Adobong Manok
Adobong Manok—Chicken en Adobe—is the Philippines' most famous dish!

2½-pound broiler chicken
3 cloves garlic minced
5 tablespoons vinegar
2 bay leaves crushed
1½ teaspoons salt
¼ teaspoon pepper
Boiling water
2 tablespoons fat
½ cup coconut cream

Cut the chicken into 2-inch pieces or have your butcher do it for you. Combine the chicken in a skillet with the minced garlic, vinegar, crushed bay leaves, salt, and pepper. Add enough boiling water to barely cover the chicken, cover the skillet, and simmer until the chicken is tender and the water has evaporated. Add the fat, turn heat to high, and fry the chicken until it is crisped and browned. Serve hot with the coconut cream in a separate dish.

Serves 4

Coconut Cream

To make coconut cream bore holes in the eyes of a coconut and drain all the liquid from the inside. Crack the coconut and grate the coconut meat. Put 1 cup of the grated coconut in several thicknesses of chesecloth and squeeze out as much liquid as you can. Squeeze the rest of the coconut 1 cup at a time.

A substitute coconut cream may be prepared by soaking 2 cups packaged coconut in 1 cup heavy cream for 1 hour. Then let it cook for 10 minutes over a low heat, cool, and squeeze the liquid through several thicknesses of cheesecloth.

Adobong Manok at Baboy

This is a combination dish containing both chicken and pork. The flavor contrasts are exotic.

5-pound roasting chicken
1½ pounds pork
1 teaspoon salt
¼ teaspoon black pepper
4 cloves garlic minced
½ cup cider vinegar
1 bay leaf crumbled
3 tablespoons peanut oil
1 cup water
1 cup coconut cream

Have your butcher chop the chicken into 2-inch pieces, bones and all. Cut the pork in 1½-inch pieces. Mix together the salt, pepper, garlic, vinegar, and bay leaf. Marinate the chicken and pork in this mixture for 30 minutes. Drain, reserving the marinade. Heat the peanut oil in a heavy Dutch oven and brown the chicken and pork in it. Add the marinade and the water. Cover and cook over a medium heat for 30 minutes or until the chicken and pork are tender and almost all the liquid has evaporated. Stir in the coconut cream. Cook 5 minutes longer.

Serves 6

Adobe
Adobe—a braised chicken—is simple and good.

4-pound chicken fryer cut into pieces
½ cup vinegar
1 teaspoon salt
¼ teaspoon pepper
2 cups water
½ cup flour
¼ cup lard

Put the chicken pieces in a kettle with the vinegar and salt, pepper, and water. Bring quickly to a boil then simmer 45 minutes covered or until chicken is tender. Drain well. Roll the pieces of cooked chicken in flour and fry until golden brown and crisp on both sides.

Serves 4

Chicken and White Squash

Tinola Sa Upo—Chicken and White Squash—is another interesting way the Filipinos have of cooking chicken. Summer squash may be used for this.

1½-pound broiler chicken
1 teaspoon salt
2 cloves garlic minced
1 small onion chopped fine
3 tablespoons lard
1 large tomato sliced
1 teaspoon fresh ginger root grated
¼ cup chopped pimientos
2 cups white summer squash cut into small pieces
Water

Have your butcher cut the chicken into 6 pieces bones and all. Rub the chicken pieces well with salt. Melt the lard in a large heavy skillet and brown the minced garlic and chopped onion in it. When nicely browned add the sliced tomato, grated ginger root, and chopped pimientos. Cook for 3 minutes. Add the chicken pieces and enough water to barely cover. Simmer covered until the chicken is almost done. Add the white summer squash and cook about 10 minutes longer or until the squash is soft.

Serves 6

Mexican Chicken

Contrary to general belief, Mexican cooking is not necessarily hot. It is well spiced, yes, but the range of dishes goes far beyond the popular tacos, enchiladas, and tamales. It is a blending of three cooking worlds: the Aztec, the Spanish, and the French. The Aztecs had a rich and enlightened culture and when Cortez finally arrived in Mexico City after the long march across Mexico the many exotic dishes on Montezuma's table came as a delightful surprise to him. Bernardo Diaz in describing the wonderful variety of foods in the native cuisine said in his journal: "His cooks had upward of thirty different ways of dressing meats and such foods as chocolate, vanilla, corn, chilis, peanuts, tomatoes, avocados, squash, beans, sweet potatoes were eaten."

Of course as soon as the Spaniards had conquered Mexico they introduced their own Spanish cooking style. They imported olive oil, wine, cinnamon, cloves, rice, wheat, peaches, apricots, and the cattle to provide beef, milk and butter. Later when Maximilian and Carlotta were put on the throne of Mexico as emperor and empress they brought sophisticated French dishes to their court.

The Mexican peon has always relied chiefly upon the local produce available to him as the basis of his diet. Corn plays a vital role and the corn dishes such as tortillas, tacos, and tamales have changed very little since Aztec times. Chili peppers too are essential to Mexican cooking as well as beans and tomatoes, which are used in many sauces. Also many herbs and spices are used, fresh coriander being one of the most in demand as a substitute for saffron.

548

Chickens too have played their role in Mexican cooking. Chicken Mole Poblano with its wonderful dark brown sauce of chili peppers and chocolate can hardly pass unnoticed. Nor can the Cazuela of Chicken—a chicken cooked in an earthenware pot over a direct fire with chili peppers and herbs and tomatoes; or possibly with the addition of fruit or vegetables and nuts. These are chicken dishes that have changed very little since the conquest of Mexico by Cortez.

Chicken Mole Poblano

Chicken Mole Poblano—Chicken in Mole Sauce—is a unique chicken dish with chocolate, chili peppers, and spices. It is supposedly the creation of Mexican nuns who devised the dish in desperation to serve to visiting church dignitaries. I doubt if sherry was used by the nuns, but it does give the sauce a more subtle flavor.

4-pound roasting chicken cut into pieces
Chicken broth
6 small green chili peppers
2 slices dry white bread
Water
½ cup chopped blanched almonds
1 teaspoon anise seeds
2 cloves garlic chopped
2 tablespoons peanut oil
1 onion chopped
2 large tomatoes peeled and diced
2 ounces bitter chocolate
3 tablespoons sugar
Pinch of cinnamon
Pinch of powdered cloves
½ cup sherry

Cook the chicken in enough chicken broth to cover for 1 hour. Remove the chicken from the kettle and keep warm. Reserve

2 cups of the chicken broth. Roast the small green chili peppers in a hot 450° oven until they are crisp and well browned. Cool, then remove seeds and chop them coarsely. Place them in an electric blender and blend fine. Toast the slices of dry white bread until they are a dark brown. Add them to the chili peppers in the blender and blend until fine. Remove to a bowl and add just enough water to make a smooth paste. Set aside.

In a pan combine the blanched chopped almonds, the anise seeds, and the chopped garlic. Broil in the oven until they are a dark brown. Shake the pan frequently while browning. When browned place in the blender and blend fine. Add to the toast chili pepper paste and set aside.

In a frying pan heat the 2 tablespoons peanut oil and when hot brown the chicken pieces quickly on both sides. Remove and keep warm. Add to the frying pan the chopped onion, diced tomatoes, and cook until the onion is soft. Blend smooth in the electric blender and then return to the frying pan. Add the blended paste mixture, the bitter chocolate, sugar, cinnamon, ground cloves, and cook over a low heat, stirring constantly, until the chocolate has melted. Add the 2 cups chicken broth and the ½ cup sherry. Cook over a medium heat for 15 minutes, stirring frequently. Add the chicken and continue cooking until just heated through. Add salt to taste and serve at once.

Serves 4

Green Chicken with Almonds
Pollo Almendrede Verde is a delicately flavored chicken dish that shows the great variety in Mexican cooking.

4 tablespoons olive oil
4-pound chicken fryer cut into pieces
1 large onion chopped fine

1 clove garlic minced
1 cup chicken broth
½ cup orange juice
½ cup sherry
1 teaspoon ground cumin
1 cup blanched almonds
1 large avocado mashed
Salt and pepper to taste

Heat the olive oil in a skillet and brown the chicken pieces well on both sides. When browned remove the chicken. Add the onions and garlic to the pan and sauté until soft. Add the chicken broth, orange juice, sherry, and ground cumin. Mix well and return the chicken to the pan. Cover and cook over a low heat for 40 minutes or until the chicken is tender. Blend the almonds fine in an electric blender. Add the mashed avocado and a little of the juice from the pan. Blend until smooth. Add to the chicken in the pan and cook for 5 minutes over a medium low heat, stirring constantly. Add salt to taste and serve the chicken in the delicate green sauce.

Serves 4

Red Chicken Fricassee with Sesame Seeds

Pipian Raje de Ajenjeli is a chicken dish that has changed very little since Aztec days.

4-pound chicken fryer cut into pieces
Chicken stock to cover
4 tablespoons chili powder
½ cup sesame seeds
1 onion chopped
2 cloves garlic minced
Pinch of cloves
Pinch of cinnamon
1 cup tomato hot sauce
Salt and pepper to taste

Put the chicken pieces in a kettle with the chicken stock and cook over a low heat until tender. Set aside and keep warm. In an electric blender combine the chili powder, sesame seeds, chopped onion, minced garlic, pinch of cloves and cinnamon, and the tomato hot sauce. Blend until smooth. Pour the blended mixture into a pan and slowly add 1 cup chicken stock, stirring constantly over a medium heat, until the sauce is of a medium thick consistency. Add the chicken pieces and cook 5 minutes longer.

Serves 4

Smothered Chicken
Tapado de Pollo is a delightful dish of chicken and fruit and vegetables.

6 tablespoons olive oil
4-pound chicken fryer cut into pieces
1 large onion sliced
2 cloves garlic minced
3 large tomatoes peeled and chopped
½ pound green peas
1 pound summer squash sliced
2 cooked apples sliced
2 pears peeled and sliced
4 slices pineapple cut in chunks
2 large bananas peeled and sliced
Salt and pepper to taste

Heat 4 tablespoons olive oil in a skillet and sauté the chicken pieces until well browned on both sides. Place a layer of the chicken pieces in a heavy dutch oven and on top of them place a layer of half the onion, garlic, tomatoes, peas, squash, apples, pears, pineapple, and bananas. Season with salt and pepper and sprinkle with 1 tablespoon olive oil. Repeat with layers of remaining chicken, vegetables, and fruit. Season with salt and pepper and sprinkle with 1 tablespoon olive oil. Cover and cook on top of the stove over a low heat for 1 hour or until the chicken and vegetables and fruit are tender. The amount of gravy will depend on the ripeness of the fruit and vegetables.

Serves 6

Pollo à la Mexicana

Pollo à la Mexicana—Chicken in the Mexican Way—This is the recipe of a Mexican friend. It is quite hot so use the Mexican red chili sauce with caution.

3 tablespoons olive oil
3 cloves garlic minced
4-pound chicken fryer cut into pieces
3 8-ounce cans tomato hot sauce
1 8-ounce can Mexican red chili sauce
1 cup canned corn kernels
Salt and pepper to taste

Heat the olive oil in a heavy pan and when hot add the minced cloves of garlic. Cook for 1 minute. Add the chicken pieces and brown quickly on both sides. Add the tomato hot sauce and the can of Mexican red chili sauce. If the red chili sauce is not available use another can of tomato hot sauce with 2 or 3 tablespoons of chili powder and add a few drops of Tabasco if you wish to make it hotter. Cover the pan and let the chicken simmer in the sauce for 40 minutes or until the chicken is tender. Add the canned corn kernels and continue cooking until just heated through. Taste for seasoning and serve the chicken hot in the sauce.

Serves 4

Mexican Chicken Cazuela

A cazuela is an earthenware pot used by the Mexicans since

ancient times for cooking purposes. The cazuela has handles at either end and a round bottom so that it can be placed directly over a fire.

4-pound chicken cut into pieces
1 teaspoon salt
⅛ teaspoon pepper
½ cup flour
3 tablespoons olive oil
3 peeled whole cloves garlic
1 large onion chopped fine
2 cups stewed tomatoes
1 8-ounce can tomato hot sauce
2 tablespoons chili powder
1 cup pitted ripe olives

Add the salt and pepper to the flour and roll the chicken pieces in the seasoned flour. Heat the olive oil in a cazuela or casserole and brown the chicken with the peeled whole cloves of garlic. When chicken is browned add the finely chopped onion. Cook until onion is soft then add the stewed tomatoes, tomato hot sauce, and the chili powder. Cover the pan and cook for 40 minutes or until the chicken is tender. Add the pitted ripe olives and cook until they are heated through. Serve the chicken from the cazuela.

Serves 4

Chicken Tacos
Tacos are small tortillas stuffed with various mixtures, rolled, fastened with a toothpick, fried in lard, and served with various sauces. They can also be stuffed and eaten without frying.

12 small tacos
1 cup chopped cooked chicken

1 tablespoon finely chopped onion
4 ounces cream cheese
2 tomatoes peeled and chopped
1 tablespoon chili powder

Mix the chopped cooked chicken, finely chopped onion, and cream cheese. When thoroughly mixed add the chopped tomatoes and the chili powder. Stuff 12 small tacos with the mixture and roll up. Fry in lard or not, as you wish.

Serves 2–3

South American Chicken

Most South American food is surprisingly good. It is highly flavored but not nearly as hot as Mexican food. Beans and rice are popular, and to a South American a meal without beans or rice as an accompaniment would be unthinkable. Corn is also served in some form at almost every meal. South Americans like elaborate meals and are particularly fond of starting off with something spicy. Many of the countries have very similar cooking styles, although the native ingredients available in individual countries have naturally influenced the cuisine.

South America has only two countries without an access to the sea, Bolivia and Paraguay, and even Paraguay is on the Paraguay River, which flows down to the sea. Bolivia is unique in that everything must reach the country by rail or air, as the roads are very poor. Consequently, with such a long coastline South Americans eat a lot of fish and have developed many unusual recipes for the preparation of fish.

Argentina is the second largest country in South America and, of course, is famous for its beef. The fertile grassy plains of the pampas covers about a fifth of the country and supports countless herds of cattle. The cattle are tended by the colorful gauchos—cowboys—whose costume is characterized by a wide silver belt, baggy trousers, and a bright scarf. Until recent times the gauchos went into the pampas with their herds for months at a time and would subsist almost exclusively upon maté—a local tea—and on beef. Whenever they felt hungry they would kill one of the steers, build a fire, and roast an enormous chunk of meat.

The people of Argentina have always eaten beef as part of their staple diet. One of their well-known dishes is a Carbonada, which is a combination of beef with fruit and vegetables. Their soups are unusual, the classic national soup being cocido, a chicken and vegetable soup stew. They have three distinct cooking styles. Spanish, a natural result of having been settled by the Spanish; classic French, which is found in the best hotels and restaurants; and the Criolla, a style based upon campfire cooking and dating back to Argentina's earliest pioneer days.

Brazil is an immense country, the largest in both area and population in South America. It is closer to Portugal than to Spain in its traditions, and of all the countries in South America only the Brazilians speak Portuguese. The Portuguese style of cooking also influences the cuisine. Another important influence upon the cooking style is that of the Africans who were brought in as slaves in the early days to cultivate the country. The national dish is feijoade, a combination of black beans with smoked pork and dried beef. The cuscus, for which Brazil is also famous, is a dish that came originally from Arabia. The principal farinaceous ingredient is cornmeal humidified with salt water and shortening, to which highly seasoned fish, meat, or poultry is added along with palm hearts, sliced tomatoes, eggs, olives, and herbs.

Chili is mostly mountainous. The snowy peaks of the Andes tower above its capital city of Santiago. During the winter season the mountain slopes draw skiers from all over the world. Bread and beans form the main diet for the ordinary Chilean. They also like thick soups of corn or rice mixed with vegetables and pieces of chicken. A popular soup called Cazoela de Ave is made of chicken, potatoes, corn, rice, onions, and spicy peppers. Owing to the long coastline they have excellent fishing and have created some unusual seafood dishes, notable among them Chape de Mariscos, a seafood soup stew.

Dishes with almond sauce are popular throughout large parts of South America and in Ecuador they combine the almond sauce with shrimps, eggs, corn, or anything else that is available. Green tangled forests cover much of Ecuador. Many of the people are descended directly from the Incas and live in the high cool valleys of the Andes. They have little variety in their food and many of their local dishes are made of corn.

Peru's contribution to great eating is a marvelous chicken and pepper dish called Aji de Pollo. The people eat a lot of fish along the coastline. They season their food highly with hot peppers. The diet of the mountain people is very simple and consists largely of potatoes and ocas, a South American herb.

Chickens are enjoyed in all the countries of South America. Easily prepared but highly flavorful poultry dishes are the general rule. Herbs and spices are used lightly but with great effect to flavor the delicate meat of the chicken. In South America they say, *"La gallina hace la cocina"*—the chicken makes the meal.

Argentine Cocido

Almost every country has some method of preparing a hearty soup with meat or poultry and vegetables. In Russia it is borsch, in France pot au feu, and in Argentina the cocido. The broth is served first with the chicken and vegetables as a main course.

1 pound chick peas (garbanzos)
1 chorizo (Spanish sausage)
1 chicken cut in half
½ pound stew beef in one piece
3 potatoes peeled and quartered
1 large yellow squash cut into thick slices
1 cup fresh or canned corn kernels
½ pound very fine noodles
Salt and pepper to taste

Soak the chick peas in cold water overnight. Drain. Place in a large kettle with the chorizo, chicken, stew beef, and water to cover. Simmer covered over low heat for 2 hours or until the meat and the chick peas are tender. Add the potatoes and cook about 30 minutes or until almost tender. Add the squash and corn and cook 10 minutes more. Cook the noodles in a separate pan according to directions on the package and add to the cocido. Taste for seasoning. First strain the broth from the stew and serve in soup bowls with a spoonful of the fine noodles in each bowl. Then remove the vegetables and beans to one platter. On another platter place the chicken halves in the center and surround with the cut-up pieces of meat.

Serves 8

Canja
From Brazil comes this unusual dish made from rice cream and chicken.

5-pound stewing hen cut into pieces
1 teaspoon salt
¼ teaspoon pepper
2 tablespoons butter
1 large onion sliced
2 cloves garlic minced
2 quarts boiling water
1 bay leaf
6 peppercorns
¼ teaspoon marjoram
3 cups chicken broth
1 cup rice
Cream

Rub the chicken pieces well with the salt and pepper. Melt the butter in a Dutch oven and brown the chicken with the onions and garlic. Drain off the butter. Add the boiling water, bay leaf, peppercorns, and marjoram. Cover and cook over a low heat for 1½ hours or until the chicken is tender. Remove the chicken, cool, and cut the chicken meat from the bones into pieces. Strain 3 cups of the chicken broth into a saucepan and let it come to a boil. Add the rice, lower the heat, and simmer for 1½ hours. Mash the rice and rub it through a fine sieve. Dilute with enough cream to make a rich creamy soup. Add the chicken and cook over a medium low heat until hot. Do not let it boil. Taste for seasoning and serve the chicken and rice cream in soup bowls.

Serves 6

Stewed Chicken, South American Style
A chicken is cooked in this manner quite often in South America.

Juice of 1 lemon
1 medium onion chopped
2 cloves garlic minced fine
¼ cup olive oil
¼ cup vinegar
½ teaspoon salt
6 whole peppercorns
2 bay leaves
1 teaspoon coriander
4-pound chicken fryer cut into pieces
1 tablespoon butter
1 can tomato paste
1 cup water

Make a marinade of the lemon juice, onion, garlic, olive oil, vinegar, salt, peppercorns, bay leaves, and coriander. Marinate the chicken in this mixture for 4 hours turning several times. Melt the butter in a skillet and brown the chicken well on both sides. Add the marinade, cover, and cook for 10 minutes.

Add the tomato paste and the water. Replace the cover and cook for about 35 minutes longer or until the chicken is tender.

Serves 4

Chicken Cuscus

Cuscus de Galinha—Brazil's famous chicken dish was transported straight from North Africa. It is made with humidified cornmeal and highly spiced with herbs. The palm hearts can be bought in many supermarkets.

4 cups white cornmeal
1 cup salted boiling water
½ cup butter
2 tablespoons butter melted
1 onion chopped fine
2 teaspoons crushed red chili peppers
4-pound stewed chicken
1½ cups chicken gravy
10-ounce can palm hearts sliced thin
3 tomatoes sliced thin
2 yellow squash sliced thin
Olive slices

Place the cornmeal in a large shallow pan and sprinkle 1 cup boiling water that has been salted over it. Mix in with a fork and place the pan in a 425° oven to bake for 2 minutes. Remove from oven and add ½ cup butter. Knead into the mixture. Melt 2 tablespoons butter in a skillet and cook the chopped onions and crushed red chili peppers until soft but not browned. Cut the stewed chicken into small pieces and discard the bones. Add to the skillet along with the chicken gravy and cook for 5 minutes. Remove from the heat and add the cornmeal mixture. Mix well. If the mixture seems too dry add a little more boiling salted water. In the bottom of a colander place a layer of tomato slices, olive slices, and some of the cornmeal mixture. Press the cornmeal mixture against the sides and bottom with your fingers. Cover with tomatoes, olives, yellow squash, and palm hearts. Alternate with the cornmeal mixture until all of the ingredients are used up. Cover the colander tightly and steam over hot water for 1½ hours or until firm. Let the cuscus set a few moments, then unmold on a serving platter.

Serves 6

Chicken Vatapa

A friend of mine lifted this unique Brazilian vatapa from a lady who had just returned from a South American tour. I have varied the ingredients slightly but I consider it one of the most unusual dishes I have tasted.

1 cup canned bay shrimp ground fine
2 cups cooked fresh shrimp
Juice of 2 lemons
4-pound chicken fryer cut into pieces
3 tablespoons butter
1 large onion chopped fine
1 clove garlic minced
1 teaspoon salt
½ cup tomato hot sauce
1 tablespoon peanut butter
1½ cups coconut milk

Grind the cup of canned bay shrimp fine. Marinate the 2 cups cooked fresh shrimp in the lemon juice for 1 hour. Melt the butter in a heavy pan and brown the chicken along with the chopped onion, garlic, and salt. When browned add the tomato hot sauce and simmer covered for 40 minutes or until the chicken is tender. Remove the chicken from the sauce, cool, and cut the meat from the bones into small pieces. Add the ground canned shrimp, the drained fresh shrimp, the peanut butter, and coconut milk to the sauce in the pan. Return the chicken to the pan and cook until thick. Serve with the following sauce.

Sauce
1½ cups shredded packaged coconut
1 cup heavy cream
1 tablespoon minced onion
Juice of ½ lemon

Soak the shredded coconut in the heavy cream for 30 minutes. Then cook it over a low heat for 10 minutes. Cool and strain through several thicknesses of cheesecloth, squeezing out as much liquid as possible. Add the minced onion and the lemon juice. Cook until just heated through and serve over the Vatapa.

Serves 6

For coconut milk see page 543.

Braised Chicken and Pork
From Puerto Rico comes Pollo Adobe—braised chicken—which is a spicy dish not to be confused with the Filipino adobe chicken.

4-pound chicken fryer cut into pieces
1 pound lean pork cut into strips
6 peppercorns crushed
3 cloves garlic crushed
3 tomatoes peeled and chopped fine
¼ cup cider vinegar
½ cup green stuffed olives
2 teaspoons salt
1 bay leaf crushed
2 cups water

Put the chicken pieces in a bowl with the lean pork strips and add crushed peppercorns, crushed garlic, tomatoes, vinegar, stuffed olives, salt, bay leaf, and 2 cups water. Let the meat stand in this marinade for 24 hours. Then place the meat and the marinade in a heavy Dutch oven and cook over a low heat for 2 hours. The liquid should be almost evaporated and the chicken and pork very tender. Serve with boiled rice.

Serves 4

Chicken in Rice Ring
From Colombia comes Gallina à la Colombiana—a chicken in rice ring.

3 tablespoons olive oil
1 large onion minced
1 cup chopped green peppers
2 cloves garlic minced
2 tablespoons minced parsley
4-pound chicken fryer cut into pieces
½ cup tomato hot sauce
1 cup dry white wine
½ cup boiling water
1 teaspoon salt
½ teaspoon dry green chili peppers
2 tablespoons melted butter
2 cups cooked rice
2 eggs well beaten
1 cup sliced toasted almonds
1 cup seedless raisins

Heat the olive oil in a heavy skillet and brown the onions, garlic, green peppers, and minced parsley until soft. Add the chicken and cook until lightly browned on both sides. Add the tomato hot sauce, dry white wine, boiling water, salt, and dry green chili peppers. Cover and cook over a low heat for

40 minutes or until the chicken is tender. Remove chicken and cut the meat from the bone into small pieces. Return the chicken meat to the sauce. Mix the cooked rice, melted butter, toasted almonds, seedless raisins, and beaten eggs together. Pour into a buttered ring mold and bake in a 350° preheated oven about 30 minutes or until set and browned. Turn out onto a serving platter and fill the center with the chicken mixture. Sprinkle the top with almonds.

Serves 6

Piquette

The last few years Marian Anderson has had a series of South American baby sitters for her two children. Marian does not speak Spanish and most of the baby sitters spoke inadequate English, but fortunately she was able to solve enough language problems with one girl from Colombia to get this recipe for piquette.

1 cup chopped onions
2 cloves minced garlic
2 tablespoons minced parsley
1 teaspoon crushed green chili pepper
1 tablespoon vinegar
1 teaspoon salt
5-pound roasting chicken cut into pieces
2 tablespoons olive oil
2 cups hot water
2 cups hot chicken broth
2 cups sliced sweet potatoes
4 ears corn cut into 2-inch pieces

In a mortar pound to a paste the chopped onion, garlic, parsley, green chili pepper, and salt. Add the vinegar and mix smooth. Coat the chicken pieces well with this mixture and place in the refrigerator to set for 24 hours. Heat 2 tablespoons olive oil in a kettle and brown the chicken well on both sides. When browned cover with the hot water and hot chicken broth. Let come to a boil then simmer over low heat for 1½ hours or until the chicken is tender. Remove the chicken from the kettle and keep hot. Add the sweet potatoes to the stock and cook until almost tender. Add the corn and cook 10 minutes longer. Serve the chicken and vegetables on a platter with the following sauce.

Sauce
½ cup cubed white bread
1 cup milk
¼ cup olive oil
1 cup onions chopped fine
1 teaspoon salt
½ teaspoon black pepper
1 cup tomato hot sauce
½ cup grated Parmesan cheese

Add the bread to the milk and mash until smooth. Heat the olive oil in a skillet and cook the onions until soft but not browned. Add the salt, pepper, and tomato hot sauce. Cook over low heat for 10 minutes. Mix in the mashed bread. Cook over a low heat 5 minutes longer, stirring constantly. Serve with the chicken and vegetables.

Serves 6

Aji de Gallina
Adena Robinson spent a summer in Peru with her daughter who works for the Peace Corps. She brought back this recipe for the marvelous Peruvian chicken and pepper dish with its spicy bread sauce.

1 teaspoon chili peppers ground fine
1 cup dry breadcrumbs
1 cup hot milk

4 tablespoons olive oil
4-pound chicken cut into pieces
1 large onion chopped fine
2 cloves garlic minced fine
1 cup tomato hot sauce
1 cup chicken stock
1 teaspoon salt
⅛ teaspoon black pepper

Soak the dry chili peppers and dry breadcrumbs in the hot milk for 30 minutes. Squeeze out excess moisture and set aside. Heat the olive oil in a Dutch oven and brown the chicken well on both sides. Remove the chicken. In the oil remaining in the pan cook the onions and garlic until soft but not browned. Add the tomato hot sauce and the chicken stock. Add the breadcrumbs and cook over a high heat for 2 minutes, stirring constantly. Add salt and pepper and return the chicken to the pan. Cover and cook over a low heat for 40 minutes or until the chicken is tender.

Serves 4

Chicken with Oranges

From Ecuador comes Gallina con Naranjas—chicken with oranges—which is a delightful, refreshing dish.

5-pound roasting chicken cut into pieces
2 cups orange juice
2 small onions minced fine
1 clove garlic minced fine
1 teaspoon chili peppers ground fine
4 tablespoons butter
1 teaspoon salt
⅛ teaspoon pepper
2 tablespoons flour
½ teaspoon sugar
2 oranges sliced thin

Mix the orange juice, minced onions, garlic, and chili pepper together in a bowl. Add the chicken pieces and marinate for 4 hours in the refrigerator. Melt the butter in a heavy skillet and brown the chicken well on both sides. Remove the chicken and add the salt, pepper, flour, and sugar to the pan. Stir until the flour begins to brown. Add the orange juice marinade and cook until thickened slightly. Return the chicken to the pan, cover, and cook over a low heat for 40 minutes or until the chicken is tender. Serve on a hot platter with the orange slices for garnish.

Serves 6

Cazuela

Argentina has the cocido and Chile has this cazuela which is half stew and half soup and hearty enough to make a meal in itself.

5-pound stewing chicken cut into pieces
½ cup flour
1 teaspoon salt
¼ teaspoon pepper
2 tablespoons olive oil
Water
1 teaspoon chili peppers ground fine
¼ teaspoon coriander
6 sweet potatoes peeled and quartered
1 pound string beans
2 cups hubbard squash peeled and cut into small squares
½ cup canned chick peas
2 ears corn cut into 2-inch pieces
Salt and pepper to taste
2 egg yolks beaten with 2 tablespoons cold water
Minced parsley

Add the salt and pepper to the flour and roll the chicken pieces in the seasoned flour. Heat the olive oil in a skillet and brown the chicken well on both sides. Remove and put in a heavy kettle with cold water to cover. Add the chili peppers and coriander. Bring to a boil, cover, and simmer over a low heat for 40 minutes. Add the sweet potatoes and cook until almost tender about 40 minutes longer. About 20 minutes after adding the sweet potatoes add the string beans and the hubbard squash. Five minutes before the chicken is done add the canned chick peas and the corn. Cook 10 minutes longer. Season to taste with salt and pepper. Add the egg yolks beaten with cold water and continue cooking over low heat until the sauce has thickened slightly. Stir constantly. Serve some of the chicken and vegetables in warm soup bowls and pour over the gravy. Sprinkle the top with minced parsley.

Cassoulet

A Cassoulet with garbanzos is a very popular South American chicken casserole.

1 pound garbanzos (chick peas)
¼ pound diced salt pork
2 cloves garlic mashed
1 large onion chopped fine
5-pound roasting chicken cut into pieces
1 teaspoon salt
¼ teaspoon pepper
2 tablespoons olive oil
1 onion chopped
2 cloves garlic minced
1 8-ounce can tomato hot sauce
1 cup dry white wine
½ pound diced ham

Soak the garbanzos overnight. Drain. Add the diced salt pork, mashed garlic, chopped onion, and water to cover. Cover the pan and simmer the chick peas over a low heat until almost tender. Drain the chick peas reserving the liquor. Rub the chicken pieces well with salt and pepper and brown well on both sides in the olive oil. Remove the chicken. Add 1 chopped onion and 2 cloves of minced garlic to the pan and cook until soft. Return the chicken to the pan and add the tomato hot sauce and dry white wine. Simmer covered for 15 minutes. Put half of the chick peas in the bottom of a casserole. Add the chicken mixture and cover with the rest of the chick peas. Add the garbanzo liquor to cover the beans and bake covered in a 325° oven for 1½ hours. Add the diced ham and bake uncovered ½ hour longer.

Serves 8

Pastel de Pollo
Pastel de Pollo is a South American chicken pie that is both different and good.

4-pound chicken fryer cut into pieces
1 teaspoon salt
½ teaspoon ground chili peppers
3 tablespoons olive oil
1 large onion chopped fine
½ green pepper chopped fine
1 clove garlic minced
1 cup tomato hot sauce
½ cup dry white wine
¾ cup pitted black olives sliced
2 cups canned corn kernels
Pastry for 1 crust pie

Season the chicken pieces with salt and the ground chili peppers. Heat the olive oil in a heavy skillet and brown the chicken with the chopped onions and green peppers and minced garlic. Add the tomato hot sauce and dry white wine. Cover and cook over a low heat for 40 minutes or until the chicken is tender. Remove chicken and when cool remove the meat from the bones and return to the sauce. If sauce seems too thin thicken with a little flour. Add the olives and corn kernels. Turn into a casserole and cover with the pie pastry. Cut several slits in the top so the steam will escape. Bake in a 400° preheated oven for 30 minutes or until the crust is nicely browned.

Serves 6

Chicken and Black Beans with Garlic Sauce

This is another recipe Marian Anderson managed to get from one of her South American baby sitters. Beans are a must to most South American families and this dish with chicken and black beans in garlic sauce is served regularly. If the black beans are unavailable use white beans.

1 pound dried black beans
4 cloves peeled garlic
1 onion cut in half
1 bay leaf
5-pound roasting chicken cut in pieces
Salt and pepper
2 tablespoons olive oil
1 clove mashed garlic

Wash the black beans and soak them overnight in cold water. Drain, cover them with fresh water, and add 4 cloves peeled garlic, the onion, and a bay leaf. Simmer covered for 30 minutes. In the meantime sprinkle the chicken with salt and pepper and brown on both sides in 2 tablespoons olive oil. Remove the chicken and pour the olive oil into the container of an electric blender. Remove the cloves of garlic, onion, and bay leaf from the bean pot. Add the garlic and onion to the olive oil and blend until smooth. Return this puree to the bean pot along with the chicken. Simmer covered over low heat for about 1 hour longer or until the beans and chicken are tender.

Serves 8

Epilogue

And so our chicken completes its journey around the globe and sails for home. It has been to France, Italy, Spain, the Middle East, the Orient; through South America and every island in the Pacific. From the scorching sands of the Sahara to the snow-capped peaks of the Alps and the bitter cold of Russia. In every land chicken is a favorite dish, and as the boat docks in San Francisco it finds the American chicken standing at the forefront of gourmet cooking. In San Francisco there are the choicest recipes from everywhere in the world, and in the great restaurants of the city chicken dishes are cooked as they are in Shanghai, Hong Kong, Paris, Madrid, Rome, Berlin, Budapest, Vienna, or anywhere else one might mention. So our globe-trotting young chicken completes its world cruise and comes home to roost at last.

Index